The Complete Guide To Public Employment

Ronald L. Krannich Ph.D

Caryl Rae Krannich Ph.D

IMPACT PUBLICATIONS

THE COMPLETE GUIDE TO PUBLIC EMPLOYMENT: Opportunities and Strategies With Federal, State, and Local Governments; Trade and Professional Associations; Consulting Firms; Nonprofit Organizations; Foundations; Research Organizations; Political Support Groups; and International Institutions

Library of Congress Cataloging-in-Publication Data

Krannich, Ronald L.
  The complete guide to public employment.

  Bibliography: p.
  Includes index.
  1. Civil service positions — United States.
I. Krannich, Caryl Rae.   II. Title.
JK716.K68   1986   353.001'03   86-80633
ISBN 0-942710-05-3 (pbk.)

For information on distribution or quantity discount rates, call 703/361-7300 or write to Sales Department, IMPACT PUBLICATIONS, 10655 Big Oak Circle, Manassas, Virginia 22111.

TABLE OF CONTENTS

PREFACE

The public sector offers numerous and exciting employment opportunities for individuals interested in pursuing public goals. However, in recent years, the public sector has been under attack from many quarters for being wasteful, unproductive, and unresponsive. Viewing government as a culprit rather than a catalyst for positive change, the critics tell public employees to do more and better with less and, at the same time, expect fewer career rewards in the form of salaries, benefits, and advancement opportunities. In short, all is not well with government employment and many public sector careers.

But there are other sides to the public employment equation which are both encouraging and positive for anyone seeking a public sector career. This is the subject of our book. For we find a very dynamic and exciting public sector offering numerous opportunities in spite of cutbacks and low morale in government. As we stress throughout this book, the public sector is much more than government employees doing the business of government. The public sector includes many nongovernmental institutions performing similar functions as government agencies. Many of these organizations chart their own public agendas with or without the help of government.

From a career development and transition perspective, numerous governmental and nongovernmental institutions are closely related to one another in terms of goals, functions, budgets, and personnel. When governments cut back, they often contract-out or devolve their functions to nongovernmental organizations which, in turn, increase their budgets, organizational infrastructures, and personnel. In fact, the trend in government is to increase budgets and expenditures but not increase in-house personnel. The implications of this trend are quite clear: limited career advancement within government and a growing public sector outside government among contracting and consulting firms, nonprofit organizations, associations, foundations, and research organizations.

We wrote this book because there is a need to bring together a comprehensive concept of the public sector related to specific how-to employment strategies and opportunities. Millions of individuals are primarily oriented to public sector employment. Many of these people want to have a positive impact on others and make a living at the same time. Yet, too often individuals seeking public sector employment are at the mercy of highly generalized and often inappropriate or inaccurate career advice based upon experiences with private sector organizations.

We have attempted to fill a major gap in the literature on job search approaches and the public sector as well as bring to life what is often viewed as a dull and boring subject. The book is designed for anyone who is interested in beginning a public service career or advancing their career among public sector organizations. In the process, we hope it helps generate renewed interest in public sector careers.

The book represents a synthesis of our collective training, research, and work experience in the public sector and job search strategies both in the United States and abroad. Much of the basic research for the book began in 1980 at the state and local levels as well as on Capitol Hill while we were both university professors in political science/public administration and speech communication respectively. During the next six years we managed to live in the fast lane as five other career books, one business communication book, numerous management training manuals and programs, geographic moves, and our international work took precedence over completing this volume. In the process, our concept of public employment underwent major changes. The result was a newly restructured book designed to respond to several key public sector institutions as well as outline useful linkages among these institutions.

Research continued and major writing began during 1983 and 1984 while we lived and worked in Thailand on several international development projects as well as counseled numerous Thais and expatriate Americans on their international careers and approaches to reentering the U.S. job market. After nearly losing the manuscript to paranoid security personnel in the Soviet Union, it returned safely to the United States where we subjected it to further expansion and revisions. The final research and writing was completed during 1985 and 1986 in Washington, DC and Northern Virginia.

Yet, the book is by no means complete. What we began we learned we could not finish within the space of a single volume. The subject is both enormous and complex, reflecting the diversity and complexity of the institutions found in American society and abroad. It requires a great deal of additional work on employment cultures of public institutions which we begin to outline as well as many others not included in our coverage. For example, when we examined Political Action Groups (PACs), we began unravelling a fascinating world of political employment little understood by people inside or outside PACs. Consequently, we only introduce the reader to the basics of PACs and point them in the right direction for initiating a job search requiring their own research into how various PACs operate.

The same is true for contracting and consulting firms. Little is known about the structure and employment cultures of these organizations. We present basic information and how-to strategies on these groups to get you properly started. Another section on international contracting and consulting provides a more in-depth look at how various firms relate to the key Federal agency for international work — the U.S. Agency for International Development.

The book is designed to link understanding to action. For how-to advice not firmly rooted in data and analysis can be useless and dangerous advice. At times we go to the top of the hill to preach the how-tos of success, but we always try to do so knowing the how-tos are based on an analysis of on-going realities and cases of success. In this sense we have attempted to be balanced and honest in our treatment of the subjects.

We dedicate this book to our readers who, in putting it into practice, should contribute to a better public sector as well as enrich their lives. You may not get rich following our advice, but if you successfully implement the information in this book, you will probably enjoy what you do and make a decent living at the same time. After all, that is what being rich and living is all about.

Most important, you need not get locked into jobs which may turn sour or become deadend careers. The pages that follow chart some important career options and strategies within the public sector which should give you the freedom to make informed choices about your future. We wish you the very best in your efforts to career and re-career within the public sector.

Ronald L. Krannich
Caryl Rae Krannich
Manassas, Virginia
April 17, 1986

INTRODUCTION

We've heard all the stories. There are no jobs available in the public sector. Government work is boring. Public servants are underpaid. This is not the time to seek public employment. Further cutbacks will occur in governments at all levels. Once you plateau your career in government, there's nothing you can do except wait for retirement. Government employees lack the necessary skills and motivation to find rewarding jobs and careers outside government. It's better to go into business.

Don't believe everything you hear. A great deal of nonsense is propagated about public careers by well-meaning individuals who do not understand government and the public sector. Baffled by complex structures and functions which appear illogical to well organized, tidy, and apolitical minds, ignorance rather than information dominates a great deal of thinking about the public sector.

This book is about improving your public sector employment I.Q. It outlines how you can find employment and advance your career within the public sector despite all the stories to the contrary. It is not your usual treatment of this subject. Some books, for example, outline how to find employment with Federal, state, or local governments. Others specify job alternatives for individuals interested in international careers. This book deals with both these areas and much more.

APPROACH

We have chosen a different approach to the subject which is as ambitious as it is comprehensive. Based on our experience in working with thousands of individuals interested in making career changes, finding public employment, and becoming involved in public issues, we see a need for a different type of book. Our presentation of this subject:

- *Combines a career alternatives perspective* (what jobs exist and where to find them) *with a job search skills perspective* (how to get a job) directly related to a series of institutions (governmental and nongovernmental) found in the public sector.
- *Explores government as an interrelated system* of 82,341 units of Federal, state, and local government as well as comprised of executive, legislative, and judicial branches of government at all levels which generate over 16 million jobs.
- *Integrates the governmental units with several nongovernmental public organizations* which are critically important to the overall functioning of the public sector.
- *Treats the public sector and the job search process from a realistic perspective* which is based upon research, cases of success, and a solid understanding of how public institutions are structured and function.
- *Links public jobs in one institutional complex with similar jobs in other institutional complexes*, so individuals can plan for career transitions among various public sector institutions.

Throughout this book we have avoided the common practice of over-simplifying processes which are inherently complex and difficult to manage. To identify where the jobs are and land a suitable public job in specific institutions and organizations require a great deal of hard work. It involves weeks of research, careful planning, and implementation through the use of telephones, letters, and meetings with individuals and organizations. Above all, it requires you to link your job search skills with a thorough knowledge of how specific institutions and organizations operate. It is necessary to adapt your job search skills to particular situations which may or may not operate according to the general advice you receive about finding a job.

BASICS

Each chapter is designed to provide you with the maximum basic information and advice on how to navigate your job search among public sector organizations. We neither claim nor attempt definitive treatments of each subject. Indeed, many of the chapters can easily be expanded into separate in-depth volumes on finding a job in a particular type of organization.

Our basic organizing principle for each chapter stresses both *understanding and action*. We attempt to provide you with a solid framework for understanding how various institutions and processes operate and then offer specific advice on how to conduct an effective job search with each organization. Wherever possible, we include useful addresses and telephone numbers for your further research. This contact information is your bridge to more in-depth information on each organization and process.

In many cases we include only a telephone number for an organization. We have done this for two reasons. First, many organizations move locations within a community, but they retain their original telephone number. Should an address change, the U.S. Postal Service only forwards mail for one year. On the other hand, should a telephone number change, you can always call Information for the new number. Second, we urge you to use the telephone in your job search. Writing letters is important in some situations, but writing letters for basic information is often inefficient and ineffective. You will consistently get better information by using the telephone than by writing letters. Letter writing takes time, and frequently you do not get replies or the written information you receive is incomplete.

Use the telephone before you write a letter. In fact, one purpose of a call may be to get the name of an individual to whom you will address the letter. A long distance telephone call may cost you a few dollars, but it will pay for itself in the long run. Our experience has been consistently positive when telephoning for job information and advice with various public institutions both inside and outside government. Most people will give you a great deal of useful information over the telephone. Most important, they will tell you to whom you should address your written correspondence. It is also advisable to use the telephone to follow-up your written correspondence.

THE PUBLIC SECTOR

Our concept of the public sector should become increasingly

useful for individuals seeking and pursuing public service careers. The public sector is much larger than just Federal, state, and local governmental units. Several private institutions work closely with government institutions in pursuing public goals. Other private institutions, especially nonprofit organizations and foundations, have their own public agendas paralleling those of government agencies. Altogether, these government and nongovernmental institutions employ over 30 million individuals.

Many individuals who enter government only view public service careers as government careers. They further compartmentalize their careers by only working within a particular office of a single agency within one unit of government. Some government employees make career transitions from one office or agency to another. A few even move from one level of government to another — from county to city, city to state, or state to Federal. Unfortunately, many of these government employees find their careers plateau at mid-age; advancement, promotion, and salary increments are very limited once one enters certain positions and ranks in government.

Other types of organizations provide job and career alternatives for government employees who either plateau their careers or wish to leave government service. While many individuals believe leaving government means going into profit-making businesses primarily oriented to sales, numerous organizations outside government perform functions similar to government. Indeed, in many cases — especially consulting firms and nonprofit organizations funded by government agencies — government functions are performed by private organizations. Only after government employees leave government and work for such organizations do they begin to see that much of the public work they had hoped to do in government is actually performed by these nongovernmental organizations.

PRIVATIZING AND CONTRACTING-OUT GOVERNMENT

Our concept of public sector employment generally follows important trends and transformations taking place within government over the past 30 years. These trends will continue within the foreseeable future. While local governments are the primary direct-service units of government, state and Federal governments tend to provide indirect services. More and more public services, including important planning and management functions, are being contracted-out to consultants and nonprofit organizations. Other functions are being privatized by transferring them to the private sector. In fact, many government employees who wish to leave government are individuals who went into government with the expectation of becoming involved in providing services in a particular public policy area. Many of these people become dissatisfied with their work, because it involves routine administrative tasks for issuing and monitoring government contracts, grants, and cooperative agreements to consultants and nonprofit organizations.

Ironically, as governments at all levels increasingly privatize as well as contract-out public services, some of the most interesting and rewarding public service jobs will be found in the private sector rather than in government agencies. As we stress throughout this book, these nongovernmental public service institutions provide numerous job and career alternatives for individuals primarily oriented toward public service careers. One important trend should continue over the next decade: government budgets may increase, but government employment will remain relatively stable, either declining or growing very little. On the other hand, the nongovernmental public service sector should experience considerable employment growth during the next decade as it becomes the major benefactor of government budgetary increases.

MOTIVATION

Individuals seek public service careers for several reasons. Money and status is not one of the driving motivations. Public service jobs provide adequate to low compensation. Unless one's fingers are in the public till, one does not get rich in the public service. Yet, many public jobs can provide very comfortable middle to upper-middle class life styles.

Many people go into the public service because they prefer the security, pay, benefits, or the nature of the work. Furthermore, many individuals enter the public service for negative reasons: do not like working in business which requires long hours, pressures to produce a profit, stress, and unpredictable security.

Whatever one's motivation, public service careers are becoming more like jobs in the private sector — longer hours, pressures to produce, stress, and less security. Therefore, it is best to enter public service careers for positive rather than negative reasons. You should have specific goals in mind which will lead to positive career experiences. If you seek public employment because you do not like other types of employment, you will most likely become unhappy in the public sector. Always start by examining your motivations and identifying what it is you want to do — not what you don't like to do.

THE BOOK

The remainder of this book examines the major components involved in acquiring public employment and making career transitions among both governmental and nongovernmental public service organizations at the local, state, Federal, and international levels. The book is divided into seven parts consisting of 28 chapters.

The four chapters in Part I provide a general orientation toward public sector institutions and job search myths and realities. These chapters introduce the concept of the public sector; examine past, present, and future employment trends; and outline career alternatives and effective approaches to finding public sector jobs.

The four chapters in Part II present the basic job search skills for organizing and conducting an effective job search among most types of organizations. These skills involve getting organized, identifying skills, stating job objectives, writing resumes and letters, networking, communicating, conducting job interviews, and negotiating salaries. The chapters stress the importance of adapting these skills to particular organizations within the public sector.

The five chapters in Part III provide an orientation for approaching government employment. They examine the advantages and disadvantages of working in government, outline key structural aspects of government institutions and the hiring process, specify how to gather information on government opportunities, and identify both formal and informal job search strategies appropriately adapted to the government hiring process.

The five chapters in Part IV outline how to find employment with executive, legislative, and judicial institutions with governments at the local, state, and Federal levels. A separate chapter examines how to best complete the key application form required for entry into Federal executive jobs — the newest version of the SF-171.

Six chapters in Part V provide a comprehensive examination of the key peripheral institutions defining the nongovernmental public sector: consulting firms, trade and professional associations, nonprofit organizations, foundations, research organizations, and political support groups. Each chapter outlines the structure of various hiring cultures and effective job search strategies which must be adapted to each institutional complex.

Part VI consists of four chapters designed for gaining employment with various public sector institutions operating within the international arena. These consist of U.S. governments, international organizations, and various peripheral groups, such as consulting firms, associations, nonprofit organizations, foundations, and research organizations. Part VI also examines important realities of international employment, including various myths, realities, life styles, and the nature of work motivating individuals to find employment in this fascinating arena.

The concluding section pulls together the previous chapters by focusing on the key to taking action — implementation. It stresses the importance of translating this book into an effective action plan which will result in rewarding public service careers.

GETTING STARTED

Chances are you chose this book because you want to learn more about getting into or advancing within the public sector. Attempting to uncover the mystery of public employment, you seek to understand what you need to know and do to be effective in finding public employment today.

Before we venture further into this subject, we suggest you do two things immediately. First, *begin orienting yourself to the public sector* by addressing several practical questions about your future:

1. How well do I understand the:
   - structures, functions, and relationships of public sector institutions?
   - relative advantages and disadvantages of working in the public sector?
   - various job search strategies and techniques appropriate for different public sector institutions?
2. To what degree will my present understanding of government and job search strategies help me find public employment?
3. What background, qualifications, and skills are best for public employment?
4. Where are the public sector jobs?
5. How long will it take me to get a job with government or other public sector institutions?
6. How do I acquire the necessary skills for success in the public sector job market?
7. How realistic am I about my capabilities to both find public employment and function well within a public environment?
8. Where do I go and what do I do next?

These questions have important personal implications for you. They require thoughtful and realistic answers to help you take effective action to acquire public employment and advance your career in the public sector.

The second thing you need to do is *begin acquiring the necessary knowledge and skills to be effective* in the public sector job market. Few people are as effective as they could be in this job market. Indeed, the realities of government and public employment are often at odds with individuals' perceptions. Lacking a clear understanding of the realities, many individuals:

- Avoid public employment altogether, or
- Use ineffective job search strategies which result in either (1) failing to find a job, or (2) finding a job inappropriate for their true capabilities and interests.

This should not happen to you. The following chapters have been carefully structured so you can acquire the necessary knowledge and skills to be effective in the public sector job market. They are based upon years of experience and success in what is one of the most fascinating, challenging, and rewarding job arenas for individuals who understand and appreciate public sector work.

PART I

EMPLOYMENT REALITIES AND STRATEGIES

What is the public sector? How many jobs are available? Where are the jobs? How do I go about finding a government job? What are my alternatives to working for government? How can I become most effective in acquiring public employment and advancing my career?

Most job seekers raise these questions. Encountering numerous organizations and hiring systems, they seek useful advice on how to simplify the job finding process in today's public sector job market. Yet, the answers to these questions are anything but simple. In the following chapters, we outline a concept of public employment to simplify understanding of this process while also recognizing the inherent complexity of the situation. Furthermore, this concept is the basis for developing the how-to strategies and tactics as outlined in each chapter of this book.

The four chapters in this section address these and other key questions. The chapters prepare you for the two major prerequisites for being effective in today's public sector job market:

- You must know the realities of public employment before venturing into this employment arena.
- You must use job search strategies appropriately designed for particular realities.

Each chapter is designed to simplify the overall complexity of public employment by placing public employment within the larger context of important job trends, perceptions, networks, and alternatives. Accordingly, this section focuses on better understanding:

- public employment trends
- common myths impeding job search effectiveness
- public sector networks and networking
- alternative job markets relating to public employment

Part I outlines a basic action orientation for developing an effective job search in today's public sector job market. The remaining sections and chapters will help you develop effective job search strategies for particular organizations at the Federal, state, local, and international levels.

One word of caution is in order before you begin these initial chapters. It is one thing to understand realities and another to apply the realities to your particular situation. As you read these chapters, be careful in relating the statistics and trends to your particular situation. The trends are based upon large amounts of data which hold true for society and organizations as a whole. They do not necessarily apply to you as the individual. Indeed, subsequent chapters are specifically designed to equip you with the knowledge and skills to get what you want in spite of general trends. The bottom line is for you to set goals and follow through with strategies to get what you want. Statistics and trends outlined in these chapters merely provide an important context within which you will develop an effective public sector job search strategy.

Chapter One
PUBLIC
SECTOR TRENDS

It is one thing to talk about working for "the public sector" and another to experience the realities and complexities of the public sector. For the public sector consists of a relatively stable and predictable set of organizations which affects the way government conducts business. Well integrated into the private sector, the public sector also is a highly decentralized, fragmented, and chaotic system. Understanding the changing nature of this system is the first step to understanding present and future employment prospects with public sector organizations.

MEMBERSHIP

The public sector consists of all organizations and institutions directly or indirectly related to the business of governing communities, states, and the nation. It includes government organizations as well as peripheral organizations primarily oriented toward and dependent upon government. These peripheral organizations are comprised of:

- Trade and professional associations involved in influencing public policy through legislative and executive agencies.
- Contracting and consulting firms with government con-

11

tracts.
- Nonprofit organizations performing public service functions.
- Foundations providing resources to other peripheral groups.
- Research organizations engaged in public-related research.
- Political support groups, lobbyists, and law firms influencing both the formulation and implementation of public policy.

Figure 1 illustrates this concept of the public sector.

FIGURE 1

THE PUBLIC SECTOR

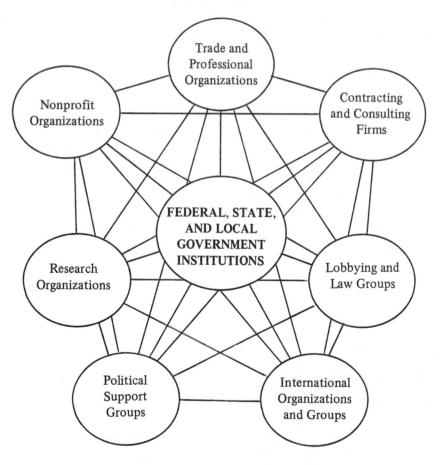

While this is not the usual definition of the public sector, it is an extremely useful one for our purposes. As you will see throughout this book, government is one of many institutions — albeit the most significant — involved in governing communities and influencing the content of public policies. Together, these institutions comprise an interrelated *network* of public sector job and career opportunities. By familiarizing yourself with this network, you will be better able to identify job opportunities and advance your public sector career.

DIMENSIONS OF GOVERNMENT

Government is the single largest employer in the United States. Nearly one in six civilian employees, or 16 million individuals, work for government organizations. Millions of other nongovernment jobs depend on providing services to government agencies. Of these, approximately three million jobs in the private sector are paid through Federal government contracts.

The civilian government complex consists of numerous units of government and public employees as outlined in Table 1.

───────── TABLE 1 ─────────		
GOVERNMENT UNITS AND EMPLOYEES, 1982		
Level	Units	Employees
TOTAL	**82,341**	**16,034,000**
Federal	1	2,875,000
State	50	3,816,000
Local	82,290	9,344,000
• Counties	3,041	1,811,000
• School Districts	14,851	4,211,000
• Townships/Towns	16,734	379,000
• Municipalities	19,076	2,424,000
• Special Districts	28,588	519,000

While these units of government are loosely related, each has separate personnel systems and hiring practices. Even within a single unit of government, several hiring systems may operate for different types of employees. Viewed as a job market, this system is highly decentralized.

The largest single category of government employees is educators (5.5 million), constituting 42 percent of the government workforce at the state and local levels. Educational positions also have been primarily responsible for recent major growth and decline trends in public employment.

Federal government employment constitutes 15.9 percent of all public employment. Nearly 98 percent of all Federal employees work for 110 executive agencies. Only six agencies employ over 80 percent of all Federal civilian employees. Table 2 summarizes the personnel size of the largest agencies.

TABLE 2
LARGEST FEDERAL AGENCIES

Agency	Employees	Percent of Total
TOTAL	**2,317,276**	**80.6**
— Department of Defense	987,890	31.6
— Postal Service	666,238	21.3
— Veterans Administration	239,625	7.5
— Department of Health and Human Services	163,921	5.3
— Department of Treasury	138,244	4.8
— Department of Agriculture	121,358	4.2

Government employment does not stop at 16 million employees attached to executive branch bureaucracies. Another 500,000 individuals occupy elected and appointed legislative and judicial positions at the Federal, state, and local levels. The government complex also includes the District of Columbia and five territorial governments. Furthermore, over 1 million individuals are employed in the armed forces. Overall, government employment approaches 18 million.

The concentration of government employees varies by geographical area. For every 1000 citizens, there are 47 state and local employees, ranging from a high of 82 per 1000 in Alaska to a low of 38 per 1000 in Pennsylvania. California alone has nearly 1.5 million state and local employees whereas Vermont has fewer than 30,000. Federal government concentration averages 13 employees for every 1000 citizens. Overall statistics for Federal civilian employees by city, state, and branch of government are presented in Appendix A.

The Federal civilian workforce is widely distributed throughout the country as well as abroad. Over 87 percent of Federal employees are located outside the Washington, D.C. Metro area. About 133,000 civilian employees work overseas, although 59,000 of these are not U.S. citizens. The State of California alone has nearly as many Federal employees as the Washington Metro area — 300,000. Since the Federal government is divided into 10 administrative regions, the regional centers of New York, Philadelphia, Boston, Chicago, Atlanta, Kansas City, Dallas, Denver, San Francisco, and Seattle have a disproportionate concentration of Federal workers, employing 36.9 percent of all Federal civilian employees. Each of the metropolitan areas in Table 3, for example, has at least 25,000 Federal employees:

TABLE 3

METROPOLITAN AREAS WITH 25,000 CIVILIAN FEDERAL EMPLOYEES OR MORE, DECEMBER 1982

City/Metro Area	Federal Employees
TOTAL	1,024,515
Washington, DC/MD/VA	348,980
New York/NJ	88,957
Philadelphia/NJ	71,122
Los Angeles-Long Beach	67,842
Chicago	66,571
San Francisco	64,006
Baltimore	52,355
Norfolk-Virginia Beach	37,006
San Antonio	36,980
St. Louis, MO/IL	35,418
Boston	35,310
Atlanta	31,149
Dallas-Ft. Worth	30,437
Detroit	29,614
Oklahoma City	28,168

While over 90 percent of government employees work for executive agencies, numerous job opportunities also are available in the developing bureaucracies of the legislative and judicial branches of government. For example, within the Federal government the legislative branch employs 39,143 individuals; the judicial branch employs 16,626. Although less visible to the public, agencies within these two branches of government have been growing rapidly in the past few years. Employment in the legislative branch has increased by more than 50 percent since 1965 (25,947). Employment in the judicial branch has nearly tripled in the same period (5,904).

GROWTH, DECLINE, AND STABILITY PATTERNS

As illustrated in Table 4, the number of units of government actually declined by 47 percent during the period 1942-1982. However, despite this decline, public employment grew at the same time.

TABLE 4
GROWTH AND DECLINE OF GOVERNMENT UNITS, 1942-1982

Level of Government	1942	1952	1962	1972	1982
TOTAL	**155,116**	**116,743**	**91,237**	**78,269**	**82,341**
U.S. Government	1	1	1	1	1
States	48	48	50	50	50
Local Governments	155,067	116,694	91,186	78,218	82,290
— Counties	3,050	3,049	3,043	3,044	3,041
— Municipalities	16,220	16,778	18,000	18,517	19,076
— Townships/Towns	18,919	17,202	17,142	16,991	16,734
— School Districts	108,579	67,346	34,678	15,781	14,851
— Special Districts	8,299	12,319	18,323	23,885	28,588

Following general population growth and labor participation trends, the long-term pattern for government employment has been toward growth. While government employment more than doubled during the past three decades, most of this growth took place at the state and local levels during the 1960s and 1970s. For example, from 1950 to 1981 state government employment increased by 253 percent; local government employment grew by 190 percent. Table 5 summarizes public employment statistics from 1950 to 1983:

TABLE 5

CHANGING GOVERNMENT EMPLOYMENT, 1960 to 1983

Level of Government	1950	1960	1970	1980	1981	1982	1983
EMPLOYEES (1,000)							
Total	6,503	8,808	13,028	16,213	15,968	15,918	16,034
Federal (civilian)	2,117	2,421	2,881	2,898	2,865	2,848	2,875
State and Local	4,285	6,387	10,147	13,315	13,103	13,071	13,159
Percent of total	66.9	72.5	77.9	82.1	82.1	82.1	82.1
State	1,057	1,527	2,755	3,753	3,736	3,747	3,816
Local	3,228	4,860	7,392	9,562	9,377	9,324	9,344
AVERAGE ANNUAL PERCENT CHANGE							
Employees, Total	.5	3.5	4.2	1.5	-1.5	-.3	.7
Federal	-8.9	.4	2.2	1.0	-1.2	-.5	.9
State	(NA)	(NA)	6.3	1.5	-.7	.6	1.8
Local	(NA)	(NA)	4.4	1.7	-1.9	-.6	.6

The most rapidly growing units of government have been special districts. Between 1970 and 1983, employment with special districts increased an average of 5 percent each year — a rate 2 to 10 times higher than all other forms of government combined.

Most public employment increases during the past three decades responded to three general changes in society:

- Post-World War II population increases requiring extensive expansion of educational facilities, highways, and other local infrastructure and services.
- The increased demand for more community and social services in relation to a generally more affluent and aging population.
- Revitalized and more liberal state legislatures and bureaucracies which played increased social advocacy roles.

Federal employment trends differed from state and local patterns. During the same period Federal employment increased by only 37 percent. All of this growth took place during the period 1950 to 1970. The period 1970 to 1981 actually witnessed a 1.0 percent decline in Federal employment. Yet, the Federal budget increased by over 1200 percent (from $40 billion to $526 billion) during the same period.

Why did Federal employment fail to grow as dramatically as state and local bureaucracies, especially given major budgetary capabilities to do so? The answer to this question relates to two general trends off-setting the need to increase Federal personnel in direct proportion to budgetary increases. First, much of the budgetary increase was in the form of *transfer payments* to states and locales: categorical and block grants and revenue sharing funds. From 1960 to 1981, Federal aid to state and local governments increased 1200 percent, from $7.0 billion to $86 billion. In 1981 the majority of aid was targeted for income security (22.5 percent), education (22.3 percent), health (19.9 percent), and transportation (14.2 percent). One of the major impacts of Federal aid was to stimulate the rapid growth of state and local bureaucracies — especially in the areas of public safety, welfare, education, health, and transportation — rather than enlarge the Federal bureaucracy. State and local bureaucracies had to increase their staffs to handle the influx of Federal funds.

Second, *private contractors and consultants* played a greater role in providing Federal government services. Contracting-out government services increased significantly during the 1960s and

1970s as Federal agencies shifted from providing direct services to obligating funds and managing contracts. Procurement became a growth industry in the Federal government. By the early 1980s a "hidden bureaucracy" of contracting and consulting firms was well entrenched in relation to the Federal government. Washington, D.C. alone — where they are frequently referred to as Beltway Bandits and Suburban Consultants — has over 700 such firms doing business with the bureaucracy. While many specialize in defense contracting, others provide services to numerous agencies, ranging from project design to delivering specific services to agency clientele. Similar firms do business with state and local governments.

An overall employment pattern in government is evident: state and local governments tend to increase personnel in response to budgetary increases; Federal budgetary increases tend to stimulate the growth of state and local bureaucracies as well as the involvement of contracting and consulting firms specializing in public services.

ENTERING A CUTBACK ERA

Since the early 1980s, the pattern of growth in state and local bureaucracies has been altered somewhat. Recessions combined with taxpayers' revolts resulted in public employment declining for the first time since the immediate post-World War II period.

Major declines in public employment began in 1980. The sharpest declines took place at the state and local levels. Between 1980 and 1981, employment in municipalities declined by 3.6 percent; counties by 2.4 percent; townships by 2.0 percent; and school districts by 1.1 percent. Only special districts registered an increase in employment — 1.7 percent. Declines were evident in all functional areas except police protection. Education experienced the greatest cutbacks; highway departments registered the largest percentage decrease in employees. Indeed, by 1981 there were 245,000 fewer government employees, representing a 1.8 percent decline at the state and local levels.

Declines in public employment during the early 1980s were fairly predictable. Cutbacks were most urgently needed for many state and local bureaucracies in the Northeast and Midwest. Hit hard by recession, the public services in these areas had become bloated during the 1960s and 1970s due to the growth of liberal social services and public employee unions. Examples of such problems abound. New York City lived far beyond its means, faced repeated financial crises, and nearly defaulted. New York State government followed a similar pattern of excessive spending in the face of declining revenues. Ubiquitous patronage in the 1970s gave Boston an average of 44.4 public employees for every 1,000 inhabitants — 76 percent above the national average!

Something had to give. In Massachusetts — a state noted for liberal programs, strong public employee unions, and high taxes — taxpayers revolted with passage of the infamous Proposition 2 1/2 ballot initiative; 40,000 jobs were eliminated from the public payroll shortly thereafter. New York City, despite strong opposition from public unions, managed to reduce its public employees from 283,000 in 1974 to 210,000 in 1982. The financially strapped cities of New York, Boston, Philadelphia, Providence, Newark, Cleveland, and Detroit began practicing a long-overdue version of "cutback management" as government jobs became increasingly insecure and unpredictable.

The Federal bureaucracy also experienced personnel declines during the 1980s. Shortly after taking office, President Reagan did what new presidents only talk about — trim the Federal bureaucracy. Reduction in Force (RIF) procedures went into effect, frightening and demoralizing thousands of Federal employees from Hawaii to Maine who began thinking the unthinkable — possible job loss and insecurity.

While nearly 60,000 Federal employees lost their jobs by 1984, the Federal government continued to hire approximately 1,000 new employees each day. In most months it hires 20,000 new employees, but in some months it has hired as many as 70,000. Instead of substantially shrinking the Federal bureaucracy, the Reagan Administration actually slowed the rate of job growth by reordering personnel priorities among and within agencies as well as between grades of officials and tinkering with a few politically vulnerable programs. For example, the Department of Health and Human Services (HHS) lost a disproportionate number of employees in weak service programs; HHS employees in GS-11 to GS-15 positions — classifications which grew dramatically during the 1970s — were more vulnerable to the personnel cuts than employees in lower grades.

Another trend is emerging during this cutback era: government budgets continue to increase but at a slower rate than in previous decades. Some government employees will be cut from the public payroll, but fewer new employees will be hired in general. However, the "hidden government" of contracting and consulting firms will continue to do business with government agencies. Many will increase their employees in direct proportion to declines in government employment.

PREDICTING THE FUTURE

Given past patterns of growth, stability, and decline in public employment, what can we expect in the future? Certain trends are evident given our knowledge of future demographic changes and basic public service needs. First, *beginning in 1983, public employment at all levels began an upward trend.* However, while public employment will most likely continue to increase, the actual rate of increase will be relatively small compared to previous decades of rapid government employment expansion. Continuing declines and no-growth patterns for government employment will take place in many states and locales through the 1980s. On an average, government employment growth will probably fluctuate from 0 to 1.0 percent each year. This is about one-half the growth rate projected for all employment in the United States between 1985 and 1990 — fluctuating from 1.4 to 1.9 percent per year. Indeed, the total percentage participation of government employment in the total labor market has been steadily declining over the past 25 years. In 1960, for example, government employment constituted 3.7 percent of the total labor force. In 1983, government employment represented 2.9 percent of the total.

Second, *education — the most predictable public employment sector — will face continuing turbulence over the next decade due to declining student enrollments in secondary and higher education.* According to U.S. Department of Labor projections, between 1978 and 1990 the demand for secondary school teachers will decline by 20.8 percent; college and university faculty will decline by 9.2 percent. On the other hand, beginning in 1985, more jobs became available in elementary education as the children of the post-World War II baby boom generation began entering schools in large numbers. Between 1978 and 1990 the demand for elementary teachers should increase by 24.9 percent. To a very large extent, the slow growth in public employment is due to changes in the structure of education. This is especially true in the case of state government employment where approximately 30 percent of all employees work in higher education institutions. As higher education enters a slow-growth and cutback period, state employment growth can expect to slow.

Third, *state and local government services and jobs will continue to increase in response to the major demographic shifts from the Northeast and Midwest into the South and West.* At the same time, several older cities and states in the Northeast and Midwest will experience further public service declines. The states of New York, Rhode Island, Massachusetts, Pennsylvania, Ohio, Michigan, and Illinois — as well as the cities of Boston, New York, Philadelphia, Cleveland, Detroit, Chicago, and St. Louis — are still adjusting to declining tax bases caused by population and industrial migration to the South and West. Governments of these states and cities will probably cutback further, because they are caught in a vicious circle: population, industries, and revenues decline at the same time costs increase for providing social services and physical infrastructure as well as for maintaining generous public employee pension plans. These cutbacks may have a more permanent impact on the bureacracies than many patchwork measures initiated in the late 1970s and early 1980s.

The good news is in the South and West and in areas where major universities are linked to high-tech industries. Population growth and industrial development will most likely continue in Florida, Texas, Oklahoma, New Mexico, Arizona, Colorado, Utah, Nevada, Wyoming, and California. Massachusetts, an extremely resilient state, will probably rebound by transforming its economy in line with its major emerging strength — high technology tied to an incredible educational complex near Boston, especially the booming Route 128 area. Ohio and Illinois may undergo similar transformations by shedding older smokestack industries in favor of high-tech industries linked to several major higher educational complexes. State and local bureaucracies in these areas will probably grow in response to increases in population, industry, and revenue. Education and public safety bureaucracies will be the major beneficiaries.

Excepting Florida and Arizona, most growth states and cities are developing around high-tech and energy industries. Since their relatively young, conservative, well educated, and affluent populations neither require nor demand extensive social services, governments in these states and cities will concentrate on developing basic infrastructure to accommodate continuing growth. As high-tech and energy industries undergo turbulent growth and decline, local government bureaucracies in these areas will be less affected because of their limited initial growth. States and cities experiencing little or no population and economic growth will most likely further shrink their bureaucracies as well as contract-out various services.

Fourth, *the Federal government will probably continue to replace personnel at the present stable, incremental growth rates of approximately 1,000 new employees each day.* Certain agencies — especially Defense, Justice, State, Veterans Administration, and Environmental Protection — are destined to grow due to Administration plans to expand these and other high priority agencies. At the same time, Reagan Administration plans to cut 40,000 Federal employees during the period 1985-1988 are aimed primarily at the middle and upper grade — GS-11 through GS-15 — positions. Employees in professional, administrative, and technical fields are most vulnerable to such cutbacks. They will face the most difficulty in receiving promotions in the coming years. Accordingly, Federal careers are likely to plateau around the GS-9 to GS-11 levels during the 1980s. As the Federal budget grows and government employment declines, private contracting and consulting firms will probably expand their businesses with Federal, state, and local government agencies.

Fifth, *public employment opportunities will be numerous regardless of overall no-growth and decline patterns in government employment.* After all, a group of 16 million government employees, with a normal annual turnover rate of 14 percent (due to resignations, retirements, deaths, and dismissals), automatically generates 2,240,000 job vacancies each year. Added to this number are a similar number of vacancies occurring among the peripheral organizations doing business with government agencies — organizations which have even higher turnover rates than government. The total number of annual job vacancies in the public sector is probably closer to 7 million.

Sixth, *government personnel procedures today are more apolitical and professional than ever before.* Except for a few patronage-entrenched states and locales, gone are the good-ole-boy days when politicians dumped incompetents into government agencies and political connections could get you a job with little or no demonstrated skills or experience. Patronage systems have given way to merit systems based upon systematic recruitment, selection, and promotion procedures. Even counties — often considered the last havens of political patronage — have become increasingly urban and highly professional. While connections are still important for getting a government job — indeed, essential for you to use — they tend to be professional in nature. The name of the game today is *professional networking* rather than using "political pull" — a significant shift in how the game is played.

Finally, *public sector jobs are increasingly technical and competitive.* Once a job market for unskilled generalists, the public sector today engages in highly technical activities requiring substantial educational and technical skills. Because of the relatively good pay and job security of government employment, many people want to work for government. Therefore, you can expect to encounter a great deal of competition from numerous candidates who possess relatively strong educational and technical backgrounds.

Knowing these trends, your task should be to identify how you can best link your skills and abilities to job vacancies in the public sector. Because of no-growth and limited-growth job situations in government, it is extremely important to carefully plan your job search. The evidence is clear: numerous job opportunities are available, but you will need to prepare well for an increasingly competitive, professional, and technical public sector job market where careers tend to plateau within a short period of time.

Chapter Two
MYTHS, REALITIES, AND PERCEPTIONS

Job and career alternatives abound in the public sector. The exact number of jobs, however, is uncertain. We know there are nearly 16 million Federal, state, and local government positions. Probably another 16 million positions are available with organizations doing business with government. Thousands of international public employment opportunities are found with the United Nations, regional organizations, consulting firms, foundations, and voluntary organizations.

If you have the necessary skills and motivation to work in the public sector, you possess the basic prerequisites for *doing* the job you want. But before you can do the job, you need some basic information on public sector employment alternatives as well as a powerful set of job search skills appropriate for various job alternatives. These become your prerequisites for *getting* the job.

This chapter develops a useful orientation toward the job market. It relates basic information on employment alternatives as well as examines the institutional setting for identifying the major job and career alternatives.

GETTING THE JOB

"Where are the jobs, and how do I get one?" Underlying these

frequently asked questions are certain assumptions about the job market. The questions anticipate easy answers to what is inevitably a complex phenomenon.

Let's answer these two questions by first examining several myths which could impede your job search. These myths also focus on important employment issues affecting both interviewers and interviewees. Based on this discussion, you should be able to start your job search in the right direction.

Most job seekers are unprepared and naive in approaching the job market; some might be best termed "job dumb." They muddle-through the job market with questionable perceptions of how it works. Combining facts, stereotypes, myths, and folklore — gained from a mixture of logic, experience, and advice from well-meaning friends and relatives — these perceptions lead job seekers down several unproductive paths. The perceptions are often responsible for the self-fulfilling prophecy of the unsuccessful job seeker: *"There are no jobs available for me."*

OVERCOMING JOB MARKET MYTHS

Twelve basic myths often prevent individuals from being effective in today's job market:

MYTH 1: *Anyone can find a job; all you need to know is how to find a job.*

REALITY: This "form versus substance" myth is often associated with career counselors. While it is sometimes a reality in an industrial society with low unemployment, it is a myth in a post-industrial, high-tech society. For example, many of today's unemployed are highly skilled in the technology of the industrial society, but they live and own homes in economically depressed communities. These people lack the necessary *skills and mobility* required for jobs in high-tech growth communities. Knowing job search skills alone will not help these people.

MYTH 2: *The best way to find a job is to respond to classified ads, use employment agencies, and submit applications to personnel offices.*

REALITY: Except for certain types of organizations, such as government, these formal application procedures are usually ineffective for finding jobs. Such approaches assume the presence of an organized, coherent, and centralized job market — but no such thing exists. The job market is highly decentralized, fragmented, and chaotic — a caricature of the overall American governmental system. Classified ads, agencies, and personnel offices tend to list low paying yet highly competitive jobs. Most of the best jobs — high level, excellent pay, least competitive — are neither listed nor advertised; they are found through word-of-mouth. When seeking employment outside government, your most fruitful strategy will be to conduct research and informational interviews on what is called the "hidden job market." In the case of government, you will need to supplement formal application procedures with informal approaches. Chapter Eight outlines how you can do this most effectively.

MYTH 3:   *Few jobs are available for me in today's competitive job market.*

REALITY: This may be true if you lack marketable skills and insist on applying for jobs listed in newspapers, employment agencies, or personnel offices. Competition in the advertised job market usually is high, especially for jobs requiring few skills. Numerous jobs with little competition are available on the hidden job market. Jobs requiring advanced technical skills often go begging. Little competition may occur during periods of high unemployment, because many people quit job hunting after a few disappointing weeks of working the advertised job market.

MYTH 4:   *I know how to find a job, but opportunities are not available for me.*

REALITY: Most people don't know how to find a job, or they lack marketable job skills. They continue to use ineffective job search methods. Opportunities are readily available for individuals who understand the structure and operation of the job market, have appropriate work-content skills, and use job search methods designed for the hidden job market.

MYTH 5: *Employers are in the driver's seat; they have the upper-hand with applicants.*

REALITY: Most often no one is in the driver's seat. Not knowing what they want, many employers make poor hiring decisions. They frequently let applicants define their hiring needs. If you can define employers' needs as *your* skills, you might end up in the driver's seat!

MYTH 6: *Employers hire the best qualified candidates. Without experience and numerous qualifications, I don't have a chance.*

REALITY: Employers hire people for all kinds of reasons. Most rank experience and qualifications third or fourth in their pecking order of hiring criteria. Employers seldom hire the best qualified candidate, because "qualifications" are difficult to define and measure. Employers normally seek people with the following characteristics: *competent, intelligent, honest, and likable.* They want *value* for their money. Therefore, you must communicate to employers that *you* are such a person. You must overcome employers' objections to any lack of experience or qualifications. Never confess your weaknesses, mistakes, or guilt. The best qualified person is the one who knows how to get the job — convinces employers to *like* him or her the most.

MYTH 7: *It is best to go into a growing field where jobs are plentiful.*

REALITY: Be careful in following the masses to the "in" fields. First, many so-called growth fields quickly become no-growth fields, such as aerospace engineering and nuclear energy. Second, by the time you acquire the necessary skills, you may experience the "disappearing job" phenomenon: too many people did the same thing you did and consequently glut the job market. Third, since many people leave no-growth fields, new opportunities may arise for you. Fourth, if you go after a growth field, you will try to fit into a job rather than find a job fit for you. After you know *what you do well and enjoy doing* (Chapter Six), and what additional training you may need, you should look for a job or career conducive to your particular mix of skills, interests, and motivations. In the long-run you will be much happier and productive finding a job fit for you.

MYTH 8:   *People over 40 have difficulty finding a good job.*

REALITY: Yes, if you apply for youth jobs. Age should be an insignificant barrier to employment if you conduct a well organized job search and are prepared to handle this potential negative with employers. Age should be a positive and must be communicated as such. After all, employers want experience, maturity, and stability. People over 40 generally possess these qualities. As the population ages and birth rates decline, older individuals should have a much easier time changing jobs and careers.

MYTH 9:   *I must be aggressive in order to find a job.*

REALITY: Aggressive people tend to be offensive and obnoxious people. Try being *purposeful* and *persistent.*

MYTH 10:   *I should not change jobs and careers more than once or twice. Job changers are discriminated against in hiring.*

REALITY: While this may have been generally true 30 years ago, it is no longer true today. America is a *skills-based* society: individuals market their skills to different organizations in exchange for money. Furthermore, since organizations are small businesses with limited advancement opportunities, careers quickly plateau for most people. For them, the only way up is to get out and into another organization. Therefore, the best way to advance careers in such a society is to change jobs frequently. Job-changing is okay as long as you demonstrate career advancement with each change. Most individuals entering the job market today will undergo several career and job changes regardless of their initial desire for a one-job, one-career life plan.

MYTH 11:   *People get ahead by working hard and putting in long hours.*

REALITY: Success patterns differ. Many people who are honest, work hard, and put in long hours also get fired, have ulcers, and die young. Some people get ahead even though they are dishonest and lazy. Others simply have good luck or a helpful patron. Moderation in both work and play will probably get you just as far as the extremes. Chapter Five outlines some realistic ways to become successful in addition to hard work and long hours.

MYTH 12:   *I should not try to use contacts or connections to get a job. I would apply through the front door like everyone else. If I'm the best qualified, I'll get the job.*

REALITY: While you may wish to stand in line for tickets, bank deposits, and loans, because you have no clout, standing in line for a job is dumb. Every employer has a front door as well as a back door. Try using the back door if you can. It works in many cases. Chapter Eight outlines in detail how you can develop your contacts, use connections, and enter both the front and back doors.

APPROACHING GOVERNMENT

While the 12 myths are relevant to the job market in general and should assist you in penetrating the public sector job market, another 12 myths are particularly relevant for government employment:

MYTH 13:   *Government agencies are not hiring.*

REALITY: Government agencies always hire. They have an average annual turnover rate of 14 percent. If they did not hire, they would collapse. The fact they don't advertise widely is no reason to believe they are not hiring. Even in cutback cycles, hiring takes place. You need to learn how to get information on job vacancies in government.

MYTH 14:   *Working for the Federal government means moving to Washington, D.C.*

REALITY: Only 13 percent of the Federal workforce is located in the Washington Metro area. The remaining 87 percent is spread throughout the country. Mainly centered around 10 regional cities, Federal employees also work in small communities, rural and remote areas, and abroad. In fact, you'll be lucky if you get to Washington!

MYTH 15:   *Competition for government jobs is so great — I don't have a chance.*

REALITY: The same is probably true for jobs in the private sector. While government employment is competitive, your chances of getting a job are excellent if you know how to best present yourself to agencies. Much of your competition is poorly organized for this job market. The key to success is learning how to make your application form, resume, and interview stand above the crowd.

MYTH 16:   *Government salaries are lower than those in the private sector.*

REALITY: This may be true if you make $50,000 or $60,000 a year — the ceilings placed on many government salaries. Comparable private sector positions may pay $100,000 a year or more. However, government salaries are very generous in the $15,000 to $40,000 annual salary ranges, especially for generalists and relatively unskilled individuals. Comparable positions in the private sector tend to pay less.

Salary inequities are more a problem for individuals making at least $50,000 a year and whose careers have plateaued in the public sector. But many of these people also are overpaid compared to similar work performed in the private sector.

MYTH 17:   *Government work is generally dull, boring, and full of red tape.*

REALITY: Work in general has dull and boring moments. Public organizations have by no means cornered the market on dull and boring jobs and red tape. Large organizations and large governmental agencies have similar organizational maladies normally associated with bureaucracy. Like many jobs in the private sector, many government jobs also are exciting, challenging, and devoid of red tape. The quality of the job depends on where you are in the organizational hierarchy and what you are doing.

MYTH 18:   *A great deal of incompetence and deadwood exists in government.*

REALITY: A great deal of incompetence and deadwood also exists in business and private industry. One major difference is that the private sector periodically cleans out its deadwood during recessions when the red ink requires cost-saving techniques. However, once recessions are over and businesses show profits, they once again acquire and keep incompetence and deadwood. The real myth is that business and private industry are substantially more efficient and effective than government. Remember, 500,000 businesses fail each year in the United States; many failures are due to mismanagement, incompetence, and deadwood. Government, on the other hand, is not allowed to fail, and thus it lacks a key imperative to clean its house. Moreover, with nearly 18 percent of the American workforce unionized, many organizations are constrained in making the necessary personnel decisions to get rid of their incompetence and deadwood.

MYTH 19:   *Government tends to hire generalists and unskilled individuals.*

REALITY: Government tends to hire all types of individuals. It more and more hires qualified specialists who can demonstrate proficiency in particular skill areas. Few government jobs are available for the unskilled.

MYTH 20:   *The best way to find a government job is to get a high score on the entrance examination.*

REALITY: High scores on entrance examinations are important, but they do not guarantee you a job. In addition, many government jobs do not require examinations. Application forms and resumes, along with recommendations and interviews, may be the only screening requirements. You will need to develop informal relations with individuals in agencies, present yourself well in writing and in person, and follow-through the application process with personal contacts. Chapters 10, 11, and 13, as well as individual government chapters (14-18), outline how to best gain entrance into government positions.

MYTH 21:   *Political patronage and personal contacts are still important in getting a government job.*

REALITY: Political patronage still exists, but it is by no means widespread. Professional selection procedures and merit systems are firmly entrenched in most governmental units. Who you know, however, can play an important and decisive role in the selection process. But the ubiquitous personal contact and the use of political pull have undergone a positive transformation: personal contacts tend to be professional contacts which help locate and screen qualified candidates. In this sense, personal contacts are important and functional for the employment process.

MYTH 22:   *Once I work for government, I will have difficulty finding work in the private sector. Business doesn't want to hire former government employees.*

REALITY:	Many government skills are directly transferable to business and industry. For example, firms doing business with government – especially contracting and consulting firms – readily hire former government employees. They need personnel who know the details of government. Indeed, a big *revolving door* exists between government and business. When you attempt to move from government to the private sector, your major problems will be in the areas of networking and communication. You must learn how to network outside government as well as present yourself in the language and style of business.

MYTH 23:	*Government employees work eight-hour days, get generous benefits, and have a great deal of security.*

REALITY:	This is true in many cases but not so in other cases. Many government employees work beyond the eight-hour day. Several Federal agencies and employees, especially in the Washington Metro area, have reputations for hard work and workaholism. Some governments are not too generous with benefits. Job security is not what it used to be. Government bureaucracies are being held more accountable for productivity, which affects work hours, salaries, benefits, and security.

MYTH 24:	*It's better to work for government than business – and vice versa.*

REALITY:	Yes, most people tend to "stand where they sit!" "Being better" is a function of which side of the fence you are sitting on or where you think the grass is greener at any particular moment. Most jobs are not inherently exciting or rewarding. They are often what you make of them. The organizational chart and job description merely give you a license to do a job. You and others will define the job, including its positives and negatives.

MAJOR REALITIES

The facts of public sector employment are often quite different from the dominant image and myths guiding job searches. At the very least, you should be aware of these realities when preparing your job search:

1. *The government hires almost every type of skilled worker.* For example, the Federal government's workforce includes approximately 150,000 engineers and architects, 120,000 accountants and budget specialists, 120,000 doctors and health specialists, 87,000 scientists, 45,000 social scientists, and 2,700 veterinarians.

2. Regardless of government cutbacks, *public employment opportunities are numerous* and will remain so in the foreseeable future.

3. Although the government hiring process is more formalized than hiring in business, *an informal hiring system also operates in government.* This informal system works similarly to the informal system in the private sector. Networking is the key to making the informal system work to one's advantage.

4. *A great deal of mystery and complexity seems to shroud the public sector hiring process;* it dissuades many highly qualified candidates from entering the public sector.

5. *It may take you longer to get a government job than a private sector job* because of more complex hiring procedures in government.

6. *Government jobs are similar to other jobs* — rewarding and unrewarding, with advantages and disadvantages. Don't expect too much or too little from public sector jobs.

7 *Government salaries in general compare favorably to private sector salaries.* With benefits included, many government salaries — especially Federal — are more generous than comparable positions in the private

sector.

8.   ***Government employees have more long-term job
     security than employees in business.*** However, they
     pay a price for this security — limitations on salary
     and career mobility. These limitations reflect the
     fact that most government employees are not ex-
     pected to be risk-takers, entrepreneurs, and produc-
     ers. The system protects them from failure.

9.   ***Successful candidates know how to best get a job
     they are qualified to perform.*** You will have a high
     probability of entering the public service if you de-
     velop the necessary skills and practice effective job
     search strategies.

     You should now have a realistic perspective from which to
begin answering the questions we posed at the beginning of this
chapter: *"Where are the jobs, and how do I get one?"* This chapter
presented a basic orientation. Chapters Three and Four provide
details on the "where" of the public sector job market. Chapters
Five, Six, Seven, and Eight outline the "how." The remainder of
the book links the "where" to the "how."

Chapter Three
OPPORTUNITY STRUCTURES FOR NETWORKING

The public sector encompasses a network of organizations and relationships centered around various governmental and public functions. From a public employment perspective, this network is an "opportunity structure" composed of numerous jobs relating to government and the public. Movement within this network takes place through a combination of personal contacts, formal application procedures, and placement services.

As you begin your job search, you should primarily concentrate on developing and using networks within this opportunity structure. This is commonly referred to as "networking" your way to a job that is right for you. This chapter outlines a framework for understanding the basic elements of these structures and specifies the necessary networking for being successful in finding a public sector job. Chapter Eight outlines detailed networking strategies for implementing your job search.

COMMUNITY NETWORKS AND LINKAGES

It is useful to view communities as made up of interacting social, economic, political, and governmental structures. Comprising a potential network of job opportunities, these structures also extend beyond single communities. Corporations, associations, and political,

37

social, cultural, and educational affiliations link individuals and organizations to other communities as well as to the state, national, and international levels. Most communities have similar networks, even though the individuals, groups, and institutions may differ.

While communities differ in many respects, the institutional actors and their games are relatively predictable from one community to another. The Yellow Pages of your telephone book, for example, identify the major players in this game: banks, mortgage companies, advertising firms, car dealers, schools, churches, small businesses, industries, hospitals, law firms, governments, and civic and voluntary groups. Each player pursues its own interests. While internal power structures exist, no one player dominates the game all of the time. Numerous groups overlap with one another because of shared economic, political, and social interests. Banks, for example, must loan money to businesses and churches. Businesses, in turn, need educational institutions for personnel, expertise, and markets. And educational institutions need businesses to absorb their graduates. Dependent upon one another, the players tend to compete, cooperate, and co-op one another to ensure the successful continuation of the game. Overlapping memberships on school boards, medical boards, and boardrooms of banks and corporations give the appearance of a centralized power structure. But power is diffused in what is essentially a decentralized and fragmented decision-making system.

These networks and opportunity structures also extend to other communities. During the past 50 years, local institutions have become integrated into a larger economic, social, cultural, and political system by means of corporations, associations, and affiliations. For example, today's small mom-and-pop shop is probably affiliated with a professional association headquartered in Washington, D.C., New York City, or Chicago. Professional associations provide a variety of support services to members: lobbying, resource and information centers, training, consulting, newsletters, journals, and insurance. The day of the large firm owned by a local family has largely passed in favor of corporations headquartered outside the community.

The organizations linked within and beyond communities comprise your opportunity structure for penetrating both the advertised and hidden job markets. You will need to identify both the organizations and the linkages by conducting research with individuals who occupy positions within the networks.

PERIPHERAL INSTITUTIONS

The basic public sector network consists of Federal, state, and local government institutions interacting with a variety of peripheral institutions. While many of the peripheral institutions actively influence the content and/or implementation of government policies, government agencies also actively influence the activities of other peripheral institutions to achieve certain public policy goals. Figure 1 in Chapter 1 outlines the basic elements and relationships of the public sector network. This network consists of six distinct groupings of interrelated nongovernmental organizations focused on public sector issues.

Trade and professional associations are good examples of major peripheral institutions involved in influencing public policy. Representing dues-paying members, these organizations either pursue a monetary interest or promote the advancement of knowledge. Many associations have permanent staffs — mainly located in state capitals, Washington, D.C., New York City, and Chicago — which lobby both legislatures and executive agencies on a full-time basis. The largest association is the American Association of Retired Persons with 16,000,000 members and a staff of 800 individuals located in Washington, D.C. Hundreds of large associations have annual budgets of more than $5 million, employ staffs of 50 or more individuals, and maintain Political Action Committees (PACs) to help fund the election or re-election campaigns of their favorite presidential and congressional candidates. In addition to providing specific services to their members, trade associations lobby legislators to influence the content of public policy. They lobby agencies to alter the implementation of legislation and agency directives. Furthermore, many of these organizations retain lawyers who influence the interpretation of public policies in the courts. These organizations are possible targets for your job search. Approximately 100,000 associations operate at the state level. Nearly 3,700 associations are located in Washington, D.C. — double the number of a decade ago.

Other groups also influence public policy. Many are single issue, ad hoc groups lacking permanent organizations and staffs. Several associations are very small and thus rely on professional association management firms to conduct their affairs. The largest and oldest such firm is the Washington-based Smith, Bucklin and Associates. Established more than 30 years ago, it currently provides services in the areas of government relations, trade show management and promotion, generic market development, public relations, statistical surveys and reporting, financial management, membership development, and travel and transportation to more than 100 small associations. While small associations offer few job opportunities relating to the public sector, the association management firms are an increasing source of public job opportunities.

A second grouping of peripheral institutions relevant to your job search are *contracting and consulting firms.* They constitute one of the most dynamic growth sectors relating to government. Thousands of these organizations specialize in various government functions and activities, from producing complex weapons systems to managing day-care centers. While many of these firms are small – with staffs of five to ten individuals – others are extremely large with staffs of over 10,000. These are the specialists and technocrats whose career paths involve circulating in and out of government (the "revolving door") as well as among firms doing government business. Most of these firms are located in the Washington, D.C.-Virginia-Maryland Metropolitan area, New York, and Chicago.

Contracting and consulting firms fall into two categories according to their size and degree of diversification. First, several firms are solely specialized in government business. Some firms specialize in a single area – construction, energy systems, procurement, mass transit, defense systems, planning, or management training. Others are diversified into several related areas, such as defense systems, energy systems, and procurement. Bechtel Corporation, for example, has over 33,000 employees in the United States and abroad. It provides government with management consulting, procurement, engineering, and construction services in such diverse fields as nuclear power, mining, irrigation, mass transit, petrochemicals, conservation, food, land management, and airport development. With nearly 100 percent of their business tied to government, these organizations tend to be vulnerable to the shifting budgetary priorities of government. Indeed, many firms specializing in a single government area went bankrupt during the recessions of the 1970s and 1980s. However, firms diversified in several government activities tend to be more stable and capable of weathering economic and budgetary cycles.

A second set of contracting and consulting firms consists of organizations doing business in both the public and private sectors. Coopers and Lybrand, a British-based multinational, for example, has offices in 97 countries and employs 30,000. They specialize in over 50 technical areas relevant to finance and management. Other examples include large corporations which maintain government contracting divisions. Major auto, aircraft, shipbuilding, and high-tech industries – such as Chrysler, Boeing, IBM, and Texas Instruments – have such divisions. Many of these firms do a great amount of work with the U.S. Department of Defense. Straddling both public and private sectors, their public divisions perform two important internal organizational functions: (1) acquire public funds for research and development activities important for future corporate development, and (2) serve as a buffer against private market fluctuations.

Texas Instruments is a case in point. During the early 1980s Texas Instruments laid off nearly 10,000 employees due to declining private market shares precipitated by its failures in the digital watch and microcomputer markets. However, its defense contracting division actually increased in both budget and personnel during this same period. This division generates important research and development activities to help Texas Instruments develop new products for the private sector market. Important research and development activities — normally scaled down during recessions — can continue given a safety net of Federal contracts.

A third major grouping of peripheral institutions are *nonprofit organizations*. While all associations and foundations as well as many consulting firms have nonprofit tax status, they are not nonprofit organizations in terms of their public orientation. Most groups we consider to be nonprofit organizations are organizations specifically structured to pursue a particular social, political, or economic cause. They receive the bulk of their funding from some combination of government grants and contracts, private foundation grants, and public donations. In contrast to associations and consulting firms which influence both the formation and implementation of public policy, government agencies often use nonprofit organizations to pursue public goals within the scope of their missions. By providing funds for various categories of programs, government becomes a major interest group of what are ostensibly private, nonprofit organizations.

Thousands of nonprofit organizations are found at the local, state, national, and international levels. At the local level, many nonprofits, such as the Salvation Army, YWCA, and the Red Cross, are known as community service organizations. Many of these and other local nonprofits are branches of national and state organizations. International nonprofits, such as CARE and Catholic Relief Services, have annual budgets of more than $250 million and staffs of more than 175 full-time employees.

A fourth category of peripheral institutions are *foundations*. These are primarily philanthropic organizations which provide funding for nonprofit organizations. However, some foundations, especially those operating in the international arena, provide services similar to nonprofit organizations. At the local level, community foundations and the United Way are most active. At the national and internaional levels, some of the larger foundations include the Lily Endowment, Rockefeller Foundation, and the Johnson Foundation.

Our fifth major category of peripheral public service institutions are *research organizations*. Many operate similarly to consulting firms, nonprofit organizations, and universities. Their basic goal is to generate new knowledge for improving the public policy process. Examples of such groups include the Rand Corporation, Stanford Research Institute (SRI), Hoover Institute, American Enterprise Institute, Brookings Institute, and the Urban Institute.

Our final category of peripheral institutions consists of several *political support, influence, and management groups*. Political Action Committees, political parties, professional lobbyists, lawyers, and political consultants are in the business of financing and winning election campaigns as well as influencing the shape of public policy. Several of these organizations are closely linked to trade associations and key personnel on Capitol Hill and in the White House.

KEY RELATIONSHIPS

Each of the six peripheral networks has its own hiring culture and formal and informal employment assistance networks. Most individuals will work for a particular type of peripheral organization and advance within the hierarchy of organizations which make up the particular group of organizations. Their career tends to focus on government, associations, consulting firms, nonprofit organizations, foundations, or research organizations.

Other individuals make career transitions from government to associations and from there to consulting firms, or from nonprofits to associations and consulting firms. Many employees of associations and consulting firms at one time worked for government. Indeed, one essential qualification for many positions is previous government experience. At the same time, many government employees previously worked for these organizations. A "revolving door" phenomenon — the movement of personnel from government agencies to peripheral public service organizations and back — is evident at all levels of government. While this phenomenon is especially visible between members of legislative institutions (committee and staff members) and businesses (particularly associations, lobbying groups, and law firms), it is less visible, but extremely prevalent, between executive agencies and consulting and contracting firms.

As you prepare for a public career or plan to advance within the public sector, you need to become more aware of both the employment networks within each institutional complex as well as networks for making transitions from one type of public organization to another. Your ability to make job moves within and between public institutions will provide you with the greatest degree of career mobility possible in the public sector.

PREVALENCE OF NETWORKS

The prevalence of these networks and the extent of public employment opportunities is mainly a function of the size and location of government institutions. Rural county governments, for example, deal with few peripheral organizations. Small municipalities are involved with local law firms and companies providing basic infrastructural engineering and construction services, such as streets, sewers, water, and public buildings. Faculty from local colleges or universities may offer limited, ad hoc consulting services in the areas of social welfare and management systems. Local governments also lobby state legislatures and executive agencies. One permanent staff member — on a part-time basis — often performs this function by shuttling back and forth to the state capital. The mayor or city manager may lobby on important issues.

At the state level, larger municipalities tend to have a permanent staff presence as well as use professional associations, lobbyists, and law firms. In addition, several consulting and contracting firms specialize in municipal contracts. Many of these firms are based in state capitals and in Washington, D.C. rather than in local communities. Cities such as New York, Chicago, and Los Angeles have their own local revolving doors. As cities increasingly privatize municipal services — such as mass transit, sanitation, and water — more opportunities should develop for consulting firms at the local level.

Opportunity networks are increasingly evident at the state level. Law firms and representatives of professional associations and interest groups lobby state legislatures and agencies. Consulting and contracting firms vie for business with state agencies. Many firms operate only within a particular state. Multi-state firms, such as Bechtel, have branch offices at the state level to generate business with state and local governments.

AT THE CENTER

Washington, D.C. has a well defined network of opportunity structures. This network provides thousands of alternative job opportunities for enterprising individuals willing to work in the nation's capital. Trade and professional associations alone employ over 80,000 individuals in the Washington Metropolitan area.

Job-changing from Congress to agencies to associations to consulting and contracting firms is a time-honored practice in Washington. The ubiquitous personal contact provides access to influential people who can be helpful in making job and career moves within and among various organizations dependent upon government business. For example, the following political and administrative institutions function as alternative opportunity structures: congressional staffs, congressional committees, congressional subcommittees, congressional bureaucracy, executive staff, departments, independent executive agencies, and independent regulatory agencies. Each of these institutions generates thousands of job opportunities and recruits on the basis of different personnel practices. Outside, but linked to, the Federal government are the five types of peripheral groups as outlined in Figure 1 of Chapter 1. A disproportionate number of these groups are headquartered in the Washington Metropolitan area. These groups provide employment and career advancement opportunities for individuals in the public sector job market.

For years Washington insiders have learned how to use these networks to advance their careers. A frequent career pattern is to work in a Federal agency for three to four years. During that time you make important contacts on Capitol Hill with congressional staffs and committees as well as with contractors and associations. Since you have specialized knowledge on the inner workings of government, you have important skills to offer other groups. And if you change jobs frequently, you may be able to advance your career quickly. Indeed, in contrast to job-changers in many other communities in the United States, the job-changer in Washington, D.C. is often seen as someone "in demand" rather than someone with an unstable employment pattern!

NETWORKING

Using specific strategies and techniques designed for acquiring information and contacts through people to move within these opportunity structures is also known as "networking." You must network to be effective in the public sector job market. Effective networking strategies and techniques are outlined in Chapter Eight. Specific networking methods for various types of public sector institutions are examined in chapters of Parts IV, V, and VI on dealing with government, the periphery, and the international arena.

Throughout the remainder of this book we examine two types of networks and networking phenomena — one you create and another already created for your use. The first is *interpersonal networks*. This involves the use of prospecting techniques to generate informational interviews which result in useful job information, advice, and referrals to other informed individuals who generate additional information, advice, and referrals within an ever expanding job search network. Similar to establishing new clients in sales, you take the initiative to develop these networks in hopes they will eventually result in sales. In the job search, "sales" are job interviews and job offers.

The second type of network and networking involves *formal job services networks*. This consists of established groups and organizations specifically designed to provide employment assistance to job seekers. These networks provide all types of assistance, from informal job clubs to job listings and placement services. Dealing with these networks involves locating the services and fully utilizing the most useful components of the services. Government agencies, as well as each of the six peripheral groups, have established various types of these networks. Some are better organized and more useful than others. Indeed, the effectiveness of some services — especially those found among trade and professional associations — provides a refreshing look at an employment phenomenon unknown to many career counselors and job seekers.

Chapter Four
JOB AND CAREER ALTERNATIVES

Numerous job alternatives are available for individuals who understand the size, structure, requirements, and trends of today's job market. Altogether, the American workforce consists of approximately 110 million jobs. According to the *Dictionary of Occupational Titles*, published by the U.S. Department of Labor, these jobs fall into nearly 20,000 categories. With approximately one-third of all jobs relating to the public sector, public employment alternatives are nearly as numerous as those in the private sector.

JOB GROWTH AND TRANSFORMATION

During the past three decades, an incredible number of new jobs were created in both the public and private sectors. This period of major demographic and economic change transformed the basic nature of the job market. Between 1955 and 1980, for instance, the number of jobs increased from 68.7 million to 105.6 million – an average annual increase of 1.5 million new jobs. During the 1970s, jobs increased by over 2 million each year. Between 1980 and 1985, 2.2 to 2.7 million jobs were created each year for an annual growth rate of 1.6 to 2.4 percent. This high rate of employment growth is expected to slow to 1.4 to 1.9 percent per year for the period 1985-1990. By 1990 the total labor force should consist of 122 to 128

46

million workers — up 17 to 22 percent from 1980.

The remarkable growth in jobs during the past decade took place despite recurring recessions and cutbacks in public employment. Both the economy and workforce underwent major transformations which have important implications for the future job market. Among these changes were shifts from:

1. Blue collar to white collar occupations.
2. Manufacturing occupations to service occupations.
3. Primarily male workforce to an increasingly balanced male-female workforce.
4. Old technology to new technology in the workplace.
5. Single job and career pattern to a multi-job and career pattern.
6. Narrow specialization to flexible specialization requiring continuous retraining.
7. A smokestack economy to a service and high-tech economy.
8. Old manufacturing centers in the Northeast and Midwest to new manufacturing, service, and high-tech centers in the South and West.

Job trends in the 1980s, which also should continue into the 1990s, appear to be in the following directions:

1. *Growth in service occupations:* Service occupations will experience the greatest growth in jobs, accounting for 16 percent of all jobs in 1990.
2. *Dynamic job growth in trade sector:* The largest total number of new jobs will be in the trade sector, reflecting its already large base. Approximately 5 to 7.2 million jobs will be created in the wholesale and retail trades.
3. *Limited job growth in manufacturing:* Manufacturing jobs will show little growth — 0.8 to 1.6 percent growth per year.
4. *Bad news for agriculture:* Agricultural jobs will continue to decline.
5. *Major job growth in several new industries:* Major growth occupations center around the information, service, and energy-related industries — computers, engineering, accounting, banking, economics, physics, and health care.
6. *Newly emerging occupational structure and language:*

New occupational structure and vocabulary is emerging around the new occupational fields of computers, robotics, biotechnology, lasers, and fiber optics.

7. *New push toward training and retraining:* Rapid economic transformations attendant with new technology is creating a fluid and changing occupational structure requiring continuous training and retraining of the workforce.

8   *Increased emphasis on part-time employment:* More part-time employment opportunities are available in response to the needs of two-career families, partial entry of many women in the labor force, home-centered work, and preference of employers for maintaining more flexible and cost-effective workforces.

9. *Emerging labor shortages:* Major labor shortages will occur in the job market due to shortage of young people (entry-level) and skilled individuals (middle and upper levels).

10. *Limited advancement opportunities:* Advancement opportunities are becoming limited due to growth of small businesses with short advancement hierarchies, postponement of retirement, continuing focus on non-hierarchical forms of organization, and already glutted managerial ranks.

11. *Rise of entrepreneurship:* Entrepreneurship is increasing with a trend toward more self-employment and new business starts; at the same time, more business failures are occurring.

12. *New patterns of retirement:* An aging workforce is increasingly evident due to fewer young people entering the job market and the tendency for delayed retirement or retirees re-entering the job market to take part-time and entry-level jobs previously held by young people.

PUBLIC SECTOR JOBS

The composition of government employment also has undergone major transformations since 1950. Similar to changes in the private sector workplace, government employs more white collar and female workers than ever before. The jobs require greater specialization, and new technologies are rapidly being introduced into the workplace.

The increase in government employment, especially at the

state and local levels, has been more dramatic than in the private sector — 361 percent increase for state governments and 289 percent increase for local governments versus 90 percent increase in the overall job market. Since 1950, Federal government employment increased by only 36 percent. While a disproportionate amount of the state and local government increase was in education — responding to the post-World War II baby boom children entering public schools — increases were across-the-board in every government occupational category. Government simply grew and grew.

Ironically, the number of governmental units dramatically declined during this same period of major growth in public employment. In the early 1950s, for example, the American governmental system consisted of nearly 150,000 units of government. Today, the same system consists of less than 83,000 governmental units. Most of the decline was due to a major reform movement in the immediate post-World War II period to consolidate school and special districts. While the consolidation eliminated nearly half of the American governmental system, it retained, in a much expanded form, one of the key dynamics of this system — executive bureaucracies which continuously increased their personnel.

These transformations as well as recent changes in government policies toward deficit spending, decentralization, and privatization of government functions has generated several trends for the public sector job market. Among these are:

1. *Slow and declining growth in state and local governments:* Growth in state and local government employment will slow; it will decline substantially in the case of secondary and higher education — the areas with the highest concentration of state and local government employees.

2. *No growth in Federal employment:* Federal employment will remain relatively stable over the next decade. Continuing efforts to control budgetary deficits will ensure recurring freezes on hiring new personnel and the creation of few new positions and programs.

3. *Continuing growth of associations and movement of headquarter operations to Washington, D.C.:* As the trade sector rapidly expands over the next decade, associations will become larger, provide more services to their members, and increase their lobbying and public relations activities. More associations will move their headquarters to the Washington Metropolitan area where they will constitute a rapidly expanding labor

market for association specialists.

4. *Consulting businesses will expand considerably at all levels:* While government employment at all levels will remain relatively stable, government budgets will continue to increase. Much of the increase will go for purchasing public services from consulting firms. Procurement will become an even bigger business within government during the next decade.

5. *Nonprofit organizations will increase the scope of their activities:* Both government and private foundations will further expand their funding of nonprofit organizations to achieve public goals largely relinquished by government agencies. Government agencies will further move to privatize public functions through these organizations.

6. *Research organizations will play a more important role in government:* Government agencies will increasingly purchase information gathering and analysis from private research organizations rather than increase their own in-house information gathering, processing, and analytical capabilities in specialized areas.

7. *Professional lobbying organizations, association management firms, and law firms representing businesses and associations will continue to expand:* As associations expand in number and size, they will require the specialized legal, management, and political services of groups organized to provide such services.

8. *International opportunities will be increasingly limited to experienced professionals:* Fewer opportunities will be available for generalists. Opportunities also will be limited for working abroad as public organizations place greater emphasis on developing local capabilities by employing and training host-country nationals to replace expatriate Americans. Except for the U.S. Peace Corps and voluntary nonprofit organizations, few entry-level positions will be available.

9. *More and more government employees will seek public service careers outside government:* As government employees experience limited career growth, plateau their careers, play routine contracting roles, and become more aware of public service careers outside government, they will seek to make successful career transitions to nongovernmental public organizations.

The overall trend for the public sector over the next decade will be slow growth in government institutions. Government spending will continue to increase, but the number of government personnel and direct services performed by government agencies will remain stable or decline. Major growth, however, will take place among most peripheral institutions. Rather than witness a shrinking public sector, over the next decade we should see rapid and dynamic growth among nongovernmental institutions involved with public policy issues. In so doing, the role of government will increasingly shift toward that of a contractor directing public funds into organizations which have the capabilities to provide public services efficiently and effectively. Government agencies will become more like interest groups as they attempt to influence the direction and activities of these nongovernmental public institutions.

GOVERNMENT INSTITUTIONS

Consisting of 82,341 units of government and over 16 million public employees and despite cutbacks and no-growth trends, today's governmental system yields numerous job opportunities in thousands of job categories. Except for many manufacturing and sales occupations, most job categories found in the private sector also have counterparts in government. Since government produces both goods and services, numerous occupational skills can be transferred from the private sector into government, and vice versa.

The major opportunities among the 16 million government jobs are mainly confined to four units of government: Federal, state, municipal, and county. Townships, school districts, and special districts yield a sizeable number of jobs, but they tend to have limited job alternatives, salaries, and advancement opportunities.

Federal employment opportunities remain relatively constant. The Federal government hires about 1,000 individuals each day. This mainly represents replacement of existing personnel who have an average annual turnover rate of 14 percent. The Federal government hires individuals in thousands of job categories. After all, it engages in a broad spectrum of activities, ranging from managing large self-contained communities, such as military bases and the Pentagon, to the more mundane and sterotypical aspects of government. Work of Federal employees includes:

- Issuing social security checks, welfare payments, and inter-governmental funds.

- Regulating private industry.
- Managing public lands and water resources.
- Extending aid to cities and states.
- Conducting research.
- Providing health care.
- Publishing books and documents.
- Stimulating entrepreneurship and business investment.
- Dispensing grants and loans.
- Regulating trade.
- Protecting minorities.
- Printing and managing money.
- Developing communication and security systems.
- Delivering mail.
- Policing individuals and organizations.
- Exploring outer space, the oceans, and polar regions.
- Gathering and analyzing demographic, economic, and social data.
- Maintaining public buildings, monuments, and cemeteries.
- Assisting the international community.
- Incarcerating criminals.
- Providing support services for all of its activities.
- Collecting artifacts and memorabilia.
- Housing public employees.
- Gathering intelligence on potential enemies.

Such a variety of activities means many types of government jobs including those for: janitors, drivers, grounds keepers, undertakers, typists, secretaries, plumbers, mechanics, typesetters, printers, teachers, scientists, researchers, policy analysts, grants specialists, case workers, lawyers, program officers, artists, movie directors, and clergymen.

State employment opportunities also run the gamet with education being the largest single category for state employment. State governments require a large variety of employees to manage increasingly complex organizational activities. Indeed, during the past two decades, state governments have asserted stronger governance roles with new and expanded functions. State governments tend to perform more indirect regulatory and administrative services than do local governments, especially in the areas of inspecting, licensing, and collecting revenue. Major direct services provided by state governments tend to be in the areas of higher education, welfare, mental health, highway maintenance and safety, and parks and recreation. Most of these state services have Federal government counterparts.

Municipal employment opportunities are tied to specific city services. While city governments are supposed to have a single bureaucracy, in practice three bureaucracies tend to function simultaneously, each in response to a particular set of local functions and constituents. The first bureaucracy relates to education. Even when education is placed under city government – rather than in special districts (45 of 50 states) – educators tend to be managed by a separate bureaucracy. This bureaucracy has its own rules and regulations as well as separate personnel and wage systems.

The second bureaucracy relates to public safety, especially police and fire. They, too, constitute a bureaucracy within a bureaucracy, structured similarly to a military organization with separate rules and regulations and personnel and wage systems. In addition, this group tends to be more highly organized and militant than other municipal employees.

The final bureaucracy includes the diverse group of remaining city employees. Relatively unorganized and specialized in particular functions, this bureaucracy has numerous subgroups which tend to be relatively autonomous. In many communities, the parks and recreation department has experienced significant growth during the past two decades.

Overall, city governments tend to be *internally decentralized and fragmented*, posing particular challenges to job seekers who often assume most job action is centralized around the personnel department. Similar situations prevail in the cases of state and Federal governments where the hiring process is largely decentralized within individual agencies.

Depending on the specific state and community, school districts, townships, and a variety of special districts may function within and around urban areas. In some cases – especially in the Northeast and Midwest – the number and variety of these local government organizations overlap and conflict in a truly mind-boggling manner. Illinois, for example, has about twice as many local jurisdictions per capita than most states – the epitome of a government jungle! Organized chaos is the fundamental characteristic of government in these areas. In spite of major and successful efforts to consolidate these units in the 1950s, an incredible number of overlapping jurisdictions, inefficiency of operations, and just pure chaos remains. Such a local government structure gives the American governmental system the image of being an essentially decentralized, fragmented, and chaotic system – an image it justly deserves.

For the job seeker, these local units of government offer numerous job opportunities. However, on the whole, they do not offer great opportunities. Because of their small size, the economies of scale do not permit them to offer generous salaries, benefits, and advancement opportunities. Managerially, they lack sufficient resources and thus are often frustrating units of government. Governmental units with substantial functions encompassing a population of about 200,000 are most likely to yield significant job opportunities. Municipalities and counties – not special districts, townships, and school districts – tend to meet this criteria.

County governments are perhaps the most overlooked units of local government. This is unfortunate, because in many cases they offer good job opportunities with adequate salaries, benefits, and advancement opportunities. Gone are the days when most counties were essentially rural and dominated by political machines. Today, the majority of counties are urban and are increasingly staffed by professionals. Indeed, recent trends in local government are to transfer more and more municipal services to the urban county level. In metropolitan areas, it makes both economic and political sense to transfer such major municipal services as police, fire, mass transit, sanitation, and education to the county level. Where politically feasible, urban county governments should grow considerably over the next two decades as a new reform movement takes hold to further consolidate local governments. The growth in urban county governments will most likely be at the expense of city bureaucracies.

Examples of these urban governments include Los Angeles County, Miami-Dade County, and Fairfax County adjacent to Washington, D.C. In the Washington, D.C. Metropolitan area alone several urban county governments in Maryland and Virginia have undergone phenomenal growth in population, revenue, and public services in the period 1960 to 1986. Montgomery (Maryland) County's budget went from $54 million to $967.6 million; Prince George's (Maryland) County's budget increased from $21.9 million to $605 million; and Fairfax (Virginia) County's budget grew from $21.1 million to $783.8 million during this 26 year period. These counties provide models for other urban counties as well as for what many observers believe is the coming consolidation movement at the local level.

PERIPHERAL GROUPS

The periphery consists of numerous institutions and organizations which regularly interact with government as well as pursue public goals. It includes both profit and nonprofit organizations as well as voluntary and nonvoluntary groups. The total number of job opportunities with these organizations is difficult to accurately estimate. A conservative figure is at least another 16 million positions are found among peripheral organizations in the public sector.

The Washington Metropolitan public sector network is a good example. Although many people still believe government employs a majority of the workforce in and around Washington, beginning in 1983 government ranked second to private business. More than 50 percent of the job opportunities in the Washington, D.C. Metropolitan area are found in the nongovernmental "service" sector — contracting and consulting firms; law and public relations firms; professional and trade associations; nonprofit organizations; foundations; and research organizations. This sector should continue to grow in direct proportion to the growth in the Federal budget.

At the state and local levels, similar growth has taken place in this nongovernmental service sector. Lacking specific data on the size and shape of the sector, our best guess is that it continues to grow in spite of state and local government cutbacks. Moreover, we expect the periphery to expand as state and local governments shift more functions to private sector organizations. Expect public employment to level off at the state and local levels, even though budgets will continue to increase. Following the pattern at the Federal level, state and local governments will probably intensify the contracting-out of public services. In addition, local governments will privatize more of their basic service functions.

While peripheral organizations at the state and local levels include associations, consulting firms, foundations, and lobbying groups, numerous nonprofit organizations are also prevalent. The United Way and Red Cross, for example, are large organizations in terms of both budget and personnel. Operating mainly in municipalities, they offer job opportunities for enterprising public sector job seekers. Hundreds of other nonprofit community service organizations also generate employment alternatives.

INTERNATIONAL ARENA

Identifying as well as structuring a job search aimed at the international public sector is often difficult to do. The international arena is extremely fragmented, and information is difficult to access. Nonetheless, numerous and exciting job opportunities exist in this arena.

The international public sector consists of many international-oriented state and local government agencies, Federal agencies, regulatory and development organizations, consulting and research firms, nonprofit organizations, international organizations, and an assortment of organizations difficult to classify. A majority of these organizations provide development assistance to Third World countries. Others focus on strengthening economic, political, and military relations among both developed and developing countries. Many are oriented toward U.S. foreign policy interests.

Both state agencies and local governments are involved in international affairs. States with international trade and tourism interests, such as California, Illinois, New York, and Florida, will have positions relevant to developing international relations. Many of these positions will be directly attached to the Governor's office or found in trade sections of commerce departments. Some large cities also have positions in their economic development departments for promoting foreign investment and tourism. Employees in those positions are expected to develop public relations approaches and establish contacts with potential clients both in the U.S. and abroad. Realizing both the reality and importance of foreign investment in the U.S., an increasing number of cities are beginning to establish international relations requiring qualified international personnel. In many large cities, World Affairs Councils – comprised of local officials, business leaders, and educators – join together in promoting local interest in international issues.

The Federal government is a major employer of international specialists. In addition to the Department of State and the Department of Defense, every department and numerous agencies have either direct or counterpart international interests requiring full-time international specialists and related support personnel. Trade negotiators, commercial officers, Foreign Service Officers, cultural affairs officers, foreign intelligence officers, agronomists, economists, policy analysts, engineers, doctors, teachers, and librarians are only a few of the many international jobs available. Within the Executive Office of the President, the Council of Economic Advisors, National Security Council, Office of Management and Budget, Office of Science and Technology, and Office of the U.S. Trade Representative have major international interests and thus employ international specialists.

Within the Executive Departments, over 100 agencies have international interests and employ international specialists. Independent and quasi-governmental agencies also have international interests and employees as do the lesser known Federal commissions, committees, and advisory groups.

Within the legislative branch of the Federal government, the House and Senate committee and personal staffs as well as the legislative bureaucracy, primarily consisting of the Congressional Budget Office, General Accounting Office, and the Library of

Congress, provide international employment opportunities.

Related to U.S. government involvement in international affairs are numerous international consulting and research firms based in the United States and abroad. The consulting firms generally provide services to government in the areas of research, management, engineering, and basic public services. The majority of these firms work in developing countries. Several research organizations also do international work directly related to the interests of the U.S. government.

The United Nations is the primary non-American international organization providing employment opportunities for Americans. The United Nations is divided into six UN organs, 15 specialized agencies, and numerous related organizations. Regional international organizations, such as the North Atlantic Treaty Organization and the Organization of American States, also provide job opportunities for enterprising job seekers.

Several nonprofit organizations, foundations, and educational and communication groups function in the international arena. They, too, offer interesting job and career opportunities for those who have the requisite skills and know-how to locate job opportunities.

Details, including addresses and telephone numbers, on the various public sector job alternatives outlined in this chapter are included in the relevant chapters of Parts V and VI. Each chapter surveys the most important resources available to untangling the chaos of the various public sector job markets.

PART II

EFFECTIVE JOB SEARCH SKILLS AND STRATEGIES

Knowing *where* the jobs are is important to your job search. But knowing *how to find a job* is even more important. Before you acquire names, addresses, and phone numbers of potential employers, you should possess the necessary job search skills and strategies for both gathering and using job information effectively.

In this section we outline the most important skills and strategies for conducting an effective job search. These are general skills and strategies appropriate for most public and private sector employment situations. In later sections of the book, we outline additional skills and strategies most appropriate for particular public sector environments.

The skills and strategies discussed in this section are directly transferable to most public sector situations. They constitute the *foundation skills and strategies* from which you must custom-design effective approaches for different public sector jobs and careers.

However, one important word of caution is in order before you plunge into this skills section and become a true-believer in such concepts as functional skills, combination resumes, referral letters, prospecting, networking, and informational interviewing. Government agencies, associations, consulting firms, foundations, and research organizations each have their own hiring cultures, consisting of both formal and informal personnel practices. Even within each group, individual organizations will differ in how they recruit, evaluate, and select individuals. Some organizations will have highly formalized application and testing procedures. Others maintain computerized talent banks which they regularly use for recruiting new personnel. Others work strictly on an informal, word-of-mouth basis. Others have developed important formal and informal networking mechanisms. And still others frequently use professional recruiting services to identity and select job candidates.

If you fail to adapt the skills and strategies outlined in the next four chapters to specific employment situations, you will encounter difficulties with your job search. Based upon your research activities, you must adapt, adapt, adapt, adapt. In the end, you will learn there is no one best approach which can be used universally for all organizations and employment situations.

Chapter Five

PREPARE
TO TAKE ACTION

Preparation for a job search involves a combination of knowledge, skills, and abilities relevant to both the job market and particular jobs. You must understand where you are going, how you will get there, and the prerequisites for successfully achieving your goals.

DEVELOP YOUR CAREERING COMPETENCIES

How well can you plan and implement an effective job search? Successful job seekers use a great deal of information as well as specific skills and strategies in getting the jobs they want. Test yourself to see what job search information, skills, and strategies you currently possess as well as those you need to develop or improve. You can easily identify your level of job search competence by completing Exercise 1.

61

EXERCISE 1

TESTING YOUR CAREERING COMPETENCIES

INSTRUCTIONS: Respond to each statement by circling which number at the right best represents your situation.

SCALE: 1 = strongly agree
2 = agree
3 = maybe, not certain
4 = disagree
5 = strongly disagree

1. I know what skills I can offer employers in
different occupations.   1 2 3 4 5

2. I know what skills employers most seek in
candidates.   1 2 3 4 5

3. I can clearly explain to employers what I
do well and enjoy doing.   1 2 3 4 5

4. I can specify why an employer should hire me.   1 2 3 4 5

5. I can gain support of family and friends for
making a job or career change.   1 2 3 4 5

6. I can find 10 to 20 hours of time each week
to conduct a part-time job search.   1 2 3 4 5

7. I have the financial ability to sustain a
three-month job search.   1 2 3 4 5

8. I can conduct library and interview research
on different occupations, employers,
organizations, and communities.   1 2 3 4 5

9. I can write different types of effective
resumes, job search letters, and thank-you
notes.   1 2 3 4 5

10. I can produce and distribute resumes and
letters to the right people.   1 2 3 4 5

11. I can list my major accomplishments in
action terms.   1 2 3 4 5

12. I can identify and target employers I want
to interview.   1 2 3 4 5

13. I can develop a job referral network.   1 2 3 4 5

14. I can persuade others to join in forming
a job search support group.   1 2 3 4 5

15. I can prospect for job leads.   1 2 3 4 5

16. I can use the telephone to develop prospects
and get referrals and interviews.   1 2 3 4 5

17. I can plan and implement an effective
direct-mail job search campaign.   1 2 3 4 5

18. I can generate one job interview for every
10 job search contacts I make.   1 2 3 4 5

19. I can follow-up on job interviews.   1 2 3 4 5

20. I can negotiate a salary 10-20% above what
an employer initially offers.   1 2 3 4 5

21. I can persuade an employer to renegotiate
my salary after six months on the job.   1 2 3 4 5

22. I can create a position for myself in an
organization.   1 2 3 4 5

TOTALS   _____

GRAND TOTAL   _____

You can calculate your overall careering competencies by adding the numbers you circled in Exercise 1 for a total composite score. If your grand total is more than 60 points, you need to work on developing your careering skills. How you scored each item will indicate to what degree you need to work on improving specific job search skills. If your score is under 40 points, you may wish to skip this and the next two chapters; go directly to the chapters on public sector employment. The remainder of this section will focus on developing your careering competencies. After completing this section, you should be well prepared to conduct your own job search in both the public and private sectors.

ACQUIRE MORE EDUCATION AND TRAINING

Do I have the necessary skills and experience employers require as prerequisites to be considered for a position? Do I need to go back to school for a degree, diploma, or certificate? These questions are frequently asked by individuals entering the job market or those making a job or career change. The questions are especially important when approaching public sector jobs. For example, many international positions require professional degrees. More specialized education programs are now offered for managing trade and professional associations.

It is difficult to provide simple answers to these questions. However, you should first know what it is you want to do. It is always best to find employment that is conducive to your particular mix of interests, skills, and abilities rather than try to locate jobs which may demonstrate your weaknesses. Second, you must conduct research to identify what skills training is really required for particular positions. Notice, we say *skills training* – not education. Although related, there is an important difference between skills training and education. Many employers are looking for specific skills rather than educational credentials. Unfortunately, most educational institutions are still oriented toward transferring disciplines and subject matter to students rather than specific skills relevant to the world of work. If you fail to keep these two points in mind, you may waste a great deal of time and money on unnecessary training or seek jobs you are unqualified to perform.

So how should you proceed? Do the necessary self-assessment and data gathering required to answer these questions. Begin by asking yourself a key question for orienting your job search: *"What do I really want to do?"* Follow the exercises in Chapter 6 to conduct a self-assessment and set goals. Once you have a clear idea of your job and career goals, you will be prepared to target your job search toward particular organizations, positions, and individuals.

Assuming you know what you want to do, your next step is to gather information to determine whether you possess the necessary skills to qualify for the job. Obviously, if you are a high school graduate wishing to become a medical doctor, engineer, lawyer, or accountant, you will need several years of highly specialized training for certification in these fields. However, if you want to become an FBI agent, just what educational background, experience, and demonstrated skills do you need? Where do you find this information?

You can begin answering these questions by consulting several publications identified in Chapter 6 on conducting job research.

Next, talk to individuals who have a working knowledge of the particular job or career you desire. Contact people in similar positions to what you are seeking. While many educators can be helpful, they should rank as a secondary information source. Few educators are objective sources for information about education and training requirements for particular jobs. Remember, most educators are relatively isolated from day-to-day job market realities. Furthermore, educators are in the business of keeping themselves employed by recruiting more students into existing programs as well as by developing new degree and certification programs. They are committed to promoting more formal education, degrees, and certification — whether or not such training and documentation is really necessary and relevant to the world of work.

If you read materials and talk to informed individuals and employers, you will quickly learn what you need to do to be successful in your job search. If you learn you must return to school for a formal degree or certificate, your information sources will identify the most appropriate type of training you should acquire as well as recommend where best to receive the training. In many cases you will find you do not need additional training to qualify for a position. Since many employers prefer conducting their own in-house training, they primarily look for individuals who are motivated, enthusiastic, and trainable.

If you must acquire new skills, keep in mind several training options:

- Public vocational education
- Private vocational education
- Employer training
- Apprenticeship programs
- Federal employment and training programs
- Armed Forces training
- Home study schools
- Community and junior colleges
- Colleges and universities

Most of these sources emphasize practical hands-on training. Private trade schools, for example, are flourishing while university enrollments are stagnant and declining — indicating a shift to practical skills training in education. Each alternative has various advantages and disadvantages, and costs differ considerably.

Public vocational education is provided through secondary, postsecondary, and adult vocational and technical programs. Many secondary schools give students vocational training in addition to the regular academic program. Postsecondary vocational education is provided for high school graduates who do not seek baccalaureate degrees. Adult vocational and technical programs emphasize retraining or upgrading the skills of individuals in the labor force.

Vocational education traditionally emphasized training in agriculture, trade, and industry. Today, the emphasis is on distribution, health, home economics, office, and technical occupations. Most programs train individuals for specific occupations outlined in the U.S. Department of Labor's *Occupational Outlook Handbook*. Approximately 18 million individuals are enrolled in vocational education programs. The numbers are expected to increase throughout the 1980s and into the 1990s.

Private vocational education is provided through approximately 7,000 institutions. Enrolling over 1 million students in 165 different programs, private vocational education is provided in seven major areas: agribusiness, marketing/distribution, health, home economics, business/office, technical, and trades and industry. Two-thirds of these schools are specialized cosmetology/barber, business/office, and flight schools. Most of these institutions are small, with fewer than 100 students, specializing in only one or two skill areas such as real estate, nursing, auto work, commercial art, or apparel.

Employer training focuses on transferring specific skills to new employees, improving employee performance, or preparing employees for new jobs. Skilled and semi-skilled workers are trained through apprenticeships, learning-by-doing, and structured on-the-job instruction. White-collar employees usually receive classroom training offered by in-house trainers, professional associations, private firms, or colleges and universities. Tuition-aid programs are used frequently by firms lacking in-house training resources.

Apprenticeship programs normally range from one to five years, depending on the particular occupational skill requirements. These programs are used most extensively in the trade occupations. Of the more than 50,000 apprenticeship completions registered with the Department of Labor each year, approximately 60 percent are in construction trades, 12 percent in metalworking, 4 percent in personal services, 2 percent in printing, and over 20 percent in miscellaneous areas. Over 300,000 individuals enroll in apprenticeship programs each year.

Federal employment and training consist of a maze of 22 programs, ranging from Trade Adjustment Assistance to programs for redwood forest lumberjacks. The major Federal programs largely function through state and local governments. Since 1983, the largest Federal program has been a public-private collaborative effort to identify training needs and develop training programs at the local level. The Jobs Training Partnership Act (JTPA) establishes Private Industry Councils (PIC's) at the local level to develop training programs in response to locally-defined needs. The successor program to the CETA programs of the 1970s, JTPA/PIC programs primarily provide vocational training for relatively unskilled and hard to employ individuals.

Armed Forces training focuses on five categories of training: recruitment, specialized skills, officer acquisition, professional development, and flight. Specialized skills training is by far the most important and extensive training conducted by the various services. Within this training category, enlisted personnel receive a great deal of technical training which can be directly transferred to the civilian work world.

Home study or correspondence schools provide several training options. Most programs concentrate on developing a single skill; others offer professional certificates and academic degrees by mail — even Ph.Ds! While some programs are of questionable quality, many are good programs. For certain people, these programs offer a convenient, inexpensive, and effective way of learning new skills. Approximately 3 million students enroll in home study courses each year. Over 1 million of them enroll in programs sponsored by the Federal government and the military.

Community and junior colleges in recent years have shifted emphasis from preparing individuals for university degree programs to equipping them with skills for today's job market. More programs now emphasize vocational or occupational curriculums, such as data processing or dental hygiene, which are typically two-year programs resulting in an associate degree. Enrollments in these and other community college programs increased dramatically during the 1970s and early 1980s. They should continue strong throughout the 1980s and into the 1990s as these colleges further adapt their programs to changing demands in the job market for different types of skilled workers at the local level.

Colleges and universities continue to provide the traditional four-year and graduate degree programs in various subject fields. While many of the fields are occupational-specific, requiring certification — such as engineering, law, medicine, and accounting — many are not. The exact relationship of degree programs to the job market varies with different disciplines. Because of this, many graduates of certain programs have had difficulty finding employment in their chosen fields. This is particularly true for students with a generalist background in the liberal arts. More recently, however, many colleges and universities have adjusted to declining enrollments by offering several nontraditional, occupational-related courses and programs.

Continuing education, special skills training courses, short courses, and workshops and seminars on job-related matters have become popular with nontraditional, older students who seek specific skills training rather than degrees. At the same time, traditional academic programs are placing greater emphasis on internships and cooperative education programs in order to give students work experience related to their academic programs.

Additional training programs may be sponsored by local governments, professional associations, women's centers, YWCA's, and religious and civic groups. As training and retraining become more acceptable to the general public, a greater number and variety of training programs will be offered by these groups.

Expect a revolution in the training field over the next decade. It will be closely related to high-tech developments. Computer-based training, similar in some respects to traditional home study programs, will become more prevalent as home computers and interactive video training packages are developed in response to the new technology and the rising demand for skills training. Much training will become "prosumer": in a decentralized information market, individuals will choose what training they most desire as well as control when and where they will receive it. With the development of interactive video training programs, individuals will manage the training process in a more efficient and effective manner than with the more centralized, time consuming, and expensive use of traditional student-teacher classroom instruction. This type of training will make much of today's education and training obsolete.

BECOME AN INFORMED CONSUMER

Several publications can help you decide which training path is most appropriate for you. If you decide you need to acquire a specific skill, consult various professional or trade associations; many can provide you with a list of reputable institutions providing skills training in particular fields. The names, addresses, and telephone numbers of all major associations are listed in the *Encyclopedia of Associations*, an extremely useful directory found in most main library reference sections.

Other sources of published information on education and training opportunities include the reference section of libraries, career planning centers, or guidance offices. Most have collections of catalogues and directories listing educational and training opportunities. Two publishing firms annually issue several useful educational directories: Barron's Educational Series and Peterson's Guides.

The National Association of Trade and Technical Schools (NATTS) publishes three useful guides to private trade and technical schools: *Handbook of Trade and Technical Careers and Training, How to Choose a Career and a Career School,* and *College Plus: Put Your Degree to Work With Trade and Technical Skills.* You can get copies of these publications by mail or telephone: NATTS, 2251 Wisconsin Ave., NW, #200, Washington, D.C. 20007, Tel. 202/333-1021.

The Apprenticeship Information Center (AIC) provides information on apprenticeship programs. It is affiliated with the U.S. Employment Service, and provides information, counseling, aptitude testing, and referrals to union hiring halls and employers. Also, write to the U.S. Department of Labor's Bureau of Apprenticeship and Training for several pamphlets dealing with apprenticeships: Inquiries Unit, Employment and Training Administration, U.S. Department of Labor, 601 D St., Rm. 8122, Washington, D.C. 20213, Tel. 202/376-2570.

If you are interested in home study and correspondence courses, the National Home Study Council issues two useful publications for surveying your options: *Directory of Accredited Home Study Schools* (free — send postcard) and *There's a School in Your Mail Box* ($6.00). Write or call: National Home Study Council, 1601 18th St., NW, Washington, D.C. 20009, Tel. 202/234-5100.

You also need to determine the quality and suitability of these programs. After all, this is a business transaction — your money in exchange for their services. As an informed consumer, you must demand quality performance for your money. Therefore, when contacting a particular institution, ask to speak to former students and graduates. Write to the Council on Postsecondary Accreditation (One Dupont Circle, Suite 305, Washington, D.C. 20036, Tel. 202/452-1433) to inquire about the school's credentials. Focus your attention on the *results or outcomes* the institution achieves. Instead of asking how many faculty have Master or Ph.D. degrees, or how many students are enrolled, ask these questions:

- What are last year's graduates doing today?
- Where do they work and for whom?
- How much do they earn?
- How many were placed in jobs through this institution?

If they can not answer these questions, they probably can not meet your needs and hence do not deserve your time, effort, and money.

Most colleges and universities will provide assistance to adult learners. Contact student services, continuing education, academic advising, adult services, or women's offices at your local community college, college, or university. Be sure to talk to present and former students about the *expectations and results* of the programs for them.

If you need further assistance, contact a local branch of the National Center for Educational Brokering (CEB). While there is no national clearinghouse to help you match your goals with appropriaate educational programs, NCEB can assist you nonetheless. NCEB counselors will help you identify your goals and career alternatives. For information on the center nearest you, write to the National Center for Educational Brokering, 325 9th St., San Francisco, CA 94103, Tel. 415/626-2378.

Other sources of information on education and training programs are the Yellow Pages of telephone directories and employers. Look under "Schools" in the telephone book. Call the schools and ask them to send you literature and application forms. Ask them how best to acquire the necessary skills for particular occupations. Most important, *thoroughly research alternatives before you invest money, time, and effort.*

Beware of education and training myths. Additional education and training is not always the answer for entry or advancement within the job market. First, you should identify what it is you want to do and then identify what it is you need to do to get what you want. Indeed, employers spend about $40 billion each year on employee training and retraining — much of which is spent because of the failure of traditional educational institutions. You may find it is best to get into a particular organization that provides excellent training for its employees. Most of your best run corporations rely on their own in-house training rather than on institutions outside the corporation. Even government is providing more and more training for its employees, although it still places a great deal of emphasis on formal educational credentials for entry into the government service.

SELECT USEFUL OPTIONS

You have two options in organizing your job search. First, you can follow the principles and advice outlined in this self-directed book. Just read the chapters and then put them into practice by following the step-by-step instructions. Second, you may wish to seek professional help to either supplement or replace this book. Indeed, many people will read parts of this book — perhaps all of it — and do nothing. Unwilling to take initiative, lacking sufficient time, or failing to follow-through, many people will eventually seek professional help to organize and implement their job search. They will pay good money to get someone else to tell them to follow the advice found in this book. Some people need this type of expensive motivation.

At the same time, we recognize the value of professional assistance. Especially with the critical skills identification and objective setting steps (Chapter 6), some individuals may need more assistance than our advice and exercises provide. If this pertains to you, by all means seek professional help.

You also should beware of pitfalls in seeking professional advice. While many services are excellent, other services are useless and fraudulent. Career planning and job assistance are big businesses involving millions of dollars each year. Many people enter these businesses without expertise. Indeed, many get into the business because they are unemployed. In other words, they major in their own problem! Others are frauds and hucksters who will take your money in exchange for broken promises. You should know something about these professional services before you venture beyond this book.

Look in the Yellow Pages of your telephone directory under these headings: Management Consultants, Employment, Resumes, Career Planning, and Social Services. Several career planning and employment services are available, ranging from highly generalized to very specific services. Most services claim they can help you. If you read this book, you will be in a better position to seek out specific services as well as ask the right questions. You may even discover you know more about finding a job than some of the professionals!

At least 10 different career planning and employment services are available to assist you with your job search. Each has certain advantages and disadvantages. Approach them with caution. Never sign a contract before you read the fine print, get a second opinion, and talk to former clients about the *results* they achieved through the service.

Public employment services are normally provided by a state agency which dispenses employment assistance and unemployment compensation. Employment assistance usually consists of job listings and counseling services. Counseling services mainly involve screening individuals for employers choosing to list low paying jobs with the agency. However, employers generally avoid this service, especially for positions requiring skills in the $18,000 plus range. Since most people using these services are unemployed, unskilled, and poor, the services have difficulty placing such people. Some experts believe these offices should be abolished because they actually exacerbate unemployment; they take people away from the most productive channels for employment — personal contacts and retraining programs. You may choose to avoid these offices. On the other hand, some state and local government agencies routinely use these services in listing job vacancies. Therefore, if you are looking for a government job, you should neither completely neglect these services nor place too much reliance on them.

Private employment agencies work for money received from applicants and employers. Approximately 8,000 such agencies operate nationwide. Many are highly specialized in technical, scientific, and financial fields. The majority of these firms serve employers since they — not applicants — represent repeat business. Employers will normally pay a placement fee. When applicants pay for the service, agencies will charge 10 to 15 percent of the applicant's first year salary. These firms have one major advantage: job leads you may have difficulty uncovering elsewhere. A good firm can be extremely helpful, particularly in highly specialized fields. But these firms can be costly, and the quality of their services varies. Be careful in how you deal with them. Make sure you understand the fee structure and what they will do for you before you sign anything. Most of these firms will not help you find a government job. Nonetheless, many of their clients represent public sector organizations working at the periphery of government.

College and university placement offices provide in-house career planning services for graduating students. While some give assistance to alumni, many do not. Most of these offices are understaffed or provide only rudimentary services, such as maintaining a career planning library, coordinating on-campus interviews for graduating seniors, and presenting workshops on how to write resumes and conduct job interviews. Check with your local campus to see what services you might use.

Private career and job search firms are organized to help individuals acquire job search skills. They will not find you a job. In other words, they teach you much — maybe more but possibly less — of what is outlined in this book. Expect to pay anywhere from $1,500 to $10,000 for this service. If you need a monetary incentive to practice what you find in this book, contract with one of these firms!

Executive search firms find employees to fill critical positions in the $30,000 plus salary range. Working for employers, they also are known as "headhunters," "management consultants," and "executive recruiters." These firms find high-level technical and managerial talent for organizations. They call you rather than you call them. If a friend or relative is in such a business or you have relevant skills, let them know you are available – and ask for their advice on how to contact employers. You may want to consult two useful books on this subject: Kenneth J. Cole, *The Headhunter Strategy: How to Make It Work For You* (New York: John Wiley and Sons) and Robert H. Perry, *How to Answer a Headhunter's Call: A Complete Guide to Executive Search* (New York: AMACOM).

Marketing services combine job search and executive search activities. Charging $2,500 or more, marketing firms usually work with individuals anticipating a starting salary of at least $25,000. These firms try to minimize one's job search time and risk. A typical operation will charge a $100 enrollment fee for developing a client's psychological, skills, and interests profiles. Next, a marketing plan is outlined and a contract signed for specific services. Assisted by a word processor, the firm develops a slick "professional" resume and mails it, along with a cover letter, to hundreds – maybe thousands – of firms. Clients are then briefed and sent to interview with interested employers. While you can save money and achieve the same results on your own by playing a similar direct-mail numbers game, these firms do have one major advantage: save you *time* by doing most of the work for you. Again, approach these services with caution.

Women's Centers and special career services respond to the employment needs of special groups. Women's Centers often sponsor basic career planning workshops and job information networks for women first entering and re-entering the workforce. Special career services arise at times for different categories of employees. Unemployed aerospace engineers, teachers, veterans, elderly, air traffic controllers, and government employees have formed special groups for developing job search skills and sharing job leads.

Testing and assessment centers provide assistance for identifying vocational skills, interests, and objectives. Usually staffed by trained professionals, these centers administer several types of tests. They normally charge from $400 to $600 per person. If our activities in Chapter 6 do not give you enough information on your skills and interests, you may wish to use some of these services. But try our exercises before you hire a psychologist!

Job fairs or career conferences are organized by employment agencies to link applicants to employers. Consisting of one or two-day hotel meetings, employers meet with applicants as a group and on a one-on-one basis. Employers give presentations on their organizations, resumes are circulated, and candidates are interviewed. Many of these conferences are organized around particular skill areas, such as engineering or computers. These are excellent sources for job leads and information — if you can get invited to the meetings. Employers pay for this service.

Professional associations often provide placement assistance for their members. Most associations list job vacancies in newsletters and organize a job information exchange at annual conferences. Others may provide a resume service, job and talent banks, and executive search services. Annual meetings are good sources for making job contacts in different geographic locations within a particular professional field. Many public employee associations provide such services for their members. The quality and effectiveness of these services will vary greatly.

Other types of career planning and employment services are growing and specializing in particular occupational fields. You may wish to use these services as a supplement to this book. Whatever you do, proceed with caution and know exactly what you are getting into. Remember, there is no such thing as a free lunch, and you often get less than what you pay for. After reading the next two chapters, you should be able to make intelligent decisions about what, when, where, and with what results you can use professional assistance. Shop around, compare services and costs, ask questions, talk to former clients, and read the fine print with your lawyer before giving an employment expert a job!

BE SUCCESSFUL

Once you begin your job search, you will discover that success is seldom determined by implementing a good plan. Nor is success due primarily to intelligence, thinking big, time management, or luck. Based on our experience, career planning success is most often associated with these 20 principles for taking action:

1. *You should work hard at finding a job:* Make this a daily endeavor and involve your family.
2. *You should not be discouraged with set-backs:* You are playing the odds, so expect disappointments and handle them in stride. You will probably encounter many "nos" before you uncover the one "yes" which is right for you.
3. *You should be patient and persevere:* Expect three months of hard work before you connect with the right job. With government, the waiting period may be as much as 18 months!
4. *You should be honest with yourself and others:* Hon-

esty is always the best policy, but don't be naive and stupid by blindly confessing your failures, weaknesses, and shortcomings to potential employers.

5. *You should develop a positive attitude toward yourself:* Nobody wants to employ guilt-ridden people with inferiority complexes. Focus on your positive characteristics and accomplishments; let others know what is right about you.

6. *You should associate with positive and successful people:* You are in the people-business, and your success will depend on how well you relate to others. Make a habit of running with winners.

7 *You should set goals:* You should have a clear idea of what you want and where you are going. Without these, you will present a confusing and indecisive image to others. Set high goals that make you work hard.

8. *You should plan:* Convert your goals into action steps that are organized as short, intermediate, and long-range plans.

9. *You should get organized:* Translate your plans into activities, targets, names, addresses, telephone numbers, and materials. Develop an efficient and effective filing system. Use a large calendar for setting time targets and recording appointments and useful information.

10. *You should be a good communicator:* Take stock of your oral, written, and nonverbal communication skills. How well do you communicate? Since most aspects of your job search involve communicating with others, and communication skills are one of the most sought-after skills, always present yourself well both verbally and nonverbally.

11. *You should be energetic and enthusiastic:* Employers are attracted to positive people. They avoid negative and depressing people who toil at their work. Generate enthusiasm both verbally and nonverbally. Check your telephone voice — it may be more unenthusiastic than your voice in face-to-face situations.

12. *You should ask questions:* Your best information comes from asking questions. Learn to develop intelligent questions that are non-aggressive, polite, and interesting to others. But don't ask too many questions or talk too much.

13. *You should be a good listener:* Being a good listener is

often more important than being a good questioner and talker. Learn to improve your face-to-face listening behavior (nonverbal cues) as well as remember and utilize information gained from others. Make others feel they enjoy talking with you, because you listen to what they say.

14. *You should be polite and courteous:* If rejected by others, thank them for the "opportunity" they gave you. Since they may later have additional opportunities, they should remember you in a positive manner. Treat gatekeepers, especially secretaries, as human beings. Don't be aggressive or too assertive. Being courteous to others won't hurt you. A thank-you note can go a long way.

15. *You should be tactful:* Watch what you say to others about other people and your background. Don't be a gossip, back-stabber, or confessor.

16. *You should maintain a professional stance:* Be neat in what you do and wear. Speak with the confidence, authority, and maturity of a professional.

17. *You should demonstrate your intelligence and competence:* Present yourself as someone who gets things done and achieves results — a producer. Employers generally seek people who are bright; hard working; responsible; can communicate well; have positive personalities; maintain good interpersonal relations; are likable; observe dress and social codes; take initiative; are talented; possess expertise in a particular area; use good judgment; are cooperative, trustworthy, and loyal; generate confidence and credibility; and are conventional. In other words, they like people who score in the "excellent" to "outstanding" categories of the annual performance evaluation. Many want God!

18. *You should not overdo your job search:* Don't engage in overkill and bore everyone with your "job search" stories. Achieve balance in everything you do. Occasionally take a few days off to do nothing related to your job search. Develop a system of inventives and rewards — such as two non-job search days a week, if you accomplish targets A, B, C, and D.

19. *You should be open-minded and keep an eye open for "luck":* Too much planning can blind you to unexpected and fruitful opportunities. Learn to re-evaluate your goals and strategies. Seize new opportunities if

they appear appropriate.

20. *You should evaluate your progress and adjust:* Take two hours once every two weeks and evaluate what you are doing and accomplishing. If necessary, adjust your plans and reorganize your activities and priorities in light of new information. Don't become too routinized and therefore kill creativity and innovation.

These principles should provide you with an initial orientation for starting your job search. As you become more experienced, you will develop your own set of operating principles that should work for you in particular employment situations.

TAKE TIME TO SAIL

Let's assume you have the necessary skills to open the doors of employers for the job you want. Your next step is to organize an effective job search. Organization, however, does not mean a detailed plan, blueprint, or road map for taking action. If you strictly adhere to such a plan, you will most likely be disappointed with the outcomes. Instead, your job search should approximate the art of sailing — you know where you want to go and the general direction for getting there. But the specific path, as well as the time for reaching your destination, will be determined by your environment, situation, and skills. Like the sailor dependent upon his sailing skills and environmental conditions, you tack back and forth, progressing within what is considered to be an acceptable time period for successful completion of the task.

While we recommend planning your job search, we hope you will avoid the excesses of too much planning. The plan should not become the *end* — it should be a flexible *means* for achieving your stated job and career goals. Planning makes sense, because it requires you to set goals and develop strategies for achieving the goals. However, too much planning can blind you to unexpected occurrences and opportunities, or that wonderful experience called *serendipity*.

We outline a hypothetical plan for conducting an effective job search. This plan, as illustrated in Figure 2, incorporates seven distinct but interrelated job search activities over a six month period. If you phase in the first four job search steps during the initial three to four weeks, and continue the final four steps in subsequent weeks and months, you should begin receiving job offers within two to three months after initiating your job search. Interviews and job

FIGURE 2

ORGANIZATION OF JOB SEARCH ACTIVITIES

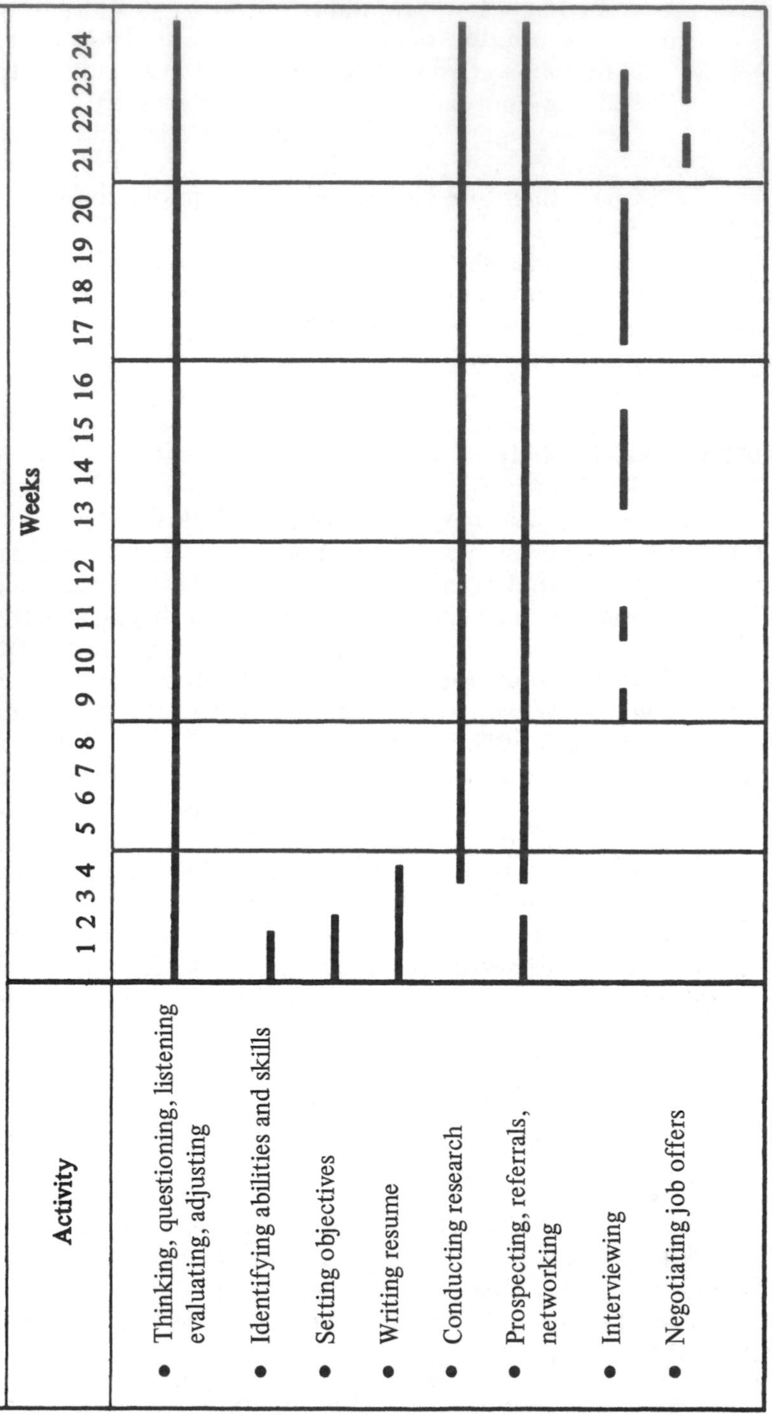

Weeks

1 2 3 4 5 6 7 8 9 10 11 12 13 14 15 16 17 18 19 20 21 22 23 24

Activity

- Thinking, questioning, listening evaluating, adjusting
- Identifying abilities and skills
- Setting objectives
- Writing resume
- Conducting research
- Prospecting, referrals, networking
- Interviewing
- Negotiating job offers

offers can come at any time — often unexpectedly — during your job search. An average time is three months, but it can occur within a week or take as long as five months. If you plan, prepare, and persist at the job search, the pay-off will be interviews and offers.

While three months may seem a long time, especially if you need to work immediately, you can shorten your job search time by increasing the frequency of each job search activity. If you are job hunting on a full-time basis, you may be able to cut your job search time in half. But don't expect to get a professional level job within a week or two. It requires time and hard work.

This hypothetical time frame is generally applicable to most nongovernmental public jobs and private sector jobs. The time frame for government jobs, however, may be much longer. When seeking government employment, you may have to wait from six to 18 months between initial application and final selection and notification. Lengthy bureaucratic selection procedures require candidates to be extremely patient when conducting a job search with government agencies. On the other hand, some government jobs require little or no waiting period.

Chapter Six

KNOW YOURSELF AND OTHERS

We assume you have the necessary work-content skills to qualify for a job interview, receive a job offer, and perform the job. If you do not, follow our skill development suggestions in Chapter 5.

In this chapter we turn to a second set of skills which you may or may not possess: job search skills. Focusing primarily on strategy and tactics, these skills are as important as work-content skills for getting a job interview and receiving a job offer. They also help advance your career once you are on the job. In this sense, they are basic job market survival skills you must acquire and practice on a continuous basis. In Chapter 5 you identified the degree to which you possessed several of these skills by completing Exercise 1 on identifying your careering competencies.

One word of caution is in order before we proceed further. The skills outlined in this and subsequent chapters do not substitute for concrete work-content skills. Form and presentation should never be confused with or replace substance. You must be able to perform the job you are being hired to do; deliver what you say you can deliver. The bottom line is that you probably won't fool enough people to get the job. However, should you fool enough and get the job, you won't keep it long. For it doesn't take long before an employer learns he or she has made a mistake by hiring someone who misrepresented credentials and qualifications — they simply don't deliver with quality performance.

JOB SEARCH SKILLS AND STEPS

Several job search skills help you prepare for face-to-face meetings with potential employers. They stress how you must (1) organize yourself and (2) communicate your value to employers. These skills also are important sequential steps required for planning and implementing an effective job search. They include:

- Identifying your strengths
- Stating your job objective
- Conducting job research
- Writing resumes and job search letters
- Dressing appropriately to meet people who have input into the hiring process
- Prospecting, networking, and informational interviewing
- Interviewing for the job
- Negotiating salary

Figure 3 illustrates the relationship of these steps to one another in the overall job search. Each step has a well defined set of rules — based upon employers' expectations and job searchers' successful experiences — you should learn and practice.

In this chapter we examine the first three job search steps — identifying strengths, stating objectives, and conducting job research. These steps focus on becoming better acquainted with yourself and your environment. They must be completed *prior to* the three image management steps in Chapter 7 — writing resumes and letters and dressing appropriately — and the three action steps in Chapter 8 — networking, interviewing, and negotiating salary.

The job search skills and steps examined in this and subsequent chapters are generally valid for acquiring both public and private sector employment. However, additional job search activities are required when seeking employment with the government and international agencies. For example, the Federal government requires all applicants to complete a standard application form — the SF-171. As we will see in Chapter 17, completing this form is a skill itself! We will address unique job search skill requirements and activities for particular public sector organizations in the appropriate chapters of Parts III, IV, V, and VI. This chapter and Chapters 7 and 8 outline the *foundation skills* for conducting an effective job search regardless of the particular setting or circumstances.

FIGURE 3

RELATIONSHIPS OF ACTIVITIES IN JOB SEARCH CAMPAIGN

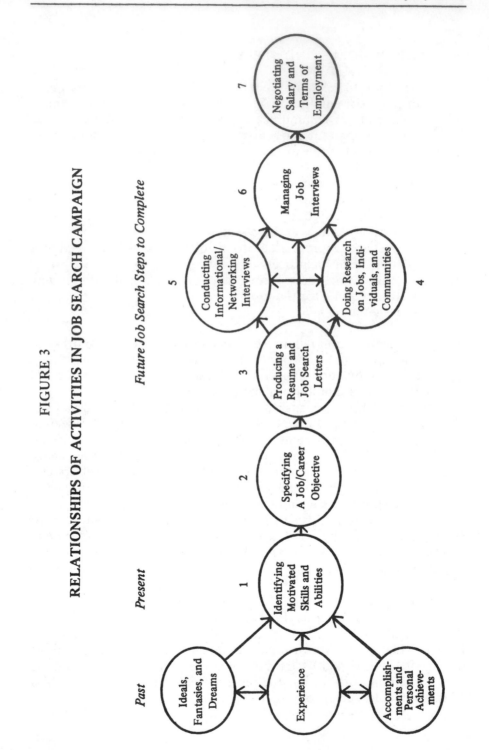

COMMUNICATING YOUR STRENGTHS

What do you do well and enjoy doing? Why should I hire you? What will you give me in exchange for this position, salary, and benefits? Although they may not directly ask you these questions, employers nonetheless want answers to these questions. It is to your advantage to prepare thoughtful answers to these basic questions before you communicate your qualifications to employers.

Put yourself in the shoes of the employer. He or she has a problem — how to select someone who will be a winner for the organization. Winners are not born every day. They have a unique set of skills and abilities employers readily seek but have difficulty both defining and finding. Contrary to popular myth, employers often do not know what type of individual they should hire or what the requirements for a particular position should be. Furthermore, most employers make less than perfect hiring decisions. Many fear they will spend a great deal of time and money selecting a candidate, yet still make the wrong hiring decision. Only after a few months of on-the-job experience with the new employee will the employer begin to confirm or reject initial hiring anxieties.

Knowing this, you should try to lower employers' hiring anxieties as well as position yourself well within the job market in relation to (1) other job seekers, and (2) your own career goals. The best way to do this is to focus on your *strengths and accomplishments*. You should communicate to employers that it is you they want to hire, because you are a winner with the necessary strengths to accomplish their goals. Unlike many other job seekers who try to *meet* the expectations of employers, you want to *raise* their expectations to your level of strengths and accomplishments. You will help employers define their needs as *your* skills and abilities.

How can you best communicate your strengths and accomplishments to employers? Start by understanding what employers want. Most seek individuals who are competent, intelligent, honest, and likable. They want to know what is both right and wrong about you — your strengths and weaknesses. While they tend to look for indicators of your weaknesses, your task is to ensure they know your strengths.

Therefore, organize your communication in direct reference to the needs and concerns of your audience. Avoid discussions of your weaknesses. Focus the employer's attention on what you do well — your strengths. A key two-part self-assessment question will orient you in the proper direction: *"What do I do well and enjoy doing?"* You want to both identify and communicate what you do best (strengths and accomplishments) and what you most enjoy doing (attitudes and values). By linking your strengths to things you enjoy doing, you should be able to present a powerful picture of purpose and enthusiasm to employers. This question also should come prior to deciding on alternative jobs and careers. Your answer to this question should direct your job search into fruitful channels. It helps identify your job objective as well as your best skills, abilities, and talents to offer potential employers.

Unfortunately, many people work against their own best interests. Unaware of their strengths, they market their weaknesses by first identifying job vacancies and then trying to fit their "qualifications" into job descriptions. This approach often frustrates applicants by presenting a picture of a job market which is not interested in them. As a result, many people attempt to acquire new work-content skills in hope of finding a job in a "growing" field, even though they do not enjoy using such skills.

Two types of skills related to your accomplishments and strengths. *Work-content skills* tend to be technical and job-specific in nature. Proficiency in typing, programming computers, operating a crane, or welding are work-content skills. They require formal training, are associated with specific trades or professions, are used only in certain job and career settings, and use a separate skills vocabulary, jargon, and subject matter for specifying technical qualifications for individuals entering and advancing in an occupation. While these hard skills do not transfer well from one occupation to another, they are critical for entering certain occupations.

A second skills category is called *functional or transferable skills.* These skills are associated with numerous job settings, are acquired through experience rather than formal training, and can be communicated through a general vocabulary. While most people have only a few work-content skills, they have numerous − perhaps as many as 300 − transferable skills. These skills enable job seekers to change jobs and careers without acquiring additional specialized education and training. These skills can be classified into two general transferable skill categories, as outlined in Table 6.

TABLE 6

TYPES OF TRANSFERABLE SKILLS

Organizational and Interpersonal Skills

_____ communicating	_____ trouble shooting
_____ problem solving	_____ implementing
_____ analyzing/assessing	_____ self-understanding

―― planning	―― understanding
―― decision-making	―― setting goals
―― innovating	―― conceptualizing
―― thinking logically	―― generalizing
―― evaluating	―― managing time
―― identifying problems	―― creating
―― synthesizing	―― judging
―― forecasting	―― controlling
―― tolerating ambiguity	―― organizing
―― motivating	―― persuading
―― leading	―― encouraging
―― selling	―― improving
―― performing	―― designing
―― reviewing	―― consulting
―― attaining	―― teaching
―― team building	―― cultivating
―― updating	―― advising
―― coaching	―― training
―― supervising	―― interpreting
―― estimating	―― achieving
―― negotiating	―― reporting
―― administering	―― managing

Personality and Work-Style Traits

―― diligent	―― honest
―― patient	―― reliable
―― innovative	―― perceptive
―― persistent	―― assertive
―― tactful	―― sensitive
―― loyal	―― astute
―― successful	―― risk taker
―― versatile	―― easy going
―― enthusiastic	―― calm
―― out-going	―― flexible
―― expressive	―― competent
―― adaptable	―― punctual
―― democratic	―― receptive
―― resourceful	―― diplomatic
―― determining	―― self-confident
―― creative	―― tenacious
―― open	―― discrete
―― objective	―― talented
―― warm	―― empathic

_____	orderly	_____	tidy
_____	tolerant	_____	candid
_____	frank	_____	adventuresome
_____	cooperative	_____	firm
_____	dynamic	_____	sincere
_____	self-starter	_____	initiator
_____	precise	_____	competent
_____	sophisticated	_____	diplomatic
_____	effective	_____	efficient

Use the following exercises to identify both your work-content and transferable skills. These self-assessment techniques stress your positives or strengths rather than identify your negatives or weaknesses. They should generate a rich vocabulary for communicating your "qualifications" to employers. Each exercise requires different investments of your time and effort as well as varying degrees of assistance from other people. We recommend using the most complete and extensive activity — the Motivated Skills Exercise — to gain a thorough understanding of your strengths.

These exercises, however, should be used with caution. There is nothing magical or particularly profound about them. Most are based upon a deterministic theory of behavior — understanding your past patterns of behavior are good predictors of your future behavior. Not a bad theory for most individuals, but it is rather simplistic and disheartening for individuals who wish to and can break out of past patterns as they embark on a new future. Furthermore, most exercises are historical devices. They provide you with a clear picture of your past, which may or may not be particularly useful for charting your future. Nonetheless, these exercises do help individuals (1) organize data on themselves, (2) target their job search around clear objectives and skills, and (3) generate a rich vocabulary of skills and accomplishments for communicating strengths to potential employers.

If you feel these exercises are inadequate for your needs, by all means seek professional assistance from a testing or assessment center staffed by a licensed psychologist (Chapter 5). These centers do in-depth testing which goes further than our self-directed, historical motivated skill exercises.

Checklist Method

This is the simplist method for identifying your strengths. Review the two lists of transferable skills outlined in Table 6. Place a

"1" in front of the skills that *strongly* characterize you; assign a "2" to those skills that describe you to a *large extent*; put a "3" before those that describe you to *some extent*. After completing this exercise, review the lists and rank order the 10 characteristics that best describe you on each list.

Skills Map

Richard N. Bolles has produced two well-known exercises for identifying transferable skills based upon John Holland's typology of work environments. In his book, *The Three Boxes of Life,* he develops a checklist of 100 transferable skills. They are organized into 12 categories or types of skills: using hands, body, words, senses, numbers, intuition, analytical thinking, creativity, helpfulness, artistic abilities, leadership, and follow-through.

Bolles' second exercise, "The Quick Job Hunting Map," expands upon this first one. The "Map" is a checklist of 222 skills. This exercise requires you to identify seven of your most satisfying accomplishments, achievements, jobs, or roles. After writing a page about each experience, you relate each to the checklist of 222 skills. The "Map" should give you a comprehensive picture of what skills you (1) use most frequently, and (2) enjoy using in satisfying and successful settings. While this exercise may take six hours to complete, it yields an enormous amount of data on past strengths. Furthermore, the "Map" generates a rich skills vocabulary for communicating your strengths to others. The "Map" is found in the appendix of Bolles' *What Color Is Your Parachute?* or it can be purchased separately in beginning, advanced, or "new" versions from Ten Speed Press. Order information on these assessment instruments also is included in the resource section of this book.

Autobiography of Accomplishments

Write a lengthy essay about your life accomplishments. This could range from 20 to 100 pages. After completing the essay, go through it page by page to identify what you most enjoyed doing (working with different kinds of information, people, and things) and what skills you used most frequently as well as enjoyed using. Finally, identify those skills you wish to continue using. After analyzing and synthesizing this data, you should have a relatively clear picture of your strongest skills.

Motivated Skills Exercise

The Motivated Skills Exercise is one of the most complex and time consuming self-assessment exercises. However, it yields some of the best data on skills, and it is especially useful for those who feel they need a more thorough analysis of their skills. Developed by Haldane Associates, this particular exercise is variously referred to as "Success Factor Analysis" or "System to Identify Motivated Skills". While you can use this technique on your own, it is best to work with someone else. Be prepared to devote from six to eight hours to this exercise. It is divided into five steps. The steps follow the basic pattern of generating raw data, identifying patterns, analyzing the data through reduction techniques, and synthesizing the patterns into a transferable skills vocabulary. You need strong analytical skills to complete this exercise on your own. The five steps are as follows:

STEP 1: Take 15 to 20 sheets of paper and at the top of each sheet write one achievement. Your achievements consist of those things you enjoyed doing and felt a sense of accomplishment in doing. These include childhood experiences as well as educational, military, recreational, home, or work-related achievements. For example, at the top of the paper you might state:

> *"I learned to play the guitar and joined a rock group while in high school."*
>
> *"I received an 'A' in physics from the toughest teacher in school."*
>
> *"I reorganized the files of our office which improved the efficiency of operations."*
>
> *"I competed in the marathon and finished in the upper third."*
>
> *"I organized a committee to investigate reducing the number of customer complaints."*
>
> *"I sang a solo in our church choir."*

STEP 2: Select from among your achievements the seven most important ones and prioritize them. Identify the factors that explain your success in each achievement. Examples of these success factors might include various aspects of managing, communicating, creating, analyzing, designing, supervising, coordinating, and problem solving. On each page write the details of your achievements — how you got involved, what you did, how you did it, and what the outcome was.

STEP 3: Further detail the "what" and "how" of your achievements by having your spouse or a friend interview you over a 60-minute period. Have them ask you to elaborate on each of your achievements and note the terminology you use to elaborate on your skills and abilities. Record your answers for each achievement on separate pieces of paper.

STEP 4: Combine the self-generated and interview data on your achievements into a single master list of success factors. Group the factors into related categories beginning with the most important factor. For example, if "supervising" is your strongest achievement, "decision-making" and "delegating" may be related to this factor. Therefore, the factors would cluster as follows:

supervising decision-making delegating	selling promoting demonstrating
creating designing initiating	decision-making managing strategizing

STEP 5: Synthesize the clusters into new combinations for projecting your past skills into the future. For example, the clusters "supervising — decision-making — delegating" and "creating — designing — initiating" may combine into a new skill category called "creative management." This is the key step in this exercise, because it begins to relate your past strengths to your future goals. It functions as a *bridge* between your

skills and your stated objective.

STATING YOUR OBJECTIVE

When you identify your strengths, you also create the necessary data base and vocabulary for developing your job objective. Using this vocabulary, you should be able to communicate to employers that you are a talented and purposeful individual who achieves *results*.

If you fail to do the preliminary self-assessment work necessary for developing a clear objective, you will probably wander aimlessly in the job market looking for interesting jobs you might fit into. Your goal, instead, should be to find a job or career that is compatible with your interests, motivations, skills, and talents. In other words, try to *find a job fit for you* rather than try to fit into a job you think looks interesting.

Job hunters with clearly stated objectives have several advantages over those who do not. Their job search is much easier and enjoyable, because they approach it with confidence and optimism. They gain greater control over the job market, because they structure the job market around their goals. They communicate a reassuring sense of purpose and self-confidence to employers who worry about hiring individuals who don't know what they want. They write well designed resumes and letters that help employers make clear choices. For employers lacking basic hiring criteria, such applicants help them better define their "needs" as the applicant's job objective.

Therefore, if you want to achieve the best results, you must have an objective *before* conducting your job search. With a clear objective, you can target your job search at specific high pay-offs in the job market. A clear objective will help you organize your job search into a coherent and manageable whole.

Objectives can be stated in many different forms. Most people think of an objective as a statement of what they would *like to do*. However, such an objective is self-centered. Employers, on the other hand, want to know what *you will do for them*. The best job objective, therefore, is an employer-centered one: state *what it is you can and will do for employers*.

Some people know precisely what they want to do and can state their objective in employer-centered terms. Others find identifying and stating a job objective to be the most difficult and frustrating aspect of the whole job search process. If you are not one of the lucky ones, here are some approaches you can use to help formulate a clear and effective objective.

Developing Your Data Base

Several practical self-directed exercises can alleviate the frustrating aspects of this task. The exercises require you to generate and analyze data about yourself. Begin thinking of your objective as being composed of several ingredients relating to your work values, skills, and knowledge of work environments. Five activities or steps will help you generate a complete set of data for stating your objective.

The first step is to *identify your work and career values* by completing several exercises:

1. List 10 things you would like to achieve before you die. Alternatively, write your obituary for the year 2010 stressing highlights or achievements of your career and life.
2. Think of 10 answers to this question: "If I had $1,000,000 I would. . ."
3. List 10 things you prefer and enjoy doing. Prioritize each item.
4. Identify 10 working conditions which you view as negative. Prioritize each condition.
5. List 10 working conditions which you view as positive. Prioritize each item.
6. Check as many of the following work values you feel are desirable in your employment:

_____ contribute to society	_____ be creative
_____ have contact with people	_____ supervise others
_____ work alone	_____ work with details
_____ work with a team	_____ gain recognition
_____ compete with others	_____ acquire security
_____ make decisions	_____ make a lot of money
_____ work under pressure	_____ help others
_____ use power and authority	_____ solve problems
_____ acquire new knowledge	_____ take risks
_____ be a recognized expert	_____ work at own pace

7. Write an essay on your ideal job. Include a weekly calendar of daily activities divided into one-hour segments. Specify your duties, responsibilities, authority, salary, working conditions, and opportunities.

The second step is to *gather information on how others see you and your goals*. Ask your spouse or two or three close friends to frankly critique both your strengths and weaknesses. You want them to respond to these questions:

- What are my strengths and weaknesses?
- How can they be improved?
- What working conditions do I enjoy?
- What are my career goals?

The third step is to examine the data you generated in the previous section of this chapter on your strengths. Include it with the information you just generated yourself and received from your spouse and friends. *Rank order which skills you most and least prefer to use in your job or career.*

The fourth step is optional, depending on whether you feel you need more information on your work values, interests, and skills. *Take one or two psychological, aptitude, or vocational tests.* Your options include:

- Strong-Campbell Interest Inventory
- Career Assessment Inventory
- The Self-Directed Search
- Temperament and Values Inventory
- Sixteen Personality Factor Questionnaire
- Edwards Personal Preference Schedule
- Myers-Briggs Type Indicators
- The Occupational View Deck
- Self-Description Inventory
- Kuder Occupational Interest Survey

Information from these tests should reinforce and validate the information you gathered from the self-assessment exercises. See a career counselor or a licensed psychologist for identifying and administering the proper tests.

The fifth step is to *test the information concerning your objective against reality and the future* by asking yourself these questions:

- Is my objective realistic?
- Can it be achieved within the next year, 5 years, or 10 years?
- Who needs my skills?
- What factors might help me or hinder me in achieving my objective?

You will further clarify your objective as you expose yourself to more job market information while conducting library research and talking to people about your skills, different jobs, and career opportunities. Procedures for gathering such information are outlined in this chapter and in Chapter 8.

Skills As Outcomes

You now should be prepared to develop a one sentence statement of your job objective. Begin by stating your objective at a general level. Next, restate it at a more specific level on your resume.

We recommend developing a *functional job objective*. Recommended by Germann and Arnold in *Bernard Haldane Associates Job and Career Building*, this type of objective includes *skills* and *outcomes*. At a general level it would appear in the following skills-outcomes framework:

> *"I would like a job where I can use my ability to (a primary skill) which will result in (an outcome)."*

If, for example, you wish to write grant and research proposals, you might state the general objective in these terms:

> *"I would like a job where my technical research and writing experience will result in new and expanded programs."*

The same objective should be re-written at a more specific level for your resume:

> *"A management consulting position where strong grantsmanship, research, and writing abilities will be used for expanding human resource development operations."*

Including both skills and outcomes, this objective is targeted toward particular employers.

As you develop your objective statement, keep in mind that employers want to know how you will achieve *their* goals. Always remember to develop a work-related objective responsive to the needs of your audience. Above all, tell employers what you have to offer — strengths, skills, competencies — and what you will do for them. Emphasize that you are a *doer* who produces concrete results.

While you have certain self-centered goals you wish to achieve for yourself, employers are less interested in what they can do for you. As many employees quickly learn, they are expendible commodities. Employers feel no need to love them, take care of them, and become sensitive to their personal and professional needs. Employment is a business transaction — their money for your talent. "You're fired!" are two words employers use to express the fact they did not get *value* for their money. Communicate your value loud and clear from the very beginning of your job search.

CONDUCTING JOB RESEARCH

You should continuously conduct research on the job market. Research will provide you with a strong knowledge base from which to plan and implement your job search. It will give you critical information for writing your resumes and letters, networking, interviewing, and negotiating salaries.

Research, the process of uncovering information, is central to every step in your job search. It should be a continuous process aimed at developing two general areas of information. First, you must understand the structure and operation of the job markets — both the advertised and hidden job markets. Second, you must acquire specialized knowledge on the key elements in the job markets — individuals and organizations. You gather this information by conducting research in libraries, by mail and telephone, and through face-to-face conversations. This research begins the first day of your job search and continues until the final day and beyond.

Advertised and Hidden Job Markets

Your research should be directed initially toward understanding the structure of the job market. The so-called job market actually consists of two structurally different arenas for locating job opportunities. Both are characterized by a high degree of decentralization. Neither should be underestimated nor overestimated.

The *advertised job market* consists of job vacancy announcements and listings found in newspapers, professional and trade journals, newsletters, employment agencies, and personnel offices. Most people focus on this market because it is relatively easy to locate, and because they believe it accurately reflects available job vacancies at any given moment. In reality, however, the advertised job market may include no more than 25 percent of actual job openings. Furthermore, this market tends to represent positions at the extreme ends of the job spectrum — low paid unskilled or high paid highly skilled jobs. The majority of positions lying between these two extremes are not well represented in the listings. And many of the advertised jobs are either nonexistent or are filled prior to being advertised.

You should spend a minimum amount of time looking for employment on the advertised job market. Monitor this market, but don't assume it represents the entire spectrum of job opportunities. Your job search time and money may be better spent elsewhere — on the hidden job market.

However, there are exceptions to this general rule of minimizing your job search time in the advertised job market. Each occupational specialty has its own internal recruitment and job finding structure. Some occupations are represented more by professional listing and recruitment services than others. For example, many professional urban government positions, such as city manager and city planner, have their own professional associations with highly developed job listing and recruitment services. Indeed, as we move into the high-tech society, greater efforts will be made to increase the efficiency of employment communication by centralizing job listings and recruitment services for particular occupational specialties. These services will be designed to reduce the *lag time* between when a job becomes vacant and is filled. Computerized job banks may increasingly be used by employers to locate qualified candidates, and vice versa. Depending on your job objective and relevant career field, you should investigate such services to determine if, indeed, they are useful for your job search.

The **hidden job market** should be the most important arena for your job search. Lacking a formal structure, this job market may encompass as many as 75 percent of all job openings at any given moment. Many employers turn to the advertised job market *after* they fail to recruit candidates on the hidden job market. The lag time between when a position becomes vacant, is listed, and then filled is a critical period for your attention and *intervention*. Your goal should be to locate high quality job vacancies on the hidden job market *before* they become listed on the advertised job market.

Your research efforts will be the key to penetrating the hidden job market. Consider, for example, the hiring problems of employers by putting yourself in their place. Start this scenario by supposing one of your employees suddenly gives you two weeks notice, or you terminate someone. Now you have a problem — you must hire a new employee. It takes time and is a risky business you would prefer to avoid. After hours of reading resumes and interviewing, you still will be hiring an unknown who might create new problems for you. Like many other employers, you want to *minimize your time and risks.* You can do this by calling your friends and acquaintances and letting them know you are looking for someone; you would appreciate it if they could refer some good candidates to you. Based on these contacts, you should receive referrals. At the same time, you want to hedge your bets or fulfill affirmative action and equal opportunity requirements by listing the job vacancy in the newspaper or with your personnel office. While 300 people respond by mail to your classified ad, you also get referrals from the trusted individuals in your network. In the end, you conduct 10 telephone interviews and three face-to-face interviews. You hire the *best* candidate – the one your former classmate recommended to you on the first day you informed her of your need to fill the vacancy. You are satisfied with your excellent choice; you are relatively certain this new employee will be a good addition to your organization.

This scenario is played out regularly in many organizations – both public and private. It demonstrates the importance of getting into the hidden job market and devoting most of your time and energy there. If you let people know you are looking for employment, chances are they will keep you in mind and refer you to others who may have an unexpected vacancy. Your research will help you enter and maneuver within this job market of interpersonal networks and highly personalized information exchanges. Chapter 8 outlines how to do this with maximum impact.

Consulting Libraries

Libraries are filled with useful job and career information. Reference and documents rooms of libraries have some of the best career resources. Career planning offices at colleges and universities have a wealth of job and career information in their specialized libraries – a wider selection than most general libraries.

Your goal should be to acquire as much written information as possible on individuals and organizations relating to your job objective. Normally this means examining directories, books, magazines, and reports. These publications will provide general surveys of occupational fields, information on particular individuals and organizations, as well as names, addresses, and telephone numbers of key individuals within organizations. At this stage you need to understand the organizations and collect many names, addresses, and telephone numbers for initiating your writing and telephoning activities.

You should start your research by examining several of the following resources normally found in the reference sections of libraries relevant to public employment:

Directories of Reference Materials

- *Ayer Directory of Publications*
- *Applied Science and Technology*
- *Directory of Directories*
- *Guide to American Directories*
- *Readers' Guide to Periodical Literature*
- *Standard Periodical Directory*
- *Ulrich's International Periodicals Directory*
- *Working Press of the Nation*

Career and Job Alternatives

- *Ad Search*
- *Advance Job Listings*
- *Affirmative Action Register*
- *The College Placement Annual*
- *Dictionary of Occupational Titles*
- *Encyclopedia of Careers and Vocational Guidance* (3 vols.)
- *Guide to Occupational Exploration*
- *Occupational Outlook Handbook*
- *Occupational Outlook Quarterly*
- *Work Related Abstracts*

Government

- *American Almanac of Politics*
- *The Book of the States*
- *Commerce Business Daily*
- *Congressional Directory*
- *Congressional Record*
- *Congressional Staff Directory*
- *Congressional Yellow Book*
- *Directory of Federal Executives*
- *Federal Register*
- *Federal Yellow Book*
- *Municipal Yearbook*
- *National Directory of State Agencies*
- *National Organizations of State Government Officials*
- *State Administrative Officials Classified By Function*
- *State Elected Officials and the Legislatures*

- *State Legislative Leadership, Committees, and Staff*
- *Taylor's Encyclopedia of Government Officials*
- *United States Government Manual*
- *Washington Information Directory*

Peripheral Public Institutions

- *The Consultants and Consulting Organizations Directory*
- *Encyclopedia of Associations* (4 vols.)
- *The Foundation Directory*
- *National Trade and Professional Associations of the United States*
- *Research Center Directory*
- *Washington* (yearly)
- *Washington Representatives*
- *Who's Who in Consulting*

International

- *Encyclopedia of Associations* (Vol. 4: "International Organizations")
- *Europa Year Book*
- *Yearbook of International Organizations*
- *Yearbook of the United Nations*

Other Resources

- Trade journals (the *Directory of Libraries* and *Subject Collections: A Guide to Special Book Collections in Libraries* compiles information on specialized business, government, and association libraries).
- Publications of Chambers of Commerce; state manufacturing associations; Federal, state, and local government agencies.
- Telephone books — especially the Yellow Pages (if not in library, contact your local telephone company which may have a telephone book collection).
- Trade books on how to get a job.

As you accumulate names and addresses from your library research, write or call individuals and organizations for further information. Many organizations will give you copies of their annual reports and related literature. Government agencies publish reports and newsletters which are worth examining. Your library may have additional job-related resources on opportunities in the local community.

Talking to People

Beware of becoming *too* preoccupied with library research. This research may give you a false sense of making progress with your job search. Stop when you feel you have enough information to begin other types of research or start other job search activities. Two weeks or 40 hours in the library should get you off to a good start. If you are examining a highly specialized field where there are few names and addresses, you may achieve a high degree of redundancy within 10 hours.

Your most productive research activity will be talking to people. Informal, word-of-mouth communication is still the most effective channel of job search information. In contrast to reading books, people have more current, and probably more accurate, information. In addition, most people are flattered to be asked for advice. They freely give it and will be happy to assist you with referrals to others. Don't hide the fact you are looking for a job, but don't ask for a job. Ask people about:

- Occupational fields
- Job requirements and training
- Interpersonal environments
- Performance expectations
- Their problems
- Salaries
- Advancement opportunities
- Future growth potential of the organization
- How best to acquire more information and contacts in a particular field
- How you can improve your resume

Techniques for conducting this type of research — referred to as networking and informational interviews — are outlined in Chapter 8.

You may be surprised how willing friends, acquaintances, and strangers give useful job information. But before you talk to people, do your library research so you are better able to ask thoughtful questions.

Knowledge is power. Research will help increase your power in the job market. You should always collect new information, revise previous conceptions, and adjust your job search efforts to new realities uncovered through your research. As you do this, your research will affect your original objective and resume as well as guide you in accomplishing the other job search steps. Your power to give some structure and coherence to the hidden job market in your area of interest should increase accordingly.

Chapter Seven

COMMUNICATE A POSITIVE IMAGE

At every stage in the job search you must communicate a positive image to potential employers. The initial impression you make on an employer through applications, resumes, letters, telephone calls, or informational interviews will determine whether the employer is interested in interviewing you and offering you a position.

Developing and managing effective job search communication should play a central role in everything you do related to finding employment. This communication takes many verbal and nonverbal forms. Your first communication with employers will most likely be by letter or in a face-to-face meeting. Job search letters often include your calling card — the resume. These documents are essentially nonverbal forms of communication.

Face-to-face meetings involve both verbal and nonverbal communication. However, the nonverbal aspect is especially important for the informational and job interviews (Chapter 8). Employers place a great deal of emphasis on how you look. Whether you like it or not, your dress and appearance play a key role in determining the outcomes of your job search.

In this chapter we examine three important nonverbal communication activities during the job search: resumes, letters, and dress. How you develop, target, and manage this communication will largely determine how far you progress through the interpersonal job search processes in Chapter 8.

WRITING RESUMES

Resumes are important tools for communicating your purpose and capabilities to employers. While many jobs only require a completed application form, you should always prepare a resume for influencing the hiring process. Application forms do not substitute for resumes.

Many myths surround resumes and letters. Some people still believe a resume should summarize one's history. Others believe it will get them a job. And still others believe they should be mailed in response to classified ads. The reality is this: *A resume advertises your qualifications to prospective employers. It is your calling card for getting interviews.*

Ineffective Resumes

Most people write ineffective resumes. Misunderstanding the purpose of resumes, they make numerous mistakes commonly associated with weak resumes and poor advertising copy. Their resumes often lack an objective, include unrelated categories of information, are too long, and appear unattractive. Other common pitfalls identified by employers include:

- Poor layout
- Misspellings and punctuation errors
- Poor grammar
- Unclear purpose
- Too much jargon
- Include irrelevant data
- Too long or too short
- Poorly typed and reproduced
- Unexplained time gaps
- Too boastful
- Deceptive or dishonest
- Difficult to understand or interpret

Your resume, instead, should incorporate the characteristics of strong and effective resumes:

- Clearly communicate your purpose and competencies in relation to employers' needs.
- Be concise and easy to read.
- Immediately motivate the reader to read it in-depth.
- Tell employers that you are a responsible and purposeful individual — a doer who can solve their problems.

Keep in mind that most employers are busy people who normally glance at a resume for only 20 to 30 seconds. Your resume, therefore, must sufficiently catch their attention to pass the 20 to 30 second evaluation test. When writing your resume, ask yourself the same question asked by employers: *"Why should I read this or contact this person for an interview?"* Your answer should result in an attractive, interesting, unique, and skills-based resume.

Types of Resumes

You have four types of resumes to choose from: chronological, functional, combination, or resume letter. Each format has various advantages and disadvantages, depending on your background and purpose. For example, someone first entering the job market or making a major career change should use a functional resume. On the other hand, a person who wants to target a particular job may choose to use a resume letter. Examples of these different types of resumes are included in Appendix B. You should refer to these examples as you read the following section. Further assistance in developing each section of your resume is found in Krannich's and Banis' comprehensive resume development book, *High Impact Resumes and Letters*.

The *chronological resume* is the standard resume used by most applicants. It comes in two forms: traditional and improved. The *traditional chronological resume* is also known as the "obituary resume", because it both "kills" your chances of getting a job and is a good source for writing your obituary. Summarizing your work history, this resume lists dates and names first and duties and responsibilities second; it includes extraneous information, such as height, weight, age, marital status, sex, and hobbies. While relatively easy to write, this is the most ineffective resume you can produce. Its purpose at best is to inform people of what you have done in the past as well as where, when, and with whom. It tells employers little or nothing about what you want to do, can do, and will do for them. This is the ultimate self-centered resume.

The *improved chronological resume* communicates directly to employers your purpose, past achievements, and probable future performance. You should use this type of resume when you have extensive experience directly related to a position you seek. This resume should include a work objective which reflects both your work experience and professional goals. The work experience section should include the names and addresses of former employers followed by a brief description of your accomplishments, skills, and responsibilities; inclusive employment dates should appear at the end. Do not begin with dates; they are the least significant element in the descriptions. Be sure to stress your *accomplishments* and *skills* rather than your formal duties and responsibilities. You want to inform your audience that you are a productive and responsible person who gets things done — a doer.

If you are changing careers or have an unstable employment history, avoid using a chronological resume. It communicates the wrong messages — you lack direct work experience, you are an unstable worker, or you have not advanced in your career. If you have such a career pattern, consider writing a functional or combination resume.

Functional resumes should be used by individuals making a significant career change, first entering the workforce, or re-entering the job market after a lengthy absence. This resume should stress your accomplishments and transferable skills regardless of previous work settings and job titles. This could include accomplishments as a housewife or house husband, volunteer worker, or Sunday school teacher. Names of employers and dates of employment should not appear on this resume.

Functional resumes have certain weaknesses. While they are important bridges for the inexperienced and for those making a career change, some employers dislike these resumes. Since many employers still look for names, dates, and direct job experience, this resume does not meet their expectations. You should use a functional resume only if your past work experience does not strengthen your objective.

Combination resumes are a compromise between the chronological and functional resumes. Having more advantages than disadvantages, this resume may be exactly what you need if you are making a career change with related experience from one career to another.

Combination resumes have the potential to both *meet* and *raise* the expectations of employers. You should stress your accomplishments and skills as well as include your work history. Your work history should appear as a separate section immediately following your presentation of accomplishments and skills in the "Areas of Effectiveness" or "Experience" section. It is not necessary to include dates unless they enhance your resume. This is the perfect resume for someone wishing to change to a job in a related career field.

Resume letters are substitutes for resumes. Appearing as a job inquiry or application letter, resume letters highlight various sections of your resume, such as work history, experience, areas of effectiveness, objective, or education, in relation to employers' needs. These letters are used when you prefer not sending your more general resume. Resume letters have one major weakness: they give employers insufficient information and thus may prematurely eliminate you from consideration.

Structuring Your Resume

After choosing an appropriate resume format, you should generate the necessary information for structuring each category of your resume. You developed much of this information when you identified your strengths and specified your objective in Chapter 6. To complete your data base for the resume, include the following information on separate sheets of paper:

RESUME STRUCTURE

CONTACT INFORMATION:	name, address, telephone number.
WORK OBJECTIVE:	refer to your data in Chapter 6 on writing an objective.
EDUCATION:	degrees, schools, dates, highlights, special training.
WORK EXPERIENCE:	paid, unpaid, civilian, military, and part-time employment. Include job titles, employers, locations, dates, skills, accomplishments, duties, and responsibilities. Use the functional language developed in Chapter 6.
OTHER EXPERIENCE:	volunteer, civic, and professional memberships. Include your contributions, demonstrated skills, offices held, names, and dates.
SPECIAL SKILLS OR LICENSES/CERTIFICATES:	foreign languages, teaching, paramedical, etc. relevant to your objective.
MISCELLANEOUS INFORMATION:	references, expected salary, willingness to relocate and travel, availability dates.

Producing Drafts

Once you generate the basic data for constructing your resume, your next task is to reduce this data into draft resumes. If, for example, you write a combination resume, the internal organization of the resume should be as follows:

- Contact information
- Work objective
- Qualifications or functional experience
- Work history or employment
- Education

Be careful in including any other type of information on your resume. Other information most often is extraneous or negative information. You should only include information designed to strengthen your objective.

While your first draft may run more than two pages, try to get everything into one or two pages for the final draft. Most employers lose interest after reading the first page. If you produce a two-page resume, one of the best formats is to attach a single supplemental page to a self-contained one-page resume.

Your final draft should conform to the following rules for creating an excellent resume:

RULES FOR EFFECTIVE RESUMES

RESUME DON'TS

- *Don't* use abbreviations except for your middle name.
- *Don't* make the resume cramped and crowded; it should be pleasing to the eyes.
- *Don't* make statements you can't document.
- *Don't* use the passive voice.
- *Don't* change tense of verbs.
- *Don't* use lengthy sentences and descriptions.
- *Don't* refer to yourself as "I".
- *Don't* include negative information.
- *Don't* include extraneous information.

RESUME DOS

- *Do* use action verbs and the active voice.
- *Do* be direct, succinct, and expressive with your langu-

age.
- *Do* appear neat, well organized, and professional.
- *Do* use ample spacing and highlights (all caps, under-lining, bulleting) for different emphases.
- *Do* maintain an eye pleasing balance. Try centering your contact information at the top, keeping information categories on the left in all caps, and describing the categories in the center and on the right.
- *Do* check carefully your spelling, grammar, and punctuation.
- *Do* clearly communicate your purpose and value to employers.
- *Do* communicate your strongest points first.

Evaluating

You should subject your resume drafts to two types of evaluations. An *internal evaluation* consists of reviewing our lists of "dos" and "don'ts" to make sure your resume conforms to these rules. An *external evaluation* should be conducted by circulating your resume to three or more individuals whom you believe will give you frank, objective, and useful feedback. Avoid people who tend to flatter you. The best evaluator would be someone in a hiring position similar to one you will encounter in the actual interview. Ask these people to critique your draft resume and suggest improvements in both form and content. This will be your most important evaluation. After all, the only evaluation that counts is the one that helps get you an interview. Asking someone to critique your resume is one way to spread the word that you are job hunting. As we will see in Chapter 8, this is one method for getting invited to an interview!

Final Production

Your final resume can be typed or typeset. If you type it, be sure it looks professional. Use an electric typewriter with a carbon ribbon. Varying the typing elements and styles can produce an attractive copy. Do not use a portable typewriter with a nylon ribbon since it does not produce professional copy. Many typists will do your resume on the proper machine for about $5 to $10.

If you choose to have your resume typeset by a printer, it may cost you from $20 to $50, depending on the printer. The final product will look very professional. However, keep in mind that some employers may think you had someone else write the resume for you because it looks *too* professional.

Whether typed or typeset, be sure to proofread the final copy. Many people spend good money on production only to later find typing errors.

When reproducing the resume, you must consider the quality and color of paper as well as the number of copies you need. By all means use good quality paper. You should use watermarked 20-pound or heavier bond paper. Costing 2 to 4 cents per sheet, this paper can be purchased through stationery stores and printers. It is important not to cut corners at this point by purchasing cheap paper or using copy machine paper. You may save $5 on 100 copies, but you also will communicate an unprofessional image to employers.

Use one of the following paper colors: off-white, light tan, light gray, or light blue. Avoid white, blue, yellow, green, pink, orange, red, or any other bright colors. Conservative, light-muted colors are the best. Any of these colors can be complemented with black ink. In the case of light gray — our first choice — a navy blue ink looks best.

Your choices of paper quality and color say something about your personality and professional style. They communicate non-verbally your potential strengths and weaknesses. Employers will use these as indicators for screening you in or out of an interview. At the same time, these choices may make your resume stand out from the crowd of standard black-on-white resumes.

You have two choices in reproducing your resume: a copy machine or an offset process. Many large copy machines give good reproductions on the quality paper you need. The offset process produces the best quality because it uses a printing plate. It also is relatively inexpensive — 2 to 5 cents per copy with a minimum run of 100 copies. Altogether, you should be able to have your resume typed and 100 copies reproduced on high quality colored bond paper for less than $25. If you have it typeset, the same number of copies may cost you $50.

Whatever your choices, do not try to cut costs when it comes to producing your resume. It simply is not worth it. Remember, your resume is your calling card — it should represent your best professional image. Therefore, put your best foot forward at this stage. Go in style; spend a few dollars on producing a first-class resume.

JOB SEARCH LETTERS

Resumes sent through the mail are normally accompanied by a cover letter. After interviewing for information or a position, you should send a thank-you letter. Other occasions will arise when it is both proper and necessary for you to write different types of job search letters. Examples of these letters, which follow this discussion, are presented in Appendix C.

Your letter writing should follow the principles of good resume and business writing. Job hunting letters are like resumes — they advertise you for interviews. Like good advertisements, these letters should follow four basic principles for effectiveness:

1. Catch the reader's attention.
2. Persuade the reader of your benefits or value.
3. Convince the reader with more evidence.
4. Move the reader to acquire the product.

Basic Preparation Rules

Before you begin writing a job search letter, ask yourself several questions to clarity the content of your letter:

- What is the *purpose* of the letter?
- What are the *needs* of my audience?
- What *benefits* will my audience gain from me?
- What is a good opening sentence or paragraph for grabbing the *attention* of my audience?
- How can I maintain the *interests* of my audience?
- How can I best end the letter so that the audience will be *persuaded* to contact me?
- If a resume is enclosed, how can my letter best *advertise the resume?*
- Have I spent enough *time* revising and proofreading the letter?
- Does the letter represent my *best professional effort*?

Since your letters are a form of business communication, they should conform to the rules of good business correspondence:

PRINCIPLES OF GOOD BUSINESS COMMUNICATION

- Plan and organize what you will say by outlining the content of your letter.
- Know your purpose and plan the elements of your letter accordingly.
- Communicate your message in a logical and sequential manner.
- State your purpose immediately in the first sentence and paragraph; main ideas always go first.
- End your letter by stating what your reader can expect next from you.
- Use short paragraphs and sentences; avoid overly complex sentences.
- Punctuate properly and use correct grammar and spelling.
- Use simple and straight forward language; avoid jargon.
- Communicate your message as directly and briefly as possible.

The rules stress how to both *organize and communicate* your message with impact. At the same time, you should always have a specific purpose in mind as well as know the needs of your audience.

Types of Letters

Cover letters provide cover for your resume. You should avoid overwhelming a one-page resume with a two-page letter or repeating the contents of the resume in the letter. A short and succinct one-page letter which highlights one or two points in your resume is sufficient. Three paragraphs will suffice. The first paragraph should state your interests and purposes for writing. The second paragraph should highlight your possible value to the employer. The third paragraph should state that you will call the individual at a particular time to schedule an interview.

However, do not expect great results from cover letters. Many professional job search firms use word processing equipment and mailing lists to flood the job market with resumes and cover letters. As a result, employers are increasingly suspicious of the authenticity of such letters.

Approach letters are written for the purpose of developing job contacts, leads, or information as well as for organizing networks and getting interviews – the subjects of Chapter 8. Your primary purposes should be to get employers to engage in the 5-R's of informational interviewing:

> *Reveal* useful information and advice.
> *Refer* you to others.
> *Read* and *revise* your resume.
> *Remember* you for future reference.

These letters help you gain access to the hidden job market.

Approach letters can be sent out en masse to uncover job leads, or they can be targeted on particular individuals or organizations. It is best to target these letters since they have maximum impact when personalized in reference to particular positions.

The structure of approach letters is similar to other letters. The first paragraph states your purpose. In so doing, you may want to use a personal statement for openers, such as *"Mary Tillis recommended that I write to you..."* or *"I am familiar with your..."* State your purpose, but do not suggest that you are asking for a job — only career advice or information. In your final paragraph, request a meeting and indicate you will call to schedule such a meeting at a mutually convenient time.

Thank-you letters may well become your most effective job search letters. They especially communicate your thoughtfulness. These letters come in different forms and are written for various occasions. The most common thank-you letter is written after receiving assistance, such as job search information or a critique of your resume. Other occasions include:

- *Immediately following an interview* — Thank the interviewer for the opportunity to interview for the position. Repeat your interest in the position.
- *Receive a job offer* — Thank the employer for his or her faith in you and express your appreciation.
- *Rejected for a job* — Thank the employer for giving you the "opportunity" to interview for the job. Ask to be remembered for future reference.
- *Terminate employment* — Thank the employer for the experience and ask to be remembered for future reference.
- *Begin a new job* — Thank the employer for giving you this new opportunity and express your confidence in producing the value he or she is expecting from you.

Examples of each type of letter are found in Appendix C.

Several of these thank-you letters are unusual, but they all have the same purpose in mind — to be remembered by potential employers in a positive light. In a job search, being remembered by employers is the closest thing to being invited to an interview and offered a job.

DISTRIBUTION AND MANAGEMENT

The only good resumes are the ones that get read and result in a job interview. Therefore, after completing a first-rate resume and job search letters, you must decide what to do with them. Are you planning to only respond to classified ads? What other creative distribution methods might you use? What is the best way to proceed?

Responding to Classified Ads

Except for government agencies, most of your writing activities should focus on the hidden job market. At the same time, you should respond to job listings in newspapers, magazines, and personnel offices. While this is largely a numbers game, you can increase your odds by the way you respond to the listings.

You should be selective in your responses. Since you know what you want to do, you will be looking for only certain types of positions. Once you identify them, your response entails little expenditure of time and effort — an envelope, letter, stamp, resume, and maybe 20 minutes of your time. You have little to lose. While you have the potential to gain by sending a letter and resume in response to an ad, remember the odds are usually against you.

It is difficult to interpret job listings. Some employers place blind ads with P. O. Box numbers in order to collect resumes for future reference. Others wish to avoid aggressive applicants who telephone or "drop-in" for interviews. Many employers work through professional recruiters who place these ads. While you may try to second guess the rationale behind such ads, respond to them as you would to ads with an employer's name, address, or telephone number. Assume there is a real job behind the ad.

Most ads request a copy of your resume. You should respond with a cover letter and resume as soon as you see the ad. Depending on how much information on the position is revealed in the ad, your letter should be tailored to emphasize your qualifications vis-a-vis the ad. Examine the ad carefully. Underline any words or phrases which relate to your qualifications. In your cover letter you should use similar terminology in emphasizing your qualifications. Keep the letter brief and to the point.

If the ad asks you to state your salary history or salary requirements, state *"negotiable"* or *"open."* Alternatively, you can include
a figure by stating a salary range 20 percent above your present
salary base. For example, if you are making $30,000 a year, you can
state this as *"in the $30,000 to $36,000 range."* Use your own judgment in addressing the salary question. There is no hard and fast
rule on stating a figure or range. A figure helps the employer screen-
out individuals with too high a salary expectation. We prefer keeping
salary considerations to the end of the interview — after you have
demonstrated your value.

You may be able to increase your odds by sending a second
copy of your letter and resume two or three weeks after your initial
response. Most applicants normally reply to an ad during the seven
day period immediately after it appears in print. Since employers
often are swamped with responses, your letter and resume may get
lost in the crowd. If you send a second copy of your application two
or three weeks later, the employer will have more time to give you
special attention. By then, he or she also will have a better basis on
which to compare you to the others.

Keep in mind that your cover letter and resume may be
screened among 400 other resumes and letters. Thus, you want your
cover letter to be eye catching and easy to read. Keep it brief and
concise and highlight your qualifications as stated in the employer's
ad. Above all, don't spend a great deal of time responding to an ad
or waiting anxiously at your mailbox or telephone for a reply. Keep
moving on to other job search activities.

Self-Initiated Methods

Your letters and resumes can be distributed and managed in
various ways. Many people shotgun hundreds of cover letters and
resumes to prospective employers. This is a form of gambling where
the odds are against you. For every 100 people you contact in this
manner, expect one or two who might be interested in you. After
all, successful direct-mail experts at best expect only a 2 percent
return on their mass mailings!

If you choose to use the shotgun method, you can increase
your odds by using the *telephone*. Call the prospective employer
within a week after he or she receives your letter. This technique
will probably increase your effectiveness rate from 1 to 5 percent.
For a good book on this subject, see John Truitt's *Telesearch: Direct
Dial the Best Job of Your Life* (New York: Macmillan or Facts on
File).

However, many people are shotgunning their resumes today. As more resumes and letters descend on employers with the increased use of word processing equipment, the effectiveness rates may be even lower. This also can be an expensive marketing method.

Your best distribution strategy will be your own modification of the following procedure:

1. Selectively identify whom you would be interested in working for.
2. Send an approach letter.
3. Follow up with a telephone call seeking an appointment for an interview.

In more than 50 percent of the cases, you will get an interview. It is best not to include a copy of your resume with the approach letter. Keep your resume for the end of the interview. Chapter 8 outlines the procedures for conducting this informational interview.

Recordkeeping

Once you begin distributing letters and resumes, you also will need to keep good records for managing your job search writing campaign. Purchase file folders for your correspondence and notes. Be sure to make copies of all letters you write since you may need to refer to them over the telephone or before interviews. Record your activities with each employer — letters, resumes, telephone calls, interviews — on a 4 x 6 card and file it according to the name of the organization or individual. These files will help you quickly access information and enable you to evaluate your job search progress.

Always remember the purpose of resumes and letters — *advertise you for interviews*. They do not get jobs. You are a stranger; most employers know nothing about you. Therefore, *you must effectively communicate your value in writing prior to the critical interview*. While you should not overestimate the importance of this written communication, neither should you underestimate it.

DRESSING APPROPRIATELY

Let's assume you present a positive image in your written and telephone communication. Based on these impressions, someone agrees to meet with you for an informational interview or invites you to a job interview. At this stage, you must convey a positive image in the way you look as well as the way you behave both verbally and nonverbally. Your appearance becomes a powerful indicator of your value to individuals who do not know you well.

Appearance is the first thing you communicate to others. Before you have a chance to speak, others notice how you dress and accordingly draw certain conclusions about your personality and competence. Indeed, research shows that appearance makes the greatest difference when an evaluator has little information about the other person. This is precisely the situation you find yourself in at the start of the interview.

Many people object to having their capabilities evaluated on the basis of their appearance and manner of dress. *"But that is not fair,"* they argue. *"People should be hired on the basis of their ability to do the job — not on how they look."* But debating the lack of merit or complaining about the unfairness of such behavior does not alter reality. Like it or not, people do make initial judgments about others based on their appearance. Since you cannot alter this fact and bemoaning it will get you nowhere, it is best to learn to use it to your advantage. If you learn to effectively manage your image, you can convey marvelous messages regarding your authority, credibility, and competence.

Some estimates indicate that as much as 65 percent of the hiring decision may be based on the nonverbal aspects of the interview. Employers sometimes refer to this phenomenon with such terms as "chemistry," "body warmth," or that "gut feeling" the individual is right for the job. This correlates with findings of communication studies that approximately 65 percent of a message is communicated nonverbally. The remaining 35 percent is communicated verbally.

Rules of the Game

Knowing how to dress appropriately for the interview requires knowing important rules of the game. Like it or not, employers play by these rules. Once you know the rules, you at least can make a conscious choice whether or not you want to play. If you decide to play, you will stand a better chance of winning by using the often unwritten rules to your advantage.

Much has been written on how to dress professionally, especially since John Molloy first wrote his books on dress for success in the 1970s. While this approach has been criticized for promoting a "cookie cutter" or "carbon copy" image, it is still valid for most interview situations. The degree to which employers adhere to these rules, however, will depend on particular individuals and situations.

Your job is to know when, where, and to what extent the rules apply to you. When in doubt, follow our general advice on looking professional.

Knowing and playing by the rules does not imply incompetent people get jobs simply by dressing the part. Rather, it implies that qualified and competent job applicants can gain an extra edge over a field of other qualified, competent individuals by dressing to convey positive professional images.

Winning the Game

Much of the general advice on how to dress for success is sound. However, there is a major flaw in most of the advice you encounter. Researchers on the subject have looked at how people in positions of power view certain colors for professional attire. Few have gone beyond this to note that colors do different things on different people. Various shades or clarities of a color or combinations of contrast between light and dark colors when worn together may be unenhancing to some individuals and actually diminish that person's "power look."

For example, the combination of a white shirt or blouse paired with a navy suit — one of the success and power looks promoted by many — will be enhancing both to the appearance and the image of power on some individuals, but will be unenhancing and actually overpower the appearance of others. Or suppose you take the advice that a medium to charcoal gray suit is a good color in the professional world. It is, but the advice to wear medium to charcoal gray only recognizes differences of light to dark. In that medium to charcoal range we could pick scores of shades of gray from very blue grays to taupe grays. The wrong gray shade on individuals can make them look unattractive, unhealthy, and even older than their age. Who wants to hire someone who appears to be in poor health?

If we combine the results of research done by John Molloy on how colors relate to one's power look and that done by JoAnne Nicholson and Judy Lewis-Crum in their book *Color Wonderful* (New York: Bantam) on how colors relate to us as unique individuals, we can achieve a win-win situation. You can retain your individuality and look your most enhanced while, at the same time, achieving a look of success, power, and competence.

Your Winning Appearance

The key to effective dressing is to know how to relate the clothing you put on your body to your own natural coloring. Let's

pose a few questions to start your thinking about color in what may
be some new ways. Ask yourself these questions:

- Can you wear black and white together and look good,
  or does that much contrast wear you?
- Can you wear navy and white together and retain your
  "power look" or does that much contrast actually diminish your look of power and authority?
- Can you wear a pure white or is a slightly cream toned
  white more flattering?
- Do you look better in clear or toned down shades of
  colors?

The answers to these questions vary with each individual and their
own natural coloring. So it is important to know what the appropriate answer is for you.

Into which category does your coloring fit? Let's find out
where you belong in terms of color type:

- *Contrast coloring:* If you are a contrast color type, you
  have a definite dark-light appearance. You have very dark
  brown or black hair and light to medium ivory or olive
  toned skin. Black men and women in this category will
  have clear light to dark skin tones and dark hair.
- *Light-bright coloring:* If you are of this color type, you
  have golden tones in your skin and golden tones in your
  blond or light to medium brown hair. Most of you had
  blond or light brown hair as children. Black men and
  women in this category will have clear golden skin in their
  face and dark hair.
- *Muted coloring:* If you are a muted color type, you have
  a definite brown-on-brown or red-on-brown appearance.
  Your skin tone is an ivory-beige, brown-beige, or golden-
  beige tone — that is, you have a beige skin with a golden-
  brown cast. Your hair could be red or light to dark brown
  with camel, bronze, or red highlights. Black men and
  women in this category will have golden or brown skin
  tones and dark hair.
- *Gentle coloring:* If you are of this color type, you have a
  soft, gentle looking appearance. Your skin tone is a light
  ivory or pink-beige tone and your hair is ash blond or ash
  brown. You probably had blond or ash brown hair as a
  child. Black men and women in this category will have
  pink tones in their skin and dark hair.

There are also some individuals who may be a combination of two color types. If your skin tone falls in one category and your hair color in another, you are a combination color type.

These color types will be referred to in the next two sections when guidelines are given for effectively combining shirts, suits, and ties for men, and skirted suits, blouses, and accessories for women to both enhance and maximize each individual's professional look.

However, if you are uncertain which hair or skin tone is yours and are hence undecided as to which color type category you belong to, you may wish to contact Color 1 Associates, Inc. at 714/545-4517 (Costa Mesa, California) or 202/293-9175 (Washington, D.C.). In addition, the *Color Wonderful* book includes a listing of professionally trained associates located nearest you.

Color 1 provides you with an individualized color chart that allows you to wear every color in the spectrum, but in your best *shade* and *clarity* as well as written material telling you how you can combine your colors for the best amounts of contrast for your natural coloring (color type).

The color chart is an excellent one-time investment considering the costs of buying the wrong colored suit, shirt, or blouse. It will more than pay for itself if it contributes to an effective interview as you wear your suit in your best shade and put your clothing together to work with, rather than against, your natural coloring. It can help you convey positive images during those crucial initial minutes of the interview — as well as over a life-time.

Male Images of Success

John Molloy has conducted extensive research on how individuals can dress effectively. Aimed at individuals already working in professional positions who want to communicate a success image, his advice is just as relevant for someone interviewing for a public or private sector job.

Except for some blue collar jobs, basic attire for men interviewing for a position is a suit. Let's look at appropriate suits in terms of color, fabric, and style. The suit color can make a difference in creating an image of authority and competence. In general, blue, gray, camel, or beige are proper colors for men's suits. Usually the darker the shade, the greater amount of authority it conveys to the wearer. Given your situation (the interview) and your audience (the interviewer), you should aim at conveying enough authority to command attention and a positive regard, but not so much as to threaten the interviewer. Hence, the medium to charcoal gray or navy blue would be good suit colors. Black, a basic funeral attire, can threaten the interviewer by conveying too much authority.

When selecting your gray, navy, camel, or beige suit, choose a shade that is enhancing to you. Should you wear a blue-gray, a taupe-gray, or a shade in-between? Do you look better in a somewhat bright navy or a more toned-down navy; a blue navy or a black navy; a navy with a purple or a yellow base to it?

In general, most people will look better in somewhat blue grays than in grays that are closer to the taupe side of the spectrum. Most people will be enhanced by a navy that is not too bright or contain so much black that it is difficult to distinguish whether the color is navy or black. When selecting a beige or a camel, select a tone that complements your skin color. If your skin has pink tones, avoid beiges and camels that contain gold hues and select pink based beiges/camels that enhance your skin color. Similarly, those of you who have gold/olive tones to your skin should avoid the pink based camel and beiges.

Should your camels or beiges be pink-toned, ivory-toned or golden-toned? If you are unsure, get the name of the Color 1 Associate nearest you and schedule an appointment. If you are going to spend a lot of money on a suit — and if you buy a good, well-made suit you are going to spend a lot of money — buy a suit that will work for you.

Your suit(s) should be made of a natural fiber. A good blend of a natural fiber with some synthetic is acceptable as long as it has the "look" of the natural fiber. The very best suit fabrics are wool, wool blends, or fabrics that look like them. Even for the warmer summer months, men can find summer weight wool suits that are comfortable and look marvelous. They are your best buy. For really hot climates, linen, or a fabric that looks like linen tests well. Normally a linen will have to be blended with another fiber, often a synthetic, in order to retain a pressed, neat look. The major disadvantage of pure linen is that it wrinkles. Avoid 100 percent polyester materials, or anything that looks like it — especially double-knits — like the plague! It is a definite negative for your look of competence, power, and success.

The style of your suit should be classic. It should be well-tailored and well-styled. Avoid suits that appear "trendy" unless you are applying for a job in a field such as arts or perhaps advertising. A conservative suit that has a timeless classic styling and also looks up-to-date will serve you best not only for the interview, but it will give you several years wear once you land the job.

Select a shirt color that is lighter than the color of your suit. John Molloy's book on appearance and dress for men, *Dress For*

Success, goes into great detail on shirts, ties, and practically everything you might wear or carry with you. We recommend Molloy's
book over others because it is based on research rather than personal
opinion and promotional fads.

However, you must take Molloy's advice one step beyond where
he takes you: keep in mind your color type. If you have contrast or
light-bright coloring, you will look great wearing your shade of white
in a shirt with your navy blue shade in a suit. But if you have muted
or gentle coloring, *this is too much contrast for you.* For muted or
gentle coloring, the combination of navy and white will visually
overpower you and you will not look your most enhanced.

If you are a muted or gentle color type, the look that gives you
the greatest power look and yet does not overpower you will be a
suit in your most flattering shade of gray worn with a shirt in your
shade of white. You can expect your white to be less of a "pure"
white (a bit more creamy) than the white a contrast or a light-bright
would wear. When you wear a navy suit, pair it with a blue shirt
rather than a white one. This combines your colors in a level of
contrast effective for your coloring.

Female Images of Success

Few men would consider wearing anything other than a suit to
a job interview — especially an interview for a managerial or professional position. Women are often less certain what is appropriate.
As a result of research conducted by John Molloy and others, the
verdict is now in. A skirted suit is the definite choice for the interview. This attire allows a woman to best convey images of professionalism, authority, and competence. Wearing a skirted suit can
initially help a woman overcome negative stereotypes that some men
still hold toward women in managerial and other professional positions.

Let's survey appropriate suits in terms of color, fabric, and
style. As in the case of men's suit, the color of your suit can help
create an image of authority and competence. The suit colors that
make the strongest positive statements for you are *your shade* of
gray in a medium to charcoal depth or *your shade* of blue in a
medium to navy depth of color. Other dark shades, such as maroon,
test well as does camel. Avoid black, which can convey so much
authority; many interviewers find it threatening. Also, avoid solid
brown. British looking tweeds and small plaids or herringbone designs in brown are acceptable, but a solid dark brown suit does not
score well in most geographical areas.

When selecting your gray, navy, camel, or any other colored

suit, follow the same rules we outlined for men: choose a shade that is enhancing to you. If you are uncertain which shades are best for you, contact a Color 1 Associate for advice.

Similar to men's suits, your suit should be made of a natural fiber or have the "look" of a natural fiber. The very best winter-weight suit fabrics are wool or wool blends. For the warmer climates or the summer months, women will find few, if any, summer weight wool suits made for them. Hence linen, blended with a synthetic so it will not look as if it needs constant pressing, is your first choice. Other fabrics, such as polyester blended with rayon, in clothing of good quality often has the definite look of linen but without the hassles of caring for real linen. But the key word here is *quality*. A cheap polyester/rayon fabric will look just that. Avoid 100 percent polyester material, or anything that looks like it — especially double-knits — like the plague it is.

Your suit style should be classic. Following similar rules as for men, women's suits should be well-tailored, well-styled, and avoid a "trendy" look unless appropriate for certain occupations. A conservative, classic suit will last for years and is an excellent investment. Indeed, you can afford to buy good quality clothing if you know you will get a lot of use from the item. When deciding on your professional wardrobe, always buy clothes to last and buy quality.

Quality also means buying silk blouses if you can afford them. Keep in mind not only the price of the blouse itself, but the cleaning bill. There are many polyester blouse fabrics that have the look and feel of silk — this is an exception to the "no polyester" rule. Silk or a polyester that has the look and feel of silk are the fabrics for blouses to go with your wool suits. Cotton blouses should generally not be paired with a wool suit. Choose your blouses in your most flattering shades and clarity of color. John Molloy's book on appearance and dress for women, *The Woman's Dress for Success Book,* goes into great detail on the blouse styles that test best as well as expands on suit colors. It includes information on almost anything you might wear or carry with you to the interview or on the job.

But remember, as in the case of men, you must take Molloy's advice one step further: keep in mind your color type. Contrast or light-bright coloring types look great wearing their shade of white in a blouse with their navy blue shade in a suit. Muted and gentle color types will find this to be too much contrast and thus overpower their natural coloring. Such a color combination actually diminishes their power look.

If you are a muted or gentle color type, why not try your coral red shade blouse with your navy suit or wear your shade of white with your gray shade suit. Once you are aware of your color type and how to best enhance it while retaining visual authority, you will find many new and flattering combinations.

Give your outfit a more "finished and polished" look by accessorizing it effectively. Collect silk scarves and necklaces of semiprecious stones in your suit colors. Wear scarves and necklaces with your suits and blouses in such a way that they repeat the color of the suit. For example, a woman wearing a navy suit and a red silk blouse could accent the look by wearing a necklace of navy sodalite beads or a silk scarf that has navy as a predominate color. The *Color Wonderful* book includes a great deal of information to help you accessorize your look geared to your color type.

The most appropriate shoe to wear with a business suit is a classic pump — closed heel and toe and little or no decoration. Not only does this shoe stand by itself as creating the most professional look, it also teams best with a business suit and is flattering at the same time. A sling-back shoe (heel open with a strap across the heel) can be worn with a suit, but will slightly diminish the wearer's professional look. Avoid shoes with both the heel and toe open as well as any sandal look. They can be beautiful shoes, but save them for evening wear. We have observed many women arriving for job interviews wearing suits, but ruining their professional image by wearing strappy sandal shoes. In general, wear shoes as dark or darker than your skirt. If not, you may draw the other person's eyes to your feet when, instead, you want them to focus on your face and on what you are saying.

You may choose to carry a purse *or* an attache case, but not both at the same time. It is difficult not to look clumsy trying to handle both a purse and an attache case, and it is likely to diminish your power look as well. One way to carry both is to keep a slim purse with essentials such as lipstick, mirror, and money inside the attache case. If you need to go out to lunch, or any place where you choose not to carry the attache case, just pull out your purse and you're off.

Buying Quality Apparel

Aside from information on what articles of apparel to wear, a word on the quality of what you purchase is in order. *Buy the best you can afford.* If you are not gainfully employed, this may seem like impractical advice. But it still remains your best advice. Two really good suits with a variety of shirts or blouses will look better from the first day you own them than four suits of inferior quality — and will out last them as well. To buy quality rather than quantity is a good habit to form.

Stretch your money by shopping sales or good discount outlets if you wish. But remember, it isn't a bargain if it isn't right for you. A suit that never quite fits or isn't exactly your best shade is not a bargain no matter how many times it has been marked down. John Molloy's books have useful hints on how to overcome a middle-class background and learn to buy good quality clothing at reasonable prices.

In addition to buying natural fibers in clothing whenever possible, invest in real leather for shoes, attache case, and handbag — if you carry one. Leather conveys a professional look and will out last the cheap looking imitations you might buy. In the end, we get what we pay for.

Chapter Eight

TAKE
POSITIVE ACTION

The job search skills discussed thus far prepare you for the most critical stages of the job search: networking, interviewing, and negotiating terms of employment. These are the face-to-face implementation stages of the job search. Specific skills and strategies are associated with success in these stages. This chapter outlines practical methods for developing the necessary interpersonal skills and for implementing the face-to-face strategies.

PROSPECTING, NETWORKING, AND INFORMATIONAL INTERVIEWS

What do you do after you complete your resume? Most people send cover letters and resumes in response to job listings; they then wait to be called for a job interview. Viewing the job search as basically a direct-mail operation, many are disappointed in discovering the realities of direct-mail — a 5 percent response rate is considered outstanding!

Successful job seekers break out of this relatively passive job search role by orienting themselves toward face-to-face action. Being proactive, they develop interpersonal strategies in which the resume plays a supportive rather than a central role in the job search. They first present themselves to employers; the resume appears only at the end of a face-to-face conversation.

Throughout the job search you will acquire useful names and addresses as well as meet people who will assist you in contacting potential employers. In both the public and private sector job markets, such information and contacts become key building blocks for generating job interviews and offers.

Since the best and most numerous jobs are found on the hidden job market, you must use methods appropriate for this job market. Indeed, research and experience clearly show the most effective means of communication are face-to-face and word-of-mouth. The informal, interpersonal system of communication is the central nervous system of the hidden job market. Your goal should be to penetrate this job market with proven methods for success. Appropriate methods for making important job contacts are *prospecting and networking*. Appropriate methods for getting these contacts to provide you with useful job information are *informational and referral interviews*.

Communicating Qualifications

Taken together, these interpersonal methods help you *communicate your qualifications to employers*. Although many job seekers may be reluctant to use this informal communication system, they greatly limit their potential for success if they do not. Swamped with 400 to 500 resumes for a single position, many employers prefer this informal system. In addition, many employers are uncertain what type of individual they should hire. By using this informal system, you help employers identify their needs, limit their alternatives, and thus make decisions and save money.

Most employers also want more information on candidates to supplement the "paper qualifications" represented in application forms, resumes, and letters. Studies show that employers in general seek candidates who have these skills: communication, problem solving, analytical, assessment, and planning. Surprising to many job seekers, technical expertise ranks third or fourth in employers' lists of most desired skills. These findings support a frequent observation made by employers: the major problems with employees relate to communication, problem solving, and analysis; individuals get fired because of political and interpersonal conflicts rather than technical incompetence.

Employers generally seek individuals they *like* both personally and professionally. Therefore, communicating your qualifications to employers entails more than just informing them of your technical competence. You must communicate that you have the requisite personal *and* professional skills for performing the job. Informal prospecting, networking, and informational interviewing activities are the best methods for communicating your "qualifications" to employers.

Developing Networks

Networking is the process of purposefully developing relations with others. Networking in the job search involves connecting and interacting with other individuals who can be helpful to you. Your network consists of you interacting with these other individuals. The more you develop, maintain, and expand your networks, the more successful should be your job search.

Your network is your interpersonal environment. While you know and interact with hundreds of people, on a day-to-day basis you probably encounter no more than 20 people. You frequently contact these people in face-to-face situations. Some people are more *important* to you than others. You *like* some more than others. And some will be more *helpful* to you in your job search than others. Your basic network may encompass the following individuals and groups: friends, acquaintances, immediate family, distant relatives, professional colleagues, spouse, supervisor, fellow workers, close friends and colleagues, and local businessmen and professionals, such as your banker, lawyer, doctor, minister, and insurance agent. You should contact many of these individuals for advice relating to your job search.

You need to *identify everyone in your network* who might help you with your job search. You first need to expand your basic network to include individuals you know and have interacted with over the past 10 or more years. Make a list of at least 200 people you know. Include friends and relatives from your Christmas card list, past and present neighbors, former classmates, politicians, business persons, previous employers, professional associates, ministers, insurance agents, lawyers, bankers, doctors, dentists, accountants, and social acquaintances.

After identifying your extended network, you should try to *link your network to others' networks.* Individuals in these other networks also have job information and contacts. Ask people in your basic network for referrals to individuals in their networks. This approach should greatly enlarge your basic job search network.

What do you do if individuals in your immediate and extended network can not provide you with certain job information and contacts? While it is much easier and more effective to meet new people through personal contacts, on occasion you may need to *approach strangers without prior contacts.* In this situation, try the "cold turkey" approach. Write a letter to someone you feel may be useful to your job search. Research this individual so you are acquainted with their background and accomplishments. In the letter, refer to their accomplishments, mention your need for job information, and specify a date and time you will call to schedule a meeting. An example of such a "cold turkey approach letter" is included in Appendix C. Another approach is to introduce yourself to someone by telephone and request a meeting and/or job information. While you may experience rejections in using these approaches, you also will experience successes. And those successes should lead to further expansion of your job search network.

Prospecting For Success

The key to successful networking is an active and routine *prospecting campaign.* Salespersons in insurance, real estate, Amway, Shaklee, and other direct-sales businesses understand the importance and principles of prospecting; indeed, many have turned the art of prospecting into a science! The basic operating principle is *probability:* the number of sales you make is a direct function of the amount of effort you put into developing new contacts and following-through. Expect no more than a 10 percent acceptance rate: for every 10 people you meet, 9 will reject you and 1 will accept you. Therefore, the more people you contact, the more acceptances you will receive. If you want to be successful, you must collect many more "nos" than "yeses." In a 10 percent probability situation, you need to contact 100 people for 10 successes.

These prospecting principles are extremely useful for your job search. Like sales situations, the job search is a highly ego-involved activity often characterized by numerous rejections accompanied by a few acceptances. While no one wants to be rejected, few people are willing and able to handle more than a few rejections. They take a "no" as a sign of personal failure — and quit prematurely. If they persisted longer, they would achieve success after a few more "nos." Furthermore, if their prospecting activities were focused on gathering information rather than making sales, they would considerably minimize the number of rejections. Therefore, this is what you should do:

- Prospect for job leads.
- Accept rejections as part of the game.
- Link prospecting to informational interviewing.
- Keep prospecting for more information and "yeses"

which will eventually translate into job interviews and offers.

A good prospecting pace as you start your search is to make two new contacts each day. Start by contacting people in your immediate network. Let them know you are conducting a job search, but emphasize that you are only doing research. Ask for a few moments of their time to discuss your information needs. You are only seeking *information and advice* at this time — not a job.

It should take you about 20 minutes to make a contact by letter or telephone. If you make two contacts each day, by the end of the first week you will have 10 new contacts for a total investment of less than seven hours. By the second week you may want to increase your prospecting pace to four new contacts each day or 20 each week. The more contacts you make, the more useful information, advice, and job leads you will receive. If your job search bogs down, you probably need to increase your prospecting activities.

Expect each contact to refer you to two or three others who will also refer you to others. Consequently, your contacts should multiply considerably within only a few weeks.

Handling and Minimizing Rejections

These prospecting and networking methods are effective. While they are responsible for building, maintaining, and expanding multi-million dollar businesses, they work extremely well for job hunters. But they only work if you are patient and persist. *The key to networking success is to focus on gathering information while also learning to handle rejections.* Learn from rejections, forget them, and go on to more productive networking activities. The major reason direct-sales people fail is because they don't persist. The reason they don't persist is because they either can't take, or get tired of taking, rejections.

Rejections are no fun, especially in such an ego-involved activity as a job search. But you will encounter rejections as you travel on the road toward job search success. This road is strewn with individuals who quit prematurely because they were rejected four or five times. Don't be one of them!

Our prospecting and networking techniques differ from sales approaches in one major respect: we have special techniques for minimizing the number of rejections. If handled properly, at least 50 percent — maybe as many as 90 percent — of your prospects will turn into "yeses" rather than "nos." The reason for this unusually high acceptance rate is how you introduce and handle yourself before your prospects. Many insurance agents and direct distributors expect a 90 percent rejection rate, because they are trying to sell specific products potential clients may or may not need. Most people don't like to be put on the spot — especially when it is in their own home or office — to make a decision to buy a product.

Selling With Sincerity

The principles of selling yourself in the job market are similar. People don't want to be put on the spot. They feel uncomfortable if they think you expect them to give you a job. Thus, you should never introduce yourself to a prospect by asking them for a job or a job lead. You should do just the opposite: relieve their anxiety by mentioning that you are not looking for a job from them — only job information and advice. You must be honest and sincere in communicating these intentions to your contact. The biggest turn-off for individuals targeted for informational interviews is insincere job seekers who try to use this as a mechanism to get a job.

Your approach to prospects must be subtle, honest, and professional. You are seeking *information, advice, and referrals* relating to several subjects: job opportunities, your job search approach, your resume, and others who may have similar information, advice, and referrals. Most people gladly volunteer such information. They generally like to talk about themselves, their careers, and others. They like to give advice. This approach flatters individuals by placing them in the role of the expert-advisor. Who doesn't want to be recognized as an expert-advisor, especially on such a critical topic as one's employment?

This approach should yield a great deal of information, advice, and referrals from your prospects. One other important outcome should result from using this approach: people will *remember* you as the person who made them feel at ease and who received their valuable advice. If they hear of job opportunities for someone with your qualifications, chances are they will contact you with the information. After contacting 100 prospects, you will have created 100 sets of eyes and ears to help you in your job search!

The guiding principle behind prospecting, networking, and informational interviews is this: *the best way to get a job is to ask for job information, advice, and referrals; never ask for a job.* Remember, you want your prospects to engage in the 5-R's of informational interviewing:

- *Reveal* useful information and advice.
- *Refer* you to others.

- *Read* and *revise* your resume.
- *Remember* you for future reference.

If you follow this principle, you should join the ranks of thousands of successful job seekers who paid a great deal of money learning it from highly-paid professionals.

Approaching Key People

Whom should you contact within an organization for an informational interview? Contact people who are busy, who have the power to hire, and who are knowledgeable about the organization. The least likely candidate will be someone in the personnel department. Most often the heads of operating units are the most busy, powerful, and knowledgeable individuals in the organization. However, getting access to such individuals may be difficult. Some people at the top may appear to be informed and powerful, but they may lack information on the day-to-day personnel changes or their influence is limited in the hiring process. It is difficult to give one best answer to this question.

Therefore, we recommend contacting a variety of people. Aim for the busy, powerful, and informed, but be prepared to settle for less. Secretaries, receptionists, and the person you want to meet may refer you to others. From a practical standpoint, you may have to take whomever you can schedule an appointment with. Sometimes people who are not busy can be helpful. Talk to a secretary or receptionist sometime about their boss or working in the organization. You may be surprised with what you learn!

The best way to initiate a contact with a prospective employer is to *send an approach letter*. An example of such a letter appears in Appendix C. Begin this letter with a personal statement, such as: *"James Chance suggested that I contact you..."* Briefly state your purpose — seek information and advice — and mention you will call at a specific time to schedule a meeting. Do not enclose a resume with this letter. Remember, your purposes are to get information, advice, referrals, and remembered. While this is not a formal interview, it may well lead to one.

Most people will meet with you, assuming you are sincere in your approach. If the person tries to put you off when you telephone for an appointment, clearly state your purpose and emphasize that you are not looking for a job with this person — only information and advice. If the person insists on putting you off, make the best of the situation: write a nice thank-you letter in which you again state your intended purpose; mention your disappointment in not being able to learn from the person's experience; and ask to be remembered for future reference. Enclose your resume with this letter.

While you are ostensibly seeking information and advice, treat this meeting as an important preliminary interview. You need to communicate your qualifications — that you are competent, intelligent, honest, and likable. These are the same qualities you should communicate in a formal job interview. Hence, follow the same advice given for conducting a formal interview and dressing appropriately for face-to-face meetings (Chapter 7).

Structuring the Informational Interview

An informational interview will be relatively unstructured compared to a formal interview. Since you want the interviewer to advise you, you reverse roles by asking questions which should give you useful information. You, in effect, become the interviewer. You should structure this interview with a particular sequence of questions. Most questions should be open-ended, requiring the individual to give specific answers based upon his or her experience.

The structure and dialogue for the informational interview might go something like this. You plan to take no more than 45 minutes for this interview. The first three to five minutes will be devoted to small talk — the weather, traffic, the office, mutual acquaintances, or an interesting or humorous observation. Since these are the most critical moments in the interview, be especially careful how you communicate nonverbally. Begin your interview by stating your appreciation for the individual's time:

"I want to thank you again for scheduling this meeting with me. I know you're busy. I appreciate the special arrangements you made to see me on a subject which is very important to my future."

Your next comment should be a statement reiterating your purpose as stated in your letter:

"As you know, I am exploring job and career alternatives. I know what I do well and what I want to do. Before I commit myself to a new job, I need to know more about various career options. I thought you would be able to provide me with some insights into career opportunities, job requirements, and possible problems or promising directions in the field of _____"

This statement normally will get a positive reaction from the individual who may want to know more about what it is you want to do. Be sure to clearly communicate your job objective. If you can't, you may communicate that you are lost, indecisive, or uncertain about yourself. The person may feel you are wasting his or her time.

Your next line of questioning should focus on "how" and "what" questions centering on (1) specific jobs and (2) the job search process. Begin by asking about various aspects of specific jobs:

- Duties and responsibilities.
- Knowledge, skills, and abilities required.
- Work environment relating to fellow employees, work flows, deadlines, stress, initiative.
- Advantages and disadvantages.
- Advancement opportunities and outlook.
- Salary ranges.

Your informer will probably take a great deal of time talking about his or her experience in each area. Be a good listener, but make sure you move along with the questions.

Your next line of questioning should focus on your job search activities. You need as much information as possible on how to:

- Acquire the necessary skills.
- Best find a job in this field.
- Overcome any objections employers may have to your background.
- Uncover job vacancies which may be advertised.
- Develop job leads.
- Approach prospective employers.

Your final line of questioning should focus on your resume. Do not show your resume until you focus on this last set of questions. The purpose of these questions is to: (1) get the individual to read your resume in-depth, (2) acquire useful advice on how to strengthen it, (3) refer you to prospective employers, and (4) be remembered. With the resume in front of you and your interviewee, ask the following questions:

- *Is this an appropriate type of resume for the jobs I have outlined?*
- *If an employer received this resume in the mail, how do you think he or she would react to it?*

- *What do you see as possible weaknesses or areas that need to be improved?*
- *What should I do with this resume? Shotgun it to hundreds of employers with a cover letter? Use resume letters instead?*
- *What about the length, paper quality and color, layout, and typing? Are they appropriate?*
- *How might I best improve the form and content of the resume?*

You should receive useful advice on how to strengthen both the content and use of your resume. Most important, these questions force the individual to *read* your resume which, in turn, may be *remembered* for future reference.

Your last question is especially important in this interview. You want to be both *remembered* and *referred*. Some variation of the following question should help:

"I really appreciate all this advice. It is very helpful and it should improve my job search considerably. Could I ask you one more favor? Do you know two or three other people who could help me with my job search? I want to conduct as much research as possible, and their advice might be helpful also."

Before you leave, mention one more important item:

"During the next few months, should you hear of any job opportunities for someone with my interests and qualifications, I would appreciate being kept in mind. And please feel free to pass my name on to others."

Send a nice thank-you letter within 48 hours of completing this informational interview. Following the example in Appendix C, express your genuine gratitude for the individual's time and advice. Reiterate your interests, and ask to be remembered and referred to others.

Follow-up on any useful advice you receive, particularly referrals. Approach referrals in the same manner you approached the person who gave you the referral. Write a letter requesting a meeting. Begin the letter by mentioning that *"Mr./Ms. ⎯⎯⎯⎯⎯ suggested that I contact you concerning my research on careers in ⎯⎯⎯⎯⎯"*

If you continue prospecting, networking, and conducting informational interviews, soon you will be busy conducting interviews and receiving job offers. While 100 informational interviews over a two-month period should lead to several formal job interviews and offers, the pay-offs are uncertain because job vacancies are unpredictable. We know cases where the first referral turned into a formal interview and job offer. More typical cases require constant prospecting, networking, and informational interviewing activities. The telephone call or letter inviting you to a job interview can come at any time. While the timing may be unpredictable, your persistent job search activities will be largely responsible for the final outcome.

Telephoning For Job Leads

Telephone communication plays a role in prospecting, networking, and informational interviewing activities. However, controversy centers around how and when to use the telephone for generating job leads and scheduling interviews. Some people recommend writing a letter and waiting for a written or telephone reply. Others suggest writing a letter and following it with a telephone call. Still others argue you should use the telephone exclusively rather than write letters.

How you use the telephone will indicate what type of job search you are conducting. Exclusive reliance on the telephone is a technique used by highly formalized job clubs which operate phone banks for generating job leads. Using the Yellow Pages as the guide to employers, a job club member may call as many as 50 employers a day to schedule job interviews. A rather aggressive yet typical telephone dialogue goes something like this:

> *"Hello, my name is Jim Baker. I would like to speak to the head of the training department. By the way, what is the name of the training director?"*

> *"You want to talk to Ms. Stevens. Her number is 723-8191 or I can connect you directly."*

> *"Hello, Ms. Stevens. My name is Jim Baker. I have several years of training experience as both a trainer and developer of training materials. I would like to meet with you to discuss possible openings in your department for someone with my qualifications. Would it be possible to see you on Friday at 2:00 p.m.?"*

Not surprising, this telephone approach generates many "nos." If you have a hard time handling rejections, this telephone approach will help you confront your anxieties. The principle behind this approach is *probability:* for every 25 telephone "nos" you receive, you will probably get one or two "yeses." Success is just 25 telephone calls away! If you start calling prospective employers at 9:00 a.m. and finish your 25 calls by 12:00 noon, you should generate at least one or two interviews. That's not bad for three hours of job search work. It beats a direct-mail approach.

The telephone is more efficient than writing letters. However, its effectiveness is questionable. When you use the telephone in this manner, you are basically asking for a job. You are asking the employer: *"Do you have a job for me?"* There is nothing subtle or particularly professional about this approach. It is effective in uncovering particular types of job leads for particular types of individuals. If you need any job in a hurry, this is one of the most efficient ways of finding employment. It sure beats standing in line at the state employment office! However, if you are more concerned with finding a job that is right for you – a job you do well and enjoy doing, one that is fit for you – this telephone approach may be inappropriate.

You must use your own judgment in determining when and how to use the telephone in your job search. There are appropriate times and methods for using the telephone, and these should relate to your job search goals and needs. We prefer the more conventional approach of writing a letter followed by a telephone call. While you take the initiative in scheduling an appointment, you do not put the individual on the spot by asking for a job. You are only seeking information and advice. This low-keyed approach results in numerous acceptances and has a higher probability of paying off with interviews than the aggressive telephone request. You should be trying to uncover jobs that are right for you rather than any job that happens to pop up from a telephoning blitz.

Using Job Clubs and Support Groups

The techniques we outlined thus far are designed for individuals conducting a self-directed job search. Job clubs and support groups are two important alternatives to these techniques.

Job clubs are designed to provide a group structure and support system to individuals seeking employment. These groups consist of about 12 individuals who are led by a trained counselor and supported with telephones, copying machines, and a resource center.

Highly formalized job clubs, such as the 40-Plus Club, organize job search activities for both the advertised and hidden job markets. As outlined by Azrin and Besalel in their book *Job Club Counselor's*

Manual, job club activities include:

- Signing commitment agreements to achieve specific job search goals and targets.
- Contacting friends, relatives, and acquaintances for job leads.
- Completing activity forms.
- Using telephones, typewriters, photocopy machines, postage, and other supplies and equipment.
- Meeting with fellow participants to discuss job search progress.
- Telephoning to uncover job leads.
- Researching newspapers, telephone books,and directories.
- Developing research, telephone, interview, and social skills.
- Writing letters and resumes.
- Responding to want ads.
- Completing employment applications.

In other words, the job club formalizes many of the prospecting, networking, and informational interviewing activities within a group context and interjects the role of the telephone as the key communication device for developing and expanding networks.

Job clubs place excessive reliance on using the telephone for uncovering job leads. Members call prospective employers and ask about job openings. The Yellow Pages become the job hunting bible. During a two-week period, a job club member might spend most of his or her mornings telephoning for job leads and scheduling interviews. Afternoons are normally devoted to job interviewing.

We do not recommend joining such job clubs for obvious reasons. Most job club methods are designed for the hardcore unemployed or for individuals who need a job — any job — quickly. Individuals try to fit into available vacancies; their objectives and skills are of secondary concern. We recommend conducting your own job search or forming a support group which adapts some job club methods to our central concept of *finding a job fit for you* — one appropriate to your objective and in line with your particular mix of skills, abilities, and interests.

Support groups are a useful alternative to job clubs. They have one major advantage: they may cut your job search time in half. Forming or joining one of these groups can help direct as well as enhance your individual job search activities.

Your support group should consist of three or more individuals who are job hunting. Try to schedule regular meetings with specific purposes in mind. While the group may be highly social, especially if it involves close friends, it also should be *task-oriented*. Meet at least once a week and include your spouse. At each meeting *set performance goals* for the week. For example, your goal can be to make 20 new contacts and conduct five informational interviews. The contacts can be made by telephone, letter, or in person. Share your experiences and job information with each other. *Critique each other's progress*, make suggestions for improving the job search, and develop new strategies together. By doing this, you will be gaining valuable information and feedback which is normally difficult to gain on one's own. This group should provide important psychological supports to help you through your job search. After all, job hunting can be a lonely, frustrating, and exasperating experience. By sharing your experiences with others, you will find you are not alone. You will quickly learn that rejections are part of the game. The group will encourage you, and you will feel good about helping others achieve their goals. Try building small incentives into the group, such as the individual who receives the most job interviews for the month must be treated to dinner by other members of the group.

INTERVIEWING FOR THE JOB

Formal job interviews are required by nearly 95 percent of all organizations. The job interview is the single most important step to getting a job offer. How well you handle this interview is more important than your previous work experience, recommendations, and educational record.

The job interview also is the most stressful job search experience. Your application, resume, and letters may get you to the interview, but you must perform well in person in order to get a job offer. Knowing the stakes are high, most people face interviews with dry throats and sweaty palms; it is a time of great stress. You will be on stage, and you are expected to put on a good performance.

How do you prepare for the interview? First, you need to understand the nature and purpose of the interview. Second, you must prepare to respond to the interview situation and the interviewer. Make sure whoever assists you in preparing for the interview evaluates your performance. Practice the whole interviewing scenario, beginning with entering the door to leaving at that end. You should sharpen your nonverbal communication skills and be prepared to give positive answers to questions as well as ask intelligent questions. The more you practice, the better prepared you will be for the real job interview.

Communication

An interview is a two-way communication exchange between an interviewer and interviewee. It involves both verbal and nonverbal communication. While we tend to concentrate on the content of what we say, research shows that approximately 65 percent of all communication is nonverbal. Furthermore, we tend to give more credibility to nonverbal than to verbal messages. Regardless of what you say, how you dress, sit, stand, use your hands, move your head and eyes, and listen communicate both positive and negative messages.

Job interviews can occur in many different settings and under various circumstances. You will write job interview letters, schedule interviews by telephone, be interviewed over the phone, and encounter one-on-one as well as panel, group, and series interviews. Each situation requires a different set of communication behaviors. For example, while telephone communication is efficient, it may be ineffective for interview purposes. Only certain types of information can be effectively communicated over the telephone because this medium limits nonverbal behavior. Honesty, intelligence, and likability — three of the most important values you want to communicate to employers — are primarily communicated nonverbally. Therefore, you should be very careful of telephone interviews — whether giving or receiving them.

Job interviews have different purposes and can be negative in many ways. From your perspective, the purpose of an initial job interview is to get a second interview, and the purpose of the second interview is to get a job offer. However, for many employers, the purpose of the interview is to eliminate you from a second interview or job offer. The interviewer wants to know why he or she should *not* hire you. The interviewer tries to do this by identifying your weaknesses. These differing purposes create an adversarial relationship and contribute to the overall interviewing stress experienced by both the applicant and the interviewer.

Since the interviewer wants to identify your weaknesses, you must counter by *communicating your strengths* to lessen the interviewer's fears of hiring you. Recognizing that you are an unknown quantity to the employer, you must raise the interviewer's expectations of you.

Answering Questions

Hopefully your prospecting, networking, informational interviewing, and resume and letter writing activities result in several invitations to interview for jobs appropriate to your objective. Once you receive an invitation to interview, you should do a great deal of work in preparation for your meeting. You should prepare for the interview as if it were a $500,000 prize. After all, that may be what you earn with the employer over the next 10 years.

The invitation to interview will most likely come by telephone. In some cases, a preliminary interview will be conducted by telephone. The employer may want to shorten the list of eligible candidates from 10 to 3. By calling each individual, the employer can quickly eliminate marginal candidates as well as up-date the job status of each individual. When you get such a telephone call, you have no time to prepare. You may be dripping wet as you step from the shower or you may have a splitting headache as you pick up the phone. Telephone interviews always seem to occur at bad times. Whatever your situation, put your best foot forward based upon your thorough preparation for an interview. You may want to keep a list of questions near the telephone just in case you receive such a telephone call.

Telephone interviews often result in an interview at the employer's office. Once you confirm an interview time and place, you should do as much research on the organization and employer as possible as well as learn to lessen your anxiety and stress levels by practicing the interview situation. *Preparation and practice* are the keys to doing your best.

During the interview, you want to impress upon the interviewer your knowledge of the organization by asking intelligent questions and giving intelligent answers. Your library and networking research should yield useful information on the organization and employer. Be sure you know something about the organization. Interviewers are normally impressed by interviewees who demonstrate knowledge and interest in their organization.

You should practice the actual interview by mentally addressing several questions most interviewers ask. Most of these questions will relate to your educational background, work experience, career goals, personality, and related concerns. The most frequently asked questions include:

TYPICAL INTERVIEW QUESTIONS

Education

- *Describe your educational background.*
- *Why did you attend _____ University (College or School)?*
- *Why did you major in _____?*
- *What was your grade point average?*
- *What subjects did you enjoy the most? The least? Why?*
- *What leadership positions did you hold?*
- *How did you finance your education?*
- *If you started all over, what would you change about your education?*
- *Why were your grades so low? So high?*
- *Did you do the best you could in school? If not, why not?*

Work Experience

- *What were your major achievements in each of your past jobs?*
- *Why did you change jobs before?*
- *What is your typical workday like?*
- *What functions do you enjoy doing the most?*
- *What did you like about your boss? Dislike?*
- *Which job did you enjoy the most? Why? Which job did you enjoy the least? Why?*
- *Have you ever been fired? Why?*

Career Goals

- *Why do you want to join our organization?*
- *Why do you think you are qualified for this position?*
- *Why are you looking for another job?*
- *Why do you want to make a career change?*
- *What ideally would you like to do?*
- *Why should we hire you?*
- *How would you improve our operations?*
- *What do you want to be doing five years from now?*
- *How much do you want to be making five years from now?*
- *What are your short-range and long-range career goals?*
- *If you could choose your job and organization, where*

would you go?
- *What other types of jobs are you considering? Other companies?*
- *When will you be ready to begin work?*
- *How do you feel about relocating, traveling, working over-time, and spending weekends in the office?*
- *What attracted you to our organization?*

Personality and Other Concerns

- *Tell me about yourself.*
- *What are your major weaknesses? Your major strengths?*
- *What causes you to lose your temper?*
- *What do you do in your spare time? Any hobbies?*
- *What types of books do you read?*
- *What role does your family play in your career?*
- *How well do you work under pressure? In meeting deadlines?*
- *Tell me about your management philosophy.*
- *How much initiative do you take?*
- *What types of people do you prefer working with?*
- *How _____ (creative, analytical, tactful, etc.) are you?*
- *If you could change your life, what would you do differently?*
- *Who are your references?*

Your answers to each question should be positive and emphasize your *strengths*. Remember, the interviewer wants to know about your *weaknesses*. For example, if you are asked *"What are your weaknesses?"*, you can turn this potential negative question into a positive by answering something like this:

> *"I sometimes get so involved with my work that I neglect my family as well as forget to complete work around the house. My problem is that I'm somewhat of a workaholic."*

What employer could hold this negative against you? You have taken a negative and raised the expectations of the employer by basically saying you are a hard and persistent worker; the organization will get more for its money than expected.

Other questions are illegal, but some employers ask them nonetheless. Consider how you would respond to them:

ILLEGAL QUESTIONS

- *Are you married, divorced, separated, or single?*
- *How old are you?*
- *Do you go to church regularly?*
- *Do you have many debts?*
- *Do you own or rent your home?*
- *What social and political organizations do you belong to?*
- *Are you living with anyone?*
- *Are you practicing birth control?*
- *Were you ever arrested?*
- *How much insurance do you have?*
- *How much do you weigh?*
- *How tall are you?*

Don't get upset and say *"That's an illegal question. . . I refuse to answer it!"* While you may be perfectly right in saying so, this response lacks tact, which may be what the employer is looking for. For example, if you are divorced and the interviewer asks about your divorce, you might respond with *"Does a divorce have a direct bearing on the responsibilities of this position?"* Some employers may ask such questions just to see how you answer or react under stress. Others may do so out of ignorance of the law.

Asking Questions

Interviewers expect candidates to ask intelligent questions concerning the organization and the nature of the work. Moreover, you need information and should indicate your interest in the employer by asking questions. Consider asking some of these questions if they haven't been answered early in the interview:

QUESTIONS YOU SHOULD ASK THE INTERVIEWER

- *Tell me about the duties and responsibilities of this job.*
- *How does this position relate to other positions within this organization?*
- *How long has this position been in the organization?*
- *What would be the ideal type of person for this position? Skills? Personality? Working style? Background?*
- *Can you tell me about the people who have been in this position before? Backgrounds? Promotions? Term-*

inations?
- *Who would I be working with in this position?*
- *Tell me something about these people? Strengths? Weaknesses? Performance expectations?*
- *What am I expected to accomplish during the first year?*
- *How will I be evaluated?*
- *Are promotions and raises tied to performance criteria?*
- *Tell me how this operates.*
- *What is the normal salary range for such a position?*
- *Based on your experience, what type of problems would someone new in this position likely encounter?*
- *I'm interested in your career with this organization. When did you start? What are your plans for the future?*
- *I would like to know how people get promoted and advance in this organization.*
- *What is particularly unique about working in this organization?*
- *Can you explain the various benefits employees receive?*
- *What does the future look like for this organization?*

You may want to write these questions on a 3 x 5 card and take them with you to the interview. While it is best to memorize these questions, you may want to refer to your list when the interviewer asks you if you have any questions. You might do this by saying: *"Yes, I jotted down a few questions which I want to make sure I ask you before leaving."* Then pull out your card and refer to the questions.

Nonverbal Communication

The interview is an image management activity. Interviewers normally make a positive or negative decision based upon the impression you make during the first four or five minutes of the interview. The major factors influencing this decision are your nonverbal cues communicated at the very beginning of the interview. Therefore, what you wear, how you look, the way you shake hands, how you smell, whether you are interested and enthusiastic, where and how you sit, and how you initiate the small talk are extremely important to the interviewer's decision. These factors may be more important than your answers to the interview questions. Your answers will tend to either reinforce or alter the initial impression.

While it may seem unfair for employers to make such snap

decisions, it happens nonetheless. Accept it as an important reality of the job search, and learn to adjust your behavior to your best advantage. Remember, those first five minutes may be the most critical moments in your job search and for your future job or career. Put your best foot forward with the most positive image you can generate.

Be sure you dress appropriately for the interview, as we suggested in Chapter 7. Other nonverbal behaviors to sensitize yourself to are how you sit, stand, and listen. You may want to think through or practice each step of the interview, from arriving to leaving. Be sure you arrive at the interview on time — 10 to 15 minutes early is best. When you enter the office area, remove your coat. On meeting the interviewer, extend your hand; women should do the same, particularly when interviewing with a male. Next, sit when and where the interviewer indicates; don't rush to a seat as if you are in a hurry to get started and finished.

Be particularly sensitive to *your listening behavior*. While the interviewer expects more than single "yes" and "no" answers to questions, the interviewer also needs nonverbal feedback in order to take you seriously. Indicate your attention and interest by maintaining frequent eye contact, nodding, smiling, and interjecting verbal responses. Listening is an active process, and effective listeners make others feel good about their communication.

Closing the Interview

Be prepared to end the interview. Many people don't know when or how to close interviews. They go on and on until someone breaks an uneasy moment of silence with an indication that it is time to go.

Interviewers normally will initiate the close by standing, shaking hands, and thanking you for coming to the interview. Don't end by saying "Goodbye and thank you." At this stage, you should summarize the interview in terms of your interests, strengths, and goals. Briefly restate your qualifications and continuing interest in working with the employer. At this point it is proper to ask the interviewer about selection plans: *"When do you anticipate making your final decision?"* Follow this question with your final one: *"May I call you next week to inquire about my status?"* By taking the initiative in this manner, the employer will be prompted to clarify your status soon, and you will have an opportunity to talk to her further.

Many interviewers will ask you for a list of references. Be sure to prepare such a list prior to the interview. Include the names, addresses, and phone numbers of four individuals who will give you positive professional and personal recommendations.

Telephone Interviews

Few people are effective telephone communicators. Several channels of nonverbal communication, such as eye contact, facial expression, and gestures, are absent in telephone conversations. People who may be dynamic in face-to-face situations may be dull and boring over the telephone. Since critical communication relating to the interview will take place over the telephone, pay particular attention to how you handle your telephone communication.

Two potential telephone interview situations may arise at any time. First, you may request an interview by calling an employer. Second, the employer may call you and conduct a screening interview over the phone. While the rules for both types of telephone conversations vary, certain principles should be followed.

When you telephone to request an interview, always know the name of the person you wish to contact. If you don't know the person's name, you can easily get the name by making two phone calls: one to the receptionist or secretary and another to the person you want to speak to. When calling the receptionist or secretary, just ask for the name of the person you wish to contact: *"Who is the head of the _____ office?"* Your second call should be directly to the person you wish to contact.

Most often your telephone calls will go through a secretary. The easiest way to avoid being screened out is to sound like you know the person or he or she is expecting your call. Do not ask: *"May I speak with Mr. Casey?"* This question often results in being screened out; a secretary next asks who you are and the nature of your business. Instead, try a more direct and authoritative statement for openers: *"This is Mary Allen calling for David Casey."* A surprising number of secretaries will put you directly through to the individual without asking you a series of screening questions.

Should the secretary want more information about the nature of your call, say you wish to make an appointment to see the person about some business. If the secretary persists in trying to identify what exactly you want, say it's "personal business." If this line of questioning fails to get you through, try to call at odd times, such as one half hour before the office opens and a half hour after it closes. Many managers arrive early and leave late — times when no one else is around to answer the telephone.

Telephone introductions are easier if you are following-up on a letter you sent earlier. You might begin by saying,

"Hello, this is Mary Allen. I'm calling in regards to the letter I sent you last week. I mentioned I would call you today to see if we could meet briefly. You may recall my interests and experience in training and development. I would like to meet with you briefly to discuss. . ."

However, if this is a "cold turkey" request-for-interview call, you may have difficulty scheduling an interview. Many employers will not invite you to a job interview based on this aggressive approach. Be straightforward, assertive, and hope for the best. Try to avoid the "give-me-a-job" mentality often associated with such calls. Use one of these opening statements to ease the aggressiveness of this call:

"I heard about the innovative work you are doing in technical training. . ."

"I've always wanted to learn more about opportunities with your organization. Would it be possible for us to get together briefly to discuss your training needs?"

"I was told you might know someone who would be interested in my background: 10 years of increasingly responsible training and development experience. . ."

It is best to write down these opening statements and refer to them in your conversation. Avoid a lengthy phone conversation. You do not want to turn this into a job interview. Your goal is to schedule a face-to-face interview. If the individual asks you interview-type questions, stress your strengths and specify an interview time.

Keep in mind that your telephone voice will be a slightly higher pitch than your normal voice. Therefore, lower your pitch and speak in a moderate volume and rate. If you vary your volume, rate, and pitch for emphasis, you will sound relatively enthusiastic and interesting over the phone.

The second type of telephone encounter, as we noted earlier, is the unexpected call from the employer who is attempting to eliminate several finalists by conducting a telephone screening interview. If you receive such a call, be prepared for questions probing both your strengths and weaknesses. Although this may be a stressful situation for you, try to sound as enthusiastic, interested, and positive as possible. Stress your strengths and try to arrange a formal interview. Keep your list of questions near the telephone so you also can interview the employer. In closing this interview, try to arrange an interview: *"I would appreciate an opportunity to meet with you to further discuss how my skills might best meet your needs. Would it be possible for us to meet briefly sometime in the next few days?"*

Many interviewers will probe salary questions with you over the phone. They want to know if you are within a realistic range for further consideration. While it is always best to keep this question to the end of the final interview, be prepared to answer it over the telephone. Based on your research, you should already know the salary range for the position. You should either respond with *"I'm open to discussions on this question,"* or state your range which also includes part of the employer's range as common ground for negotiations. Use this question as the basis for requesting an interview. Mention that you need more information on the position. Out of fairness to the employer, he or she needs to know more about you and your value. A job interview would be most appropriate at this time.

You can prepare for these telephone conversations. Role play them with a friend. Tape-record various conversation scenarios, but do not look at each other during these conversations. Have someone else critique the tape and discuss how you might improve your telephone answers and questions.

Dealing With Objections

Interviewers must have a healthy scepticism of job candidates. They expect people to exaggerate their competencies and overstate what they will do for the employer. They sometimes encounter dishonest applicants, and many people they hire fail to meet their expectations. Being realists who have made poor hiring decisions before, they want to know why they should *not* hire you. Although they do not always ask you these questions, they think about them nonetheless:

- *Why should I hire you?*
- *What do you really want?*
- *What can you really do for me?*
- *What are your weaknesses?*
- *What problems will I have with you?*

Underlying these questions are specific employers' objections to hiring you:

- *You're not as good as you say you are; you probably hyped your resume or lied about yourself.*
- *All you want is a job and security.*

- *You have weaknesses like the rest of us. Is it alcohol, sex, drugs, finances, shiftlessness, petty politics?*
- *You'll probably want my job in another 5 months.*
- *You won't stay long with us.*

Employers raise such suspicions and objections because it is difficult to trust strangers in the employment game and they may have been "burned" before. Indeed, there is an alarming rise in the number of individuals lying on their resumes or falsifying their credentials.

How can you best handle employers' objections? You must first recognize their biases and stereotypes and then *raise* their expectations. You do this by stressing your strengths and avoiding your weaknesses. You must be impeccably honest in doing so. Take, for example, the question *"Why are you leaving your present job?"* If you have been fired and you are depressed, you might blurt out all your problems:

> *"I had a great job, but my crazy boss began cutting back on personnel because of budgetary problems. I got the axe along with three others."*

You might be admired for your frankness, but this answer is too negative; it reveals the wrong motivations for seeking a job. Essentially you are saying you are unemployed and bitter because you were fired. A better answer would be:

> *"My position was abolished because of budget reductions. However, I see this as a new opportunity for me to use the skills I acquired during the past 10 years to improve profits. Having worked regularly with people in your field, I'm now anxious to use my experience to contribute to a growing organization."*

Let's try another question reflecting objections to hiring you. The interviewer asks:

> *"Your background bothers me somewhat. You've been with this organization for 10 years. You know, its different working in our organization. Why should I hire you?"*

One positive way to respond to this probing question is to clearly communicate your understanding of the objection and then give evidence that you have resolved this issue in a positive manner:

"I understand your hesitation in hiring someone with my background. I would too, if I were you. Yes, many people don't do well in different occupational settings. But I don't believe I have that problem. I'm used to working with people. I work until the job gets done, which often means long hours and on weekends. I'm very concerned with achieving results. But most important, I've done a great deal of thinking about my goals. I've researched your organization as well as many others. From what I have learned, this is exactly what I want to do, and your organization is the one I'm most interested in joining. I know I will do a good job as I have always done in the past."

Always try to avoid confessing weaknesses, negatives, or lack of experience. You want to communicate your strengths and positives loud and clear to the interviewer. Be honest, but not stupid!

Follow-Up

Once you have been interviewed, be sure to follow through to get nearer to the job offer. One of the best follow-up methods is the thank-you letter. An example is included in Appendix C. After talking to the employer over the telephone or in a face-to-face interview, send a thank-you letter. This letter should be typed on good quality bond paper. In this letter express your gratitude for the opportunity to interview. Re-state your interest in the position and highlight any particularly noteworthy points made in your conversation or anything you wish to further clarify. Close the letter by mentioning that you will call in a few days to inquire about the employer's decision. When you do this, the employer should remember you as a thoughtful person.

If you call and the employer has not yet made a decision, follow through with another phone call in a few days. Send any additional information to the employer which may enhance your application. You might also want to ask one of your references to call the employer to further recommend you for the position. However, don't engage in overkill by making a pest of yourself. You want to tactfully communicate two things to the employer at this point: (1) you are interested in the job, and (2) you will do a good job.

SALARY NEGOTIATIONS

Salary is one of the most important yet least understood considerations in the job search. Many individuals do well in handling all interview questions except the salary question. They are either too shy to talk about money — nice people don't talk about salaries — or they believe you must take what you are offered because salary is predetermined by employers. In some cases — especially government — salaries are specified for each position and thus are non-negotiable. But even in government, what is specified is often a salary *range*. Lacking experience in negotiating salaries, public employees generally do not know the first step to dealing with money questions. as a result, many applicants are paid much less than they are worth. Over the years, they will lose thousands of dollars by having failed to properly negotiate their salaries.

Government salaries are normally listed with specific position descriptions. Since most salaries outside government are negotiable and even within government negotiation is possible within a limited range, the salary question may arise at any time. Employers like to raise the question as soon as possible in order to screen candidates in or out. You, on the other hand, want to deal with the salary question toward the end — after you learn more about the job and demonstrate your value to the employer. Your goal should be to get a job interview and job offer as well as negotiate as high a salary as possible.

Strategies

A standard salary negotiation scenario is for the employer to raise the question: *"What are your salary requirements?"* You should turn this question around by asking the employer: *"What is the normal range in your organization for a position such as this as well as for someone with my qualifications?"* The employer will either try again to get you to state a figure by restating the original question or reveal the actual range. Expect a frank answer most of the time. If the employer indicates a range, the rest of the salary negotiation is relatively simple.

Having done your homework on salaries and knowing what you are worth and what the employer is willing to pay, you are now ready to do some friendly but earnest haggling. If, for example, the employer says his range for the position is $25,000 to $28,000, you might respond by saying *" $28,000 is within my range."* If his range is much more or less than you anticipated, avoid being emotional or overly positive or negative. Disregard the bottom figure and concentrate on working from the top by putting his highest figure into the bottom of your range. For example, if he says "$25,000 to $28,000," you should move the top figure into your $28,000 to

$33,000 range. By doing this, you create common ground from which to negotiate or you neutralize the salary issue until later negotiations.

However, if the employer does not state a range or states only a single figure, such as $28,000, rely on your salary research or multiply this figure by 25 percent to arrive at a figure for negotiation. Thus, the $28,000 figure now becomes your $35,000 expectation. Respond by saying, *"I'm thinking more in terms of $35,000."* A $7,000 difference should give you room for negotiation. If you state $42,000, you may appear unreasonable, unless you can support this figure based upon your salary research on comparable positions. But your previous salary research should result in stating a reasonable salary range which can be documented for similar positions in this or other organizations.

Employers may praise their "benefits" package prior to talking about a cash figure. Be wary of such benefits. Most are standard and thus come with the job regardless of the salary figure you negotiate. Unless you can create some special benefits, such as an extra two weeks of paid vacation each year, you should focus your attention primarily on the base salary figure.

Raising the Base

The salary figure you negotiate will influence subsequent salaries with this and other organizations. In fact, many employers figure your present worth based on your salary history; they simply add 10 to 15 percent to what you made in your last job to arrive at your new salary. If you were a $15,000 a year teacher, such a procedure will discriminate against you and your talents. Since as a teacher you were working at a depressed salary, you may have difficulty justifying a major salary increase in the eyes of most employers. In this case, you need to change the rules of the game. Disregard your salary history and, instead, focus on both your worth and the value of the position to the employer — not on what the employer can get you for. On the other hand, if you are coming from a $40,000 a year job to a $30,000 one, you must convince the employer that you will be happy with a salary decrease — if, indeed, you can live with it. Many employers will not expect you to remain long if you take such a salary cut; thus, they may be reluctant to offer you a position.

Renegotiations

You should make sure your future salary reflects your value.

One approach to doing this is to reach an agreement to renegotiate your salary at a later date, perhaps in another six to eight months. Use this technique especially when you feel the final salary offer is less than what you are worth, but you want to accept the job. Employers often will agree to this provision since they have nothing to lose and much to gain if you are as productive as you tell them.

However, be prepared to renegotiate in both directions — up and down. If the employer does not want to give you the salary figure you want, you can create good will by proposing to negotiate the higher salary figure down after six months, if your performance does not meet the employer's expectations. On the other hand, you may accept this lower figure with the provision that the two of you will negotiate your salary up after six months, if you exceed the employer's expectations. It is preferable to start out high and negotiate down rather than start low and negotiate up.

Renegotiation provisions stress one very important point: you want to be paid on the basis of your performance. You demonstrate your professionalism, self-confidence, and competence by negotiating in this manner. More important, you ensure that the question of your monetary value will not be closed in the future. As you negotiate the present, you also negotiate your future with this as well as other employers.

Acceptance

You should accept an offer only after reaching a salary agreement. If you jump at an offer, you may appear needy. Take time to consider your options. Remember, you are committing your time and effort in exchange for money and status. Is this the job you really want? Take some time to think about the offer before giving the employer a definite answer. But don't play hard-to-get and thereby create ill-will with your new employer. How you interview and negotiate your salary will influence how well you get along with your employer on the job.

While considering the offer, ask yourself several of the same questions you asked at the beginning of your job search:

- *What do I want to be doing five years from now?*
- *How will this job affect my personal life?*
- *Do I want to travel?*
- *Do I know enough about the employer and the future of this organization?*
- *Are there other jobs I'm considering which would better meet my goals?*

Accepting a job is serious business. If you make a mistake, you could be locked into a very unhappy situation for a long time.

If you receive one job offer while considering another, you will be able to compare relative advantages and disadvantages. You also will have some external leverage for negotiating salary and benefits. While you should not play games, let the employer know you have alternative job offers. This communicates that you are in demand, others also know your value, and the employer's price is not the only one in town. Use this leverage to negotiate your salary, benefits, and job responsibilities.

If you get a job offer but you are considering other employers, let the others know you have a job offer. Telephone them to inquire about your status as well as inform them of the job offer. Sometimes this will prompt employers to make a hiring decision sooner than anticipated. In addition, you will be informing them that you are in demand; they should seriously consider you before you get away!

Some job seekers play a bluffing game by telling employers they have alternative job offers even though they don't. Some candidates do this and get away with it. We don't recommend this approach. Not only is it dishonest, it will work to your disadvantage if the employer learns that you were lying. But more important, you should be selling yourself on the basis of your strengths rather than your cleverness and greed. If you can't sell yourself by being honest, don't expect to get along well on the job. When you compromise your integrity, you demean your value to others and yourself.

Your job search is not over with the job offer and acceptance. One final word of advice. Be thoughtful by sending your new employer a nice thank-you letter. As outlined in Appendix C, this is one of the most effective letters to write for getting your new job off on the right foot. The employer will remember you as a thoughtful individual whom he looks forward to working with.

The whole point of our job search methods is to clearly communicate to employers that you are competent and worthy of being paid top dollar. If you follow our advice, you should do very well with employers in interviews and in negotiating your salary as well as working on the job.

PART III

APPROACHING GOVERNMENT

Whether you plan to work for a Federal agency or a county office, you need to know how to best approach individual governmental units. You can apply most of the job search strategies and techniques outlined in Part II to the public sector, but you must make certain adjustments in the case of government. Given the decentralized, fragmented, and chaotic nature of government, hiring procedures follow a similar structure; they differ between and within levels and units of government. Knowing how to get a job in Boston City Hall, for example, provides little guidance when applying for a job with Cook County, the State of Wisconsin, or the Federal government.

The chapters in this section provide a general orientation toward the government hiring process. Part Four examines uniquenesses and provides details on how to find a job with each level of government.

The five chapters in this section outline how you can best prepare for approaching government agencies in general. The first rule is to *know yourself*. Why do you want to work for government? How realistic are your expectations in light of both government employment realities and your motivational pattern?

The second rule is to *know your audience*. What do you know about the particular government agency you wish to work for? Who are they? What do they do, where, how, and with what effects? How do they hire? What job search strategies and techniques are most appropriate for particular agencies?

The final rule is to *custom-design your job search* in response to what you learned from rules one and two.

In the end, there is no substitute for acquiring both self-knowledge and knowledge of your audience and then linking this knowledge to an appropriate action plan designed for particular government agencies. If you do this, you should have no problem successfully navigating your job search through the chaos of government.

Chapter Nine

CONSIDER THE POSITIVES AND NEGATIVES

All jobs have their positives and negatives, advantages and disadvantages, pros and cons. Your decision to seek government employment should be partly based on a realistic assessment of the positives and negatives in relation to your skills and motivational patterns. If not, you may be in for a real surprise once you land the job. This chapter is designed to minimize surprises and place wishful thinking in a realistic perspective by carefully assessing where you may be going.

FACING REALITY

What's it like working for government? How does it differ from work in the private sector? Is it true what they say about government jobs? These questions are difficult to answer given the diversity of over 82,000 governments in the United States. Such diversity makes it especially difficult to generalize across all units and agencies of government. For example, since many county and municipal governments are small, they have similar advantages and disadvantages as small organizations: few high-level opportunities, slow advancement, limited mobility, low pay, numerous responsibilities.

On the other hand, the Federal government is a large organization with many employment advantages and disadvantages generally associated with large organizations: bureaucracy, red tape, specialization, loss of identity, mobility, career advancement, specialization, good pay and benefits. While it is easy to stereotype government, stereotypes are only true in some cases.

MAJOR ADVANTAGES

Many people seek government employment because they are motivated by various perceived advantages. Among these are:

1. *Salaries:* Government salaries are relatively good compared to comparable positions in the private sector. This is especially true in the case of many Federal employees and for lower level, unskilled employees and generalists who are often overpaid for their level of skills and effort. However, as we will see shortly, this advantage becomes a disadvantage in many skilled areas and for individuals in high-level managerial positions. Salaries in these cases are not as competitive. But, in general, government salaries are good to excellent for comparable positions and value of labor in the private sector.

2. *Benefits:* Government benefits are good to excellent. The Federal government has one of the most generous pension plans available anywhere. Many state and local governments provide excellent pension plans, tuition assistance, medical insurance, and paid vacation and sick leave.

3. *Work Hours:* Government employees basically work an 8-hour day and a 40-hour week. Their evenings and weekends are normally free for other pursuits. In fact, many people seek government employment precisely because they are tired of working stressful 60 and 80 hour weeks, seven days a week, in the private sector.

4. *Working Conditions:* Since government is not profit driven, the work is relatively stressless. While there are deadlines to meet and individual employees sometimes encounter incompetent superiors, government work involves a great deal of on-going routines. Indeed, higher educators are noted for occupying one of the least stressful occupations of all!

5. *Job Satisfaction:* Many public employees are relatively satisfied with their jobs. They find the work rewarding in both monetary and personal terms. There are far more employees willing to make government a career than there are those who want to leave government for jobs in the private sector. Especially at the local level, many public employees enjoy the direct contact they have with the public in providing needed services. This intangible "opportunity to serve the public" is rewarding for many people.

6. *Security:* Government jobs are some of the most secure jobs found anywhere. Few government employees lose their jobs due to budgetary cutbacks, elimination of their offices or jobs, or incompetence. Even in the worst of economic times, government employees will adapt to potential job loss by finding more secure government positions. To be fired in government is unusual, unless one is obviously incompetent, rebellious, or corrupt.

7. *Advancement and Promotions:* Many public employees function within merit personnel and equal opportunity systems which assure relative fairness in promotions and advancement. Well defined grievance procedures protect government employees from whimsical and capricious bosses. Especially in large government agencies, the promotion hierarchy tends to be well defined and open to individuals who perform well.

DISTINCT DISADVANTAGES

Public employment also has several disadvantages which discourage individuals from seeking government employment as well as motivate others to leave government for the private sector. Many of these disadvantages are directly related to the advantages:

1. *Salaries:* While government salaries in general are good to excellent, in certain cases they are not. Many skilled workers in high-demand occupations are underpaid when compared to their counterparts in the private sector. This is especially true in the case of medical, engineering, and computer personnel. High-level managers normally cannot exceed arbitrary salary ceilings set by legislatures. Therefore, these individuals may experience few financial rewards

for performing well in their jobs.

2. *Limited Career Mobility:* Especially in small governmental units, the advancement hierarchy may be limited. In larger governmental units it may be difficult to move to other government positions because of a narrow skill specialty which is programmed for a particular office within an agency.

3. *Bureaucracy:* Government work in many agencies and units lacks challenges, involves a great deal of red tape, does not encourage initiative and creativity, and may involve working with deadwood. While these are characteristics of many large organizations, they may be more pronounced in government because government lacks clearly defined and measurable goals to achieve and measure performance. In addition, government employees are not expected to be creative risk-takers.

4 *Politics:* Government by its very nature is political. But many people have a low tolerance for politics and thus find such environments frustrating and stressful. Good ideas often become compromised to the political interests of representatives, interest groups, and fellow bureaucrats. Such a political environment frequently conflicts with individuals' professional values which stress finding the one best solution.

5. *Limited Extra Income Opportunities:* Government employees have few opportunities to make additional income either on or off the job. Except in the case of faculty in higher education, who are often permitted and encouraged to both "daylight" and "moonlight", most public employees are expressly prohibited from engaging in such extracurricular income generating activities. Government employees must learn to live within their salaried incomes.

6. *Few Perks:* Government employees receive few on-the-job perks normally associated with large organizations — car, expense accounts, and memberships. At best, government jobs come with a basic office — built by the lowest bidder and often windowless — equipped with a desk, chair, telephone, typewriter, secretarial assistance, and access to a copy machine.

7. ***Status and Public Attitudes:*** Public employees are not held in high esteem, because they are not seen as doers who accomplish things of monetary value. Many individuals have negative attitudes toward public servants. They often view them as living off the public dole and being overpaid and underworked.

8. ***Sense of Powerlessness:*** Much of government work is frustrating. Employees often find difficulty in deriving on-the-job satisfaction which is normally attendant with the nature of the work itself. A great deal of work gets processed, but concrete accomplishments are difficult to identify and little satisfaction is derived. In large agencies employees may feel like a clog in the wheel. They view their work as somewhat meaningless since it does not appear to accomplish anything of importance.

9. ***Plateaued Careers:*** Many public employees find their career plateaus quickly in government due to a combination of limited career mobility, short advancement hierarchies, and arbitrary salary ceilings. A great many public employees in the age range of 38 to 45 suffer from what Marilyn Moats Kennedy identifies as the Killer Bs: Blockage, Boredom, and Burnout. They feel they have advanced as far as they can possibly go; many have lost interest in their work. They have job security and they are paid well, but they dislike their jobs because their government careers have essentially stalled in terms of promotions, salary increments, responsibilities, and rewards for performance. These are the career distressed who do not look forward to another 20 years in their present jobs and careers.

WEIGHING THE ALTERNATIVES

Many observers may tell you the advantages of government service outweigh the disadvantages and vice versa. Others will tell you government work is challenging and exciting — the best possible career to enter. Don't believe everything you hear. Few people are lucky enough to have challenging and exciting jobs they love. Most jobs are a mixture of advantages and disadvantages, high points and low points. Try as we can to make work more challenging, exciting, and enjoyable, many jobs will remain dull and stressful. There simply is no objective way of determining the best alternatives for you. It largely depends on the individual. You do the best you can in terms of self-assessment, research, and planning. Then you acquire work experience which may or may not fulfill your career aspirations.

In many respects, government work is very similar to work in other small or large organizations. If you work for a small private firm, you are less likely to use your specialized skills on a full-time basis. You must learn to be adaptive, do things you may not particularly enjoy or be skilled in doing, but these are things you must do in order to get the work done. Chances are you operate in a situation that is understaffed, stressful, and not conducive to innovation. You are always trying to get the basics done. For individuals who like to practice only their specialty skills, such work environments are inherently frustrating and unstable. They tend to bring out one's weaknesses rather than enhance one's strengths. On the other hand, for individuals who enjoy challenges which come with developing and doing many different things, such a work environment may be ideal.

Large bureaucracies are found in both the public and private sectors. In this particular type of organization individuals tend to be conservative; they are more oriented toward maintaining existing patterns than with innovation, creativity, and risk-taking; and they play the games necessary to survive and advance within the hierarchy. Many individuals — especially entrepreneurial types — are ill-suited for such work environments. They would enjoy and prosper more in settings which permitted them greater freedom and control over their work. In fact, entrepreneurial types who are oriented toward the public sector, are probably better off working for a well staffed small government organization or joining small and adaptive nongovernmental organizations which work with government.

Unfortunately, thousands of public employees are unhappy with their jobs precisely because their skills and motivational patterns are not conducive to the various work environments found in government. While at one time their jobs may have been exciting and challenging, their jobs today have changed, or they themselves have changed. As individuals acquire experience and their values, goals, and work situations change, many find themselves in different types of careers than they had previously enjoyed or anticipated for the future. These individuals might be happier in different jobs and careers if they were willing and able to make a career transition from government to the private sector. But good salaries, benefits, and security convince them to stick it out rather than change to jobs and careers which would be more appropriate for their particular mix of skills and motivations.

You can avoid becoming one of these career plateaued or displaced public employees if you do the proper self-assessment, gather information on alternative jobs and careers with different types of public organizations, and realistically assess whether or not a particular public sector job is best for you. In the end, only you can determine what will fulfill your needs.

THE COMPARABLE WORTH DEBATE

Debates have gone on for years concerning whether public employees are overpaid or underpaid. Understandably, if you are a public employee, you may feel you are underpaid. After all, you know many other people who make more money than you — and you feel you are just as hard a worker. On the other hand, if you work in the private sector, you may feel public employees are overpaid. What do they produce given their generous salaries, benefits, and work environments? The stereotyped government employee may be the postal employee most citizens encounter on a regular basis. Needless to say, the old adage that most people "stand where they sit" operates when evaluating the relative worth of public employees.

Many governmental units regularly study comparable salaries in the private sector in order to bring government salaries in line with the competition. In addition, several studies have been commissioned to review data concerning the question of Federal salaries. For example, the president's Advisory Committee on Federal Pay reported in November of 1980 that salaries of Federal white-collar workers were 1 to 2 percentage points behind similar positions in the private sector. At the higher levels the salary gaps were considerable: salaries of top executives were on an average 7 percent behind comparable positions in the private sector; in some cases the lag was as much as 46 percent. Yet, government statistics showed the average Federal white-collar worker earned $5,000 more than the private sector counterpart. However, skill requirements were higher for the Federal employee. Other studies have shown that Federal employees receive better pay and benefits than their private industry counterparts.

Given the inconclusive and contradictory conclusions of the various studies, it is difficult to conclude one way or the other on how government salaries compare with private industry salaries. The problem with most studies and debates is in establishing the criteria for comparability of positions. Many public employees possess specialized skills on the inner workings of government which are not directly transferable to the private sector. While these individuals may be white-collar workers earning $40,000 a year as a welfare analyst, in reality they would have difficulty finding a comparable level job in the private sector. Indeed, one of the best indicators of comparable worth is what public employees actually do once they leave government for positions in the private sector. No studies have used actual career transitions as the basis for determining comparable worth.

Our experience with public employees tends to support the overpaid theory. Even though many government officials feel they are underpaid and some studies support this belief, most appear overpaid when they go job hunting in the private sector. When they begin marketing their public sector skills in private industry, many more individuals must take salary cuts than receive salary increases. Only after job hunting in the private sector do many public employees change their views about being underpaid. However, this situation will vary with different types of positions. For example, teachers are generally underpaid, and they can find employment in the private sector which pays better — but normally they must change their field of work. The same is true for many public safety positions. Individuals in these occupations must change careers in order to substantially increase their salaries in the private sector.

Chapter Ten

UNDERSTAND THE STRUCTURE OF GOVERNMENT

The American governmental system is highly decentralized, fragmented, and chaotic. It is characterized by a high degree of overlapping functions and redundant structures. As such, it presents a confusing picture to many individuals expecting to encounter a well defined, rational system of governance.

If it were a simple and rational structure, the American governmental system would be centralized with well defined points of decision-making and entry for government jobs. One would expect to respond to job announcements or submit applications to a personnel office which, in turn, would make hiring decisions. Indeed, most governments project an image of rational hiring by maintaining the appearance of unified and centralized recruitment and selection processes.

Your task is to understand how governments are internally structured to hire individuals. Once you understand this structure, as well as the attendant recruitment processes, you will be well on the road to developing a realistic and effective job search with government.

DECENTRALIZED STRUCTURE

America's passion for decentralized political and governmental structures is offset by its commitment to achieving greater efficiency and effectiveness in government. To be efficient and effective yet decentralized and fragmented at the same time is one of the great American dilemmas of government. In trying to have their cake and eat it, American governments are adept at presenting pictures of rational organizations responding efficiently and effectively to public needs. This image of performance may or may not have a direct relationship to the day-to-day realities of government.

Underlying the facade of organizational efficiency and effectiveness are numerous organizational jungles and management nightmares. Not only do government units overlap with one another and duplicate functions, internally they often are loosely structured with a great deal of autonomy given to individual departments and offices. The extreme case of such highly decentralized organizations is state universities which are basically confederations of competing factions, i.e., departments and programs, held together by a common budget, organizational name, and college catalog. Each department functions as a relatively autonomous organizational entity which hires its own faculty, sets its own performance standards, and decides its own fate. Loyalty and identity to one's larger profession takes precedent over commitment to the immediate institution, including an individual's department!

Other government institutions may not be as extremely decentralized as universities, but they are decentralized nonetheless. City governments, for example, tend to be organized along functional lines: police, fire, education, health, recreation, welfare, etc. Each department will have its own set of rules and regulations, professional standards and loyalties, and personnel practices. Each functional grouping of employees tends to be affiliated with large state and national professional associations. Large groupings of employees may belong to public unions. Similar to universities, they are largely held together by a common budget, name, and public relations brochure. Several of the departments will be geographically separated from the others — with their own buildings and grounds — and largely function as governments within governments. The education and public safety bureaucracies most likely will function separate from one another as well as from the city government bureaucracy in general. In fact, city managers and mayors in both small and large communities often experience difficulty in controlling these departments because of their highly decentralized nature.

State and Federal governments function along similar decentralized lines. Each agency and department maintains its own personnel offices and recruitment practices. While state civil service commissions and the United States Office of Personnel Management develop personnel recruitment and performance standards and provide training and limited recruitment services to individual agencies and offices, most hiring takes place within particular agencies. And even within agencies, hiring tends to be decentralized to the actual operational units which have the hiring needs.

FORMAL AND INFORMAL HIRING SYSTEMS

Formal organizational charts outline the basic skeleton of organizations. They indicate how organizations, under the best of circumstances, should operate according to formal authority and responsibilities. These charts are good starting points for understanding the basic structure of government. These are not, however, to be taken too seriously as indicators of how government actually functions. For within all organizations, informal structures and processes operate in spite of the formal organizational chart. Indeed, most individuals within organizations neither understand nor are interested in the formal organizational chart. Many would be hard pressed to either locate or explain the chart! Rather, they behave according to the administrative and social processes and precedents which they are most familiar with and which are identified as "the organization" within their minds.

Identifying and explaining the formal organizational chart is the easy part of conducting a job search with government. Most government offices will have a government operations manual, annual report or telephone directory outlining the formal structure and functions of government. Within the Federal government the *U.S. Government Manual, Federal Yellow Book, Congressional Yellow Book, Federal Directory, Congressional Directory,* and the *Washington Information Directory* adequately outline such information.

The informal structure, on the other hand, is the most important for identifying on-going realities but also the most difficult to identify and understand. It requires research on who does what, where, when, and with what effects. It involves using investigative skills to uncover the ongoing realities of organizations. The results of such investigation often uncover the negative side of organizations — the deadwood, the powerful and powerless, the injustice, and the perversions — as well as positive opportunities for you. Such investigations strip away the pictures of performance portrayed in the public relations brochures and plant one's feet firmly on the ground by reaffirming what most observers of formal and informal organizations have learned over the years: organizations are organizations are organizations; they differ considerably in terms of their structures, functions, goals, and outcomes. Some are exciting places to work, while others are simply dreadful. Most are difficult to change in the short-run.

Unfortunately, most job seekers develop job search strategies and expectations aimed at the formal organization and the picture of performance projected for public consumption. Few ever delve into the inner workings of government to uncover the informal structure that really determines how things get done and by whom. Such information is usually acquired while on the job — after one has made a commitment to the organization. In many cases, the informal structure may be at considerable variance with what initially appeared to be the organizational reality. You should try to avoid any on-the-job surprises which could have been revealed prior to taking a particular job.

You need to identify and use the informal structure to your advantage prior to joining an organization. Part of your research should focus on understanding this structure. While most government organizations will have a similar formal structure, their informal structures may be considerably different. You will not know this until you do some intelligence work on an organization. The following generalizations are valid for most government organizations. They will help you conduct your own investigation of government agencies in an intelligent manner:

1. *Most government personnel offices do not perform important hiring functions.* Their primary function is to communicate vacancies of operational units, process applications and inquiries, conduct testing, initially screen applications to pass on to the operating unit, and generally engage in routine personnel functions such as maintaining personnel files, putting employees on the payroll, and conducting limited training. They do some hiring, but normally for low level positions with which operational units would rather not be bothered.

2. *Hiring decisions are made at the operational levels.* Identifying vacancies, recruiting candidates, screening, and selection — are primarily made by operational units. Managers and supervisors within an office are the key decision-mak-

ers. They are the first to identify personnel needs, worry about whom to hire, and select the best individual to meet their needs. While they will share some of the hiring functions with personnel offices — normally administrative overhead and regulatory functions (issuing vacancy announcements, conducting testing and screening, ensuring equal opportunity) — they maintain a certain degree of hiring autonomy to ensure that the formal procedures will give them what they want. Appealing to higher level authorities or using political pull to force hiring decisions on these lower levels will be strongly resisted. Such actions threaten the very autonomy of operating units.

3. *Lengthy application procedures may or may not be necessary.* Many government jobs can be filled immediately without undergoing a lengthy recruitment and selection process. For example, it is not unusual for congressional staff aids to walk into a congressman's office and be hired on the spot! However, most positions will involve a waiting period precisely because the personnel office must follow a formal procedure, even though the operating unit may have already decided on a candidate prior to initiating the formal selection procedures.

4. *In spite of claims to the contrary, many government jobs are "wired" for particular individuals.* Vacancy announcements and equal opportunity procedures may make the hiring process look open, competitive, and legitimate, but operating units continue to engage in the notorious practice of wiring positions. This involves the informal preselection of candidates. Individuals are informally recruited for a position and then the qualifications are written around the individual so that in the end he or she will be the best qualified candidate from the pool of qualified applicants. As many as 70 percent of all government vacancies may be partly wired, or at least less than fully open and competitive. A simple fact of life operates among those who do the wiring and hiring: they seek stability, predictability, and control over the hiring process. By all means, they wish to avoid the surprise of hiring an unknown quantity who may or may not work out for a position. For it is better to know and like your future employee ahead of time than to engage in a recruitment crap-shoot sponsored by a personnel office that doesn't really understand your needs. After all, people

in personnel don't have to live with the new employee! Wiring is not an illegal practice since the formal hiring process does take place according to the rules and regulations and the final selection takes place within this system. But unethical? Perhaps. Unfair? Certainly. Illegal? Of course not. This is the government hiring business as usual. And it takes place in most units of government to some degree.

TAKING ACTION

Given these guidelines to the informal hiring process in government, we suggest you do the following:

1. *Do not be deceived by appearances.* Many people exaggerate their abilities, usefulness, and performance. Use your eyes and intuition as well as your ears when researching government organizations. Your goal should be to learn as much as possible about the informal organization. You want to know: How do things get done around here? Who makes the decisions? What kind of work environment is this? Do people enjoy their work? Who is on the "ins" and "outs"? While difficult questions to answer as an outsider, progress toward answering them will reveal a great deal of useful information for organizing your job search targeted on particular agencies.

2. *Contact the personnel office and properly observe the formal application procedures,* but do not have high expectations or spend a great deal of time trying to get a job through this source. Personnel offices should be treated as a necessary step, but not the only one.

3. *Conduct research with the people who make the hiring decisions* — the managers and supervisors in the operating units. If they have a vacancy and they like you, they may even promote you by wiring a position around your experience and qualifications or at least making sure your application is forwarded by personnel.

4. *Decide how you want to play the job search game.* Some people love to network, drop names, and talk about themselves. They have no qualms about being the subject of wiring, and they believe in the ethics and efficacy of "pulling

their own strings." This works and is acceptable behavior for many people. On the other hand, this approach may not be for you. People do get good jobs without networking, wiring, or pulling strings. But also be aware that many of your competitors are practicing these job search techniques for getting the job they want. You are at a disadvantage. Your odds at getting a job may not be as good as they could be, but you have to live with yourself, and some things may not come naturally, are personally objectionable, or make one feel uncomfortable. That is your choice. We merely outline alternative choices and suggest different probabilities for success.

Chapter Eleven
KNOW THE HIRING PROCESS

The hiring process varies for each of the 82,000 plus units of government. Each has its own formal and informal systems for recruiting, screening, and selecting candidates. As noted in Chapter Ten, expect the structure of hiring to follow the general structure of government — decentralized, fragmented, and chaotic — both between and within governmental units.

LINKING TWO PROCESSES

Most governmental units will follow several similar *formal steps* in the hiring process. These are specified in civil service regulations, personnel manuals, and merit criteria. They include:

1. Announce vacancies.
2. Accept applications.
3. Administer examinations.
4. Review credentials.
5. Select group of qualified finalists.
6. Conduct interviews.
7. Offer job to one candidate.
8. Place new employee on payroll.

At the same time, an informal hiring process may supplement or reinforce the formal process. This *informal process* will:

1. Communicate hiring needs through networks of friends and colleagues.
2. Conduct conversations, discussions, or informational interviews with prospective candidates.
3. Pre-select one or two interesting candidates.
4. Coach candidates on how to best complete the formal application and testing procedures in order to become the best qualified and/or develop the position description and selection criteria around the qualifications of a particular individual, i.e., "wire" the position.
5. Select the pre-selected candidate.

These two processes, in effect, are linked together. Hence, the informal hiring process works only if it is closely tied to the formal process. Given elaborate rules and regulations required by government agencies to ensure equity, fairness, and objectivity in identifying and selecting the best qualified individuals, candidates must enter through the front door and complete the necessary steps to become formally eligible. At the same time, the informal back door operates similarly to most non-governmental hiring practices. It enables individuals to use the job search skills outlined in Chapter Five through Eight: network, conduct informational interviews with hiring personnel, and circulate resumes. In fact, many managers and supervisors appreciate meeting individuals who use such self marketing techniques, because it gives them important information and ideas for specifying their own personnel needs and requirements.

The effective job candidate learns to link the formal and informal hiring processes, as illustrated in Figure 4. While involving separate skills and strategies, the two processes come together at the eligibility and interview stages.

Therefore, when seeking government employment, you must develop an additional set of job search skills aimed at the formal hiring process. This involves being able to locate information on vacancy announcements, complete applications, take the necessary tests, and handle the formal selection interviews.

VACANCY ANNOUNCEMENTS

Vacancy or position announcements are one of three types of job related announcements issued by government agencies. The

FIGURE 4

LINKING FORMAL AND INFORMAL HIRING PROCESSES IN GOVERNMENT

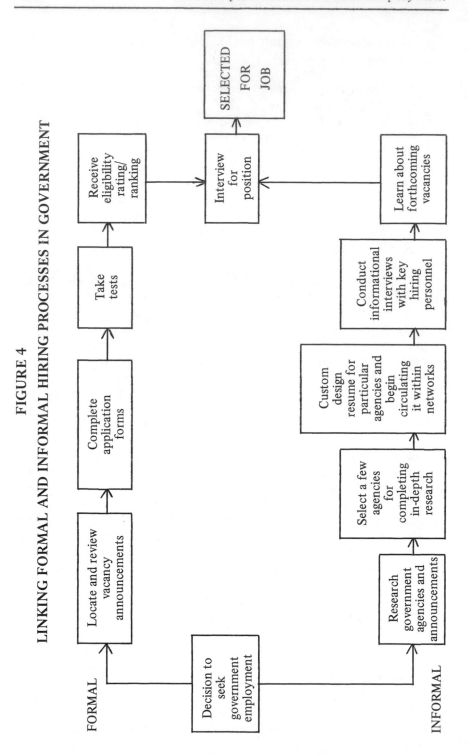

others include open announcements and examination announcements. *Open announcements* — most frequently used for positions with high turnover rates — permit applications to be submitted and considered at any time. *Examination announcements* state that a particular entrance exam will be given on specific dates and that individuals must apply to sit for the exam. Personnel offices normally issue all three types of announcements.

Government agencies regularly announce vacancies through personnel offices. The personnel office, in turn, may decide to distribute the announcement to numerous sources or restrict distribution to certain locations and publications. For example, at the state and local levels many high-level professional and technical positions are routinely listed in regional and nationwide professional newsletters, journals, and job banks. Among these information sources are:

- *Affirmative Action Register*
- *APWA Reporter* (American Public Works Association)
- *The City-County Recruiter* (Clearinghouse for Government Personnel)
- *ICMA Newsletter* (International City Management Association)
- *The Job Finder: A Checklist of Openings for Administrative and Governmental Research Employment*
- *JobMart* (American Planning Association)
- *Jobs Available: A Listing of Employment Opportunities in the Public Sector*
- *Mountain Plains States' Job Bank*
- *NAHRO Monitor* (National Association of Housing and Redevelopment Officials)
- *New England Administrative, Professional, Technical Job Bank*
- *Public Administration Times* (American Society for Public Administration)
- *The State Recruiter* (Clearinghouse for Government Personnel)

Most positions found in government are associated with some professional organization which provides job information and referral services. Contact information for these and other publications are included in Appendix D. For comprehensive and detailed listings of job information sources, see S. Norman Feingold and Glenda Ann Hansard-Winkler, *900,000 Plus Jobs Annually: Published Sources of Employment Listings* and Daniel Lauber, *The Compleat Guide to*

Jobs in Planning and Public Administration. Both books are included in the resource section at the end of this book.

At the Federal level the 1000 plus vacancies occurring each day are announced through a variety of sources. No single Federal government office compiles a listing. The most comprehensive listings of job vacancies are compiled biweekly by three private firms:

- Federal Research Service
- Federal Jobs Digest
- Federal Employment Bulletin

Information on these firms and their publications is included in Chapter Sixteen.

Most vacancy announcements in government will have limited distribution. The extent of distribution is unpredictable because individual agencies and hiring officials decide on how and where to disseminate such information. Distribution may take the form of a one-page announcement posted on a personnel office or cafeteria bulletin board. Wider distribution might include listing a vacancy in the local newspaper. Except for hard to fill high-level and technical positions requiring specific experience and skills, most government offices have little incentive to widely broadcast their vacancy announcements. Most will do the minimum advertising required to fulfill affirmative action and merit system requirements.

Since there is no single source you can consult to give you a comprehensive listing of alternative vacancy announcements at any particular time, your strategy for gathering information may include several alternative approaches:

1. Survey specific professional journals and newsletters for job listings.
2. Subscribe to a particular job listing or job bank service.
3. Telephone or write to particular agencies for vacancy announcements (these come in a variety of names — Personnel Office, Civil Service Commission, Merit System, Department of Labor, Employment, or Manpower).
4. Visit government job information centers, personnel offices, libraries, and cafeterias to ask questions and survey bulletin boards.
5. Contact the hiring agency directly for vacancy information.
6. Register with the State Employment Office in order to get access to their job information bank.

The most effective strategy will be to focus your job search on a particular government agency. For example, After conducting a great deal of research, you may decide you really would like to work for the United States Information Agency (USIA). However, this is a big agency, performing numerous functions, with thousands of employees.

The question is: Where do you want to work doing what within USIA? You must be specific. The personnel office as well as the private job listing services will include several USIA announcements. But during your research, you should identify a particular office within USIA within which you want to find employment. Take, for example, the Office of Private Sector Programs within the Bureau of Educational and Cultural Affairs. Focusing on this office, you should consult the *Federal Yellow Book, The Directory of Federal Executives,* of the *USIA Telephone Directory* for names and phone numbers of key people you should contact for information about vacancies. In this case, try both the Office of Personnel (in USIA this is located in the Bureau of Management and is divided into domestic and foreign service personnel divisions – two separate personnel systems functioning within USIA) and the program unit – the Office of Private Sector Programs. After a few phone calls to these offices, you should have a specific name and phone number for monitoring vacancy announcements. Most people will refer you to the proper individual and office. If you are persistent and ask the right questions for information, you will get what you want. But it will take a few phone calls.

The general rule, then, is to focus on specific positions within specific offices of specific agencies and government units. Always move your information gathering activities to the lowest level at which hiring decisions are made. In other words, you must use a decentralized job search strategy to be effective in decentralized governmental systems. Job listings and job banks do just the opposite: they centralize the job information function by coordinating the chaos of job announcements. If you come at this from a shotgun approach, i.e., *"Where are all the jobs I might fit into?"*, you may wander aimlessly, sinking before you swim, in the incredible morass of government agencies and offices.

Knowledge of specifics is power in this job finding game. It is best to start with the assumption that vacancy announcements with government offices are available only to those who are interested and willing to expend the time and energy to find them. It requires a great deal of initiative and perseverance on your part. The initiative will involve frequent use of the telephone, research by mail and in libraries, and your physical presence in offices. While you will find the telephone to be the most efficient approach, your physical presence will be the most effective approach. Job listings and job banks, although easy to access, are less effective sources of information. By the time you locate a job vacancy through these sources, chances are it has already been filled through the informal system or it will generate a great deal of competition. You must learn to "read" vacancy announcements to determine if they are wired for someone. This reading skill can only be acquired through experience in the informal system.

APPLICATIONS

Most government organizations require applicants to complete a standard application form when applying for a particular position or for a class of positions. This will range from a simple one-page biodata form to the more complex Standard Form-171 (SF-171) used in the Federal government. You must carefully complete this application form since it is one major determinant of whether you will be selected as a finalist and scheduled for an interview.

Most applications follow a similar format and include the same categories of information. In Chapter Seventeen on Federal employment, we examine the SF-171 in detail since it is the most widely used standardized application form in government, and it must be customized to be effective.

Let's examine the typical application form and suggest some useful guidelines for completing it. Chances are you will walk into a personnel office, request job vacancy information, and be asked to complete the application form immediately. If this happens, you need to have all the necessary information with you. Therefore, be sure you have a copy of your resume with you as well as the necessary biodata to complete the applications. Better still, take the application form with you so you have adequate time to thoroughly answer the questions. To do it properly, you may need to spend three to four hours completing the application form.

The standard application categories include many which should already appear on your resume. Most applications request the following:

1. Contact information (names, addresses, telephone numbers)
2. Position(s) sought
3. Social security number
4. Citizenship
5. Military status/service/preference
6. Examinations taken

7. Education and training completed
8. Work experience
9. Special skills and qualifications
10. Disabilities
11. Criminal record
12. Salary sought

The first thing you should do is ask for two copies of the application form or make a photocopy on which to draft a completed application. Then read the application thoroughly, and develop a strategy for making this application an outstanding document of your experience, qualifications, skills, and accomplishments which are directly focused on the stated qualifications. Assume the stated qualifications will also become the evaluation criteria. The more you write directly to those qualifications, the better your evaluation.

Application forms should be completed similarly to the SF-171. The most important sections are education and training, work experience, and special skills and qualifications. Unfortunately, most application forms are designed for the ease of the evaluator and the convenience of the filing system and thus do not give you much room to detail your accomplishments — at best, one to two inches. Following our advice in Chapter Seventeen, customize these sections of the application form by stressing your skills and accomplishments. Avoid discussing only formal duties and responsibilities as normally found in position descriptions. Assuming you have conducted research on the job you are seeking, your discussion of education, training, work experience, and special skills and qualifications should focus on the skills required for the particular job. These requirements are normally outlined in personnel manuals and position descriptions. Try to eliminate extraneous information which may distract an evaluator or appear as a weakness. You should choose those things that will enhance your application in direct relationship to the requirements of the job.

When addressing the salary questions, state "open" or write in the civil service classification or rating code. In so doing, the reader will assume you will accept the salary specified for the particular position.

Be sure you answer all questions and fill in all the blanks. If something does not apply, write in "N/A" (Not Applicable). Otherwise, evaluators may assume you did not follow instructions and left the application incomplete. Avoid giving them a reason to be negative toward your application and thus screen you out from eligibility.

Type the application form neatly, sign and date it, and attach

the necessary customized add-on sheets which detail your qualifications in direct reference to the position specifications. Also, attach
a copy of your resume if it is designed to further reinforce the application. A little redundancy at this point may be helpful. Your
resume will probably be easier to read and better focused than the
application form you were forced to complete. The resume allows
you to present yourself in the best light possible. While it may not
help your application, it can't hurt, and it just may give you an
extra edge over your competition!

EXAMINATIONS

Once you have completed and submitted the application, the
next step will be for someone to evaluate it to determine if you (1)
meet the minimum qualifications to take an entrance examination,
(2) should be placed on an eligibility list, or (3) notified for an interview. In many cases, the application is, in effect, the test. It is reviewed, evaluated, scored, and ranked with other applications. Points
are given for all those items you stressed in the customized sections
of your application.

In other cases, one must pass a test or a series of tests in order
to get on an eligibility list. Different types of tests are designed to
measure general aptitude, specific skill levels, physical abilities, and
health status.

You can and should prepare for government tests similarly to
college entrance exams. Your local library or bookstore may have
copies of practice tests or they can refer you to the proper sources.
Almost all tests governments administer to applicants are in some
practice form. Arco Publishing, for example, publishes numerous
self-directed practice test books for a variety of positions with
Federal, state, and local governments. Many of these books are good
investments.

At the same time, try to gather as much information as possible
about the particular test to be administered. Many governmental
units will issue a booklet or handouts which describe the test, present
sample questions, and outline the rules for scoring the test. For
example, some scoring rules are designed to discourage guessing and
thus severely penalize you for wrong answers. You need to know
this before taking the examination.

On the day of the test, be sure you are rested, arrive at the
testing site early, read the instructions carefully, and move along as
rapidly as possible. Many people do not do well on tests because
they fail to manage their test-taking time well. Should you not do

well on the test, all is not lost. Many agencies permit you to re-take the test at some later date.

ELIGIBILITY

After submitting your application and completing the necessary testing, expect at least six weeks before you hear whether you have been placed on an eligibility list or register. City governments normally take longer to respond than state and county governments. In many cases this will be a long, drawn-out process of waiting, waiting, and waiting. Make sure you continue job search activities in the meantime.

Types of elibility lists will vary from government to government. The standard eligibility process consists of the personnel office ranking all applicants and selecting five or more best qualified candidates, as measured by the evaluation of their applications and examination scores, to submit to the operating unit or officials responsible for completing the hiring process. These individuals, in turn, select those individuals they wish to interview.

At this stage the formal and informal hiring processes converge. What often happens is that a program supervisor has already identified someone she is interested in, even prior to initiation of the formal recruiting procedures. After helping the candidate move through the formal hiring procedures — by providing tips on how to enhance the application form and take the test — this same individual is called for an interview and often hired. In some cases the formal hiring process may result in identifying candidates who are better qualified than the one being sponsored. In this case, the hiring officials may choose the unknown candidate because he or she would better meet the needs of the office.

INTERVIEWS

If you are selected and scheduled for an interview, follow the interviewing tips we outlined in Chapter Eight. This is the most important step in the employment process. Everything you did prior to this step has been focused on getting the interview. How well you conduct yourself in the interview will largely determine if the job will be offered to you.

Government hiring officials are no different from other employers when it comes to interviewing candidates. They want *value*. They seek individuals who are competent, intelligent, honest, and likable. You need to communicate your value to the interviewer(s). Above all, you must communicate who you are, what you can and will do, and where you are going.

Make sure you also communicate that you are *knowledgeable* about the organization and operations. But be very careful in how you communicate your knowledge and competence. Many public employees still feel their particular agency, office, and operations are *unique*. They believe knowledge and experience acquired on some other problem or in another organization may not transfer well to their situations.This bias toward being different or unique is probably more a function of the extreme insulation government employees experience within the bureaucracy, as well as their need to feel important, than an objective measure of reality. Few government operations, in fact, are unique, and many government employees could learn a great deal by talking to others in different offices and agencies. But since they still believe they are unique, make sure you respond to their need to know that you know something about them, but not that you know more than they do.

By no means should you indicate during an interview that you have some general textbook knowledge or experience from elsewhere which you will apply to this program and office to deal with a specific problem. If you demonstrate your knowledge and competence in this manner, the interviewers may view you as naive and stupid. After all, they are a unique operation! Somewhere during the interview you should clearly state that you know they are unique; your approach would be adapted to their uniquenesses. For this statement you should receive a great deal of support. It could make the difference between you and other candidates interviewing for the job.

Chapter Twelve
GATHER INFORMATION FOR APPLICATION

Knowledge is always power when conducting a job search. This is especially true when seeking public employment. While there is a great deal of general information on government and periphery institutions, you will need to do a considerable amount of research to uncover the detailed information necessary to locate the job you want as well as communicate effectively with the hiring officials. In this chapter we identify several important information sources you should consult prior to applying for a position.

INFORMATION NEEDS

Your research should focus on answering five major questions for organizing your job search:

1. What are the jobs?
2. Where are the jobs?
3. Who has the power to hire?
4. How does organization and program X operate?
5. What do I need to do to get a job with organization X?

The first two questions can be answered by consulting various directories and books found in most libraries and the specialized job listing services and job banks we identified in Chapter Eleven and Appendix D. The last three questions can only be answered by talking with knowledgeable people associated with the organization. You need to probe as much as possible for details in order to focus your job search on particular organizations, positions, and individuals.

WHAT ARE THE JOBS?

This question can be answered by consulting several books and directories in the reference and government sections of your local library. The Department of Labor publishes several useful resources for surveying various job titles. At a minimum you should examine:

- *Dictionary of Occupational Titles*
- *Occupational Outlook Handbook*

Your library might also carry the following books which examine public sector jobs:

- *Careers in State and Local Government,* John Zehring (Garrett Park Press)
- *Opportunities in State and Local Government Careers,* Neale Baxter (National Textbook)
- *Opportunities in Federal Government Careers,* Neale Baxter (National Textbook)

National Textbook Company and Arco Publishing Incorporated publish several books relevant to specific career areas in government:

- *Opportunities in Federal Government Careers*
- *Opportunities in Fire Protection*
- *Opportunities in Government Service*
- *Opportunities in Law Careers*
- *Opportunities in Law Enforcement and Criminal Justice*
- *Opportunities in Library and Information Science*
- *Opportunities in Paralegal Careers*
- *Opportunities in Recreation and Leisure*
- *Opportunities in Teaching*
- *Opportunities in Transportation*
- *Your Career in Court Administration*
- *Your Career in the Foreign Service*
- *Your Career in Health Care*
- *Your Career in the International Field*

- *Your Career in Local, State, and Federal Government*
- *Your Career in the Military*
- *Your Career in Medical Technology*
- *Your Career in Teaching*

These and other useful guides to government are listed in the resource section at the end of the book.

In addition to conducting library research on identifying different jobs, you can write or visit various government personnel offices for detailed information on different jobs. State personnel offices, for example, will send you information on job titles, descriptions of duties and responsibilities, entrance requirements, and salaries and benefits if you write directly to them requesting the information.

At the local level you can write or visit the personnel departments of various units of government to acquire position description information. This office may publish a brochure or handbook or provide looseleaf handouts on particular positions. Remember, many units of local government may have several personnel systems operating simultaneously. Police and fire departments may have separate personnel departments. While most school systems are set up as special districts, relatively independent of city and county governments, in five states they are part of city or county governments. In these cases, the city or county education department will maintain a personnel system separate from other departments.

At the Federal level you should visit the Federal Job Information Centers (FJIC) which are located in 50 cities throughout the United States. These centers list position vacancies, including position descriptions. In addition, FJICs have a book which is the bible for getting information on particular positions: *Qualification Standards for White-Collar Positions Under the General Schedule.* It consists of two looseleaf binders and a volume on blue-collar positions. Position descriptions written in the language of personnel offices are included for white-collar jobs (the X-118 manual) and blue-collar jobs (the X-118A manual). You may have difficulty getting access to these volumes since FJIC personnel tend to guard them as internal documents. However, you should be able to see them by requesting to examine the books in their office. If they refuse to give you access, you can always request the information through the Freedom of Information Act.

A final source of information on identifying different types of public sector jobs is the most basic and important — talk to someone in a position that interests you. Ask them about:

- What they do.
- How they got their job.
- Advantages and disadvantages.
- Duties and responsibilities.
- A typical day on the job.
- Advancement opportunities.
- Salaries and benefits.
- The future.

Most people will be more than happy to discuss their work with you and provide you with important tips on how to enter the public service.

WHERE ARE THE JOBS?

This question can be answered by consulting several directories as well as many of the resources identified in the previous and subsequent sections, Chapter Eleven, and Appendix D. Several directories identified in Chapter Six provide addresses for locating various units of government and personnel offices. The most important ones include:

Counties:	*The County Year Book*
Municipalities:	*The Municipal Year Book*
States:	*National Directory of State Agencies* *The Book of the States*
Federal:	*United States Government Manual* *The Federal Yellow Book* *The Congressional Yellow Book* *The Congressional Directory* *Directory of Federal Executives* *Washington Information Directory*
Overall:	*Taylor's Encyclopedia of Government Officials*

Most of these directories are found in the reference sections of your local library.

One of the easiest sources of job listings to access is referenced in your telephone directory. Many county, city, and state personnel offices maintain an Employment Hotline or Employment Information Jobline. You dial the number and a recording describes a list of positions available for a particular week and provides the necessary application information. Check your telephone book under the particular governmental unit, and call the number. The recording should include all available positions, from city manager to clerk typist.

Another source of information worth examining are case studies of various units of government and agencies. In almost every state some enterprising scholars, journalists, or concerned citizens have written books and articles on county and municipal governments as well as specific local and state agencies and programs. Several excellent books have been written on Federal agencies, the most popular being TVA, FBI, CIA, Justice, Energy, and Interior. Such works help specify some of the major issues facing these agencies as well as their internal structure and work cultures.

You might also try to acquire copies of telephone directories for various units of government. All government organizations will have an in-house telephone directory — the one document that seems to hold the organization together. This is an invaluable source of information on the internal structure of the organization as well as key contact points for making your telephone calls and visiting offices. Many of these telephone directories are organizational roadmaps. They may include a recent organizational chart, a functional breakdown of the agency by section, room number, and telephone number, and an alphabetical listing of employees with their room and telephone numbers. The Federal government actually publishes and sells telephone directories for each department. You can get these publications by writing to:

Superintendent of Documents
U.S. Government Printing Office
Washington, DC 20402

Most telephone directories sell for under $10.

Governmental units and agencies produce tons of information, much of which is relevant to your job search and which is available upon request. Most publish or print organizational charts, current listings of their personnel and office locations, and statistical breakdowns of who does what and where. Some of this information is in the form of published directories, whereas other information is in the form of brochures, or looseleaf stapled pages. For example, if you want the names and addresses of key foreign service personnel abroad, the Foreign Affairs Information Management Center of the

U.S. Department of State maintains a Publishing Services Division. This unit publishes a small pocket-sized, but extremely useful, directory entitled *Key Officers of Foreign Service Posts: Guide for Business Representatives.* Regularly updated and including useful foreign mailing tips, this directory can be purchased directly from the U.S. Government Printing Office for $3.75. A little probing on your part — either by telephone or personal visit — should uncover the information you need. However, you will need to get this type of information from offices other than personnel. Most government organizations have a public information office or ombudsman whose job is to respond to such requests for information. In some counties, towns, and cities, you may need to call the county executive's, commissioner's, mayor's, or city manager's office for this information.

Your final source of information on the "where" of government consists of the people you talk to by telephone and in person. Use your telephone extensively in gathering such information. Personal visits are the most useful for getting in-depth information, but the telephone is by far the most efficient way of gathering information. If you are reluctant to make "cold calls" to strangers, we suggest you read two good books on how to overcome your shyness and become more effective on the telephone:

- *Telesearch: Direct Dial the Best Job of Your Life,* John Truitt (Macmillan or Facts on File)
- *Reach Out and Sell Someone*, Gary S. Goodman (Prentice-Hall)

Both books are included in the resource section at the end of this book.

WHO HAS THE POWER TO HIRE?

This question also will take some research effort on your part. You already know three things important for answering this question:

1. Personnel offices are in charge of conducting part of the hiring, but usually not the most important parts.
2. The program supervisors in the operating units are normally the key hiring people.
3. Several directories list the names, addresses, and telephone numbers of key government people.

Yes, what is generally the case may not be true all of the time. For example, personnel offices in many units of government may play the central role in the hiring process. Indeed, some city managers have strengthened the role of their personnel departments in order to gain greater control over relatively autonomous city agencies. In most government organizations the personnel offices will be responsible for recruiting and selecting certain types of positions.

Therefore, you need to conduct research on the particular organization that interests you. You need to ask specific questions concerning who normally is responsible for various parts of the hiring process:

- describing positions
- announcing vacancies
- receiving applications
- administering tests
- selecting eligible candidates
- choosing whom to interview
- offering the job

If you ask these questions about a specific position, you will quickly identify who has what powers to hire. Chances are the power to hire is shared between the personnel office and the operating unit. You cannot neglect the personnel office, and in some cases it will play a powerful role in all aspects of the hiring. Your research will reveal to what degree the hiring function has been centralized, decentralized, or fragmented within a particular unit of government.

HOW DOES ORGANIZATION AND PROGRAM X OPERATE?

This question is answered by using three information gathering approaches:

1. Reading literature on the agency.
2. Attending meetings to observe, make contacts, and ask questions.
3. Interviewing informed individuals.

Most agencies and units of government have a great deal of printed matter about their operations. Most of this information is available to the public, although some may be easier to access than others. A good starting point is the annual budget. Depending on what type of budget operates — line item, performance, PPBS, or zero-base — the budget should both raise and answer numerous questions. Most budgets tell you who is getting how much, where, and for what anticipated results. In addition, many agencies have their programs periodically evaluated. Program review or evaluation reports should be available through the planning, program evaluation, or central administration office. These reports will give you a good feel for not only what the agency or unit is doing, but also its problems and suggested solutions. Other useful printed materials include project documents, training manuals, and operations handbooks for individual offices. You should get access to many of these documents to learn what is really going on.

Another useful source of information is public meetings of officials. In addition to revealing a great deal of information on the agency or unit of government, these meetings offer an opportunity for you to identify key decision-makers as well as meet them in public. At the local level, these meetings include various board meetings and public hearings on schools, zoning variances, streets, transportation, health, revenue sharing — you name the activity; there is always a meeting somewhere, sometime. City council meetings, while often boring, do involve key city officials as well as representatives of interest groups and contractors. These are good places to observe the workings of government and make contact with several nongovernmental groups doing business with government.

At the state and Federal levels, meetings of officials abound, from legislative and congressional committee hearings to public hearings on agency programs. In Washington, D.C., for example, each day the *Washington Post* publishes the major upcoming meetings on Capitol Hill and in agencies. Thousands of meetings go on within each agency every week. You can contact the public affairs office to find out what meetings are being held when, and which ones are open to interested observers.

WHAT DO I NEED TO DO
TO GET A JOB WITH ORGANIZATION X?

This final question will be answered by following our advice on prospecting, networking, and informational interviewing we outlined in Chapter Eight. This question can only be answered by talking to people who know both the formal and informal hiring practices. As noted earlier, in government the formal system is usually well defined in terms of applications, tests, eligibility lists, and interviews. You can get this information by calling or writing the personnel office.

But in most cases, you must go beyond the formal system and personnel office in order to learn how best to conduct your job search. This means talking to people in the operational unit. Our experience is that most people in the program offices are relatively open and easy to talk with. They are interested in learning about potential candidates prior to initiating the rather lengthy, time-consuming, and frustrating formal recruitment process. These busy people do not have a great deal of time to spend on the hiring process, since this is not one of their formal duties and responsibilities. Therefore, information that would help them ease the hiring burden may be welcome. Contrary to what many job seekers may think, if done properly, the informational interview is not an imposition on hiring personnel. You are helping them arrive at a decision while they are helping you gain important knowledge for improving your job search. If they like you, chances are they will give you useful tips on how to get a job in their organization. There is no better information and advice than that given by the individual who will play a major role in the hiring process.

WHAT DO I DO WITH THIS INFORMATION?

Your information gathering tasks involve locating important information, analyzing it, and presenting it in a *usable* form. Gathering information for "understanding" is necessary. But you must move from understanding to *application.* After analyzing and synthesizing your research findings, you must incorporate the information into an effective strategy for improving your job search. The information needs to be:

1.   Incorporated into an outstanding resume and application forms targeted toward specific positions.
2.   Converted into effective prospecting, networking, and informational interviews.
3.   Used for conducting excellent job interviews.

This means you must make incremental movements toward achieving your stated goals. More specifically, you must *discipline yourself* to pick up the telephone and make three to five telephone calls each day. You must get behind your typewriter or word-processor and knock out three letters each day. Above all, you must take to the street, pounding the pavement and "pressing the flesh," for job leads and interviews.

Information gathering is one important step in the job search process. More important, on a regular basis you must manage a set of discrete job search activities which are closely related to one another. Without taking action based on your research, you may "understand" a great deal, but you will go nowhere. Knowledge becomes power when it is converted to effective action.

Chapter Thirteen
USE APPROPRIATELY ADAPTED TECHNIQUES

The job search techniques identified in Chapters Six, Seven, and Eight work for most job situations in either the public or private sectors. However, you must adapt these techniques to the particular governmental units and agencies you encounter. Your research should be the basis for determining to what degree you should adjust your strategies and techniques.

HIDDEN VERSUS ADVERTISED JOB MARKETS

When dealing with government, you cannot make the assumption that 80 percent of the jobs are found on the hidden job market. This simply is not true. Public service personnel systems are structured to ensure that no jobs are hidden from public view; nearly 100 percent must be advertised. Therefore, the difference in strategy is that you want to both identify job vacancies before they are advertised and effectively target those that are advertised. This requires greater attention to the formal advertised job market.

The real challenge in government is in both locating and working the advertised job market. Information and communication on job vacancies is chaotic and inherently difficult to obtain given the decentralized nature of government units and agencies within units. As noted earlier, agencies may be required to publicize job vacancies, but they also may decide to limit the scope of advertising to a few selected bulletin boards in the personnel office and public library. Your task is to develop an effective strategy aimed at *coordinating information* within this formal advertised job market. The strategy involves monitoring publicized sources of government job listings. This may require a combination of subscribing to job listing services and job banks, visiting job centers, telephoning personnel offices and agencies for the lastest job vacancy information, and periodically visiting key sites where job vacancy announcements are most likely to be posted.

WORKING THE FORMAL HIRING PROCESS

Once you have located job vacancies, you must follow the formal procedure in order to become eligible and selected for an interview. This means properly completing application forms – complete all blanks, date and sign it, and submit it within certain time frames – taking the proper tests, and monitoring your progress within the formal system. In some cases your application will be automatically forwarded to offices with vacancies you are eligible for. In other cases you may become eligible for a class of positions, but your application will not be autonomically forwarded. Once a job vacancy occurs, you must take the initiative – or "apply" – with your eligibility rating and application form. If this happens, you must continuously monitor the job vacancies – both through the formal listing sources and the informal system of personal contacts.

WRITING RIGHT WITH DEPTH

The language of government tends to be more technical and jargonistic than the language of private business. Try to identify the language being used in particular agencies and use some of the terminology on your application form and resume.

You definitely should develop a resume even though most government positions only require completion of an application form. In some cases, especially for high-level positions, you will be required to submit a resume in lieu of an application form. In other cases, you should attach your resume to the completed application. You should do this for two reasons. First, most application forms are designed by personnel offices to yield basic accounting data for merit system and affirmative action requirements. They are not structured to present your qualifications in direct relation to the requirements for a particular position. As such, your strengths often become buried in a great deal of extraneous information, such as your social security number, military status, schools attended, and criminal record. When you attach the resume to the application form, you begin highlighting and communicating the most important information to the hiring officials. You control what information should be emphasized in direct relation to the position requirements. You lose this control when you are forced to complete an application form.

You also should try to customize the application as much as possible, especially the "Experience" section. Most government application forms ask you to list your "duties and responsibilities." The problem with such instructions is that the application forms ask candidates to regurgitate formal position descriptions. These descriptions merely tell one what you are *supposed* to do — not what you *actually* do or your accomplishments. Therefore, when responding to the "Duties and Responsibilities" section, stress your accomplishments rather than your assignments.

Your choice of language is important when completing applications and writing resumes for government audiences. Be careful in using the highly generalized and "soft" language of functional and transferable skills with government agencies. Try to be as specific as possible about your accomplishments or achievements in direct relation to specific jobs. You need to include the "where" and "when" along with the "what." The organization and language of an *improved chronological resume* are best suited for government audiences when developing a resume and completing an application form. Quite frankly, most functional resumes are weak resumes which tend to communicate little beyond some highly generalized skills. They do not distinguish you from millions of other individuals who basically say the same thing about themselves. On the other hand, public employees are used to looking for "the details." They look for content and depth, which includes formal job titles, names of employers, and dates of employment.

NETWORKING ADJUSTMENTS

Networking works just as well — if not better — in the public sector as it does in the private sector. However, you will need to make some adjustments for particular agencies.

For example, being public organizations with public servants, most government agencies have formal information dissemination offices established to respond to all types of questions and requests. Most are relatively open. Since they have no competition, they have nothing to hide. Indeed, some offices are security problems because they give away too much information!

In addition to personnel offices, you should contact public information, public affairs, and/or ombudsman offices. These offices will give you a great deal of information, including printed materials and names and phone numbers of key individuals you should contact. Often it is much easier to call one of these offices for the information than play detective by using time consuming prospecting and networking techniques which will probably yield the same referrals. Telephone one of these offices and ask whom you should speak to about a particular position or job field. Chances are they will give you the name and telephone number of the key person. This procedure eliminates a lot of wasted time networking for the same information.

Once you have located the right people to talk to, then it's time to network. Follow the same procedures we suggested in Chapter Eight. At this stage your goals should be to:

1. *Identify positions which may become vacant before they are formally advertised.* If you can locate such positions, you will have more time to do the necessary research and make key contacts for preparing an outstanding application which should qualify you for eligibility in the formal hiring system. In some cases you may even become "sponsored" for the vacancy by the people you meet while networking.

2. *Gather information for making critical decisions about government jobs.* The basic problem you and others face in both the public and private sector job markets is either the lack of job information or incomplete information on the what, where, when, and how of getting a job. Your networking activities become information gathering and coordinating activities. You basically take to the telephone lines and streets to centralize a job information system which is extremely decentralized, fragmented, and incomplete.

PART IV

MOVING INTO GOVERNMENT

You face numerous alternatives when seeking a government job. You must decide which level of government you prefer: Federal, state, or local? While most jobs are with the executive bureaucracy, numerous opportunities also are available with the legislative and judicial branches of government. And within each branch, bureaus and offices offer several job options.

Part IV examines several choices available to you as well as effective strategies for landing a job with various governmental units at each level. Each chapter is designed to provide you with a basic understanding of various levels and branches of government and equip you with practical strategies for landing the job you want. Chapters Fourteen, Fifteen, and Sixteen focus on local, state, and Federal government. Chapter Seventeen examines the special application form — the SF-171 — required for Federal employment. The principles identified in this chapter are generally relevant to application forms for state and local government. Chapter Eighteen focuses on employment in the legislative and judicial branches and on Capitol Hill.

Chapter Fourteen

LOCAL GOVERNMENTS

Local governments in the United States are comprised of a variety of government institutions which make up the overall quilt-patch pattern of American government. These governments represent the type of governmental system the Founding Fathers explicitly designed: a safe (from tyranny) system where no one majority rules, one which checks and balances itself by dividing and overlapping powers and functions at different levels. Altogether this system employs 9,344,000 individuals or just under one-tenth of the total American work force. Given an annual turnover rate of 14 percent, coupled with an annual growth rate of nearly 1 percent, local government units offer numerous job opportunities to those who understand how to find a job. Given the highly decentralized and fragmented nature of these governments, you must conduct research on the what, where, and who of particular local government units in order to best understand them.

DIVERSITY OF UNITS

Local governments come in numerous categories, types, shapes, and sizes. They are truly a diverse collection of local governing authorities divided into five categories:

┌───┐

─────── **LOCAL GOVERNMENT UNITS** ───────

1. *Counties:* These local units of government function in all parts of the country except Connecticut, Rhode Island, and the District of Columbia. Normally the largest governing unit in terms of area next to state governments, 3,041 counties employ 1,811,000 individuals who provide services to nearly 200 million people. Once primarily a rural form of government, today the majority of counties are urban. Some counties have taken over the functions of municipalities (Miami-Dade County). Counties are referred to as "parishes" in Louisiana and "boroughs" in Alaska.

2. *Municipalities:* Incorporated for urban areas, these 19,076 units of government employ 2,424,000 individuals. While most municipalities are political subdivisions of counties, in a few states where city-county consolidation has taken place, certain municipalities are independent of counties (cities in Virginia) or they have taken over the functions of counties (Baltimore, Baton Rouge, Indianapolis, Jacksonville, Nashville, Philadelphia, St. Louis, San Francisco). Depending on the state, municipalities are variously referred to as "cities," "towns," "villages," and "boroughs."

3. *Townships:* These political subdivisions of counties are found in 20 states, mainly in the New England, Mid Atlantic, and Midwest states. Altogether 16,734 townships employ 379,000 people who provide special services to about 20 percent of the American population. Some states refer to these units of government as "towns" (Wisconsin, New York, and New England), "plantations" (Maine), and "locations" (New Hampshire). Townships are governed by elected boards of supervisors or trustees and share powers with county governments and other jurisdictions.

4. *School Districts:* Both independent and dependent school districts function throughout the United States. Independent school districts have their own elected boards, revenue base, and administrative organization. These function everywhere except in Virginia, Maryland, North Carolina, Hawaii, Alaska, and the District

└───┘

of Columbia. Dependent school systems are partly under the control of state, county, and municipal governments. Altogether 14,851 school districts employ 4,211,000 individuals.

5. *Special Districts:* These units of government function to provide special services not provided by other units of government. While nearly 2,000 of these units are multi-purpose districts, most specialize in performing a single function. The most frequently performed functions, in rank order, include: fire protection, water supply, soil conservation, housing, drainage, cemeteries, sewerage, school buildings, irrigation and water conservation, parks and recreation, hospitals, flood control, highways, libraries, natural resources, and other functions. Depending on the state, special districts also are referred to as "authorities," "boards," or "commissions." These 28,588 units of government employ 519,000 individuals. Sometimes school districts also are included in this category since they are essentially single-purpose special districts.

Different governing systems are used for different types of local governing units. Most counties, for example, use the commission, council-administrator, or council-elected executive form of government. Municipalities are of four types: weak major-council, commission, strong mayor-council, or council-manager form.

The five types of local governing authorities are by no means structured in a logical and efficient manner. Most have developed over time in response to state legal requirements, local needs, and political convenience. In most states, one unit of government will overlap with another. For example, counties perform some functions within municipalities, and townships may encompass school districts, counties, and municipalities. Illinois has one of the most concentrated, diverse, overlapping, and confusing systems of local government whereas Virginia has the most streamlined and logical system. However, even Virginia's much praised system of city-county consolidation gives rise to overlapping and shared functions. For example, Prince William County Government, which provides services for one of the fastest growing counties in Northern Virginia, is composed of five types of agencies which are, to varying degrees, under the control of a County Board of Supervisors and County Executive:

1. Staff and the Board of County Supervisors
2. State/Local Cooperative Agencies
3. Agencies With Administrative Boards
4. Offices Reporting to the County Executive
5. Departments Reporting to the County Executive

In addition, several other offices and agencies function as part of this county government: constitutional offices (Offices of the Clerk of the Circuit Court, Commonwealth's Attorney, Sheriff), agencies involved in the administration of justice, sanitation districts, and the School Board. The personnel office in this county government provides administrative support for recruiting individuals for many — but not all — county government positions. Typical of so many other local units of government, this county government exhibits a high degree of internal fragmentation along representational and functional lines.

COMMON FUNCTIONS

Local governments have one major characteristic in common which distinguishes them from state and Federal governments. Local governments are street-level governments that do the nitty-gritty work necessary to keep communities functioning. They maintain close contact with citizens, because they are basically service delivery units providing specific services in specific neighborhoods: sanitation, fire and police protection, education, health, street lighting and maintenance. Their cadres of street-level bureaucrats are on the firing line with citizens, politicians, local media, and interest groups. This is the action-filled level of government. For many public employees, local government is where one finds the action and excitement of public service. These small to large communities provide opportunities for individuals to work closely with citizens and elected representatives, experiment with public policies, and see the results of their efforts.

The major local government function is education. Altogether 54.8 percent of local government officials are in education. Of the 5,125,000 employees, 3,313,000 are classroom teachers. This education bureaucracy requires a $7 billion payroll each year of which $5.4 billion goes to teachers' salaries. Table 7 summarizes the distribution of local government functions by employees and payrolls.

TABLE 7

Local Government Employment and Payrolls, 1983

Function	Employees		Payroll	
	1000s	Percent of total	1000s	Percent of total
1. Education	5,125	54.8	7,018	54.5
– Teachers	(3,313)	(35.5)	(5,414)	(42.0)
2. Health and Hospitals	730	7.8	929	7.2
3. Police Protection	595	6.4	1,000	7.8
4. Fire Protection	310	3.3	477	3.7
5. Highways	284	3.0	384	3.0
6. Public Welfare	221	2.4	269	2.1
7. Parks and Recreation	220	2.4	212	1.6
8. Sanitation and Sewerage	215	2.3	314	2.4
9. Financial Administration	187	2.0	233	1.8
10. Natural Resources	37	0.4	44	0.3
11. All others	1,420	15.2	1,999	15.5

OPPORTUNITIES AND POSITIONS

The best local government opportunities will be found in the larger, more diverse, and financially well endowed units of government. These consist of the large urban county governments, municipalities of 100,000 population or more, and large school districts. Small counties, towns, townships, and special districts, while affording unique public service opportunities and a chance to be a "big fish in a small pond," usually do not provide much career advancement nor offer competitive salaries. If you work for one of these units of government and you wish to advance your career and salary, you will most likely have to resign and move to a larger unit of government. In many respects, the ideal unit of government encompasses an urban area of 200,000 to 500,000 people. Governments of this size have sufficient resources and opportunities to allow individuals to make local government a professional career.

You should uncover opportunities most closely in line with your interests and skills when you do research on various units of government. You may find a position which is ideal for you. If you seek career advancement, the small units of government will provide you with important local government experience which you can transfer to larger units of local government. After all, many city managers, county executives, police chiefs, and superintendents of schools started their careers in small communities.

The largest number of positions and opportunities will be found in the most labor intensive units and departments of government. "Teacher" is still the largest single occupational category at all levels of government. In terms of departments and offices within local government, the largest offices tend to be police, fire and rescue, health, social services, finance, development, libraries, parks and recreation, and general services. However, many of the jobs in these offices are for low-level clerical and other support personnel. An example of a county government would include the following distribution of personnel by agency, office, and department shown in Table 8:

TABLE 8

Example of Personnel Distribution in a County Government

Agency	Personnel	
	Full-Time	Part-Time
1. County Attorney	9	0
2. County Executive	15	0
3. Department of Extension and Continuing Education	13	0
4. Department of Health	72	0
5. Electoral Board and General Registrar	6	16
6. Community Mental Health, Mental Retardation and Substance Abuse Services Board	80	0
7. Park Authority	58	25
8. Library	71	0
9. Social Services	94	0
10. Community Corrections	3	0
11. Office of Consumer Affairs	8	0
12. Office of Economic Development and Tourism	6	0
13. Office of Emergency Services	0	0

14.	Juvenile Detention Home	27	0
15.	Office of Management Information and Audit	30	0
16.	Office of Personnel	26	0
17.	Office of Planning	34	0
18.	Office of Project Management	4	0
19.	Office of Telecommunications	9	0
20.	Office of Youth	2	0
21.	Development Administration Department	87	0
22.	Finance Department	73	0
23.	Fire and Rescue Services Department	116	400 Volunteers
24.	General Services Department	66	0
25.	Police Department	272	87
26.	Public Works Department	39	

Distribution of positions will vary depending on the functions of each local government vis-a-vis other governmental units as well as to what extent part-time and volunteer personnel are used or services have been contracted-out to private firms. For example, several small and rural communities, as well as large cities such as Virginia Beach (population 300,000+), maintain volunteer fire departments. In other communities refuse collection may be contracted-out to local collectors or performed only by private companies. In still other communities a local function normally performed by a municipal government may, instead, be performed by the county government, i.e., parks and recreation, libraries, corrections, mental health. In other cases the same functions may be shared between units of government.

Since local governments perform numerous housekeeping and development functions, they offer a variety of white and blue-collar opportunities which are similarly found in large organizations in the private sector. These include white-collar and professional jobs for:

WHITE-COLLAR AND PROFESSIONAL JOBS

- Accountants
- Computer programmers
- Data processers
- Doctors and nurses
- Equal opportunity officers
- Draftsmen
- Program analysts
- Dietitians

- Engineers
- Fire fighters
- Lawyers and attorneys
- Planners
- Police officers
- Secretaries
- First-line supervisors
- Mid-level managers
- Extension agents
- Communications operators
- Systems analysts
- Legislative clerks
- Probation officers
- Tax assessors
- Naturalists
- Traffic analysts
- Museum workers
- Investigators
- Recreation supervisors
- Medical technologists
- Housing counselors
- Budget analysts
- Real estate specialists
- Librarians
- Clerks
- Social workers
- Contracts and procurement officers
- Chemists
- Morgue attendants
- Court reporters
- Tax analysts
- Supply officers
- Food processors
- Employment specialists
- Architects
- Horticulturalists
- Teachers and trainers

The following blue-collar positions also are well represented throughout local government units:

BLUE-COLLAR JOBS

- Laborers
- Guards
- Signal shop foremen
- Carpenters
- Welders
- Stock workers
- Car wash operators
- Inspectors
- Park maintenance persons
- Brick masons
- Street maintenance persons
- Zoo keepers
- Sewer maintenance persons
- Bus drivers
- Mechanics
- Plummers
- Water pump operators
- Custodians
- Painters
- Refuse collectors
- Electricians
- Pool managers
- Landscape architects
- Parking meter collectors
- Tree trimmers
- Heavy equipment operators

These and many other positions relevant to local government are described in *The Dictionary of Occupational Titles*.

Most units of government classify positions according to educational requirements, duties, responsibilities, and salary ranges. When conducting your research, you should examine the job classifications to identify the various options available. Each position will require a certain level of qualifications ranging from years of formal education, training, and certification to years of comparable experience. If you examine and analyze these job classifications and attendant descriptions, you should be able to identify formal entrance requirements, possible career advancement opportunities, and potential long-term earnings.

EFFECTIVE STRATEGIES

There is no single best strategy for getting a job in local government. Each of the 82,290 local jurisdictions has a different hiring system — both formal and informal — which you must identify through your research. These systems range from very informal and personal hiring practices in a small township or rural county to a highly professionalized merit system in the large urban counties and municipalities. In some cases, you can still pull political strings to get a job through local political machines, relatives, friends, and acquaintances. The local township supervisor, commissioner, city council member, or mayor may sponsor you for a position on either his or her staff or within a department.

There are no hard and fast rules for approaching local governments. It depends on several factors: How well developed is the formal hiring process? How political is the local bureaucracy? How professional are both elected representatives and government employees? How is the hiring process structured in relation to competitive, merit and equal opportunity criteria? In some cases, especially for blue-collar positions, you may be able to apply for a non-civil service position and be hired and placed on the payroll within two weeks. However, in most cases, you will find the application and selection processes to be lengthy, taking anywhere from six weeks to eight months. In some cases, especially for police and fire positions, recruitment takes place once a year. If you miss the examination date, you must wait another year before being considered for eligibility.

In any case, you should pursue both a formal and informal job search strategy. Your research and networking activities should reveal useful information about the local hiring culture, particularly on who appears to have the power to hire. For the sake of a simple example, let's assume the operating unit has the power to hire, and the personnel office provides standard information dissemination and application processing functions. In this typical case, all job vacancy announcements will originate in the operational unit, but they will be formally announced and processed through the personnel office. You can easily begin your job search with a telephone call. You call a special telephone number to get a tape recorded listing of vacancies for which the personnel office is accepting applications. Your next step is to visit the personnel office. However, if the local government does not maintain a tape recording or provide such information over the telephone, your first step then should be to visit the personnel office. This office will give you an application form as well as a listing of position descriptions and hiring criteria for the same positions outlined on the recorded telephone message.

Local government vacancy announcements issued by personnel offices typically include the following information on both salaried and hourly positions issued by one county government:

— TYPICAL LOCAL GOVERNMENT JOB VACANCIES —

ASSISTANT TO THE   Position # 800-85
COUNTY EXECUTIVE   Office of the
G-28/Low $30s   County Executive
This position is responsible for providing support services and performing administrative activities for the County Executive; to undertake assignments in all areas of County government as directed by the County Executive; must have excellent communication skills. Requires Bachelor's degree or equivalent in public administration or related field with 3-5 years increasingly responsible local government experience; a minimum of two years supervisory experience at department director level or above or other comparable level is desired in addition to an MPA or MBA. Minimum beginning salary low $30s, depending on experience and education, plus excellent fringe benefits. Apply with cover letter and resume to Personnel Director (include address and telephone number for personnel office)

CIVIL ENGINEER II   Position # 823-6R
(Four Positions)   DDA
Negotiable $
County of 170,000 is a rapidly developing jurisdiction. Candidates will have the opportunity to contribute to the dynamics of that growth, and to make a positive impact on the quality of life in the jurisdiction. Successful candi-

dates should have analytical and creative problem solving skills, and be willing to work with the community to assure quality development. Duties consist of working within a team setting, reviewing development plans for compliance with County policies and regulations, and working with other County and State agencies. Requirements for the position include: thorough knowledge of civil engineering principles and their modern application to the design and construction of land development projects; familiarity with new stormwater management design methods and operation of hydraulic computer models; and ability to express ideas clearly and concisely, both orally and in writing. Minimum qualifications: Bachelor's degree or equivalent in civil engineering, with eligibility for registration as a professional engineer; and 2-3 years in professional engineering work, including supervisory experience. Please state salary requirements. Salary negotiable depending upon personal qualifications.

CLERK TYPIST II   Position # 1115-3
G-10-1/$12,067   Planning
Requires high school graduate or equivalent, supplemented by a course in typing; and 1-2 years clerical and typing experience. Must pass 55 wpm typing test before closing date. Duties include, but are not limited to the following: assisting the receptionist; typing; filing; coordinating zoning text amendments for public hearings; serving as the key clerk typist for zoning violations; revenue handling; some data entry/retrieval; and maintaining logs. Successful candidate should have word processing experience or interest in learning word processing. Some overtime required. Apply by: 11/15/85

DATA CONTROL   Position # 1108-1
TECHNICIAN   Community Services
G-15/$15,401-$16,818   Board
Temporary full-time position available for 6 months working with Director, Management Information Services in Community Services Board. Requires high school graduate or equivalent including course work in data processing and 2 years experience in data control functions and computer operations. Duties include: reviewing data input and output for accuracy, assisting data entry personnel, collecting data from contract agencies, coordinating flow of projects

and assisting in preparation of technical reports. Experience in HP-3000 and HP-150 preferred but not required; ability to work independently. Apply by: 11/08/85

DEPUTY ANIMAL Position # 000083-100
WARDEN Animal Control Bureau
G-17-1/$16,980
Requires high school graduate or equivalent with 1-2 years experience in the care of animals and/or dealing with the public. Polygraph, background investigation, physical examination, and valid driver's license required. Apply by: Eligibility List

POLICE OFFICER I Position # 000083-92
G-16/$16,172 Police Department
Applicants must be 21 years old, high school graduate or equivalent and possess a motor vehicle operator's license. Applicants must pass written, polygraph, psychological and physical examination and a background investigation.

CHILD SUPERVISOR I Position # 400-85
(Male) Juvenile Detention Home
G-15-1/$7.40 Hour
Temporary, part-time. Seeking qualified *male* relief worker to supervise male detainees. Requires two years of college, or high school graduate with three years experience working with children or teenage groups. Flexible schedule, no less than 4-5 days a month, shift includes 7:00 a.m. — 3:00 p.m.; 3:00 p.m. — 11:00 p.m.; 11:00 p.m. — 7:00 a.m. Must pass pre-employment physical.

CROSSING GUARDS
$174.84/Bi-weekly Police Department
Part-time. Openings in the four areas of county. Valid driver's license, automobile, and telephone required. Must pass pre-employment physical. If interested, contact Lt. Smith for applications, between 9:30 a.m. and 2:30 p.m., Monday-Friday, at 333-2222.

CUSTODIAN I Position # 201-85
G-7-1/$5.34/Hour General Services
Hours: 5:00 p.m. - 10:00 p.m., Mon-Fri. Requires any combination of education and experience equivalent to completion of the 8th grade. Must pass pre-employment physical. Apply by: Eligibility List

In order to learn about such vacancies, you must constantly monitor the listings issued by the personnel office. These offices normally compile all position vacancies and announce them as a group every week. If you call the personnel office on Monday morning, you may get the latest listing of job vacancies for the week. The positions outlined above were included in a six-page weekly handout for a suburban county of 170,000 residents.

Should you identify a position which both interests you and for which you are qualified, the next step is to complete the application. Follow the useful hints we outlined in Chapter Twelve, as well as in upcoming Chapter Seventeen on the SF-171, on completing an outstanding application. Next, take any tests required. While you wait for the results, continue your research with the hiring officials. Make sure you communicate to them that you are interested in and qualified for the position and that you have completed the formal application process. Should they like you in particular and you appear equally qualified compared to other candidates, your chances of being selected for the position will be excellent.

USEFUL RESOURCES

Your best resource for conducting research on particular units of local government will be the local governments themselves. Most local authorities publish a general information guide or organizational manual for public distribution. You can normally get a copy of this publication by calling or visiting the public affairs office or, depending on the particular unit of government, the superintendent of schools', county executive's, mayor's, or city manager's office. Your local public library also should have such information on file. If not, ask the librarian for assistance. The librarian should be able to direct you to the proper sources for detailed information on the inner workings of the local government, including organizational charts, functions of units, position descriptions, job classifications, personnel, and salary ranges.

Other, more general but broader in scope, sources of information on local governments include *The County Year Book*, which includes profiles on individual counties and names and phone numbers of over 12,000 county officials. Similar information is included on municipalities in *The Municipal Year Book*. Most libraries have copies of both reference books.

Several professional associations of local government officials can provide information on employment opportunities in local governments. Each functional group of local government employees has its own professional association at the national level, normally headquartered in Washington, D.C., New York City, Chicago, or Los Angeles; many have state branches. The major such associations which include local government employees are:

ASSOCIATIONS OF LOCAL GOVERNMENT EMPLOYEES

- American Institute of Architects
- American Institute of Certified Public Accountants
- American Institute of Planners
- American Planning Association
- American Public Transit Association
- American Public Welfare Association
- American Public Works Association
- American Society for Public Administration
- American Water Works Association
- International Association of Chiefs of Police
- International City Management Association
- International Personnel Management Association
- Municipal Finance Officers Association
- National Association of Counties
- National Association of Housing and Redevelopment Officials
- National Association of Regional Councils
- National Association of Tax Administrators
- National Association of Towns and Townships
- National League of Cities
- National Municipal League
- National School Boards Association
- United States Conference of Mayors

Another useful source of information on local governments is public employee associations and unions which primarily engage in collective bargaining. These are some of the fastest growing and most militant public employee organizations in the United States:

MAJOR PUBLIC EMPLOYEE ORGANIZATIONS

- American Federation of Police
- American Federation of State, County, and Municipal Employees
- American Federation of Teachers
- Fraternal Order of Police

- The International Brotherhood of Teamsters, Chauffeurs, Warehousemen and Helpers of America
- The International Association of Fire Fighters
- National Teachers Association

Contact information for these and other associations of local employees is included in Appendix E. Additional information on these associations is available in the *Encyclopedia of Associations*, which is available in the reference section of most libraries.

Chapter Fifteen
STATE GOVERNMENTS

Finding a job with state governments is similar to finding a job with Federal and local governments. During the past three decades, state governments have become increasingly professionalized. In most cases, entrance into state government jobs follows well defined formal procedures which adhere to equal opportunity, affirmative action, and merit hiring criteria. Jobs are increasingly competitive, requiring written applications, testing, and lengthy screening processes and waiting periods.

What exactly do state governments do? What types of jobs are available? How do you gain entrance to the job you want? This chapter addresses these questions by focusing on various opportunities available and effective strategies for getting a job with state governments.

FUNCTIONS

With the exception of foreign policy and national defense, state governments perform similar functions as Federal and local governments combined. One step removed from the street-level nature of local government, state governments provide numerous services to populations within their jurisdictions. While local governments place primary influence on providing elementary and second-

213

ary education, health, and police and fire protection services, the 3,816,000 state employees place primary emphasis on providing higher educational, health, highway, and correctional services. Table 9 summarizes the distribution of state government employees by state. Table 10 summarizes the distribution of state government functions by employees and payrolls.

TABLE 9

State Government Employees By State, 1983

State	Employees	State	Employees
Alaska	76,000	Nevada	13,000
Alabama	23,000	New Hampshire	20,000
Arizona	49,000	New Jersey	100,000
Arkansas	43,000	New Mexico	43,000
California	319,000	New York	272,000
Colorado	59,000	North Carolina	103,000
Connecticut	54,000	North Dakota	18,000
Delaware	20,000	Ohio	149,000
Florida	128,000	Oklahoma	74,000
Georgia	96,000	Oregon	54,000
Hawaii	46,000	Pennsylvania	143,000
Idaho	18,000	Rhode Island	27,000
Kansas	51,000	South Carolina	65,000
Kentucky	66,000	South Dakota	18,000
Louisiana	103,000	Tennessee	76,000
Maine	24,000	Texas	217,000
Maryland	87,000	Utah	35,000
Massachusetts	87,000	Vermont	12,000
Michigan	151,000	Virginia	116,000
Minnesota	72,000	Washington	92,000
Mississippi	47,000	West Virginia	41,000
Missouri	71,000	Wisconsin	81,000
Montana	20,000	Wyoming	12,000
Nebraska	35,000		

Source: U.S. Bureau of the Census

——————— **TABLE 10** ———————

State Government Employment and Payrolls, 1983

Function	Employees		Payroll	
	1000s	Percent of Total	1000s	Percent of Total
1. Education	1,666	43.7	1,989	37.2
— Teachers	495	13.0	914	17.2
2. Health and Hospitals	670	17.6	953	17.8
3. Highways	243	6.4	393	7.3
4. Public Welfare	176	4.6	263	4.9
5. Natural Resources	159	4.2	232	4.3
6. Financial Administration	119	3.1	184	3.4
7. Police Protection	76	2.0	145	2.7
8. Parks and Recreation	29	0.1	34	0.1
9. Sanitation and Sewerage	1	-	1	-
10. All Others	676	1.8	1,151	21.5

Source: U.S.Bureau of the Census

Approximately one of every 25 workers in the United States is employed by state governments. While education remains the largest function of state governments, the state role in education tends to be more support and administrative than direct service in nature. Higher education is primarily controlled and administered by state governments. However, only 22.9 percent of all individuals performing state educational functions are classroom teachers. The remaining 77.1 percent provide support for higher education and administer intergovernmental programs to assist education programs at the local level. By contrast, 39.3 percent of all local officials in education are classroom teachers.

Health is another major function of state governments. While local governments concentrate 7.8 percent of their personnel (730,000 employees) on various health programs, state governments assign 17.6 percent of their personnel (670,000 employees) to these programs. The difference is in economies of scale. The health function is shared by state and local governments. Except in large urban areas, local governments concentrate on providing basic health services, such as family planning, dental, maternal and child health, general medical and emergency, food inspection, solid waste, sewage disposal and drinking water inspection, birth and death recordkeeping, pharmaceutical, and mental health and retardation. On the other hand, state governments maintain most public hospitals (50 percent of all hospitals), laboratories, medical schools, long-term psychiatric hospitals, and related health facilities. In many states and locales, basic health care functions will actually be performed by state employees who work within a county or municipality. Partially funded by local governments, they are state employees providing health maintenance services within the local government jurisdiction.

Highways are another major state government function. State governments have developed and maintain a large and costly infrastructure for road transportation. Highway departments absorb 6.4 percent of all state government personnel and 7.3 percent of the total state government payroll.

During the past fifteen years employment in state government overall has increased while some functions have declined. Employment in state highways, for example, has declined. On the other hand, employment in state corrections — especially since 1980 — has grown considerably above the norm. For the period 1970-1980, the state government functions in Table 11 registered varying degrees of employment increases and decreases.

TABLE 11

State Employment By Major Functions, 1970-1980

Function	Total Employment		Annual %
	1970	1980	Change
Higher Education	1,093,637	1,474,326	3.0
Hospitals	450,382	577,721	2.5
Highways	301,898	258,377	-1.6
Natural Resources	150,817	191,948	2.4
Corrections	91,505	153,086	5.3
Public Welfare	99,489	173,909	5.7
Financial and General			
Government Administration	145,429	239,225	5.0
All Other Functions	370,416	573,871	4.5

FRAGMENTED STRUCTURES

Traditionally state governments were extreme examples of weak, fragmented, and largely incapable governing institutions. Powers were divided among numerous constitutionally elected officers within the executive branch so that no one individual or office could centralize power. State governments became known as relatively powerless and inept institutions, breeding grounds for corruption and incompetence. Access to a state government job was largely a function of whom you knew; especially useful were one's connections with elected officials.

The old days of state governments have changed dramatically. During the past 30 years most state governments have increased their institutional capabilities. Most state governments have rewritten their constitutions, reformed their governmental structures around a limited number of constitutional officers, and streamlined the courts and bureaucracy. Various reform movements, emphasizing the values of efficiency, effectiveness, and a politically neutral bureaucracy, have left a profound imprint on the structure of state governments today. Governors have more power, bureaucrats are more professional, and civil services regulate the hiring and firing of personnel.

Despite major reform efforts, state governments have not been completely reformed along the lines of a centralized, unified executive. Governors' powers are proscribed by legal restrictions on tenure in office, weak veto and appointive powers, and the presence of competing constitutional officers. Off-setting the weak executive is a relatively powerful and independent bureaucracy made up of a confusing array of offices, agencies, bureaus, commissions, and boards. The majority of this so-called state bureaucracy is not under the formal control of the executive. Instead, the majority of agencies are controlled by the legislature! This type of fragmentation affects the hiring process regardless of the presence of civil service regulations and merit criteria. In some cases, agencies and commissions operate as independent governments within government. Highway departments, for example, are difficult to control in many states. Other agencies are the political property of certain legislative committees. In the end, no one seems to govern in many state governments.

State governments are by no means the same in terms of structure, functions, and hiring practices. In the Midwest, for example, the states of Michigan, Wisconsin, and Minnesota have reputations for being more program-oriented, with relatively strong civil service systems limiting the role of party patronage in influencing the hiring process. On the other hand, Illinois, Indiana, and Ohio are more political; interest groups and political parties are relatively strong, and they tend to be more job-oriented than in many other states. Given these differences, there are no hard and fast rules for best approaching the hiring process in state governments. Again, you must do your research on the particular state that interests you. Your research will determine to what degree the formal and informal hiring processes operate as well as the role of "political pull" in landing certain jobs.

Approaching state government is unlike approaching any other government because of the fragmentation both between and within the various branches of government. Well developed legislative and judicial branches offer job opportunities relating to legislative and judicial affairs. Fragmented bureaucracies under the partial control of both the legislative and judicial branches offer a variety of opportunities normally associated with executive bureaucracies in government.

LEGISLATIVE OPPORTUNITIES

During the past 30 years, state legislatures have become more full-time and professional. Especially in large states, such as California, New York, Pennsylvania, Illinois, and Ohio, legislatures have developed information processing and administrative infrastructures to manage their affairs. Each state legislature has created legislative agencies. The most common ones include:

- *Legislative Reference Services:* These offices assist the legislature with research on legislative matters.
- *Bill Drafting Services:* These offices are established by state legislatures to draft bills for legislative action.
- *Legislative Councils:* These offices are staffed by professional researchers who provide timely information to the legislature (also include Legislative Reference Services and Bill Drafting Services in some states). These offices range in size from five employees in South Carolina to over 200 in Pennsylvania.
- *Budgeting and Audit Staffs:* Offices with these staffs provide the legislature with budget and audit services.

In addition, specialized staffs, focusing on particular policy issues of various Senate and House standing committees, also function in state legislatures.

Typical of the various legislative agencies and standing committees is the example of the Texas state legislature. Many of the following standing committees and agencies have assigned staffs:

TEXAS STATE LEGISLATURE, 1985

Senate Officers and Staff Services

House of Representatives Officers and Staff Services

- President
- President Pro Tem
- Secretary
- Sargeant at Arms

- Speaker
- Speaker Pro Tem
- Sargeant at Arms
- House Study Group

Senate Standing Committees

- Administration
- Criminal Justice
- Economic Development
- Education
- Finance
- Health and Human Resources

- Intergovernment Relations
- Jurisprudence
- Natural Resources
- Nominations
- State Affairs

House Standing Committees

- Agriculture and Livestock
- Appropriations
- Business and Commerce
- Calendars
- County Affairs
- Criminal Jurisprudence
- Cultural & Historical Resources
- Elections
- Energy
- Environmental Affairs
- Financial Institutions
- General Investigating
- Government Organization
- Higher Education
- Science and Technology
- State Affairs
- State, Federal and International Relations

- House Administration
- Human Services
- Insurance
- Judicial Affairs
- Judiciary
- Labor and Employment Relations
- Liquor Regulation
- Local and Consent Calendars
- Natural Resources
- Public Education
- Public Health
- Retirement and Aging
- Rules and Resolutions
- Transportation
- Urban Affairs
- Ways and Means

Legislative Agencies

- Legislative Audit Committee
- Legislative Budget Board
- Legislative Library Board
  (includes Legislative
  Reference Library
  services)

- Sunset Advisory Commission
- Texas Legislative Council
  (includes Data Processing,
  Document Production,
  Legal, and Research
  Divisions)

While most of these staffs are developed to provide general information gathering, analysis, and policy proposals to state legislatures as a whole, individual legislators also maintain personal staffs. Similar to personal staff members of U.S. Congressmen, state level personnel staff members perform numerous functions ranging from highly personal services, such as babysitting for a legislator, to more professional services, such as responding to constituent inquiries and drafting a piece of legislation to be sponsored by the legislator.

Legislatures are one of the most exciting arenas of government. They are the most important centers of power at the state level. They make laws, control large segments of the bureaucracy, and are the stepping stones to higher political and administrative offices.

State legislatures also are challenging arenas for job seekers. Personal and committee staff members have little control over their agendas. Work and workloads vary depending on what pops up from the legislative arena at any particular time. Legislative staffs are notoriously understaffed and overworked. Long hours, crisis management, and pressure to perform are indicators of the particular life style associated with legislative jobs. Few people make legislative work a career. Two to five years normally affords enough experience and contacts to move on to other public employment. The other employment may be in a good state government job secured through political connections, a position with an interest group doing business with the legislature, or a job at the Federal level with the U.S. Congress or in an executive agency. The state legislative experience often pays off in terms of future opportunities in the public and/or private sector.

State legislatures do not have well developed systems for recruiting personnel for staff positions. Except in cases where specific scientific, technical, and policy expertise is required and such positions are advertised, the political process is still the major route to securing most legislative jobs. Personal staff positions are acquired through word-of-mouth and by contacting a state legislator or his or her staff members. But there is little mystery in securing such positions. You do not necessarily need to know someone or get referred for these positions. When a vacancy occurs — which frequently happens due to the pressures of the job and the high turnover of young staff members wishing to continue their educations — if you are available and your skills appear appropriate, you may be hired immediately. While some state legislatures will have a formal placement service for collecting resumes and dispensing job vacancy information, your best approach is to make direct and personal contact with individual legislators and their staffs. You want to plug into the word-of-mouth job networks which play a central role in the hiring process. Call them on the telephone, visit them in their offices, leave your resume, and follow-up on your contacts. Timing is critical. You can be sure most legislators will not advertise staff vacancies or needs. They will first check their networks and the resumes they have on hand. If you make a good impression both on paper and in person, you should have a good chance at getting one of these jobs. Remember, all states except Nebraska have two-house legislatures. Be sure to conduct your job search in both houses.

However, keep two things in mind when looking for a legislative job. First, not all state legislatures have a wide range of job opportunities. Small states, such as New Hampshire and Vermont, have very few legislative job opportunities. Professional staff assistance is limited and personal staffs are extremely small — perhaps nonexistent. Second, these jobs do not pay well. While some jobs may appear glamourous, many are basic clerical jobs — answering telephones, sorting mail, and responding to inquiries. Boredom and burnout are frequent occurances. The high road of legislative drama involved with tackling big issues is reserved for very few people. Nonetheless, legislative work is an excellent stepping stone for working in agencies and private organizations doing business with the state. The experience and personal contacts for future networking are invaluable benefits of such work. A two year investment in legislative work can pay off handsomely in the long run.

JUDICIAL ARENA

The judicial bureaucracy is the smallest of all. A highly fragmented system, the states attorney's office and the state court system comprise the basic entry points into the judiciary. Many positions in this system either require legal training as a lawyer or paralegal or are basically clerical and support staff positions.

The typical structure of a state judicial system includes four levels of courts:

─── STATE JUDICIAL SYSTEM ───

- *Supreme Court:* stands at the apex of the state court system. Also known as the Supreme Judicial Court or Court of Appeals in some states.
- *Intermediate Appellate Courts:* All but 15 states have these courts. Depending on the state, they are variously referred to as Court of Appeals, Superior Court, Appellate Division of Supreme Court, Court of Criminal or Civil Appeals, or District Court of Appeals. These courts primarily review the decisions of lower courts.
- *Trial Courts of General Jurisdiction:* These courts try major criminal and civil cases. They are referred in some states as Circuit Courts, District Courts, Court of Common Pleas, Chancery Courts and Superior Courts.
- *Trial Courts of Limited Jurisdiction:* These courts deal with minor cases, their judges have the least legal training, and the political process is important to staffing these courts. Trial courts vary widely in terms of names and types: Juvenile Courts, Justice Courts, Probate Courts, Small Claims Courts, Orphan's Courts, Courts of Oyer and Terminer, and City and Town Courts.

While most courts divide their work into civil and criminal cases, the Office of Circuit Court also performs numerous non-court legal functions: issues marriage licenses, registers wills and probate, records land titles, files suits, and maintains the criminal and civil court dockets.

States attorneys, elected at the county level, prosecute all criminal cases in the lower courts. A typical states attorney's office might consist of an elected states attorney, eight assistant attorneys, a secretary, and four clerical support staff. Hiring practices will vary by state and local jurisdiction. For example, the state attorney's office may use the county personnel office for announcing vacancies and screening candidates especially for the support staff positions. However, for the professional legal positions, the informal system is most important. Lawyers tend to use word-of-mouth to identify candidates. They "spread the word" among their colleagues and fellow alumni to locate qualified candidates. The most they formalize the hiring process is when they contact the local bar association. In the end, the informal networks will be decisive in determining who gets the job.

At the state level, a similar hiring pattern operates for the supreme, appellate, and lower courts. The State Supreme Court maintains a personnel office, but this office normally does not hire for positions outside its office. It provides administrative support and gives guidelines to hiring offices. The general district and juvenile courts, which may have staffs of 20 or more, will do their own hiring. However, they normally coordinate position vacancy announcements through county or city personnel offices.

Entry into these courts is best approached by monitoring the county personnel offices and contacting individual judges and court personnel who normally identify personnel needs and make the final hiring decisions. School ties and the ole boy/girl system will operate more in hiring for positions in the state judiciary than in the executive bureaucracy. Consequently, your best approach, again, is to research the organization, contact individuals through referrals and informational interviews, and leave copies of your resume. Be sure to regularly follow up to see if and when vacancies may occur.

EXECUTIVE BUREAUCRACY

The state executive bureaucracy hires for similar positions found at the local and Federal levels. They employ general administrative and clerical personnel as well as white and blue-collar specialists ranging from scientists to prison guards. Thousands of jobs will fall into the following functional and service areas that the Council of State Governments uses to classify state administrative officers:

FUNCTIONAL JOB AREAS IN STATE GOVERNMENT

Adjutant General	Governor
Administration	Health
Aeronautics	Higher Education
Aging	Highway Patrol
Agriculture	Highway Safety
Air Quality	Highways
Alcoholism	Historic Preservation
Archives	Horse Racing
Arts Council	Housing Codes
Attorney General	Housing Finance
Banking	Human Resources

Budget
Chief Justice
Child Labor
Child Welfare
Civil Rights
Coastal Zone Management
Commerce
Community Affairs
Comptroller
Consumer Affairs
Corrections
Court Administration
Criminal Justice Data
Criminal Justice Planning
Data Processing
Developmental Disabilities
  Council
Developmental Disabled
Disaster Preparedness
Drug Abuse
Economic Opportunity
Education
Educational Television
Elections Administration
Employee Relations
Employment Services
Energy Resources
Environmental Protection
Ethics
Exceptional Children
Fair Employment
Federal-State Relations
Finance
Fish and Game
Food Protection
Foreign Trade
Forestry
General Services
Geology
Secretary of State
Securities
Social Services
Soil Conservation
Solid Waste

Industrial Development
Insurance and Investments
Juvenile Delinquency
Labor
Labor and Industrial Relations
Libraries (Law, Public, State)
Licensing
Lieutenant Governor
Liquor Control
Lotteries
Manpower
Mass Transportation
Medicaid
Mental Health
Mental Retardation
Mining
Motor Vehicle Registration
Municipal Affairs
Natural Resources
Occupational Safety
Oil and Gas Regulation
Ombudsman
Parks and Recreation
Parole
Personnel
Planning
Post Audit
Pre-Audit
Press Secretary
Printing
Public Defender
Public Lands
Public Utilities
Purchasing
Railroad Safety
Railroads
Retirement (Public Employees)
Retirement (Teachers)
Savings and Loan
Urban Renewal
Veterans Affairs
Veterinarian
Vital Statistics
Vocational Education

State Fair	Vocational Rehabilitation
State-Local Relations	Water Quality
Taxation	Water Resources
Telecommunications	Water Supply
Textbook Approval	Weights and Measures
Tourism	Welfare
Transportation	Women
Treasurer	Workers Compensation
Unemployment Compensation	

Most state bureaucracies have a central personnel department, or merit system, which performs the normal hiring functions of announcing vacancies, accepting applications, administering tests, screening candidates, and forwarding eligibility lists and applications to hiring officials. Most of these offices are charged with the responsibility of seeing that the hiring process follows equal opportunity, affirmative action, and merit selection criteria.

Your best strategy for getting a job with a state agency is to use both the formal and informal systems. You should:

1. *Regularly monitor the job listings issued by the personnel department:* You can do this by telephone, letter, or personal visit to various public locations where announcements are posted. Personnel departments issue position vacancy announcements similar to those found with local governments. They may be issued every week, 10-days, or two weeks in the form of an "Employment Opportunities Bulletin."

2. *Complete all required application forms:* These will vary depending on the particular agency and position. The state personnel offices should be able to give you information on what application forms are required by particular agencies and positions.

3. *Take all required tests:* These may be a combination of written, oral, physical, and polygraph tests, depending on the requirements of different agencies positions.

At the same time, using the informal system, you should:

4. *Research state agencies:* You do this by consulting

numerous published sources and informed individuals.

5.   *Contact individuals in the agencies for information and referrals:* You do this by conducting informational interviews with agency employees with whom you discuss your interests and skills, and seek advice and referrals.

With enough persistence in the informal system, as well as attention to the details of the formal system, you should be successful in locating a job appropriate for your interests and skills.

We do not advise you to pull political strings to get a state government job. At the same time, we do not advise you against doing so. Political pull still plays a role in state government, as it does in all levels of government. But you must be careful when to use it. Most agencies will respond to the use of professional connections to gain information on your skills and abilities. Most will resist political pressures to hire a particular individual.

On the other hand, many positions in state government are appointive positions. They go with the spoils of elective office. Individuals in these positions will have discretion to hire staff members. Political connections will probably work for these positions.

However, the general rule is to know your state organization. There is no substitute for conducting research on the hiring process. If you are thorough in your research, you will learn which positions with which agencies should be approached through the political system.

COMPENSATION

State government salaries are usually better than local government salaries, but not as generous as Federal government compensation. In general, the larger the unit of government, the better the compensation. Large cities tend to pay their officials at comparable rates to state officials. However, a considerable amount of diversity is apparent between and within state governments. In Texas, for example, elected and appointed officials are paid very respectable salaries, but public employees are poorly paid. Tennessee and South Carolina, two of the poorest states in the nation (ranking 44th and 45th respectively in terms of per capita income), pay their public employees well.

Average full-time pay varies considerably from state to state. In 1982, for example, the monthly earnings of state employees in

Alaska averaged $2,407 whereas employees in Mississippi averaged
$1,191. The average monthly salary of all state employees was
$1,625, about 20 percent less than the average earnings of Federal
employees. The average monthly salaries for employees of each
state government are presented in Table 12.

─────── TABLE 12 ───────

Average Monthly Salaries
of State Government Employees, 1982

State	Salary	State	Salary
Alaska	$2,407	Connecticut	$1,521
California	2,063	Alabama	1,520
Minnesota	1,912	Virginia	1,520
Michigan	1,903	Oklahoma	1,505
Wyoming	1,875	Vermont	1,503
Nevada	1,867	Massachusetts	1,499
Arizona	1,780	Maryland	1,488
New York	1,745	Kansas	1,478
Washington	1,738	Tennessee	1,476
Illinois	1,734	New Mexico	1,473
Colorado	1,730	Maine	1,470
Indiana	1,722	Florida	1,469
Wisconsin	1,716	Georgia	1,436
New Jersey	1,714	South Dakota	1,432
Montana	1,699	Delaware	1,431
Ohio	1,670	Kentucky	1,417
Iowa	1,655	South Carolina	1,412
Oregon	1,647	North Carolina	1,400
Hawaii	1,645	Louisiana	1,394
Texas	1,644	Arkansas	1,361
AVERAGE	1,625	Missouri	1,301
North Dakota	1,616	New Hampshire	1,295
Rhode Island	1,595	Nebraska	1,293
Idaho	1,595	West Virginia	1,272
Utah	1,578	Mississippi	1,191
Pennsylvania	1,570		

SOURCE: Book of the States, 1984-85.

KEY RESOURCES

Several excellent resources are available to take the mystery out of state governments. One of the most useful resources is *The Book of the States.* Published by the Council of State Governments (Iron Works Pike, P. O. Box 11910, Lexington, KY 40578), the book provides timely articles and statistical summaries on the legislative, judicial, and executive branches of state governments as well as the intergovernmental system which relates state governments to the Federal and local governments. The Council of State Governments also publishes four other volumes which are essential reading for anyone interested in state employment:

- *National Organizations of State Government Officials*
- *State Administrative Officials Classified By Function*
- *State Elected Officials and the Legislatures*
- *State Legislative Leadership, Committees, and Staff*

Each volume lists the names and addresses of key individuals. For example, if you are interested in seeking a job on a state legislator's staff, you should consult the volume entitled *State Elected Officials and the Legislatures* for the names and addresses of each legislator in each house of each state. If you are interested in working for a legislative agency or standing committee of the state House or Senate, consult the volume entitled *State Legislative Leadership, Committees, and Staff* for the names and addresses of the key people you should contact.

The Council of State Governments also publishes several other materials which should be useful in your research:

- *State Government News* (monthly magazine)
- *State Government* (quarterly journal)
- *State Government Research Checklist*
- *The Conference Calendar* (lists monthly meetings between the Council and state officials)
- *Backgrounder Series* (brief reports on state government)
- Research Reports
- Suggested Stage Legislation

A few other directories are available on state government. Most are very general. Among the most popular are:

- *The National Directory of State Agencies* (Information Resource Press)

- *State Information Book,* Susan Lukowki and Cary T. Grayson, Jr. (eds.) (Potomac Books Inc.)

Some of the best sources of information on particular career fields in state government are the professional associations of state employees. Among these are:

ASSOCIATIONS OF STATE GOVERNMENT EMPLOYEES

- Academy of State and Local Government
- American Association of State Highway and Transportation Officials
- Association of State and Interstate Water Pollution Control Administrators
- Association of State and Territorial Health Officials
- Association of State and Territorial Solid Waste Management Officials
- Conference of Chief Justices
- Conference of State Court Administrators
- Council of State Community Affairs Agencies
- Council of State Governments
- Council of State Housing Agencies
- Council of State Planning Agencies
- Education Commission of the States
- National Association of State Alcohol and Drug-Abuse Directors
- National Association for State Information Systems
- National Association of Secretaries of State
- National Association of State Auditors, Comptrollers, and Treasurers
- National Association of State Boards of Education
- National Association of State Budget Offices
- National Association of State Comptrollers
- National Association of State Departments of Agriculture
- National Association of State Mental Health Program Directors
- National Association of State Purchasing Officials
- National Association of State Treasurers
- National Association of Tax Administrators
- National Center for State Courts
- National Conference of Commissioners on Uniform State Laws
- National Conference of Lieutenant Governors

- National Conference of State General Service Officers
- National Conference of State Legislatures
- National Governors' Association
- National State Auditors Association
- State and Territorial Air Pollution Program Administrators
- State Auditor Coordinating Council

Contact information on these and other associations of state and local officials is found in Appendix F. *The Encyclopedia of Associations* provides further details on each association.

In the end, your single best source of information will be the people you meet who answer your questions and volunteer useful tips on how the system works in a particular state, branch of government, agency, or office. If you ask a great number of questions about the employment process and specific jobs, you will be rewarded for your efforts with information you can use in getting the job you want.

Chapter Sixteen
THE FEDERAL GOVERNMENT

For many job seekers, the Federal government is where the action is. Pay is good; benefits are excellent; in spite of occasional Reductions in Force, security is virtually guaranteed; many jobs are exciting; and more status and prestige is afforded Federal employees than state and local officials.

But getting a job with the Federal government is another matter. This level of government appears complex and confusing. Competition is fierce, applications are complex, and the hiring process takes time. Hiring systems are not uniform. The legislative, judicial, and executive branches each have their own hiring systems. Within the executive branch, the U.S. Postal Service, CIA, Foreign Service, and other agencies have their own hiring systems. And certain agencies and positions are exempted from standard personnel regulations.

This chapter is designed to bring simplicity and clarity to what is inherently a complex and confusing phenomenon. In this chapter we focus on the executive bureaucracy. Chapter Seventeen takes an in-depth look at the SF-171, the Federal government's version of a written application form. Chapter Eighteen examines employment opportunities on Capitol Hill, both in the legislature and the growing congressional bureaucracy, and in the judiciary.

231

STRUCTURE

The Federal government employs 2.9 million civilians who move nearly $1 trillion each year into more than 82,000 state and local governments, 120 countries, and an enormous private sector of vendors, contractors, and nongovernmental organizations. The business of this government is incredible. It staffs and manages whole communities, such as the Pentagon and military bases at home and abroad. It is literally a cradle to the grave government: delivering babies; providing day care services; extracting taxes; educating, hiring, and retiring individuals; providing social security and health care; and burying the dead.

Federal employees work for over 100 different agencies in the three branches of government. The executive branch is divided into three types of agencies:

- The Executive Office of the President
- The Departments
- Independent Agencies

While each agency has its own personnel office, the Office of Personnel Management (OPM), an independent executive agency, stands at the apex of the Federal personnel system. This office is responsible for issuing government-wide personnel regulations; providing support services to agencies, such as managing the application, testing, and screening processes; providing training services; and assisting agencies in meeting their personnel needs.

Table 13 summarizes employment distribution by branches and major agencies of government.

TABLE 13	
Federal Civilian Employment By Agency, 1983	
Agency	**Total Employees**
TOTAL	2,876,263
Legislative Branch	**39,143**
Congress	19,806
U.S. Senate	7,361
U.S. House of Representatives	12,445

Architect of the Capitol	2,246
General Accounting Office	5,296
Government Printing Office	5,763
Library of Congress	5,308
All Other	724
Judicial Branch	**16,626**
United States Courts	16,293
Supreme Court	333
Executive Branch	**2,820,494**
Executive Office of the President	*1,621*
White House Office	384
Office of Management and Budget	611
Council of Economic Advisors	33
Council on Environmental Quality	11
National Security Council	60
All other	522
Executive Departments	**1,729,153**
Agriculture	123,987
Commerce	35,576
Defense	1,026,461
Education	5,268
Energy	17,229
Health and Human Services	147,162
Housing and Urban Development	12,996
Interior	79,582
Justice	58,869
Labor	19,083
State	23,961
Transportation	62,959
Treasury	126,020
Independent Agencies	
ACTION	524
American Battle Monuments Commission	392
Board of Governors, Federal Reserve System	1,551
Civil Aeronautics Board	441
Commission on Civil Rights	259
Environmental Protection Agency	11,931
Equal Employment Opportunity Commission	3,183

Export-Import Bank, U.S.	335
Farm Credit Administration	308
Federal Communications Commission	1,897
Federal Deposit Insurance Corporation	3,660
Federal Emergency Management Agency	2,509
Federal Home Loan Bank Board	1,534
Federal Labor Relations Authority	290
Federal Mediation and Conciliation Service	359
Federal Trade Commission	1,323
General Services Administration	29,586
International Communications Agency	7,983
International Trade Commission	420
International Commerce Commission	1,245
Merit System Protection Board	524
National Aeronautics and Space Administration	22,784
National Credit Unit Administration	615
National Endowment for the Arts	277
National Labor Relations Board	2,726
National Science Foundation	1,257
National Transportation Safety Board	337
National Regulatory Commission	3,534
Office of Personnel Management	6,369
Panama Canal Commission	8,356
Peace Corps	1,026
Pension Benefit Guaranty Corporation	466
Railroad Retirement Board	1,565
Securities and Exchange Commission	1,897
Selective Service System	284
Small Business Administration	5,100
Smithsonian Institution	4,696
Soldiers' and Airmen's Home	990
Tennessee Valley Authority	37,181
U.S. International Development Cooperation Agency	5,418
U.S. Postal Service	663,027
Veterans Administration	238,739
All other	2,822

SOURCE: U.S. Office of Personnel Management

The total Federal government workforce represents 17.9 percent of all public employees. Eighty–seven percent of Federal employees work outside the Washington, D.C. Metropolitan area, including 133,000 who work abroad. The three largest civilian employers are Defense, Postal Service, and Veterans Administration, which employ 35.7, 23.1, and 8.3 percent of the total employees respectively.

Federal employment has been relatively stable over the past 25 years. Between 1960 and 1980 Federal employment increased by 22.9 percent, for an average annual increase of 1.1 percent. In 1981 Federal employment actually decreased by 67,000 and by another 39,000 in 1982. Agencies experiencing the major cutbacks in the early 1980s were the Departments of Agriculture, Commerce, Education, Housing and Urban Development, Labor, and Transportation; Environmental Protection Agency, Federal Emergency Management Agency, Federal Trade Commission, General Services Administration, Interstate Commerce Commission, Office of Personnel Management, Small Business Administration, and the Tennessee Valley Authority. But in 1983 Federal employment began to increase once again. The judicial branch, the Departments of Defense, Interior, Justice, Treasury, and the U.S. Postal Service and Veterans Administration have steadily increased the number of employees throughout this period. Table 14 summarizes the growth and decline of Federal civilian employment for the three branches of government:

TABLE 14

Growth and Decline of Federal Civilian Employment
1960 - 1983

Year	TOTAL (1,000)	Percent of U.S. employed	Executive — Total (1,000)	Executive — Defense (1,000)	Legis-lative (1,000)	Judicial (1,000)
1960	2,430	3.7	2,403	1,042	23	5
1965	2,539	3.6	2,507	1,038	25	6
1970	2,928	3.7	2,891	1,195	30	7
1975	2,882	3.4	2,834	1,036	37	10
1979	2,897	2.9	2,844	970	40	13
1980	2,987	2.9	2,933	972	40	14
1981	2,910	2.9	2,855	986	40	15
1982	2,871	2.9	2,816	1,019	39	16
1983	2,878	2.9	2,823	1,033	39	16

SOURCE: U. S. Office of Personnel Management

COMPETITIVE AND EXEMPTED SERVICES

The Federal civil service classifies positions into competitive or exempted services. The majority of Federal government positions are in the *competitive service*. These positions fall under the civil service regulations, codified in the Civil Service Reform Act of 1978, which are administered by the Office of Personnel Management. At the same time, Congress, the judiciary, and several agency positions are exempted from these regulations. Executive agencies classified in the *exempted services* include:

EXEMPTED SERVICES

- Central Intelligence Agency
- Defense Intelligence Agency
- Executive Protective Service (Secret Service — Uniformed Branch)
- Federal Bureau of Investigation
- Federal Reserve System, Board of Governors
- General Accounting Office
- International Development Agency
- National Science Foundation (only scientific, engineering, and a few high-level managerial positions are exempted)
- National Security Agency
- U.S. Nuclear Regulatory Commission
- Postal Rate Commission
- U.S. Postal Service
- U.S. Department of State (Skilled specialists and experienced secretaries only; all others must apply to take the foreign service exam.)
- Tennessee Valley Authority
- United States Mission to the United Nations
- Veterans Administration, Department of Medicine and Surgery

---

These agencies have their own set of personnel procedures for hiring and managing personnel. Therefore, individuals apply directly to these agencies rather than go through OPM.

Exempted positions are positions which are not subject to OPM standards. These positions include:

- Professional and Administrative Careers (PAC) – GS-5 through GS-7
- Teachers in Department of Defense overseas dependent schools
- Attorneys
- Doctors, dentists, and nurses with the Veterans Administration
- Scientists and engineers with the National Science Foundation
- Chaplains with the Veterans Administration and Justice Department
- Drug enforcement agents

CLASSIFICATIONS, PAY SYSTEMS, AND SEX

The total Federal workforce is divided into two major classification systems. White-collar professional, administrative, scientific, clerical, and technical employees are paid according to the *General Schedule* (GS), which is graded from GS-1 to GS-18 and uniformly applied throughout the Federal government. Table 15 summarizes the pay rates on the General Schedule.

TABLE 15

THE GENERAL SCHEDULE
Effective through 1986

	1	2	3	4	5	6	7	8	9	10
GS-1	$ 9,339	$ 9,650	$ 9,961	$10,271	$10,582	$10,764	$11,071	$11,380	$11,393	$11,686
2	10,501	10,750	11,097	11,393	11,521	11,860	12,199	12,538	12,877	13,216
3	11,458	11,840	12,222	12,604	12,986	13,368	13,750	14,132	14,514	14,896
4	12,862	13,291	13,720	14,149	14,578	15,007	15,436	15,865	16,294	16,723
5	14,390	14,870	15,350	15,830	16,310	16,790	17,270	17,750	18,230	18,710
6	16,040	16,575	17,110	17,645	18,180	18,715	19,250	19,785	20,320	20,855
7	17,824	18,418	19,012	19,606	20,200	20,794	21,388	21,982	22,576	23,170
8	19,740	20,398	21,056	21,714	22,372	23,030	23,688	24,346	25,004	25,662
9	21,804	22,531	23,258	23,985	24,712	25,439	26,166	26,893	27,620	28,347
10	24,011	24,811	25,611	26,411	27,211	28,011	28,811	29,611	30,411	31,211
11	26,381	27,260	28,139	29,018	29,897	30,776	31,655	32,534	33,413	34,292
12	31,619	32,673	33,727	34,781	35,835	36,889	37,943	38,997	40,051	41,105
13	37,599	38,852	40,105	41,358	42,611	43,864	45,117	46,370	47,623	48,876
14	44,430	45,911	47,392	48,873	50,354	51,835	53,316	54,797	56,278	57,759
15	52,262	54,004	55,746	57,488	59,230	60,972	62,714	64,456	66,198	67,940
16	61,296	63,339	65,382	67,425	69,468*	71,511*	73,554*	75,597*	77,640*	
17	71,804*	74,197*	76,590*	78,983*	81,376*					
18	84,157*									

*The rate of basic pay payable to employees at these rates is limited to the rate payable for level V of the Executive Schedule, which would be $68,700.

Trade, labor, and other blue-collar workers — 70 percent of whom are employed by the Departments of Army, Navy, and Air Force — are paid on the *Federal Wage System* (Wage Grade — WG). Grades range from WG-1 to WG-15 and the pay in each grade varies for each of 137 geographical areas. Altogether 2,319,000 Federal employees are classified as WG. Other pay systems operate for the Senior Executive Service — management and executive positions at the GS-16 to GS-18 levels — the U. S. Postal Service, and a few other positions.

The Federal workforce is predominately male. While 35 percent are female, a disproportionate number of women occupy the lower-level administrative and clerical positions. Table 16 summarizes the characteristics of Federal government employment:

---- TABLE 16 ----

Characteristics of Federal Civilian Employment, 1983	
Characteristic	Employment
Male	1,790,000
Female	964,000
Full-time	2,497,000
Other	257,000
Competitive service	1,685,000
Excepted service	1,069,000
White-collar	2,319,000
Blue-collar	435,000

JOB TYPES AND ALTERNATIVES

The Federal government hires individuals for five categories of jobs. These consist of:

1. *Professional Occupations:* These require knowledge of a field of science or specialized education and training at a

level equal to a bachelor's degree or higher. Examples of these skilled specialists include engineers, accountants, biologists, and chemists. Engineers (90,000) and nurses (35,000) are the largest professional groups with the Federal government.

2. *Administrative Occupations:* These require increasingly responsible experience or a general college level education. Examples include personnel specialists and administrative officers.

3. *Technical Occupations:* These are associated with a professional or administrative field, but they are non-routine in nature. Examples include computer technician and electronic technician.

4. *Clerical Occupations:* These involve work which supports office, business, or fiscal operations. Examples include clerk-typist, mail and file clerk.

5. *Other Occupations:* All other occupations not classified as professional, administrative, technical, or clerical. Includes many blue-collar and trade occupations, such as painters, carpenters, and laborers.

The Federal government has as many different types of positions as the private sector. A complete list of positions would take up the remainder of this book. Therefore, we will examine the major classifications as well as identify those positions which employ the largest number of individuals.

The Office of Personnel Management, using a numerical code, classifies all General Schedule positions into 22 occupational groups and families. These include.

CLASSIFICATION OF GS POSITIONS

- GS-0000 Miscellaneous Occupational Group
- GS-0100 Social Science, Psychology, and Welfare Group
- GS-0200 Personnel Management and Industrial Relations Group
- GS-0300 General Administrative, Clerical, and Office Group
- GS-0400 Biological Sciences Group

- GS-0500 Accounting and Budget Group
- GS-0600 Medical, Hospital, Dental, and Public Health Group
- GS-0700 Veterinary Medical Science Group
- GS-0800 Engineering and Architecture Group
- GS-0900 Legal and Kindred Group
- GS-1000 Information and Arts Group
- GS-1100 Business and Industry Group
- GS-1200 Copyright, Patent, and Trade-Mark Group
- GS-1300 Physical Sciences Group
- GS-1400 Library and Archives Group
- GS-1500 Mathematics and Statistics Group
- GS-1600 Equipment, Facilities, and Service Group
- GS-1700 Education Group
- GS-1800 Investigation Group
- GS-1900 Quality Assurance, Inspection and Grading Group
- GS-2000 Supply Group
- GS-2100 Transportation Group

Wage System occupations also are classified into groups and families. These consist of 36 WG categories:

CLASSIFICATION OF WG POSITIONS

- WG-2500 Wire Communications Equipment Installation and Maintenance Family
- WG-2600 Electronic Equipment Installation and Maintenance Family
- WG-2800 Electrical Installation and Maintenance Family
- WG-3100 Fabric and Leather Work Family
- WG-3300 Instrument Work Family
- WG-3400 Machine Tool Work Family
- WG-3500 General Services and Support Work Family
- WG-3600 Structural and Finishing Work Family
- WG-3700 Metal Processing Family
- WG-3800 Metal Work Family
- WG-3900 Motion Picture, Radio, Television and Sound Equipment Operation Family
- WG-4000 Lens and Crystal Work Family
- WG-4100 Painting and Paperhanging Family
- WG-4200 Plumbing and Pipefitting Family

- WG-4300   Pliable Materials Work Family
- WG-4400   Printing Family
- WG-4600   Woodwork Family
- WG-4700   General Maintenance Operations Work Family
- WG-4800   General Equipment Maintenance Family
- WG-5000   Plant and Animal Work Family
- WG-5200   Miscellaneous Occupations Family
- WG-5300   Industrial Equipment Maintenance Family
- WG-5400   Industrial Equipment Operation Family
- WG-5700   Transportation/Mobile Equipment Operation Family
- WG-5800   Transportation/Mobile Equipment Maintenance Family
- WG-6500   Ammunition, Explosives, and Toxic Materials Work Family
- WG-6600   Armament Work Family
- WG-6900   Warehousing and Stock Handling Family
- WG-7000   Packing and Processing Family
- WG-7300   Laundry, Dry Cleaning, and Pressing Family
- WG-7400   Food Preparation and Serving Family
- WG-7600   Personal Services Family
- WG-8200   Fluid Systems Maintenance Family
- WG-8600   Engine Overhaul Family
- WG-8800   Aircraft Overhaul Family
- WG-9000   Film Processing Family

White-collar GS positions employing the largest number of individuals are:

WHITE COLLAR POSITIONS

- Accountants and auditors (GS-510) - 21,000
- Administrative assistants and officers (GS-341) - 8,368
- Air traffic control specialists (GS-2152) - 16,000
- Budget analysts or officers (GS-560) - 9,800
- Civil rights analysts (GS-160) - 5,000
- Computer specialists (GS-334) - 30,000
- Contract representative (GS-962) - 9,000
- Contract and procurement specialists (GS-1102) - 21,000
- Criminal investigators (GS-1810 and GS-1811) - 20,000
- Economists (GS-110) - 5,500

- Engineers (GS-800 series) - 90,000
- Equipment specialist (GS-1670) - 9,000
- Financial institution examiners (GS-570) - 5,000
- Foresters (GS-460) - 6,700
- Internal revenue officers (GS-1169) - 5,700
- Lawyers (GS-905) - 17,000
- Loan specialists (GS-1165) - 5,000
- Management analysts (GS-343) - 11,700
- Nurses (GS-610) - 35,000
- Personnel management specialists (GS-201) - 9,000
- Physicians (GS-602) - 9,700
- Physicists (GS-1310) - 4,500
- Production controllers (GS-1152) - 6,800
- Program analysts (GS-345) - 13,500
- Quality assurance specialists (GS-1910) - 13,000
- Social insurance representatives and administrators (GS-105) - 22,500
- Social insurance claims examiners (GS-993) - 11,000
- Supply management specialists (GS-2003) and inventory management specialists (GS-2010) - 14,423
- Teachers (GS-1710) - 14,500
- Training instructors (GS-1712) - 6,200

Blue-collar occupations, both under the GS and WG systems, which employ the largest number of individuals include:

BLUE-COLLAR POSITIONS

- Accounting technicians (GS-525) - 20,000
- Aircraft mechanics (WG-8852) - 12,000
- Claims clerks (GS-998) - 15,000
- Clerks (GS-300 and GS-500 series) - 300,000
- Clerk-typists (GS-322) - 63,000
- Computer operators (GS-332) - 10,000
- Data transcribers (GS-356) - 12,400
- Electricians (WG-2805) - 13,000
- Electronics mechanics (WG-2604) - 17,000
- Engineering aides and technicians (GS-802) - 59,500
- Financial administration workers (GS-503) - 11,600
- Firefighters and other fire protection workers (GS-081) - 10,800
- Food service workers (GS-7408) - 14,900

- Forestry technicians and smoke jumpers (GS-462) - 15,000
- Heavy mobile equipment mechanics (WG-5803) - 10,000
- Janitors or porters (GS-3566)
- Laborers (WG-3502) - 15,900
- Machinists (WG-3414) - 13,900
- Mail and file clerks (GS-305)
- Maintenance mechanics (WG-4749) - 10,000
- Medical technicians (GS-600) -26,000
- Nursing assistants (GS-621) - 35,000
- Personnel clerks and assistants (GS-203) - 12,300
- Pipefitters (WG-4205) - 15,900
- Reporting stenographers, shorthand reporters, and clerk stenographers (GS-312) - 11,300
- Secretaries (GS-318) - 82,900
- Sheet metal mechanics (WG-3806) - 13,300
- Supply clerks and technicians (GS-2005) - 31,500
- Tax accountants and examiners (GS-592) - 14,400
- Warehouse workers (WG-6907) - 24,800

For more information on these positions, see Neale Baxter's *Opportunities in Federal Government Careers,* the Department of Labor's *The Dictionary of Occupational Titles* and *The Occupational Outlook Handbook,* and publications and handouts issued by the Office of Personnel Management and personnel offices of individual agencies.

STRATEGIES

Successful Federal job applicants know how to cut through the confusing and frustrating hiring process. What separates them from unsuccessful candidates is their:

- Knowledge of individual agencies, personnel processes, and job openings.
- Skill in developing and marketing a good application which clearly communicates their experience, qualifications, and strengths to agencies.
- Patience, persistence, and drive in seeing the process through to the end.

You should begin your job search with a thorough understanding of both the formal and informal hiring processes in the Federal government. While you can get a job by only following the formal system of announcements, tests, and applications, your odds will improve considerably if you also pursue jobs in the informal system of prospecting, networking, informational interviews, and referrals. In the end, your success will depend on how well you *relate* the formal and information systems to one another.

The structure of the Federal hiring process is similar to the structure of American governments in general — exhibits an incredible amount of decentralization, fragmentation, overlap, redundancy, and chaos. The hiring system is anything but logical, efficient, and effective. For example, if you want a research intelligence position, the CIA is only one of many agencies performing these functions. The Defense Intelligence Agency in the Department of Defense, Intelligence and Research Bureau in the State Department, and the National Security Council in the Executive Office of the President, and the Federal Bureau of Investigation (FBI) essentially do the same type of work. The congressional bureaucracy, through the Federal Research Division of the Library of Congress, also engages in similar functions. These agencies duplicate each other and contribute to the overall redundancy of the Federal government.

Other occupations also are represented in numerous agencies which overlap and duplicate each other. Take, for example, investigative work. Almost every department has its own police and/or investigative force — not just the FBI. In the case of personnel training opportunities, most large agencies have their own training sections which conduct in-house training — not just the Office of Personnel Management. Such redundancy is uncovered when you conduct your informational interviews. Indeed, personnel at the CIA will tell you to talk to their friends at the Defense Intelligence Agency or the Intelligence and Research Bureau in the State Department — agencies they may have worked for prior to moving to the CIA. Trainers at OPM will direct you to fellow professionals in the various Departments and Independent Agencies who also conduct training. And, as we will see in Part IV, such networking leads to similar positions in the private sector with contracting and consulting firms as well as associations that do business with various government agencies.

While redundancy may be a waste of taxpayers' money, it may also contribute to the overall effectiveness of government by providing important internal checks and balances on policy. Whatever its costs and benefits, in a job search you need to recognize and use redundancy to your advantage. You do this by contacting several agencies for information and referrals on job opportunities in the same functional areas. Remember, no single agency of government performs a unique function. Counterpart functions will be found in several agencies. Your job is to do the necessary research to uncover the counterparts.

Decentralization also should be used to your advantage. Your contacts should be developed with key personnel in the operating units or program offices — where the hiring decisions are finally made. Since units tend to be isolated from one another because of decentralization, you should conduct several informational interviews within and between agencies. In fact, it is not unusual to discover that one office does not know what another office is doing, even though it is in the same agency, housed in the same building, and even located next door!

The formal structure of hiring in the Federal government overlays a great deal of decentralization, fragmentation, and chaos. It presents a deceptive picture of a centralized, organized, coordinated, and efficient government personnel system. This image initially encourages people to apply but then intimidates them sufficiently enough to dissuade many from following through. Do not be intimated or dissuaded from achieving your objective. The key to success is in understanding the system and using this understanding to your benefit.

The Office of Personnel Management, formerly known as the Civil Service Commission, is an independent executive agency. It stands at the center of the Federal government's merit personnel system. Many people — including some OPM employees — believe you must apply for Federal jobs through this agency. This is true in nearly 50 percent of the cases, but it is not true for over 1 million Federal positions. All Federal agencies hire their own personnel. In so doing, they may receive direct assistance from OPM in the form of announcing vacancies, scrutinizing applications, and screening candidates. The degree of involvement varies with agencies, and depend on several factors, such as classification as exempted positions or the degree of organizational capabilities the agency has to conduct their own hiring. Nonetheless, for most Federal positions, you will have to deal directly with the Office of Personnel Management.

Since the Federal personnel reforms of January 1980, OPM has been decentralizing several personnel functions to individual agencies. But decentralization has not been uniform. Some agencies are capable of hiring whereas others are still more dependent upon OPM for assistance. In other cases, OPM's role increasingly is marginal to the hiring process. Overall, OPM performs general support functions for agencies, such as providing information and assisting them in the selection and training processes.

OPM does perform one essential function for your job search campaign: dispenses information on procedures and opportunities. In addition to its 10 regional headquarters, OPM's Federal Job Information Centers (FJICs) are located in 50 cities, including Guam and Puerto Rico, which are considered subregional centers or key geographical locations for dispensing Federal employment information. However, you should approach these FJICs with some degree of caution and healthy skepticism. The major functions of FJICs are to provide information on job opportunities in particular agencies, hand out application forms (SF-171s), and conduct testing for lower-level entry positions (GS-1 through GS-5). OPM representatives at the FJICs will tell you to follow the formal procedures; most deny the existence of an informal system or, at best, they will not endorse it. This is understandable, because their job is to promote the formal system rather than help you learn the most effective methods for penetrating the bureaucracy. They are the promoters, managers, and keepers of long employment lines. A complete listing of these centers is included in Appendix G.

OPM outlines the formal hiring system by advising candidates to follow thess steps:

FORMAL APPLICATION PROCESS

1. *Acquire position vacancy announcements and application forms:* Go to the FJIC for listings of job openings and information on procedures for getting a Federal job. This results in a pile of literature and a SF-171 form. Alternatively, OPM may advise you that the particular position you desire does not fall within the scope of OPM procedures, such as exempted positions and agencies.

2. *Follow instructions in announcements:* Each announcement will give specific instructions on application deadlines, position description, qualifications, content of application package, tests required, and application procedures.

3. *Complete your application:* This is the SF-171 — the Federal government's version of an obituary resume or application form — and send it to OPM for a rating.

4. *Take any required tests:* These will be listed on the position announcements as well as specified by OPM.

5. *Wait for OPM to evaluate your qualifications:* Once you complete the SF-171 and submit it to OPM, evaluators will examine it and give you a rating based on the information supplied in the SF-171.

6. *Wait for OPM to submit your name to an agency:* If you are applying for a specific position through OPM, and if you are one of the best qualified, OPM automatically sends your application to the agency. Alternatively, the agency may request your name from OPM's list of eligible candidates.

7. *Submit your application directly to the agency:* Alternatively, a position announcement may request you to submit your application package directly to the agency personnel office. In this case, you must have a OPM rating included with your completed SF-171.

8. *Wait for the agency to call you for an interview:* Agencies normally select three candidates to interview.

9. *Wait to be selected:* If you are interviewed, you will need to wait some time before the agency makes its final selection decision.

The one common theme running throughout this formal hiring process is that you must *wait*. Indeed, you must have a great deal of patience and perseverance from the moment you review a vacancy announcement to the time you are selected for a position.

While this is a very logical, and seemingly efficient, hiring process, it is not particularly effective for the individual. Passive waiting is not a good job search strategy. If you follow OPM's advice, your chances of getting a job are about as good as responding to newspaper want ads or standing in line at an employment firm — very limited. There is a great deal of mystery to this process which OPM does not reveal to the public. Remember, the Federal government hires approximately 1,000 people each day. But the FJICs only list a few of these positions and usually only those positions available in their particular region or city as well as all positions classified as Senior — Level (certain GS-13 through GS-15 positions) and a few Senior Executive Service positions. In other words, the FJICs may not provide you with useful information on the availability of jobs in particular agencies at your level of qualifications. There is a good reason for this. OPM does not know what positions are available beyond the limited number reported to OPM. In fact, no one in the Federal government knows all the positions vacant on a particular day, week, or month. The Federal government simply does not keep such information on itself.

Given OPM's lack of information on specific job openings, you must directly contact the personnel offices of each agency for a complete listing of vacancies. Alternatively, three private firms — the Federal Research Service, Inc., Federal Jobs Digest, and the Federal Employment Bulletin — every two weeks compile and publish catalogs of approximately 3,000 vacancies at the GS-5 levels and above. While these publications are relatively comprehensive, they miss many positions which are listed only on the bulletin boards of agency personnel offices, circulated to a limited number of government offices, or posted outside agency cafeterias and snack bars.

Your alternatives to spending $6.50 for a single issue of the "Federal Career Opportunities Report" (Federal Research Service), $29 for a six issue subscription to "Federal Jobs Digest," or $130 for 26 issues of the Federal Employment Bulletin are most unattractive. The Federal job information structure definitely favors individuals who physically are located in the Washington, D.C. Metropolitan area or in regional cities and have the time and patience to telephone or walk from one agency personnel office or cafeteria bulletin board to another. If you live outside Washington or the regional cities, you encounter serious problems. You can visit your FJIC every week or telephone every agency every week for information on vacant positions. After spending $200 a week on long-distance telephone calls, the $6.50, $29, or $130 for the job listing services will seem cheap and convenient. Moreover, you will avoid travelling to an FJIC and standing in line for limited information. The FJIC is mainly designed to help people apply for the GS-1 and GS-5 entry-level positions or for blue-collar positions. Visit the FJICs, but beyond acquiring a copy of the SF-171 and learning the formal application procedures, don't expect them to be useful in your job search. Again, the Federal government is highly decentralized and fragmented within and between agencies. Your job will be to centralize and coordinate those aspects of the Federal government job market that interest you. No one — including private employment and executive search firms — can do this for you. If they claim they can, don't believe them. In short, you must take your own action if you are to be effective in getting a Federal job.

TAKING EFFECTIVE ACTION

The informal Federal hiring system is similar to the informal systems found at the state and local government levels. Since agencies continually face personnel problems because of normal turnover, they must recruit periodically. A personnel need is first identified in the operating unit and then communicated to the agency personnel office where it is formally announced in accordance with merit, affirmative action, and equal opportunity considerations. During the lengthy formal process of announcing the position, gathering SF-171s, and selecting candidates, agency personnel often try to hedge against uncertainty by looking for qualified personnel in the informal system. This means giving information on the vacancy to friends and acquaintances in their networks in the hope of attracting qualified candidates. Fearing the unknown, officials often welcome an opportunity to meet informally with a candidate, especially in the format of an informational interview.

If your timing is right, you may uncover a pending vacancy in an operating unit. Again, the personnel office will be the last to learn about the vacancy in the agency. Furthermore, the position description may be written around your resume and SF-171 or the agency may assist you in customizing your SF-171 in line with the position description. If agency personnel send you to their personnel office to rework your SF-171, this is a good signal that you are under serious consideration for a position. Although we have no accurate figures on the phenomenon of "wiring" positions, it probably occurs in many GS-13 and above positions. Some observers, such as Richard Irish (*Go Hire Yourself an Employer*) estimate that 95 percent of these positions are filled through agency "promotion." Such practices arise from certain personnel fears of agencies. Many agency heads wish to avoid leaving critical personnel problems to chance decisions of low-level officials in personnel offices.

The informal system consists of following the same general job search steps we outlined earlier as well as adapting them to the Federal personnel setting:

THE INFORMAL JOB SEARCH

1. *Research Federal agencies:* The more information you can gather on agency work and personnel procedures, the better your chances of getting a job with an

agency.

2. ***Focus on a few agencies for intensive research:*** Specific jobs are found in specific agencies. The more details you gather at the level of the hiring officials, the better the probability of getting a job.

3. ***Conduct informational interviews with agency personnel:*** Make contacts with officials in the hiring units. Seek information, advice, and referrals. Take copies of your resume *and* SF-171 with you to these interviews and leave copies for future reference.

4. ***Apply for agency vacancies with a customized SF-171:*** Develop a customized SF-171 according to our advice in Chapter Seventeen. Use this version of the SF-171 when applying for agency vacancies.

5. ***Arrange interview with the hiring supervisor:*** If you pass the formal screening process with your customized SF-171 and other documents, and hiring personnel in the operating units like you, you should be called for an interview and, hopefully, offered the job.

Revising James Hawkins' *(The Uncle Sam Connection)* model of the Federal employment process in Figure 5, we outline the formal and informal systems of Federal employment as well as the relationship between the two for positions at the GS-9 to GS-15 levels.

We do not recommend mobilizing partisan political "pull" with agencies. Bureaucrats in general do not like to respond to blatant political pressures from elected officials. Such strategies may work wonders at some state and local units of government where the "good ole boys" are still powerful — but be careful with the Feds. There are exceptions, however. Perhaps you know a congressman who is on a powerful budget or appropriations committee affecting a particular agency. The congressman and his or her legislative assistants may know key people in the agency, and they will write you a standard letter of introduction. But do not expect miracles to happen with such a letter or by dropping names of big shots. In fact, the President of the United States only directly controls 2,000 of 2.9 million civilian government positions. Even the President may not be able to help you with the relatively autonomous and resistant bureaucracy!

FIGURE 5

RELATIONSHIP OF FORMAL AND INFORMAL FEDERAL EMPLOYMENT PROCESSES

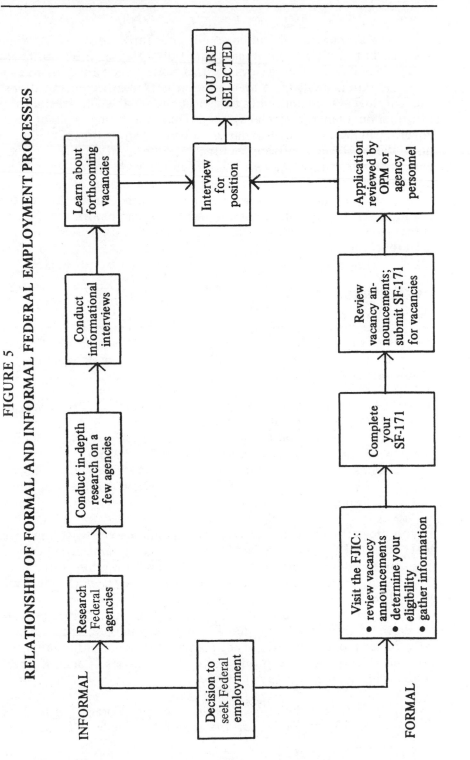

Federal bureaucrats understand and thrive on the informal system, but political patronage and political pull are considered tacky, if not illegal, these days. In this respect, government bureaucrats are no different from their counterparts in other organizations: the informal system continues to yield more reliable and trustworthy information than the formal system. Thus, the hiring goals of most government agencies are similar to those of other organizations in both the public and private sectors: hire the most qualified person who is *competent, intelligent, honest, and likable*. Indeed, the 1980 personnel reforms, which are based upon the model of the private sector, already have decentralized many hiring decisions to the agency level. In this sense, conducting a job search with the Federal government is remarkably similar to conducting a job search in the private sector.

USEFUL RESOURCES

Numerous resources are available to research the Federal hiring process as well as individual agencies. For a good overview of Federal government opportunities and job search strategies, examine the following books:

> *How to Get a Federal Job or Survive a RIF*, David Waelde (Washington, DC: FEDHELP Publications, 1984).
> *Opportunities in Federal Government Careers*, Neale Baxter (Northbrook, IL: National Textbook, 1985).
> *Directory of Employment Opportunities in the Federal Government*, Stephen E. Vogel (New York: Arco Publishing, 1985).

If you are particularly interested in intelligence careers with the CIA, FBI, NSA, DIA, the Drug Enforcement Agency, and related agencies, an excellent resource is David Atlee Phillips, *Careers in Secret Operations: How to Be a Federal Intelligence Officer* (Stone Trail Press, 1984).

Two excellent, and extremely inexpensive, publications provide a wealth of information on the Federal personnel system, particularly on employee benefits, labor-management relations, health and retirement systems, and promotions and transfers. Each of these volumes is updated annually:

> *Federal Employees' Almanac*, Joseph Young (ed.). Send $3.50 (or $4.25 for first class) to: Federal Employee's

Almanac, P. O. Box 7528, Falls Church, VA 22046. You
can call them at 703/533-3031.
Federal Personnel Guide. Send $2.75 ($4.00 for first class)
to: Federal Personnel Guide, P. O. Box 274, Washington,
DC 20044.

Both organizations publishing these books also publish useful newsletters. Joseph Young's weekly *Federal Employees' News Digest*
costs $16 for 6 months, $32 for one year, or $60 for 2 years. An-
other weekly newsletter, the *Federal Personnel Weekly News
Up.Date,* is available on a subscription basis at $25 for one year and
$46 for two years. For further information and subscriptions to
these two newsletters, write to:

Federal Employees' News Digest Inc.
P. O. Box 6028
Falls Church, VA 22046

FPG Weekly News Up.Date
P. O. Box 274
Washington, DC 20044

As noted previously, the Federal government does not maintain a current listing of all jobs available in the Federal government.
Instead, three private firms — the Federal Research Service, Inc.,
Federal Jobs Digest, and the Federal Employment Bulletin — track
Federal job vacancies and publish bi-weekly catalogs of job vacancies available throughout the government. These job listing services
provide the most comprehensive collection of vacancies available
anywhere. *Federal Career Opportunities* costs $6.50 per copy or
$36 for 6 issues, $70 for 12 issues, or $146 for 26 issues. Most issues
run about 64 pages and list 3400+ jobs at the GS-5 through Senior
Executive Service, jobs abroad, application process and contact
information, part-time and temporary positions, and "how to"
articles on job hunting techniques. In addition, the Federal Research
Service, Inc. publishes a monthly newsletter, *Federal Career Insights:* six monthly issues is $33.50 and an annual subscription is
$67. For information and subscriptions to either publication, write
or call:

Federal Research Service, Inc.
P. O. Box 1059
Vienna, VA 22180
Tel. 703/281-0200

Another private firm publishes a similar bi-weekly listing of Federal jobs as well as a *Federal Jobs Kit*. Each issue contains about 3000 jobs for all professions and occupations, including blue-collar jobs. Subscription rates are $29 for six issues, $54 for 12 issues, and $110 for 25 issues. For further information and subscription, you can write or call their toll-free number:

> Federal Jobs Digest
> 325 Pennsylvania Avenue, SE
> Washington, DC 20003
> Tel. 800/824-5000

The Federal Employment Bulletin also publishes a bi-weekly listing of Federal job vacancies. This publication lists jobs by grade and includes a useful index of job titles. The publication sells for $5.75 per issue, $22 for 4 issues, $42 for 8 issues, or $130 for 26 issues. For subscription or more information, contact:

> Federal Employment Bulletin
> P. O. Box 11715
> Washington, DC 20008
> Tel. 202/667-3050

A weekly newspaper, *The Federal Times*, also lists Federal job vacancies. Write to them at 475 School Street, SW, Washington, D.C. 20024, Tel. 202/554-7100. Other Federal jobs will be listed in the classified and/or business sections of local newspapers.

Individuals seeking legal opportunities with Federal agencies can subscribe to a special job listing service. The Federal Reports, Inc. publishes a monthly listing of attorney and law-related job opportunities in the Federal government as well as with other public and private employers in Washington, D.C., throughout the United States, and abroad. Subscription rates for this publication are $30 for three months, $50 for six months, and $90 for one year. Write or call them at:

> Federal Reports, Inc.
> 1010 Vermont Ave., NW, Suite 408
> Washington, DC 20005
> Tel. 202/393-3311

You can also contact agency personnel offices directly to get information on vacancies. Several offices maintain a job hotline with a recorded message of current vacancies. Appendix H lists the names and telephone numbers of these offices.

Many Federal government positions require passing a written examination for eligibility. Arco Publishing (215 Park Avenue, South, New York, NY 10003, Tel. 212/777-6300) has produced several self-study guides to help individuals prepare for various civil service examinations at all level of government. Among the many titles relevant to Federal employment, for example, are:

- *Civil Service Administrative Tests*
- *U. S. Postal Service*
- *Mail Handler-Postal Service*
- *Treasury Enforcement Agent*
- *General Test Practice of 101 U.S. Jobs*
- *How to Get a Clerical Job in Government*
- *Bookkeeper-Account Clerk*
- *Complete Guide to U.S. Civil Service Jobs*
- *Federal Clerk Steno Typist*

Several useful publications are available in the reference section of your local library. These are primarily directories which provide an overview of the structure of the Federal government as well as provide the names and addresses of key individuals within each agency. Among the most important directories are:

- *U.S. Government Manual*
- *Federal Staff Directory*
- *Federal Yellow Book*
- *Taylor's Encyclopedia of Government Officials*
- *Washington Information Directory*
- *Directory of Federal Executives*
- *Washington 86: A Comprehensive Directory of the Key Institutions and Leaders of the National Capital Area*

The Office of Personnel Management and the U.S. Government Printing Office publish several informative brochures and books you may wish to examine. OPM produces 22 brochures called "FED FACTS Pamphlets" on various aspects of the Federal personnel system. The ones most relevant to your job search include:

- FED FACTS 2: "Political Activity of Federal Employees"
- FED FACTS 3: "The Civil Service Retirement System"
- FED FACTS 5: "The Federal Merit Promotion Policy"
- FED FACTS 7: "The Federal Wage System"
- FED FACTS 13: "Reductions in Force in Federal Agencies"

- FED FACTS 15: "Federal Labor Relations"
- FED FACTS 16: "Pay Under the General Schedule"
- FED FACTS 17: "The Cost of Living Allowance of Federal Employees"
- FED FACTS 18: "The Intergovernmental Mobility Program"
- FED FACTS 19: "How Your GS Job is Classified"
- FED FACTS 20: "Merit System Principles and Prohibited Personal Practices"

Each brochure costs either $1.75 or $2.00, depending on the particular FED FACT. OPM distributes them free if you happen to be in one of their information offices. It may be more convenient for you to purchase them directly from the Superintendent of Documents, U.S. Government Printing Office, Washington, DC 20402. If you write to them, also ask for their catalog of publications on government jobs and personnel. You may, for example, want to purchase a telephone directory on a particular agency that interests you. Remember, the U.S. Government Printing Office is the largest publisher, printer, and bookstore in the country. It produces a wealth of reports and useful guides on the various functions and agencies of government. And they are eager to sell their publications!

You should also write or call the personnel offices of the agency that interests you. Many of these officials have publications describing various jobs and careers. For example, the U.S. Immigration and Naturalization Service of the Department of Justice publishes a question and answer brochure on becoming a Border Patrol Agent. The brochure addresses the major concerns of most applicants: duties, qualifications, conditions of employment, written and medical examinations, appointments, training, uniforms, career advancement, benefits, and special retirement.

Another useful source of information on Federal jobs are the numerous Federal and postal employee unions and organizations. Names, addresses, and telephone numbers of these groups are included in Appendix I. Additional information on these and other related associations is found in the *Encyclopedia of Associations*.

Chapter Seventeen
WRITING AN EFFECTIVE SF-171

The Personal Qualifications Statement, or Standard Form 171 (SF-171), is to the Federal government what application forms and resumes are to the rest of the work world. It is the single most important document and marketing tool in the Federal hiring process. How well you both complete and distribute this form will largely determine how well you do in the Federal job market.

Writing and distributing an effective SF-171 requires important skills you can learn. This chapter provides a basic orientation on how to develop and manage your SF-171. Keep in mind that a well written SF-171 becomes effective only when it is distributed in the proper channels. Indeed, many people learn to write an outstanding SF-171, but they fail to effectively market it to the proper individuals and agencies.

As this book went to press, the Office of Personnel Management had begun to introduce a new version of the SF-171. It was printed but not generally available. Individuals were instructed to use the previous form until present supplies are depleted.

While not substantially different from the previous version, the new SF-171 form does have a few stylistic and content changes you need to observe. Consequently, our major discussion of the SF-171 focuses on the form currently in use. In addition, we include a special section on changes found on the new form.

In order to fully benefit from the following discussion, you need to have a copy of the SF-171 in front of you. You can get a copy by contacting the personnel office of any Federal agency or one of OPM's Federal Job Information Centers. Copies of the form also are included in several resources mentioned at the end of this chapter. We do not include a copy of this form because the print is too small to further reduce for this book.

THE DOCUMENT

The SF-171 can be intimidating and less than revealing of your qualifications — but only if you let it become so. Criticized for being too long, and not particularly informative, and occasionally revised to be less intimidating, the basic SF-171 lives on nonetheless.

Despite numerous criticisms aimed at this form, you need to turn what is potentially a negative situation into a positive by restructuring the form to clearly communicate your qualifications. It should perform the same central function as a resume — advertise you for a position. If you complete the SF-171 according to our advice, you will overcome one of the major obstacles to acquiring Federal employment.

The SF-171 is a four-page application form. It appears deceptively simple to complete, but it is an extremely complex document for those who know its value. Many people pay $100 or more to have professionals assist them in completing the SF-171. Others are able to complete the form in less than an hour by filling in the blanks in long hand. Those who know the importance of the SF-171 should spend hours — indeed a few days — in putting together an effective SF-171.

The SF-171 is more than just a statement of your qualifications. It is the basis for determining several important outcomes in the Federal hiring process:

- *It is the basis for determining your eligibility for specific positions:* The SF-171 is examined and given a point rating by OPM examiners. This Notice of Rating is then matched with the minimum ratings required for specific positions. Once you have your rating, you are free to apply for Federal positions.

- *It must accompany your application for positions with specific agencies:* In addition to the OPM evaluation, agency evaluation panels carefully examine the SF-171 when ranking eligible candidates.

- *It determines if you will be called for an interview:* Like a resume, the SF-171 advertises your qualifications to potential employers. It is your single most important calling card for getting a job interview.

- *It determines your pay level if you are hired:* Since the SF-171 determines your rating, it also determines in which grade step you will be placed on the salary scale.

Not all positions require the SF-171. Each job vacancy announcement will specify what application forms need to be submitted to OPM or the agency. In the case of Wage Grade jobs, applicants complete a job interest card or a special application form rather than the SF-171. However, most government positions will require the SF-171.

KEY PRINCIPLES

When completing your SF-171, keep in mind that you are writing to three different audiences which have three separate goals:

Audiences	*Goals*
1. OPM examiners	Set eligibility rating
2. Agency evaluators	Rank candidates
3. Hiring officials	Select candidate for an interview

Unlike a resume, which is aimed at getting the interview, your SF-171 must fulfill all the other requirements before having its final impact — receive a call for an interview and if hired largely determine pay.

How, then, do you write an effective SF-171 which will satisfy all audiences? Several basic principles should be followed when completing this document:

PRINCIPLES FOR COMPLETING THE SF-171

1. *Read the instructions carefully:* A simple and obvious principle, but many people forget the simple and obvious and end up making costly mistakes.

2. *Type the form:* A typed form communicates a certain degree of professionalism. Be sure your typing is neat

and clean.

3. *Draft your SF-171:* Develop work sheets for each section. Only after condensing your data base from these sheets should you complete a final copy.

4. *Develop a master copy:* Leave items 1, 2, 13, signature, and date blank. You will complete these items when you actually submit a copy of your SF-171 for a particular position. Never sign your original copy.

5. *Complete all blanks:* Unanswered blanks mean incomplete applications and raise negative questions. If a question does not pertain to you, write in "N/A" (Not Applicable) rather than leave it blank.

6. *Customize several items by attaching continuation or add-on sheets:* Especially customize the most important items for a rating — 21 and 22 on "Experience" and "Special Qualifications."

7. *Be concise and well organized:* A well organized SF-171 should not run more than 10 pages. Edit your writing so that each word counts.

8. *Use a good writing style:* Use the active voice and action verbs to describe your skills, abilities, and accomplishments. Your descriptions should be easy and interesting to read.

9. *Focus on your accomplishments when describing your work experience:* Formal duties and responsibilities are normally found in position descriptions and they are important to rating your SF-171. However, you should also go one step further by stating specific accomplishments that go beyond the formal duties and responsibilities.

10. *Include relevant volunteer experience:* If this experience relates to the job you are applying for, include it in a separate experience block (Item 21).

11. *Check your spelling, grammar, and neatness:* Your SF-171 should be perfect in every way possible. Spell-

ing and grammatical mistakes communicate negative
messages to employers.

12 *Emphasize the most important information:* You can
emphasize by putting the most important information
first, underline, capitalize, or bullet items. Avoid
excessive use of such emphasizing devices.

There are two keys to developing an effective SF-171. First,
you should customize the SF-171 beyond its standard four-page
format. Second, you should use a functional-skills vocabulary in
describing your experience. If you describe your experience on the
SF-171 in the same manner you describe it in a resume, your SF-171
will conform to the best advice available on how to write an effective SF-171.

There are two ways to customize your SF-171. One method is
to expand the length of each section (experience, honors, special
qualifications) in order to provide more detailed information. You
do this by clipping and pasting the section headings to separate
sheets of paper or purchase customized forms. Copies of these new
sheets become customized sections of your SF-171. Complete these
expanded sections in as much detail as possible. The "Experience"
section is the most critical, and it requires a great deal of time and
effort.

Another way to customize your SF-171 is to rewrite the "Experience" sections to respond specifically to the qualifications outlined in a particular job vacancy announcement. Read each announcement carefully and then use similar skills terminology in your
SF-171. If you customize your SF-171 in this manner, you must
retype the "Experience" sections for each vacancy announcement.
While this is a time consuming process, it is the most effective
approach for addressing the exact qualifications for a particular
position.

COMPLETING THE FORM

Let's critically examine each item on the SF-171. We start at
the top and work through each item, including how to customize
the various sections.

ITEM 1: *Kind of Position You Are Filing For.*

Leave this item blank on your original form. Complete it with the appropriate announcement number and job title when you submit a copy of your form in response to a particular announcement.

ITEM 2: *Options For Which You Will Be Considered.*

Also leave this item blank. You won't know the answer to this question until you respond to a particular announcement which actually lists the options or you may elect to put in a general qualifying statement, such as "All" or "Any."

ITEMS 3 and 4: Home and Work Phone.

Self-explanatory. While you may not wish to be contacted at work, most people in personnel are discrete when contacting individuals with their present employers. Include both numbers. A simple rule to follow is "don't play hard to get."

ITEM 5: *Sex.*

Self-explanatory. Put an "X" in the appropriate gender box.

ITEM 6: *Other Last Names Ever Used.*

Include names you have used in previous jobs so your previous employment history can be verified. It also is a good idea to note in the "Experience" section (Item 21) the name you used while employed in a particular organization. Note the name you used in parenthesis at the bottom of the first section on "Name and address of employer's organization" (NOTE: employed under name of _____)

ITEM 7-10: Name, Address, Birthplace, Birth Date, and Social Security Number.

Self-explanatory, except Item 7 is not printed on the form. Use your current address or one which is your most permanent or predictable one for receiving mail. If you change your address after submitting the SF-171, make sure you give your new address to OPM and the agency.

ITEM 11: *Previous Federal Government Civilian Employment.*

Self-explanatory. It asks for your highest grade, classification series, job title, and inclusive dates. Be sure to include *all* of this information. An example would be: GS-470-11, Soil Scientist. When in doubt, contact your former agency personnel office for the details. If no previous Federal experience, enter "N/A."

ITEM 12: *Current Application Status.*

If you previously submitted an SF-171 and still have a current rating, complete all of the requested information. You may wish to attach a photocopy of your rating. If you do not have a rating, enter "N/A" (Not Applicable). This particular item is more important than it appears, especially when you begin marketing yourself via the SF-171 to agencies. We will have more to say about this item in the next section on marketing strategies.

ITEM 13: *Lowest Pay or Grade You Will Accept.*

Leave this item blank on your original. Include this information on the copy you submit to OPM and the agency. Specific information is included on the vacancy announcements of agencies. OPM is more concerned with judging your eligibility within a certain range. You will be considered for the pay and grade levels you specify as well as any above those levels. You will not be considered for lower levels unless you include them in your range. So you must decide on what lower ranges you are willing to consider.

ITEM 14: *Availability.*

> Leave this item blank on your original but specify a date — month and year — on the copies you submit to OPM and the agencies.

ITEM 15: *Temporary Employment.*

> You must decide if you are willing to take temporary employment. You do not receive the same benefits as full-time, permanent employees. However, many Federal employees got their foot in the door by stating "Yes" to this question. You can always say "Yes" and then change your mind when you see exactly what "Temporary" means for a specific position. This is not a commitment to temporary employment. Rather, it is an indication of your willingness to be flexible. You can always say no if offered a temporary position!

ITEM 16: *Consideration For Employment With Other Public Organizations.*

> This is your decision. You may want to leave this blank on your original copy and complete it when you submit the form to OPM and the agencies.

ITEM 17: *Location of Employment.*

> This is up to you. The more open you are to options, the more you will be considered for jobs in different locations. However, if you only want to work in the Washington, D.C. Metropolitan area or in Hawaii, specify these locations in the appropriate blank and boxes.

ITEM 18: *Willingness to Travel Overnight.*

> This is up to you. Some government jobs require travel. Specify the degree to which you will put up with extensive travel.

ITEM 19: *Part-Time Positions.*

Similar to Item 15, this is your decision. Part-time positions are ideal for many people. For others, part-time positions are a foot in the door.

ITEM 20: *Veteran Preference.*

Nearly 50 percent of all male Federal employees are former veterans who receive a 5 to 10 point advantage in their eligibility ratings. Spouses, widows(ers), and mothers of veterans also receive preference under this category. Be sure to complete the requested information if you are eligible for this preference. If you claim a 10-point preference, you will need to complete and attach Standard Form 15 and other required documentation as specified in this form.

ITEM 21: *Experience.*

This is the most important section of the SF-171. At this point you need to customize the form. While examiners will carefully examine each section of Item 21, the form allows you to describe three positions (A, B, C) and provides 1 1/4 inches of space to describe your duties, responsibilities, and accomplishments. If you provide this information using only the space allotted, you will do poorly on your rating.

It is perfectly acceptable — indeed expected at the agency and program level — for you to re-work this section of the SF-171. However, OPM examiners are not that pleased since they review over 2 million of these forms each year! But they will not discriminate against you for being so thorough and enterprising.

Customizing involves two types of activities, one physical, another analytical. The physical part requires clipping and pasting the original form onto continuation sheets or purchasing customized forms available through private sources identified in the resource section of this chapter. Your general rule of thumb should be to expand your most recent position (A) to a full one to two-page customized form. Your second most recent position should be put on a one-half to full-page customized form. All other positions should be described in at least one-half page. Positions of more than 15 years ago can be summarized under a single category on one-half page. Insert these continuation sheets between pages 2 and 3 of the SF-171. Make sure that this customizing does not result in an SF-171 of more than 10 pages!

The second customizing activity involves tailoring your work experience descriptions to the specific vacancy announcements and position descriptions. The two most important sources for doing this are:

- *OPM's X-118 Handbook.* Available through the FJIC's, this book details the experience required for various positions. Examiners use this book and thus relate well to its language. You should look at this book to get the proper language to use in your descriptions.

- *Vacancy announcements.* These listings detail the experience and skills required. Examine them carefully and try to pull as much as possible from your past work experience that directly relates to the requested qualifications. The more you can write your descriptions around the exact specifications for the positions, the better your chances of receiving a high rating and ranking.

This is not the time and place to engage in creative writing or throw functional skills language into this section in hopes that you can cover your lack of experience and skills. OPM and hiring agencies want the details and content — not the fluff that often appears on functional resumes. Use powerful action verbs and skills language, but do so around specific duties, responsibilities, and accomplishments. In the end, this section of your SF-171 should approximate an improved chronological resume. If you don't have the requisite experience and skills, don't waste your time and others' by applying for a position beyond your level of experience. A "can do" attitude is okay and should be encouraged, but it runs into the hard reality of evaluation criteria which is specified in terms of duties, responsibilities, accomplishments, and salaries. For example, a general responsibility may be "supervised division reports." This can mean anything from "typed and filed two 10-page reports each month" to "supervised a staff of 20 researchers and writers in producing five 100-page reports each month." There is a difference especially when the one individual's salary was $16,000 a year and the other's was $45,000 a year, even though both supervisory jobs sound the same at a highly generalized level. Evaluators want to know the details of your experience.

The actual writing of this section should follow the same basic advice we gave in Chapter Seven on writing combination and improved chronological resumes. However, a few adjustments are necessary:

- *Start with your most recent job and work in reverse chronological order:* You should include voluntary work relevant to your rating.
- *Give inclusive employment dates.* Account for any periods of unemployment exceeding three months. Hopefully, you were doing something relevant to your knowledge and skills.
- *Provide as much salary data as possible.* This is one of the most important pieces of data on your form. The more you can report, the better your rating. The figure you state can be above your base salary. Annualize special fees or commissions. If you are a former educator or a Peace Corps Volunteer, you need to do some creative thinking on how to get your salary figure up to a level more commensurate with your abilities.

If not, the Federal rating system will discriminate against you. You can avoid some discrimination by engaging in creative arithmetic. Use your last salary and add 10 percent to get your current value. Obviously Peace Corps Volunteers and teachers have a problem with this system in terms of getting ahead! For example, you may have made $18,000 a year as an educator, but your skill level should be $38,000 with the Federal government. If you put down $18,000 as your last salary, you will probably be considered for a $24,000 level Federal job, at best. Try to annualize your teaching salary by including other income, such as a $200 a day consulting fee, to get a more accurate picture of your worth. Your salary figure will be held against you if you don't do something about it. But be sure you can document these figures.

- *Give an appropriate reason for leaving.* In the "Reason for leaving" box, follow a general rule for all aspects of your job search: be honest but not stupid. If you had trouble on your last job, were fired, or resigned because you hated the job, put in a positive statement such as "further career advancement." That is most likely true and it doesn't raise unnecessary questions about your abilities.
- *Provide a positive position title.* You can be creative in this box. Many positions do not have formal titles or the titles are somewhat negative or misleading. If this is your case, create a title which most accurately reflects your work in a positive manner. If you were a housewife, you may want to include this as a position title or change it to "Volunteer" if you were heavily involved in volunteer work. In your "description of work" section, be sure to identify the details of your volunteer work, especially those duties, responsibilities, and accomplishments that directly relate to the

position you seek. Always avoid stating "unemployed." This signifies doing nothing when, in fact, you may have been doing a great deal during a period of unemployment. "Housewife," "house husband," or "volunteer" are always more preferable choices for positions than "unemployed."

ITEM 22: *Special Qualifications and Skills*

This category stresses your initiative, creativity, leadership, and communication skills. You may also wish to use continuation sheets for this box since you have less than one inch of space for presenting this information. You should include the following data in this section:

1. *Special skills:* What other things can you do that did not appear in the job descriptions of Item 22? If you have computer, typing, or special communication skills, include these since they are useful in most work settings.
2. *Patents and inventions:* Include creations that would qualify as inventions or were patented.
3. *Publications:* List complete bibliographic information on your most important publications, publishing activities, or writing experience. This category enables you to specify your written communication abilities — a highly sought after skill in many organizations.
4. *Public speaking experience:* List what you have done, with whom, where, and when. If your list is extremely long, summarize the speeches into categories.
5. *Membership in professional or scientific societies.* Give names of organizations as well as the dates and extent of your participation, especially if you played significant leadership and management roles.
6. *Hobbies:* Include only serious, job related hobbies. Revealing that you play "Trivial

Pursuit" does not strengthen your SF-171 or your image!

7.   *Other.* Anything you can think of that will strengthen your qualifications. It should be a skill or product outcome. Remember, communication and analytical skills are some of the most important ones you can emphasize.

This section also asks you to include any special licenses or certifications you received (B) along with the dates and licensing authority (C). A final section asks you to specify your level of typing and shorthand skills (D). Complete all of these sections even though they may not seem relevant to your career goals.

ITEM 23:   *Education*

This section is self-explanatory in terms of specifying schools attended, majors, credit hours, and degrees received. However, be as thorough as possible since education does count a great deal in the evaluation process. You may want to attach a continuation sheet or complete OPM Form 1170/17 in lieu of completing this cramped section. But be sure to refer the reader to the attachment with a statement such as "See continuation sheet 2.3" or "See attached Form 1170/17."

Section G on "Other schools or training" should include all types of educational experiences besides those already listed. Include workshops, correspondence courses, military training, and other types of training experiences which relate to your qualifications and skills for the job you seek. Avoid inclusion of educational experiences unrelated to your goals. Be sure to include names, dates, places, hours, certifications, and other pertinent information.

ITEM 24:   *Honors, Awards, and Fellowships.*

Again, you may need to customize this section

with another continuation sheet. Include details on all official recognition you have received for your talent and accomplishments.

ITEM 25: *Foreign Languages.*

Complete the blanks for specifying your level of foreign language proficiency. Be sure to describe how you acquired your language skills and your experience in Item 34.

ITEM 26: *References.*

List three references, including their addresses, phone numbers and occupations. Be selective by choosing only those who can speak highly of you and who are aware that you are applying for a job. It would be good to first call them, inform them of your plans, and ask for their permission before including their names in this section.

ITEMS 27-33: *Citizenship, Convictions, Termination, and Retirement Benefits.*

Self-explanatory. Check the "Yes" or "No" box depending on which is true in your case.

ITEM 34: *Detailed Answers*

Include details on any previous items requiring clarifications. Be sure to explain your language training and use (from Item 25). If you answered "No" to Item 27 or "Yes" to Items 28-33, you must provide details in this section.

You must sign and date the SF-171 at the end of page four. But do not sign and date your original copy. When you submit a copy of your form, you must provide an original signature — not a photocopy.

Once you have finished drafting each section of the form, try to condense it as much as possible without sacrificing content and appearance. Use bullets, caps, and underlining for emphasis — but don't overdo these devices. Neatly type each section — single-spaced with eye-pleasing margins and subheadings.

The continuation sheets must be inserted between pages 2 and 3 of the form. Make sure you refer to the appropriate continuation sheet for each item requiring this additional information. In addition, the continuation sheets must be the size of the original form or in an 8 1/2 x 11 size. At the top of each continuation sheet include your name, birth date, and announcement number or position title. Put page numbers in the bottom left hand corner starting with 2.1 and running them sequentially to 2.5 or 2.6. But no more than a total of 10 pages of which six would be continuation sheets.

Pay particular attention to the details of completing this form. Failure to observe any of the rules may result in lowering your rating as well as delaying your application. Forgetting simple things, like dating the form, signing it in ink, or putting your name on the continuation sheets, can negate what is otherwise an outstanding SF-171.

DISTRIBUTION

Now that you have created an excellent SF-171, what do you do next? You must get it into the proper hands for evaluation, rating, and screening. Hopefully your SF-171 will be your ticket to job interviews and a job offer.

Your SF-171 should be targeted toward three audiences:

1. *OPM evaluators:* They review the form and give you a Notice of Rating which permits you to apply for certain level positions within agencies. Without this rating, agencies cannot process your application. So your first step is to get your rating through OPM.

2. *Agency personnel offices:* They receive your SF-171 as well as other required materials as requested in the agency's job vacancy announcement. The personnel office then evaluates your application package to determine your eligibility and ranking. When you send your SF-171 to an agency, you must complete Items 1, 2, and 13 — the position title, number, options, and salary — which appear on the vacancy announcement. Without this information, the agency personnel office cannot process your application.

3. *Program office:* The program office receives the application packages and selects those who should be

contacted for interviews. Normally at least the three top candidates will be interviewed. The program office may request a particular candidate by name if the application was properly submitted and meets the criteria for eligibility.

After receiving your OPM Notice of Rating, you have two distribution choices. First, as you monitor job vacancy announcements, you submit your SF-171 and other required forms and wait. It is not necessary — indeed, not recommended — to send a cover letter or resume along with your package. As you monitor, submit, and wait, you may want to experiment with other distribution approaches.

The second major distribution approach is to shotgun your SF-171 to many agencies. This is a direct-mail game similar to scattering resumes to unknown organizations and individuals. Don't expect more than a normal direct-mail response rate — 2 percent. If you elect to go this route, enclose a cover letter along with your SF-171. Always address it to a particular individual in a program office — not to someone in the personnel office. Hopefully, you identified these names through your agency research efforts. You may get lucky and uncover an impending vacancy with this approach. At the same time, you may help employees improve their SF-171s by sending them an unsolicited example of an outstanding SF-171!

Whichever method you choose, be sure to send your SF-171 in a 9 x 12 envelope rather than in a No. 10 business envelope. A nice flat SF-171 is always preferable to one that was folded.

EVALUATING YOUR PRODUCT

Once you have completed your SF-171 and are ready to distribute it, you should evaluate it. Look over your SF-171 in relation to the evaluation criteria in Table 17.

TABLE 17

Evaluation of SF-171 Production and Distribution

Characteristic	Presence		Actions Needed
	Yes	No	
Overall Appearance			
1. Neat			
2. Easy to read			
3. Looks professional			
4. Typed			
5. Reproduced as clean, clear, and straight copies			
Continuation Sheets			
1. In proper order between pages 2 and 3			
2. Name, birth date, position at top			
3. Page numbers at bottom left			
4. Referenced in appropriate items			
5. Same size paper as SF-171			
Individual Items			
1. Items 1, 2, 13, signature, and date left blank on original			
2. All other items completed in detail			
3. Not more than 10 pages in length			
Writing Style			
1. Concise			
2. Uses subheadings			
3. Emphasizes most important information			

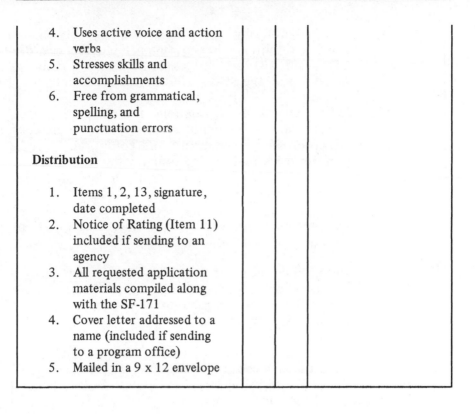

4. Uses active voice and action verbs
5. Stresses skills and accomplishments
6. Free from grammatical, spelling, and punctuation errors

Distribution

1. Items 1, 2, 13, signature, date completed
2. Notice of Rating (Item 11) included if sending to an agency
3. All requested application materials compiled along with the SF-171
4. Cover letter addressed to a name (included if sending to a program office)
5. Mailed in a 9 x 12 envelope

THE NEW SF-171

Beginning in 1986 the Office of Personnel Management began phasing in a revised version of the SF-171 we just discussed. Once present supplies of the old form are exhausted, the new SF-171 will be used by all applicants. In the meantime, either version can be used, depending on which one is available through agency personnel offices, the FJICs, and the General Services Administration — the agency responsible for issuing the form. As a result, different agencies will use different forms during this transition period. We suggest using the newest form if you can obtain a copy.

The new SF-171 differs from the previous form in five respects:

1. The name of the form has been changed from "Personal Qualifications Statement" to "Application For Federal Employment."

2. The new form is more inviting to read because of

changes in format, graphic design, type style, and color. Exhibiting a less cluttered look, the new SF-171 again runs four pages but includes a fifth optional page — the SF-171A Continuation Sheet.

3. Instructions and explanations for completing each section have been simplified in response to previous criticisms of its complexity and confusion. In addition, most instructions are found within each relevant section thus making it easier to follow for completing each section.

4. Less information is requested since two questions have been dropped as unnecessary.

5. A continuation sheet — the SF-171A — is built into the form for including information on "Work Experience." This was designed to eliminate the need to request additional forms.

Most of the changes are stylistic in nature. In issuing this new form, OPM has attempted to both give the form a more "modern" look and deal with a few recurring criticisms of past forms. The new form is divided into 10 major sections:

- General Information
- Availability
- Military Service and Veteran Preference
- Work Experience
- Education
- Special Skills, Accomplishments and Awards
- References
- Background Information
- Additional Space For Answers
- Signature, Certification, and Release of Information

In addition, the numbering of items within each section has changed. Therefore, the item-by-item discussion in the previous section must be aligned with a different numbering system in the new SF-171. Table 18 summarizes the item changes:

--- **TABLE 18** ---

ITEM DIFFERENCES BETWEEN OLD AND NEW SF-171

Items in Old SF-171	Equivalent Items in New SF-171
1. Kind of position	1. What kind of job are you applying for?
2. Options	2. Which jobs are you applying for?
3. Home phone	8. same
4. Work phone	9. same
5. Sex	7. same
(7.) Name, address	5. same
9. Birth date	4. same
10. Social security number	3. same
11. Federal government employee status	10. same
12. Application with OPM	11. same
14. Availability date	12. same
15. Temporary work	16. same
17. Work location preference	14. same
18. Willingness to travel	17. same
19. Part-time work	15. Willingness to work different hours
20. Veterans preference	18-22. same
21. Work experience (room for 3 positions, 8 lines each)	23-24. Under "Work Experience section (room for 2 positions, 13 lines each, plus continuation sheet — SF-171A — for 2 additional positions with 13 lines each)
22. Special qualifications and skills	32-34. same
23. Educational background	25-31. same
24. Honors, awards, fellowships	36. same
25. Languages	35. same
26. References	37. same
27-33. "Yes/No" background questions	38-46. same
34. Additional answers	47. same
--- Signature	48. same
--- Date	49. same

Some changes have occurred for a few items. For example, two items have been dropped from the old to the new SF-171 since they took up space and generated extraneous information:

    Item 8:   Birthplace
    Item 16:   Interest in other government and public employ-
                 ment (local, state, congressional, international)

Two other items remain under the same numbering system:

    Item 6:   Other names used
    Item 13:   Lowest pay you will accept

The only other content changes occur among the "Yes/No" questions of the fourth page. Item 28, 29, and 30 of the old form specified a five-year time frame for indicating whether one was fired from previous jobs and an exclusion of reportability for fines of $50 or less for traffic offenses. Under the new form, the time frame has been increased to 10 years and fines of $100 or less must be reported.

One other feature of this new form needs to be addressed. While OPM has included the customized SF-171A with this form to indicate additional positions under "Work Experience" (Item 24), this new inclusion is not a significant improvement for many Federal job seekers. In fact, it only permits you to describe a total of four positions with 13 lines for each work description. While this is an improvement over the old form, which provided room for only three positions with eight lines for each work description, you still need more space to adequately communicate your skills and accomplishments relevant to each job. Therefore, you also should customize this new form according to our previous discussion, even though the SF-171A is attached to the SF-171. The information required in the "Work Experience" section is identical to that requested in the "Experience" section (Item 21) of the old SF-171.

Following our guidelines, you should have a sound SF-171 that presents your best skills, abilities, and accomplishments to potential Federal employers. Your original SF-171 should be the baseline from which you continue to revise, update, and strengthen your SF-171. Once you land the job you want, you should revise your SF-171 each year. After all, you need to use the SF-171 to advance on the job.

USEFUL RESOURCES

Several private firms provide training seminars on how to write an effective SF-171. In the Washington D.C. Metropolitan area, most of these seminars are listed in the Monday business supplement of the *Washington Post* under the weekly career section of the business calendar. Two open universities in Washington, D.C. occasionally offer short (2-3 hour) courses for under $25 on completing the SF-171. Contact them for their most recent schedule of classes: First Class (Tel. 202/797-5102) and Open University (Tel. 202/966-9606).

The Federal Research Service, Inc. — a well established and highly reputable organization — regularly schedules an SF-171 seminar entitled "Top Notch SF-171 Prep: Key to Federal Jobs and Advancement" during the spring and fall of each year. The cost for this seminar is $97.00. For more information, write or call:

> Federal Research Service, Inc.
> P. O. Box 1059-W
> Vienna, VA 22180-1059
> Tel. 703/381-0200

Several good self-directed books also outline the mechanics of completing an effective SF-171. We enthusiastically recommend Patricia Wood's, *The 171 Reference Book* (Maynard, MA: Work Books, Inc.). Now in its third edition, this book represents the most thorough treatment of the SF-171. It provides step-by-step instructions, includes examples of both the old and new forms, and outlines good examples of effective SF-171s. Most importantly, it is written by someone who has been through the process and who demonstrates the street-smarts involved in writing for OPM evaluators and agency personnel and program offices. Patricia Wood also publishes *The 171 Writing Portfolio* and the *Expanded 171 Form* for those who do not wish to produce their own homemade customized continuation sheets. For information on training and production services directly related to *The 171 Reference Book*, contact:

> Patricia B. Wood and Kathryn Troutman
> The Resume Place, Inc.
> 818-18th St., NW, 6th Fl.
> Washington, DC 20006
> Tel. 202/737-8637

Another solid treatment of the SF-171 is included in Dave Waelde's *How to Get a Federal Job or Survive a RIF* (Washington, DC: FEDHELP Publications). Similar to Wood's book, Waelde walks through each section of the SF-171 offering sound advice on what to do and not to do. He includes worksheets and examples for completing the SF-171.

The Federal Research Service, Inc. also publishes two products which are useful for producing an effective SF-171. A brief booklet, *Federal Job Winner's Tips: Guide to the Federal Job Application* ($4.00), gives useful tips on completing the SF-171. Their *Federal Job Application Forms Kit* ($3.50) includes an SF-171, customized SF-171 pages, general purpose performance appraisals, education supplement forms, and a handy SF-171 preparation checklist.

The Federal Jobs Digest (325 Pennsylvania Avenue, SE, Washington, DC 20003, Tel. 800/824-5000) produces a *Federal Job Kit* which includes sample SF-171s, instructions, and continuation sheets. Individuals receive this kit when they subscribe to the *Federal Jobs Digest*.

A final useful resource is a new videotape on the SF-171 available through the *National Job Market*. The tape shows how to complete each section of the new SF-171. Selling for $71, the tape can be ordered by contacting:

> National Job Market
> P. O. Box 286
> Kensington, MD 20895
> Tel. 301/946-8910.

Chapter Eighteen

THE LEGISLATIVE BRANCH, CAPITOL HILL, AND THE JUDICIARY

The Federal legislative branch employs nearly 40,000 individuals; the Federal judiciary employs nearly 17,000. While the largest number of individuals work for Congress (19,806), nearly 20,000 individuals work for four legislative agencies: Architect of the Capitol (2,246), General Accounting Office (5,296), Government Printing Office (5,763), and the Library of Congress (5,308). Other legislative agencies include the Congressional Budget Office (200), Office of Technology Assessment (200), U.S. Botanic Gardens (60), and the Copyright Royalty Tribunal (7). The Supreme Court employs less than 400, but the remaining Federal courts employ over 16,000 individuals.

Legislative agencies generally follow similar formal recruitment procedures as executive agencies: position announcements, application forms, testing, eligibility lists, and interviews. However, being constitutionally separate from the executive branch, the legislative branch sets its own rules and regulations for recruitment and selection. While most executive agencies classify their positions according to the General Schedule and use OPM for determining eligibility and screening candidates, each legislative agency develops its own recruitment procedures separate from the GS Schedule and OPM operations. Furthermore, Congress uses its own recruitment procedures which are less structured and more personal in nature than recruitment in either executive or legislative agencies. The Federal

281

judiciary, however, is less structured; its hiring practices tend to follow a more personal approach commonly associated with jobs and careers in the legal profession.

This chapter outlines the basic principles for acquiring a job in two of the most overlooked areas of the Federal government — the legislative and judicial branches. It examines legislative agencies, congressional organizations, the Supreme Court, U.S. Courts, and supporting organizations.

LEGISLATIVE AGENCIES

The legislative branch maintains its own bureaucracy to perform general housekeeping functions (Architect of the Capitol), provide information for decision-making and dissemination purposes (Library of Congress and Government Printing Office), and check the executive branch (General Accounting Office). These agencies are relatively small in terms of personnel and budgets, but they offer numerous opportunities for enterprising job seekers.

Functions

The General Accounting Office (5,296 employees) performs important congressional oversight functions. It is responsible for conducting audits of Federal agencies and issuing reports on how to improve the efficiency and effectiveness of government. It checks to what degree agencies have spent funds allocated by Congress. In so doing, it employs hundreds of individuals with specialties in accounting, economics, and operations research.

The Library of Congress (5,308 employees) is Congresses' information arm as well as the nation's largest and most comprehensive library. It employs hundreds of librarians and subject matter specialists. The Congressional Research Service, for example, is organized to provide congressional committees with information and conduct specialized studies. The Federal Research Division is Congresses' equivalent to the CIA and the Defense Intelligence Agency.

The Government Printing Office (5,763 employees) is the government's central printer and bookstore. It daily prints all major documents, such as the *Congressional Record* and the *Federal Register*, as well as pamphlets, magazines, reports, directories, and books commissioned by individual agencies.

The Congressional Budget Office (200 employees) provides Congress with budgetary data, analyzes fiscal alternatives, conducts budgetary studies, and forecasts government spending. This office provides an important congressional check to similar functions performed by the Office of Management and Budget in the Executive Office of the President.

The Architect of the Capitol (2,246 employees) is responsible for the maintenance of all congressional buildings and grounds.

The United States Botanic Garden (60 employees) collects, cultivates, and grows a large variety of plants for public expeditions. It provides facilities for educational groups interested in the botanic garden.

The Office of Technology Assessment (200 employees) is one of the newest legislative agencies, founded in 1974. Its major role is to help Congress respond to the use of new technologies in society.

Recruitment

Each legislative agency recruits its own personnel. Consequently, you will need to contact each agency to learn their particular procedures for announcing vacancies and selecting personnel. For example, the General Accounting Office issues vacancy announcements through its Recruitment and Examination Branch (202/275-6185). In addition, it maintains a daily recorded message of job vacancies (202/275-6017).

The Library of Congress issues position vacancy announcements. If you want information on specific position vacancies, you can call the Recruitment and Placement Office at 202/287-5627; they will mail you the announcement. You can also walk into this office to get copies of current vacancy announcements.

The Government Printing Office has been operating under a hiring freeze since September 1981. While they used to have a recording of daily vacancies, this service has been discontinued. Contact the Employment Branch (202/275-2951) for information on vacancies.

The Congressional Budget Office provides job vacancy information by telephone (202/226-2621) or by visiting their Personnel and Security Office.

The U.S. Botanic Garden recruits its personnel through the Personnel Office of the Architect of the Capitol. Contact this office for vacancy announcements on both offices by calling 202/225-1231.

The Office of Technology Assessment normally collects resumes for individuals who are interested in working in this office. You can call their Personnel Office at 202/224-8713 for job vacancy information. However, you can send them a resume and cover letter at any time. The office normally circulates resumes among staff members and keeps them on file for one year.

The Copyright Royalty Tribunal is so small and specialized that it virtually has no job vacancies. While it is supposed to have five appointed commissioners, five confidential assistants, and one General Council, at present it only has three commissioners, three assistants, and a General Council. The only opportunities available are with the Volunteer Law Clerk Program — nonpaid internships for law students in the Washington, D.C. Metropolitan area.

Your best job search strategy with these legislative agencies will be to contact the personnel offices for job vacancy information, complete any application forms required, submit your resume, and make informal contacts with key agency personnel. Follow the same procedures we outlined for the informal job search process in executive agencies.

CAPITOL HILL

Finding a job with Congress requires an intimate knowledge of the congressional hiring process. Both the House and Senate maintain placement offices to primarily collect resumes. But the relatively unstructured and highly personal nature of the congressional hiring process requires knocking on doors, making personal contacts, and networking for jobs. However, before doing so, you must understand the structure of Congress and the various opportunities available. For, in the end, job hunting with Congress involves 535 personal staffs and over 300 committees and subcommittees which have their own hiring practices and salary structures. In this sense, Congress consists of over 835 separate hiring systems!

Congressional work is not for everyone. Each year approximately 40 percent of all congressional employees leave for other work. While much of the work is interesting and challenging, for many people it is stressful and financially unrewarding. Few people make congressional work a career. For many, it is an important stepping stone to other types of public service work. Yet, this high turnover rate provides numerous opportunities for enterprising individuals who wish to get some "Hill" experience.

Personal Staffs

Most congressional job opportunities are with personal staffs or committee staffs. There are 535 personal staffs — one each for each member of Congress (100 in the Senate and 435 in the House of

Representatives). Each of these staffs are divided into Washington-based staffs and home-district staffs. The normal Washington staff consists of 18 full-time and four part-time employees cramped into four to six small offices in the Russell Senate, Dirkson Senate, Rayburn House, Longworth House, or Cannon House Buildings as well as in Senate and House Annex buildings. The home-district offices are relatively small. They are usually staffed by political loyalists who are primarily oriented toward maintaining a positive image and promoting the reelection of their bosses. In the process of doing this, they respond to a great deal of constituent and interest group pressures.

The Washington-based personal staffs are organized to perform several functions for representatives. Research and subject matter specialists work closely with the Representative in the legislative arena. They follow legislation, conduct research, and draft bills. Other members of the staff function as ombudsmen, responding primarily to constituent inquiries and interest groups. And still others specialize in promoting the present image and future re-election of their boss and performing general housekeeping functions. An experienced Administrative Assistant, or AA, heads this staff.

Many personal staffs operate similar to boiler-room operations. Office space is extremely limited, work loads are unrealistic, most jobs are understaffed, and much of the work is reactive in nature. Little time is available for long-term planning and thoughtful analysis. A recent management study of congressional staffs conducted by the Congressional Management Foundation, for example, found congressional staffs in the following situation:

- Congressional workloads have grown dramatically:

  - A 2000% increase in constituent mail between 1970 and 1980; volume of mail from constituents increased from 14.6 million to 300 million letters.
  - An increase in bills introduced from 7,611 in the 84th Congress to 14,594 in the 96th.
  - An increase in roll-call votes from 147 in the 84th Congress to 1,834 in the 96th.
  - A 100% increase in both constituent casework and congressional hearings in this period — members' casework for constituents doubled to 10,000 cases per year.

- 60% of staff time is devoted to answering mail .

- The average congressional staffer is limited to 30 square feet of working space — compared to 64 square feet in the private sector.

- Congressional offices are extremely noisy, crowded with paper and files, and subject to occasional electrical failures.

- Average staff salaries are less than those with Federal executive agencies and in the private sector.

Given the nature of the work, working conditions, and salaries, no wonder there is a 40 percent turnover rate each year! Indeed, in the same study, 24 percent of congressional offices said they had difficulty in recruiting qualified staff members with Hill experience.

The Washington personal staffs are comprised of different types of individuals who perform various legislative and administrative-management functions. Figure 6 outlines the typical hierarchical structure of these personal staffs. The exact titles of staff members will vary from office to office. For example, a "Secretary" may sometimes be called a "Personal Aide" or a "Legislative Assistant" is called "Personal Staff."

The Congressional Management Foundation regularly monitors congressional staff positions, issues position descriptions, and conducts annual salary studies. Major congressional staff positions and salary information for 1985 included the following:

MAJOR PERSONAL STAFF POSITIONS

Administrative Assistant/Executive Assistant (AA): The key staff person who is responsible for overall office functions, supervision of projects, district and Hill politics and personnel. Average salary is $52,036.

Chief or Principal Legislative Assistant (LA): Directs legislative program or manages the Member's committee work, including committee prep work for hearings, witnesses, testimony, and legislative proposals, as well as general issues, oversight and initiatives, floor work, etc. Average salary is $35,098.

Legislative Assistant: Assists the LA with legislative matters. Average salary is $22,580.

Legislative Correspondent: Responsible for responding

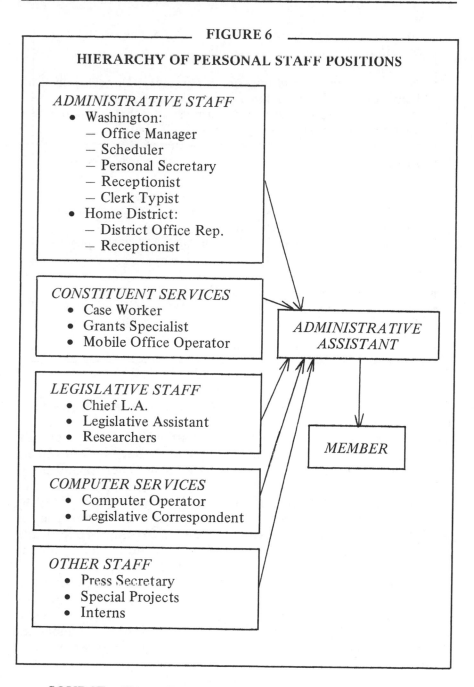

FIGURE 6

HIERARCHY OF PERSONAL STAFF POSITIONS

ADMINISTRATIVE STAFF
- Washington:
  - Office Manager
  - Scheduler
  - Personal Secretary
  - Receptionist
  - Clerk Typist
- Home District:
  - District Office Rep.
  - Receptionist

CONSTITUENT SERVICES
- Case Worker
- Grants Specialist
- Mobile Office Operator

LEGISLATIVE STAFF
- Chief L.A.
- Legislative Assistant
- Researchers

COMPUTER SERVICES
- Computer Operator
- Legislative Correspondent

OTHER STAFF
- Press Secretary
- Special Projects
- Interns

ADMINISTRATIVE ASSISTANT

MEMBER

SOURCE: Kerry Dumbaugh and Gary Serota, *Capitol Jobs* (Washington, D.C.; Tilden Press, 1982), p. 47.

to correspondence from constituents. Average salary is $16,559.

Press Assistant/Communications Director: Directs publicity for Member by issuing press releases, radio and T.V. spots, newsletters, newspaper columns, speeches, schedule announcements, etc. Average salary is $27,851.

Federal Grants Assistant/Projects Coordinator: Responsible for obtaining Federal financial assistance for the home district by helping local government entities and hometown applicants to obtain funds. Provides information on programs, deadlines, helpful agency officials, and general clarification of decisions. Average salary is $22,741.

Caseworker (Washington): Handles constituent casework: initial problem identification, contacts with agencies, follow-up letters, and case resolution. Average salary is $23,855.

The Administrative Assistant (AA) is a very prestigious position requiring a great deal of management and political expertise. This individual, as well as most other staff members, may or may not be from the Representative's district. Rather, staff members tend to be hired on the basis of their legislative expertise and political skills in Washington rather than on their loyalty to the district back home. The most important expertise involves the ability to conduct research, analyze, write, communicate, organize, meet deadlines, and work under extreme pressure. Writing is one of the most highly valued skills. You can quickly acquire subject matter expertise if you already possess these communication skills.

Salaries range from $10,000 to $68,700 a year. According to a 1985 salary survey conducted by the Congressional Management Foundation, the average House salary was $24,132 — just below the average white-collar Federal salary of $25,247. Table 19 summarizes the normal ranges and average salaries for various congressional staff positions:

TABLE 19		
SALARY RANGES AND AVERAGES FOR CONGRESSIONAL STAFF POSITIONS, 1985		
POSITION	NORMAL RANGE	AVERAGE
• Administrative Assistant	$40,000-68,000	$52,000
• Chief Legislative Assistant	$25,000-46,000	$35,000
• Legislative Assistant	$16,000-30,000	$23,000
• Legislative Correspondent	$14,000-20,000	$17,000
• Executive/Personal Secretary	$19,000-36,000	$22,000
• Office Manager	$20,000-38,000	$27,000
• Receptionist	$12,000-20,000	$16,000
• Press Assistant	$20,000-37,000	$28,000
• Research Assistant	$12,000-24,000	$16,000
• Systems Manager	$15,000-24,000	$18,000
• Computer Operator	$13,000-23,000	$18,000
• Federal Grants/Project Asst.	$16,000-33,000	$23,000
• Caseworker (Washington)	$14,000-32,000	$24,000
• Caseworker (District)	$14,000-24,000	$18,000
• Office Secretary (Washington)	$12,000-20,000	$17,000
• Office Secretary (District)	$10,000-20,000	$15,000
• Appointments Secretary	$16,000-28,000	$22,000
• District Representative	$21,000-45,000	$33,000
• District Aide	$10,000-28,000	$19,000
• Mobile Office Operator	$12,000-23,000	$17,000

The Congressional Management Foundation study also found that congressional staff benefits vary considerably from office to office as well as compared to Federal executive agencies and companies in the private sector. Less than half of congressional offices give their employees Cost of Living Adjustments (COLA's). Merit raise systems operate in 77 percent of congressional offices. Most employees receive at least 2-3 weeks vacation, and 43 percent of congressional offices provide additional vacation time for staff members who have worked in their offices for three years or more. Only 41 percent of congressional offices have a sick-leave policy, but 81 percent of the offices allow at least six weeks of paid maternity leave. Written staff policies are found in 61 percent of the congressional offices.

Getting a job on a Representative's personal staff requires a great deal of persistence, perseverance, and luck. While there is a high turnover rate, there also is high competition for these staff positions. Some offices will receive 1,000 resumes for a single vacancy. They regularly receive unsolicited resumes from job seekers who "shotgun" Capitol Hill with their paper qualifications. Many individuals wish to work for a particular Representative and thus they continually monitor staff vacancies in one office. Others are eager to work anywhere on the "Hill" so they can get experience to strengthen their resume and make important contacts.

While there are several congressional placement services available to help job seekers circulate their resumes, your best job search strategy will be to make personal contacts with key people on the Hill. You must plug into the word-of-mouth networks. The key person you need to know — the one who normally has the power to hire — is the Administrative Assistant. Above all, research individual staff offices to identify impending vacancies and to determine who has the power to hire.

Since you do not have to be from a Representative's district to get a personal staff job, 535 personal staffs offer similar job opportunities for you. Given the lack of a central personnel office for these staff positions, your most effective job search strategy will involve networking. You must contact individual offices to identify job vacancies and advertise your qualifications. The Washington-based positions are biased toward individuals who are physically present in Washington and who can make the necessary networking telephone calls and personal visits.

Your job search will go much easier if you know someone who knows a Representative. This person, in turn, can give you an introduction and recommendation. Using this contact, you can call a Representative's office and ask to speak to the AA or his or her assistant. You want to conduct several informational and referral interviews. Mention that Mr. or Ms. Smith *"recommended that I contact you concerning possible staff vacancies on Capitol Hill."* Ask for an appointment to discuss your interests. Be sure to make this a general request for information rather than ask for a job on the AA's staff. Chances are there are no vacancies at present, but the AA and other staff members often know about vacancies on others' staffs. When a vacancy does arise, it is frequently filled through word-of-mouth referrals. If you happen to be in the right place at the right time, you may be considered for the position.

The high turnover rate on Capitol Hill virtually assures that hiring will be done on ad hoc, emergency bases. The more you can get into the networks to let people know about your interests, skills, abilities, and availability, the better your chances of getting a job.

If you don't know someone to start networking on Capitol Hill, at least call your Representative. His or her staff should, as a courtesy to a constituent, get you started by providing you with useful advice on how to initiate a "Capitol Hill" search. They may give you names of people to talk to and review your resume for future reference. At the same time, you can use the "cold turkey" approach: call a Representative's office and point-blank ask *"Who makes the hiring decisions in this office?"* Once you get this information, try to get an appointment to see this person. If you can't get an appointment, try someone else on the staff who will at least give you information and job leads.

Since the job search on Capitol Hill primarily involves networking, it will take time, and you can expect numerous deadends and rejections. However, you must continue networking until your timing is right in relation to unexpected vacancies. Remember, competition for Capitol Hill positions is very keen. When you land a job, most likely it will occur unexpectedly because the whole hiring process is somewhat chaotic and unpredictable.

Committee Staff

The bulk of Congresses' work is done through various committees: standing, select, joint, and ad hoc. Standing committees are permanent committees with full time professional staffs. These staff members conduct research, write reports, and draft legislation for committee members. The committees also are subdivided into subcommittees which have their own staffs. Altogether, there are more than 300 committees and subcommittees in both the House and Senate. Table 20 identifies the major committees and subcommittees for the House.

TABLE 20

HOUSE COMMITTEES AND SUBCOMMITTEES

Standing Committees	Subcommittees

AGRICULTURE
- Conservation, Credit, and Rural Development
- Cotton, Rice, and Sugar
- Department Operations, Research, and Foreign Agriculture
- Domestic Marketing, Consumer Relations, and Nutrition
- Forests, Family Farms, and Energy
- Livestock, Dairy, and Poultry
- Tobacco and Peanuts
- Wheat, Soybeans, and Feed Grains

APPROPRIATIONS
- Agriculture, Rural Development, and Related Agencies
- Commerce, Justice, State, and Judiciary
- Defense
- District of Columbia
- Energy and Water Development
- Foreign Operations
- HUD — Independent Agencies
- Interior
- Labor-Health and Human Services-Education
- Legislative
- Military Construction
- Transportation
- Treasury-Postal Service-General Government

ARMED SERVICES
- Investigations
- Military Installations and Facilities
- Military Personnel and Compensation
- Procurement and Military Nuclear Systems
- Readiness
- Research and Development

	• Seapower and Strategic and Critical Materials
BANKING, FINANCE, AND URBAN AFFAIRS	• Consumer Affairs and Coinage
	• Domestic Monetary Policy
	• Economic Stabilization
	• Financial Institutions Supervision, Regulations and Insurance
	• General Oversight and Investigations
	• Housing and Community Development
	• International Development Institutions and Finance
	• International Finance, Trade, and Monetary Policy
BUDGET	(Task Forces rather than Subcommittees)
	• Budget Process
	• Community and Natural Resources
	• Defense and International Affairs
	• Economic Policy
	• Health
	• Human Services
	• Income Security
	• State and Local Government
DISTRICT OF COLUMBIA	• Fiscal Affairs and Health
	• Government Operations and Metropolitan Affairs
	• Judiciary and Education
EDUCATION AND LABOR	• Elementary, Secondary, and Vocational
	• Employment Opportunities
	• Health and Safety
	• Human Resources
	• Labor-Management Relations
	• Labor Standards
	• Postsecondary Education
	• Selection Education
ENERGY AND COMMERCE	• Commerce, Transportation, and Tourism
	• Energy Conservation and Power
	• Fossil and Synthetic Fuels
	• Health and the Environment
	• Oversight and Investigations

	• Telecommunications, Consumer Protection, and Finance
FOREIGN AFFAIRS	• Africa • Arms Control, International Security and Science • Asian and Pacific Affairs • Europe and the Middle East • Human Rights and International Organizations • International Economic Policy and Trade • International Operations • Western Hemisphere Affairs
GOVERNMENT OPERATIONS	• Commerce, Consumer, and Monetary Affairs • Employment and Housing • Environment, Energy, and Natural Resources • Government Activities and Transportation • Government Information, Justice, and Agriculture • Intergovernmental Relations and Human Resources • Legislation and National Security
HOUSE ADMINISTRATION	• Accounts • Elections • Office Systems • Personnel and Police • Procurement and Printing • Services
INTERIOR AND INSULAR AFFAIRS	• Energy and the Environment • General Oversight, Northwest Power, and Forest Management • Mining and Natural Resources • National Parks and Recreation • Public Lands • Water and Power Resources
JUDICIARY	• Administrative Law and Governmental Relations

- Civil and Constitutional Rights
- Courts, Civil Liberties, and the Administration of Justice
- Crime
- Criminal Justice
- Immigration, Refugees, and International Law
- Monopolies and Commercial Law

MERCHANT
MARINE AND
FISHERIES

- Coast Guard
- Fish and Wildlife
- Merchant Marine
- Oceanography
- Oversight and Investigations
- Panama Canal and Outer Continental Shelf

POST OFFICE
AND CIVIL
SERVICE

- Census and Population
- Civil Service
- Compensation and Employee Benefits
- Human Resources
- Investigations
- Postal Operations and Services
- Postal Personnel and Modernization

PUBLIC WORKS
AND
TRANSPORTATION

- Aviation
- Economic Development
- Investigations and Oversight
- Public Buildings and Grounds
- Surface Transportation
- Water Resources

RULES

- Rules of the House
- The Legislative Process

SCIENCE AND
TECHNOLOGY

- Energy Development and Applications
- Energy Research and Production
- Investigations and Oversight
- Natural Resources, Agriculture Research and Environment
- Science, Research and Technology
- Space Science and Applications
- Transportation, Aviation and Materials

SMALL BUSINESS	• Antitrust and Restraint of Trade Activities Affecting Small Business
	• Energy, Environment and Safety Issues Affecting Small Business
	• Export Opportunities and Special Small Business Problems
	• General Oversight and the Economy
	• SBA and SBIC Authority, Minority Enterprise and General Small Business Problems
	• Tax, Access to Equity Capital and Business Opportunities
STANDARDS OF OFFICIAL CONDUCT	no subcommittees
VETERANS' AFFAIRS	• Compensation, Pension, and Insurance
	• Education, Training and Employment
	• Hospitals and Health Care
	• Housing and Memorial Affairs
	• Oversight and Investigations
WAYS AND MEANS	• Health
	• Oversight
	• Public Assistance and Unemployment Compensation
	• Select Revenue Measures
	• Social Security
	• Trade

In addition, there are several House Select Committees with subcommittees and task forces:

- Select Committee on Aging
- Select Committee on Children, Youth, and Families
- Select Committee on Hunger
- Permanent Select Committee on Intelligence
- Select Committee on Narcotics Abuse and Control

The Senate has similar committees, subcommittees, and task forces. Most are counterparts to the House organizations.

Committee and subcommittee work is both interesting and hectic. Many staff members receive a great deal of job satisfaction because they help formulate important legislation. At the same time, these jobs involve long hours attendant with unrealistic work loads and deadlines.

Since each committee and subcommittee focuses on a particular policy area, many of these professional positions require highly qualified subject matter specialists. While many members of personal staffs are young and inexperienced generalists, in contrast, committee and subcommittee staff members tend to be older and experienced specialists. Committee and subcommittee staff positions also tend to pay better than personal staff positions.

Similar to finding a job on a personal staff, getting a job on a committee or subcommittee staff requires a great deal of networking, persistence, and perseverance. There are no formal hiring procedures, and hiring practices will differ from one committee to another. Therefore, you need to do a great deal of research on each committee and subcommittee in determining the best job search strategies.

Professionalism, along with politics, play key roles in getting committee and subcommittee positions. The most important hiring individual is the Chair of the committee or subcommittee. If the Chair is a Democrat, the committee and subcommittee staff members will most likely be Democrats. If the chair shifts from a Democrat to a Republican, the staff too will change. Therefore, entry into these positions begins with the Chair of the committee or subcommittee.

When conducting a job search with these committees and subcommittees, it is best to start with the committee or subcommittee chairperson's AA. This individual usually will be responsible for staffing his or her bosses' committee or subcommittee. Use a similar networking approach as you would use in landing a personal staff position. Research the committee or subcommittee, try to get a contact to the Chair, contact the AA for an informational interview, and request information, advice, and referrals to this Representative's committees or subcommittees. If you have sufficient subject matter expertise, are persistent, and indicate a political preference, you will be in a strong position for landing one of these jobs.

Changing the Guard

One of the best times to conduct a "Capitol Hill" job search is immediately following a congressional election. Newly elected members need to quickly form a staff in Washington. Should House and Senate majority control shift from one political party to another, numerous job vacancies will arise in the various committees and subcommittees. If you closely monitor congressional elections and identify newly elected members, you will locate individuals who have immediate staffing needs. Although they will bring a few of their district-level campaign workers and loyalists to Washington for key staff positions, they must recruit other staffers from among the pool of applicants based in Washington.

Your best strategy is to call the newly elected Representative's office as soon as you learn he or she has been elected. Your goal should be to arrange an interview rather than send a resume. After all, the Representative may receive hundreds of unsolicited resumes from past and present Capitol Hill staffers who are either losing their jobs because of election defeat or are looking for greener, and less stressful, pastures.

USEFUL RESOURCES

Several useful resources are available to guide you through the congressional maze. You should begin by reading a wonderful insider's guide to finding a job on Capitol Hill:

> *Capitol Hill: An Insider's Guide to Finding a Job in Congress*, Kerry Dumbaugh and Gary Serota (Washington, D.C.: Tilden Press).

This book is both a primer on the internal structure of Congress and a how-to guide to pulling the right strings. It includes a wealth of useful information, including tips on "Hill speak," networking strategies, and names and addresses of bars and restaurants most frequented by congressional staffers.

After orienting yourself with *Capitol Jobs*, you should begin targeting various personal, committee, or subcommittee staffs. Begin by consulting the following directories for the names, addresses, and telephone numbers of key representatives, staff people, and committees and subcommittees:

- *The American Almanac of Politics*
- *Congressional Yellow Book*
- *Congressional Staff Directory*
- *Congressional Directory*

The House and Senate also publish telephone directories which you should consult.

You may wish to leave a copy of your resume with the nonpartisan congressional placement offices. These offices provide job application, interview, and referral services for both personal staff and committee positions. The House Placement Office is located in House Annex # 2, Room H2-220. This office encourages individuals to walk in for information. It asks you to complete an application form and talk to staff members. Its interviewing hours are from 10:30 a.m. to 4 p.m., Monday through Friday. You can call them at 202/225-7000.

The Senate Placement Office is located in the Russell Senate Office Building, Room SR-B26. Similar to the House Placement Office, this office operates on a walk-in basis. Interviewing hours are 10:00 a.m. to 3:30 p.m., Monday through Friday. However, it is closed between noon and 1:00 p.m. each day, and interviewing stops at 2:00 p.m. on Friday. You can call them at 202/224-0167.

However, these offices are not designed to find you a job. Providing assistance only, these placement offices primarily collect resumes and forward them upon request to various offices which already have numerous unsolicited resumes. They can give you useful tips on the recruitment process on Capitol Hill. Therefore, it does not hurt to cover all bases by contacting these offices and getting your resume in their files.

The Congressional Management Foundation (CMF) monitors personnel developments on Capitol Hill. Each year it publishes a survey of job descriptions and salaries with congressional offices as well as conducts numerous seminars for Hill staffs. CMF will provide advice and tips on how to best find a job on Capitol Hill. You can contact them at:

> Congressional Management Foundation
> 333 Pennsylvania Ave., SE
> Washington, DC 20003
> Tel. 202/546-0100

Two other resources provide useful financial information on various staff positions. *The Report of the Clerk of the House*, published quarterly, provides details on the financial structure of each Representative's office. It will give you all the information you need for researching House salaries. You can get a free copy from the House Document Room (H226). A similar document, *The Report of the Secretary of the Senate*, is available on Senate staff salaries. It is free for the asking through the Senate Documents Room (B04) in the Hart Senate Office Building.

A variety of other publications are available on various aspects of Congress. Before venturing into this arena, you should have a thorough understanding of the structure and functions of the House and Senate. Your local library should have such basic reference works as the *Congressional Directory, Congressional Staff Directory,* and the *Congressional Yellow Book.* They also should have the *Congressional Quarterly, The Almanac of American Politics,* and several books on how Congress works and how to lobby Congress. The lobbying books are especially useful, because they are written in a how-to format. They reveal the internal structure of congressional organizations and outline useful strategies for influencing each organization — strategies which can be directly adapted to your job search. You, in effect, want to lobby congressional organizations with your resume, experience, skills, and personality.

THE JUDICIARY

The judicial branch consists of the Supreme Court, a variety of U.S. Courts, and supporting organizations. Altogether, these organizations employ 16,636 individuals. Finding employment within the judiciary is similar to finding employment in the legislative branch.

The Supreme Court is a relatively small organization, employing 333 individuals. Court employees consist of the Clerk of the Court, Marshall, Reporter of Decisions, Press Officer, Librarian and their staffs as well as messengers and security officers. These individuals are appointed by the Court. Law clerks, on the other hand, are appointed by the Justices.

The Clerk of the Court has the largest staff, consisting of more than 30 individuals. The Marshall of the Court is responsible for seating arrangements, paying the Justices' salaries, and dispersing court funds. The Reporter of Decisions has general editing, printing, and publication responsibilities relevant to court opinions. The Press Officer provides public information. The Librarian is responsible for maintaining a 250,000 volume library. Messengers are selected by the Marshall of the Court; they replaced the former page system and work directly with the Justices. Approximately four law clerks provide staff assistance to each justice.

Several other individuals and groups work directly with the court, but they are not court employees. These consist of:

- *Office of Solicitor General:* The third highest ranking Department of Justice official who is responsible for representing the Federal government before the Supreme Court.

- *Supreme Court Bar:* Admits 6,000 individuals to the Supreme Court Bar each year.

- *U.S. Judicial Conference:* The "Board of Trustees" for the Federal judicial system. Receives staff assistance from the Administrative Office of the U.S. Supreme Court.

- *Administrative Office:* Supervises the administration, salaries, and benefits of Federal court support personnel — except the Supreme Court. Prepares and submits budgets of all U.S. district courts as well as the 11 circuit courts of appeal. Staff of nearly 500.

- *Federal Judicial Center:* The research, training, and development arm of the Federal judiciary. Staff of over 100.

- *Supreme Court Historical Association:* Nonprofit group organized to educate the public about the Federal judiciary. Staff of fewer than 10.

The bulk of job opportunities with the Federal judiciary are found among the various U.S. courts located throughout the United States. Altogether, they employ 16,293 individuals or 98 percent of all judicial branch employees. These consist of:

- *U.S. Courts of Appeal*

  - 11 Circuit Courts
  - Federal Circuit Court
  - District of Columbia Circuit Court
  - 80 U.S. District Courts

- *Other Courts and Special Groups*

  - Temporary Emergency Court of Appeals
  - U.S. Claims Court
  - U.S. Court of International Trade
  - District Panel on Multidistrict Litigation
  - U.S. Tax Court
  - Regional Court Organizations

Each of these courts and organizations employs two types of individuals: legal specialists and administrative support staff.

Finding employment opportunities with the various courts

and supporting organizations of the Federal judiciary requires a great deal of investigation and networking on your part. Remember, this is the legal field where many positions require formal legal training, law degrees, and bar certification; access to employment tends to follow the "ole boy" system of classmate, alumni, and law firm connections. Job vacancies tend to be announced through the informal word-of-mouth system. Without a law degree, numerous connections, and a link into the word-of-mouth system, you may have difficulty gaining access to many jobs in this arena.

Nonetheless, enterprising job seekers can gain access by developing a job search particularly geared toward the unique characteristics of the Federal judicial system. The first thing you need to do is to understand how the Federal judiciary is structured and functions. A good starting point is to refer to Want's *Federal-State Court Directory* (Want Publishing Co., 1511 K St., N.W., Washington, D.C. 20005, $12.95). This directory provides an overview of the structure of the court system. You also may want to call the Supreme Court Public Information Office (202/479-3211) for information on the various judicial organizations. They can refer you to the necessary sources. From there, you should directly contact each judicial organization — both court and support groups — for information and advice. In the case of Federal courts outside Washington, D.C., contact the court directly as well as the local bar association or law school for information and advice. Many law schools maintain placement offices which can provide advice on how to best approach the Federal circuit and district courts within their geographic area.

PART V

WORKING
ON THE PERIPHERY

Many government employees have little knowledge of work-life outside their agency. For them, looking for employment outside government is a frightening experience replete with possible rejections and failure. Lacking appropriate job search skills and information on nongovernmental job opportunities, they may fail to make career transitions to rewarding jobs outside government. However, this need not happen if they understand their skills, use effective job search techniques, and locate job vacancies among appropriate public organizations.

Each year thousands of individuals make successful transitions from government to the private sector. How they do it is no big secret. For many, the first step is to identify organizations that seek the skills of government employees. The most logical groups are those doing business with government agencies. Many of these "organizations on the periphery" maintain close relations with agencies, hire former government employees, and are major beneficiaries of government budgets. Other public organizations receive financial support from sources outside government for the purpose of affecting how government conducts its business.

Numerous public service opportunities are available with organizations outside government. These organizations range from nonprofit foundations and charitable organizations to lobbyists, professional associations, and consulting firms. They all have one thing in common: they operate in a public policy arena. Some directly initiate policies for improving the welfare of communities. Others influence both the content and implementation of governmental policies.

The five chapters in this section outline public employment opportunities with various organizations functioning on the periphery of government. Many of these organizations provide exciting and rewarding job opportunities for individuals primarily oriented toward public sector work. The chapters outline a basic orientation for gaining access to the networks which provide entry to the organizations.

Chapter Nineteen
THE NEW
PUBLIC SECTOR

The normal definition and understanding of the public sector is government consisting of various executive, legislative, and judicial organizations. However, numerous nongovernmental organizations operate in the public arena. These organizations constitute a network of employment opportunities for individuals interested in public sector jobs and careers.

TYPES OF ORGANIZATIONS

The new public sector consists of literally thousands of organizations engaged in some form of public activity. The activities include:

- Representing and supporting trade, professional, social, and political groups.
- Providing contractual services to government agencies.
- Promoting social programs.
- Influencing the content of public policy.
- Performing public functions.
- Financing and promoting the political candidacies of elected officials.

305

Most nongovernmental organizations engaged in public activities have permanent, full-time staffs. Many are headquartered or maintain offices or representatives in the Washington, D.C. Metropolitan area where they have ready access to legislators and bureaucrats as well as a pool of experienced and talented personnel to run their organizations.

The major types of organizations consist of:

- Contracting and consulting firms

- Trade and professional associations

- Nonprofit organizations

- Foundations and research organizations

- Political support groups and lobbyists

While these are private organizations, all deal with government or each other in some manner. For example, consulting firms, research organizations, and foundations partly depend on government funding for their livelihoods. Trade and professional associations, lobbyists, and law firms represent the interests of their members and clients among legislators and agencies. Nonprofit organizations are often partly funded by government, and they too attempt to influence the shape and implementation of public policy. Political Action Committees and political parties mobilize resources from trade and professional associations to advance the candidacies of elected officials.

NETWORKS

The various nongovernmental organizations also constitute a network of employment opportunities for enterprising job seekers. Since most organizations perform similar functions in different specialty areas, job seekers can readily move within and among nonprofit organizations, trade and professional associations, contracting and consulting firms, and government organizations. A public career path for an individual in Washington, D.C. might consist of the following job moves:

1.   Research analyst with a nonprofit organization —
     2 years

2. Legislative assistant on Capitol Hill — 2 years
3. Policy analyst with a Federal agency — 5 years
4. Legislative liaison with a trade association — 3 years
5. Fund raiser with a Political Action Committee — 2 years
6. Senior associate with a consulting firm — present job

While such changes in jobs may appear to be evidence of job hopping, each new job is most likely a logical move up the public sector career ladder. After all, jobs on Capitol Hill do not lend themselves to congressional careers. Long-term employment within Federal agencies does not result in major career advancement nor exceptional financial rewards. Since many associations are small, they provide limited career advancement. Nonprofit organizations often pay poorly. And consulting firms may be small and family-owned and thus offer limited promotions. In such a public employment environment, career advancement takes place by making several job moves among different types of public organizations.

The end result, or final career pattern, for the public career-minded job changer may be 20 years of "public service" experience with six different organizations followed by establishing one's own contracting, consulting, or lobbying firm. Such an individual will have valuable public experience and important contacts for launching what will hopefully become an exciting and rewarding self-employment career.

JOB HOPPING THROUGH THE REVOLVING DOOR

Many observers refer to such a career pattern as "job hopping" and the public job networking and change phenomena as "the revolving door." Used in the pejorative, these terms nonetheless accurately describe the phenomena. However, there is nothing inherently wrong with job hopping through the revolving door. These are facts of worklife for career advancement in the public sector. For many people, staying with one organization for many years is a career death sentence. Especially if you work for small organizations, job hopping is the best way to advance your career. While on occasion the revolving door results in obvious conflicts of interest, on the whole it is probably functional for government. Many of the functions required by government must be contracted-out to organizations with specific government skills and experience. The only way these organizations can acquire the necessary skills and experience is to hire individuals who know the details of government. And who knows government better than former government employees?

THE SUCCESSFUL PUBLIC JOB SEEKER

Successful public job seekers understand and use the networks within and between public sector organizations. They know the what, where, and how of finding jobs in what appears to be a maze of different types of organizations. In making the transition from government to the private sector, they learn how to write excellent resumes and network for job openings according to the principles outlined in Part II for conducting an effective job search.

If you seek employment with these nongovernmental organizations, you should first visit your local library and consult four excellent directories:

- *Encyclopedia of Associations*
- *The Consultants and Consulting Organization Directory*
- *The Foundation Directory*
- *Research Center Directory*

These directories will provide you with a good overview of public organizations employing millions of public-oriented individuals. Each directory provides invaluable information on thousands of organizations, including names, addresses, telephone numbers, contact persons, functions, activities, and size of organization. If you spend a day or two in the library surveying these key volumes, you will quickly identify numerous organizations providing alternative job opportunities for someone with your interests and skills.

Several other directories provide useful information on job opportunities in this public arena. Some, but not all, libraries will have these books:

- *Career Guide to Professional Associations*
- *Directory of National Trade and Professional Associations in the United States*
- *Directory of Professional and Trade Organizations*
- *The Professional and Trade Association Job Finder*
- *Washington Information Directory*
- *Washington Representatives*

Each of the following chapters further discusses the use and content of these and other resources.

Once you have completed your library research, you should be prepared to begin contacting organizations by telephone, letter, or in person. The following chapters will assist you in developing an approach most appropriate for each type of organization.

Chapter Twenty
CONTRACTORS AND CONSULTANTS

Much of what gets done in government is actually done through consultants and contractors. During the past 25 years more and more government services and programs have been contracted-out to private firms. Indeed, as governments enter a period of limited personnel growth, the trend for the remainder of the 1980s and 1990s appears to be in the direction of even greater use of consultants and contractors to get the business of government done.

ROLES

Consultants and contractors play important roles in providing services to government. All branches of government use these services for several reasons:

1. They require specialized information not available through their present staffs.
2. They need special services and products only available from the private sector.
3. It is often more cost-effective to contract-out services than to increase the number of agency personnel to provide the services in-house.
4. Many services are short-term and thus can be most

quickly and effectively performed by outside consultants.

At the state and local levels, contractors may provide sanitation
services, road construction, health care, and building construction
and maintenance. At the Federal level these firms run a variety of
Federal programs, conduct numerous studies, and regularly supply
agencies with every conceivable type of durable and nondurable
goods from pencil sharpeners to submarines.

Almost every job found in the private sector will be performed
in government. Ironically, these government jobs are performed by
private firms on contract with government agencies. Therefore,
much of the work of government employees involves obligating
funds and administering contracts to private firms rather than provide direct government services.

Contractor services are performed at the contractor's or
agency's site. In many cases, an agency will provide office space for
a contractor's staff which then performs services in offices adjacent
to agency personnel. In many government buildings it is difficult to
identify who is a government employee or a contractor occupying
government offices.

UNDERSTANDING THE PROCUREMENT PROCESS

Local governments are the major direct service units in American government. Local officials provide services to citizens in specific
neighborhoods. Being labor intensive units of government, local
governments employ millions of individuals as teachers, police
officers, and public works and sanitation officials. Outside local
government, public services are less direct, involving fewer face-to-
face contacts between citizens and public employees. At the Federal
level, employees are the most removed from direct contact with
citizens. Federal employees tend to be disproportionately engaged
in the process of developing programs, obligating funds, and monitoring programs implemented by state and local officials and private
contractors.

The work of consultants centers around the procurement process. Procurement is the process by which government acquires
goods and services. Well defined rules and regulations govern the
process by which agencies can contract-out various services. In many
state and local jurisdictions this process is poorly structured, weakly
regulated, and subject to a great deal of mismanagement, conflicts
of interest, and corruption. It is not uncommon, for example, to

find elected officials and public employees steering contracts to friends and relatives and receiving kickbacks from the "ole boy" networks. Consequently, competition for government contracts is most limited at the state and local levels. Private firms tend to "colonize" agencies by maintaining long-term relations with key individuals in agencies who prefer their services to any other outside competitors. In communities where universities have a major presence, professors from the local institution often develop special relations with local government agencies, especially with their former students who are in positions to award contracts to their mentors.

Procurement at the Federal level is a different matter altogether. While local and state governments tend to provide a large number of street-level services through their public safety, public works, and highway departments, Federal employees do not. Direct services tend to be contracted-out to private consulting and contracting firms. The Federal government strictly regulates the procurement process through a well defined set of general regulations:

- Federal Acquisition Regulations (FAR)
- Competition in Contracting Act of 1985 (CICA)

In addition, each agency develops more detailed regulations based upon each section of the FAR and in line with the CICA. Altogether, over $200 billion a year flows from the Federal government to the private sector through this process.

One major result of the Federal procurement process has been to create competition among consulting and contracting firms. For example, all goods and services amounting to $10,000 or more ($25,000 in the case of the Department of Defense) must be procured through competitive bidding or negotiation processes. This normally takes the form of sealed bids for equipment or negotiations with agency personnel for services. Once a procurement need is identified and defined by agency personnel, contractors are identified and the procurement process follows specific rules and procedures. If a service is for less than $10,000, contracting officials must contact at least three firms for competitive bids. If the amount is more than $10,000, then the officials must issue a Request for Proposal (RFP). An announcement must be published in the *Commerce Business Daily* (CBD) for at least 30 days. During that time firms request copies of the solicitation which outlines the Statement of Work and evaluation criteria for judging proposals. Firms normally have 30 days to develop and submit detailed proposals. Once proposals are received and reviewed by contracting officers and technical personnel, an award is made to the firm receiving the highest evaluation on both technical and cost criteria. This may take anywhere from one to three months after the closing date for submitting proposals.

While all Federal agencies are supposed to follow these rules for ensuring competition, informal systems also operate to limit competition. Many agencies prefer working with a single contractor and thus they "wire" RFPs to favor one particular contractor. This is done by specifying in both the Statement of Work and the evaluation criteria various requirements which only one firm is likely to meet. An example of this practice is a recent RFP received by the authors from a military base. The solicitation requested proposals to provide career planning services to military spouses located near a specified city in a remote area of the United States. While the RFP had to be advertised in the CBD and proposals received over a 30-day period, an interesting amendment was issued which severely limited competition. Among 10 new evaluation criteria for judging offerors' resumes, it included the following minimum criteria:

- A list of all *(City X)* employers with whom the bidder has an established working relationship.

- The ability to prepare a variety of resume' styles and appropriate selective marketing brochures. This should be demonstrated with an attachment showing a minimum of 12 resumes or marketing brochures which the service provider has personally prepared.

Obviously only a few firms — perhaps only one — could meet such specific evaluation criteria. Not surprisingly, the firm to win the contract would probably be based in the specified city and previously did work with the individuals responsible for developing the RFP. They may have written the Statement of Work and evaluation criteria for the program officials!

"Wiring" contracts by specifying narrow evaluation criteria and developing unique Statements of Work is a notorious practice found throughout the Federal government. Certain agencies have reputations for engaging in such practices more than other agencies. Officials continue to play these games as long as no one protests. After all, contractors do not want to get the reputation for being "difficult" and thus quickly become persona non grata among contracting officials who prefer doing "business as usual." However, occasionally protests are lodged and solicitations are invalidated. Indeed, the authors protested a procurement training solicitation issued by one Federal agency in August, 1985. The solicitation was published in the *CBD* but the closing date was 12 days after it appeared — an obvious violation of the FAR and CICA which require a minimum of 30 days. Certain officials in the agency were trying to obligate funds for Fiscal 1985 and had wired the RFP for a particular firm. When we protested this violation, we learned there were obvious competing political factions among the contracting officials and technical personnel. They both knew they were in violation of the rules, but one had forced the other to attempt this improper procurement. Had we not protested, the funds would have been obligated and the favorite contractor of certain agency personnel would have received a nice end-of-the-year-spending windfall. Our protest was upheld and the funds were not obligated. Needless to say, we are probably persona non grata with certain individuals in this agency.

But compared to state and local governments, competition in contracting is more prevalent at the Federal level. Indeed, the new FAR and CICA rules may have far reaching implications in undermining many of the informal "wiring" practices which have gone on for years in some Federal agencies.

FLUIDITY IN HIRING

It is extremely important to understand this procurement process if you are interested in working for consulting and contracting firms. The process creates a job market situation which is very fluid, unstable, and unpredictable. A typical organizational structure is outlined in Figure 7.

Many firms keep a small *core staff* which is employed full-time to respond to RFPs and manage a lean organizational infrastructure. As contracts are won, they hire two types of additional personnel — often on a consulting basis — for implementing the contract. *Associates* normally work closely with the core staff on several projects; these individuals are relatively loyal to the firm and are given a disproportionate amount of contract work as individuals or subcontractors. *Consultants* are less closely linked to the firm; they have specific skills not found with the core staff or associates, and they tend to freelance with several such firms. Therefore, many positions with these firms are short-term positions tied to specific contracts, ranging from one month to one or more years. Most contracts are for one year with options to renew contracts up to two to three years before resubmitting them for open competition.

Given this structure, you must consider whether you want a full-time organization position or a contract-specific position as

FIGURE 7

TYPICAL STRUCTURE OF A SMALL AND FLEXIBLE CONSULTING FIRM DOING GOVERNMENT CONTRACT WORK

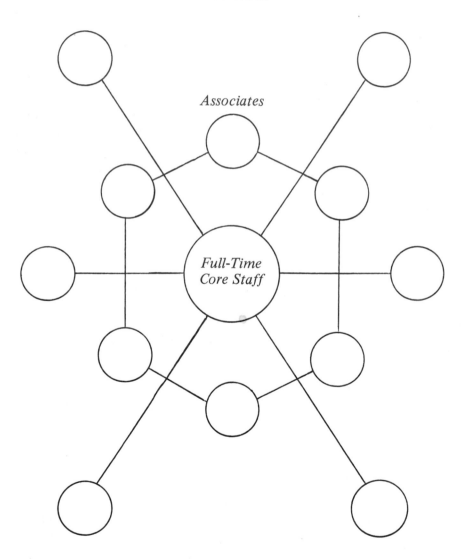

either an associate or consultant. An organization position may be more stable and predictable, but not necessarily so. For example, most contracting and consulting firms are small organizations employing fewer than 25 individuals. Many specialize in a particular government function and work primarily with a few agencies. Given the highly competitive nature of their work, many of these firms find they must staff-up and staff-down rapidly depending on which contracts they receive. If they receive a large contract, they may need to more than double or triple their staff overnight. If they lose a large contract, everyone except the president may go off the payroll and, instead, work on a daily consulting basis. For many small firms, contracting work is a feast or famine business.

On the other hand, large firms with several large contracts — especially defense contractors — will maintain a relatively large permanent staff. They normally can afford to do this, because their overhead and profits are greater on larger contracts. Furthermore, procurement officials find it difficult to estimate and monitor the costs of large contracts. But recent revelations about alleged contracting abuses by such noted firms as General Dynamics and General Electric have created a new element of instability among these large and stable contractors. They have violated one of the most important unwritten rules of the contracting business — do not get your contracting practices, however legal or illegal, exposed in the news media and thus endanger the careers of agency personnel.

THE FIRMS

Consulting and contracting firms working with the Federal government are frequently referred to as the "Beltway Bandits," a reference to both their physical location near the suburban Beltway (Route 495) and occasional revelations of contracting abuses. Over 700 contracting and consulting firms operate in the Washington, D.C. Metropolitan area. They provide a vast array of services to government agencies. Most, however, specialize in one or two government functions, such as training government personnel, operating service programs, and developing new weapons systems. The size of these firms will range from one individual operating from a basement or study to 1000 or more employees occupying 250,000 square feet of office space at $15 per square foot. While many of the firms are located in the Washington, D.C. Metropolitan area, they also are found in major cities throughout the country. In contracts involving research and development activities, more than 100 universities compete for contracts. The University of California, Los

Angeles, for example, plays a key role in the development and operation of America's nuclear weapons systems at the Los Alamos "campus" in Alamagordo, New Mexico. A large number of defense contractors and specialized research and management organizations are located around Seattle, San Francisco, Los Angeles, Dallas, Houston, Chicago, Minneapolis, Boston, and New York.

LOCATING OPPORTUNITIES

Several useful information sources are available for locating opportunities with various contracting and consulting firms. The single most comprehensive source of names, addresses, phone numbers, and annotated descriptions of firms is found in *The Consultants and Consulting Organizations Directory* and *Who's Who in Consulting* (Detroit: Gale Research Company). Most libraries have current editions of the three-volume *Directory*. It lists nearly 3,000 consulting firms according to the following categories:

1. Agriculture, Forestry, and Landscaping
2. Architecture and Interior Design
3. Arts and Entertainment
4. Business and Finance
5. Data Processing, Telecommunications, and Information Services
6. Education and Personal Development
7. Engineering, Science, and Technology
8. Environment
9. Health, Medicine, and Safety
10. Human Resources
11. Management
12. Manufacturing/Industrial/Transportation Operations
13. Marketing and Sales
14. Social Issues and Concerns

Since these volumes include all types of consulting firms, regardless of their public or private orientation, you will need to read through the various annotated descriptions to find which firms are primarily involved in government contract work. An example of a typical entry under the "Human Resources" section is:

BERGSTRALH-SHAW-NEWMAN, INC.
16220 Frederick Road, Suite 500   Phone: (301) 948-9580
Gaithersburg, MD 20877   Founded: 1978

Branch Office(s): Harrisburg, Pennsylvania; Dover, Delaware; Salt Lake City, Utah; Manila, Philippines. *Principal Executives:* Kermit L. Bergstralh, President; M. Ed Shaw, Senior Vice President; Robert B. Newman, Senior Vice President; Eugene L. Rowen, Vice President. *Purpose and Activity:* Designs, develops and implements management improvements and in-house training programs for highway, transportation and public works agencies in the United States, Canada and other countries. Services include department-wide performance and organizational reviews, management system designs, manpower and personnel management improvements, personnel classification plans, employee performance appraisals, salary plans and training materials production. Training production includes video-tapes, slide-tapes, other audiovisual materials, instructors' guides and trainee workbooks.

Although this is the best directory of such firms, keep in mind it does not include all contracting and consulting firms — only those willing to reveal information on their operations to Gale Research Company. Many firms do not want to publicize their operations through this or other public information resource directories. Consequently, you will have to locate these firms through other resources and investigative efforts.

If you are interested in working for firms which primarily focus on state and local government, you should contact the appropriate contracting office to get a list of the firms doing business with particular governmental units and agencies. In fact, this will be your most important source of information. You will learn who has what contract, for how long, and for how much. This information should be public information in most jurisdictions. In addition, you should look at the contractor's work — be it a report or other type of product — to gain information on the work being performed by the firm. Such information will give you something concrete to talk about with representatives of the firm once you decide to conduct an informational interview.

At the Federal level your information sources on contracts are numerous. One of your best sources is the *Commerce Business Daily* (*CBD*), which is available in most libraries. Issued five days a week, this Department of Commerce publication lists information on all upcoming competitive contracts for $10,000 or more as well as contracts awarded to particular firms for the amounts of $25,000 or more. You should pay particular attention to the "Contract Awards" section. This section identifies which firms receive contracts for what amounts. A good job search strategy is to continuously monitor who receives contracts and contact the firm when you see an award made in your area of expertise or interest. But you must do this immediately upon seeing the announcement since there is a few weeks of lag time between when a contract is awarded and when it is announced in the *CBD*.

We suggest this *CBD* job search strategy because typically firms operate in the following manner. The firm submits a proposal complete with a management structure, job descriptions, and resumes. But once they receive the award, the proposed staff changes due to the unavailability of some individuals proposed. At this time, the contractor must find new personnel and get them approved for the contract. In other words, the contractor now has a personnel problem or vacancy which must be filled immediately. If your qualifications and timing are right, you may find a job very quickly with such a firm. At the same time, you will make an important contact which could lead to having your resume included in other proposals. Most contractors are happy to receive resumes since they are continuously in need of personnel to propose for and staff new projects. Indeed, many contractors maintain in-house resume or talent banks. Staffing-up is always a problem employers prefer to solve before it becomes a major project implementation issue with clients.

You should also monitor the section of the *CBD* dealing with impending contracts. Once you become familiar with various specialty areas within the consulting business, you can nearly predict which firms will submit proposals for which projects. Knowing this, you can call a firm and mention your interest and availability in being included in their proposal. They may even offer you a short-term contract to. help write the proposal should you have such interests and skills. In some cases, individuals manage to get included in two or more proposals for the same contract, thus better ensuring they will get the work once the contract is awarded. Some firms have no problems with your inclusion in competitors' proposals while others frown on such opportunism. But in the contracting game, where competition is heavy, the basic goal is to get the contract and cash flowing.

Another source of information on contractors is the Contracts Office in each agency. Some offices may provide you with a listing of firms doing contract work with their agency. Also, ask the officials which contractors are doing what and who you might contact.

Sometimes these individuals are very open with such information and will make several useful suggestions. On the other hand, agency officials may guard this information as private and confidential, even though it is public information. In this instance, you may have to formally request the information through the Freedom of Information Act.

You will find that some firms largely specialize in one function in a single agency whereas other firms do contract work in one or many functional areas with several agencies. For example, if you are interested in working for a firm in the field of energy or environmental protection, you should contact the Contracts Office at the Department of Energy or Environmental Protection Agency for a list of contractors. Once you have this information, you will know whom to contact. The firms working with these agencies also may be doing similar work in other agencies and in private industry. Call the firms and let them know you are interested in working for them. Try to set up an appointment for an interview. Make sure you get your resume in their file. Indeed, many firms refer to this file when they need personnel for new projects. While they may not have a vacancy at the time you contact them, they very well may submit a proposal which results in a position for you.

Many consulting firms also periodically place employment ads in the newspaper in either the classified or business sections. In the case of the Federal government, most consulting firms will place job listings in the *Washington Post*, especially the Sunday edition. You should monitor these sections of the newspaper. However, don't expect to get a job by responding to these ads. Many firms periodically place such ads in order to increase the number of resumes for their files. Sometimes they are in the process of bidding on a project, so they advertise for resumes to put in a particular proposal. If you manage to get your resume in the proposal and the firm wins the contract, you have a job. But more often than not, such ads are fishing expeditions with no particular vacancy available at the time of the ad.

PROFESSIONAL POSITIONS

Most contracting firms hire individuals with strong analytical, communication, and technical skills. Given the nature of consulting work, consultants are hired as problem-solvers. They must quickly analyze situations, devise plans of action, and often implement projects. Such activities require a great deal of analytical skill and the ability to communicate to clients both orally and in writing. Projects continuously require flows of paper — workplans, monthly reports, memos, evaluations, studies — between the consultants and clients. If you are both a good and fast writer, stress these facts to potential employers. They especially need quick thinking, fast writers.

While most firms hire general support staff positions for word-processors, receptionists, secretaries, and accountants, most continuously seek technical specialists. Defense contractors hire a disproportionate number of engineers, systems analysts, and computer specialists. Research firms hire policy analysts with skills unique to specific programs and agencies. Other firms need specialists in a variety of areas. If you survey the *Commerce Business Daily* notices, you will quickly get a sense of which technical specialties are in demand.

It is much easier to break into a consulting firm if you have previous government experience in a specialty area involving contractors. Your special knowledge and contacts with agency personnel will make you very marketable among firms working in your area. Indeed, much of the revolving door with government involves employees leaving an agency and working for the same contractor they previously worked with in the agency. These individuals become key contact people and informants for the firm. Furthermore, since agency personnel usually think they are unique and thus outsiders cannot possibly understand their problems, situations, and needs, they prefer working with one of their own.

Educational qualifications also are important with consulting firms. They prefer individuals with MAs and PhDs because government places emphasis on educational qualifications of contractors' personnel when awarding contracts. After all, agency personnel working with contracts tend to be well educated — many have MAs and PhDs. When it comes to educational background, they prefer working with consultants who are at least their equal or have higher educations. At the very minimum, a BA degree is expected.

But how do you break into the consulting game if you don't have government experience, technical skills, or higher education? If you have strong analytical and writing skills, you should be able to land a position. These firms continuously need such skills. Often they find their technical personnel with government experience cannot write. Therefore, they must have on their staff individuals who can write and edit. If you get into a firm based on your analytical and writing skills, you may be able to quickly pick up the technical aspects of the work and in time be able to work directly with clients on projects. In the meantime, you will probably stay in the background providing support for technical personnel.

This is a very basic and typical pattern of how individuals

break into the government consulting business and become specialists in a short time even though they lack experience as a government employee. In the long run, the best skill to have is an ability to work with government agency personnel who are suspicious of outsiders and who feel their agency is unique. They respond best to firms they feel recognize their uniqueness, respond to their problems, and can be trusted. Responsiveness and trust are perhaps the most important elements in developing and maintaining a good consultant-client relationship. You can only acquire these qualities and skills by being a consultant. On-the-job experience in interacting with clients is the basic requirement for becoming an effective consultant. Education and previous government experience will not be enough.

INDEPENDENCE AND NETWORKS

If you are thinking of starting your own independent consulting business on either a part-time or full-time basis, you should talk to consultants who have taken this road. They can provide you with useful tips on avoiding the pitfalls of independence as well as suggest useful strategies for becoming successful. You might also read a few of the ever increasing number of how-to books on entering the consulting business. Among the more recent titles are:

- *Cashing In On the Consulting Boom*
- *How to Become a Top Consultant*
- *How to Succeed As an Independent Consultant*
- *Marketing Your Consulting and Professional Services*

Information on these titles is included in the resource section at the end of this book.

Several professional networks can provide information on consulting job opportunities. Many consultants belong to professional organizations in their specialty areas. These organizations often list job vacancies with consulting firms. Within many of these associations, consultants form their own interest groups or sections to focus on various aspects of consulting work. For example, the American Psychological Association has a Division of Consulting Psychologists. Many local chapters of the American Society of Training and Development have a Consultants' Section. These groups regularly meet to exchange ideas and promote their interests and themselves. Some associations specialize in consulting. For example, several professionals have formed their own professional organizations:

- Academy of Health Care Consultants (Chicago)
- American Association of Hospital Consultants (Arlington, VA)
- American Association of Political Consultants (Baltimore)
- American Consulting Engineers Council (Washington, DC)
- American Society of Agricultural Consultants (McLean, VA)
- Association of Management Consultants (Milwaukee)
- Institute of Management Consultants (New York City)
- National Association of Public Employer Negotiators and Administrators (Chicago)
- National Council of Professional Services Firm (Washington, DC)

Several other organizations publish directories of consultants and consulting organizations as well as newsletters in various specialized fields. If you are interested in management consulting, for example, you may want to contact Consulting News, an organization which publishes two newsletters (*Consultant News* and *Executive Recruiter News*) and three directories (*Directory of Management Consultants, Directory of Executive Recruiters,* and *International Directory of Executive Recruiters*): Consultant News, Templeton Road, Fitzwilliam, NH 03447 or call 603/585-2200 or 585-6544.

Chapter Twenty-One
TRADE AND PROFESSIONAL ASSOCIATIONS

America is an organizational society. Most individuals belong to an average of three different organizations. Some manage memberships in 15 or more organizations.

A particularly unique characteristic of American organizations is the ease with which one can join and participate in organizations. Most require little involvement on the part of the individual other than writing a check for annual membership dues. For writing a check, you receive a membership card, magazine, newsletter, and perhaps special offers for insurance and travel. In addition, your name and address are sold to other organizations which send mailings on how to become a member of their organization too.

Since most associations promote the interests of their members by influencing government policies, they become involved in the political process. In this sense, they are public organizations maintaining close relationships with elected representatives and government agencies.

This chapter examines associations involved with influencing government. While many Americans work for organizations which are members of these associations, thousands of other Americans work directly for the associations. They are responsible for seeing that the association serves the best interests of its members. How one goes about locating an association and finding a staff job with one of these organizations are the subjects of this chapter.

THE ORGANIZATIONS

National trade and professional organizations consist of various types of organizations such as trade associations, labor unions, and professional, scientific, and technical societies. While no exact statistics are compiled on the number of such organizations, best estimates put the number at approximately 40,000 associations in the United States. The largest number operate at the state and local levels — more than 100,000 at the state level alone. Approximately 7,000 are national associations with numerous affiliated regional groups and local chapters.

Associations differ according to their orientations. Trade associations, for example, provide assistance to businesses; they are mainly concerned with promoting members' products and services. These consist of representatives from retail (35 percent), service (20 percent), and manufacturing (15 percent) industries. Professional associations tend to be primarily oriented to advancing and applying knowledge and setting professional standards. Scientific societies are organized to promote knowledge for knowledge's sake. Labor unions promote the economic and social well-being of their members.

The size of associations varies from a few members to millions. The powerful Motor Vehicle Manufacturers Association, for example, has only 10 corporate members whereas the American Association of Retired Persons has more than 16,000,000 individual members. Staff size also varies from one part-time employee to over 800 full-time employees. Large associations have annual budgets of over $2.5 million and staffs of 50 or more people. Medium-sized associations have annual budgets between $500,000 and $2.5 million and staffs of between 11 and 50 employees. Small associations have annual budgets under $500,000 and staffs of fewer than 10 people. Altogether, over 250 associations have annual budgets exceeding $5 million. Another 325 associations have annual budgets between $2 million and $5 million.

The largest concentration of associations is in the Washington, D.C. Metropolitan area. Approximately 2,500 associations or 32 percent of all national associations are headquartered there. Approximately 19 percent are headquartered in New York City, 18 percent in Chicago, and the remaining 31 percent in other cities throughout the United States, especially in San Francisco, Los Angeles, Cleveland, and Philadelphia. The percentage of associations moving to the Washington, D.C. area has increased dramatically during the past 15 years. In 1971, for example, only 19 percent of national associations were headquartered in Washington, D.C.; 26 percent were located in New York City. The movement to Washington, D.C. is in recognition and response to the significant role national legislation plays for members of trade and professional associations. Today, more than 3,700 associations are active in Washington, D.C. The largest concentration is found along Connecticut and L Streets in downtown Washington. However, more associations are moving into suburban Washington communities. Alexandria, Virginia, for example, is now home to over 150 national associations. In fact, the number of associations in Alexandria increased from 40 in 1981 to 150 in 1986!

ASSOCIATION MANAGEMENT FIRMS

Job opportunities are by no means limited to the associations themselves. Over 200 association management firms provide a variety of management services to small associations on a contractual basis: government relations, legal counseling, membership recruitment, accounting, data processing, records management, research and intelligence, and publications. The grandaddy of these firms — Fernley and Fernley of Philadelphia — was established in 1886. The largest association management firm today is Smith, Bucklin and Associates with offices in Chicago and Washington, D.C. In the association management business for more than 30 years, this firm provides services to more than 100 clients.

If you are interested in working for association management firms, you should conduct research on how they are structured and function. For example, some of these firms represent only a single association. Other firms are considered multi-management firms since they handle several associations. These firms are found throughout the United States — not just in Washington, D.C. The major multi-management firms — in charge of at least four associations — are:

——— MAJOR ASSOCIATION MANAGEMENT FIRMS ———

Name	Telephone Number	State
• American Fraternal Programmers	305/891-9800	FL
• Association Headquarters	609/234-9155	NJ
• Association Management, Inc.	202/429-9440	DC
• Association Services Corporation	913/266-7014	KS

- Association Services International, Inc.   913/262-4510   KS
- Baxter Associates, Inc.   203/323-3143   CT
- William S. Bergman Associates, Inc.   202/452-1520   DC
- Bostrom Management Corporation   312/644-0828   IL
- The Breeden Company   312/724-7700   IL
- The Cate Corporation   703/860-8127   VA
- Clemons and Associates   301/665-1276   MD
- CM Services   312/858-7337   IL
- Davis/Replogle & Associates   213/937-5514   CA
- George K. Degnon Associates, Inc.   703/556-9222   VA
- H.H. Dolan and Associates   312/864-8444   IL
- Doyle Associates Inc.   703/642-5858   VA
- J. Edgar Eubanks and Associates
  Association Management Services   803/252-5646   SC
- Executive Management Services Corp.   516/825-6673   NY
- Executive Consultants   703/938-7433   VA
- Fernley and Fernley, Inc.   215/564-3484   PA
- Fitzgerald Management Corp.   312/525-3644   IL
- Martin Fromm and Associates   816/444-3500   MO
- G & T Management Inc.   212/867-4480   NY
- The Guild Associates, Inc.   617/266-6800   MA
- Hauck & Associates   202/452-8100   DC
- The Hill Group   202/296-9200   DC
- Humes and Associates Inc.   312/346-1000   IL
- Anthony J. Janetti   609/589-2319   NJ
- The Robert H. Kellen Company   404/252-3663   GA
- Kinder Association Managers   714/979-6316   CA
- Lurie/Murphy & Associates   312/763-7350   IL
- Messervey & Company   312/693-0990   IL
- Payne and Associates, Inc.   202/783-1222   DC
- Penn Michael Management   201/521-4441   NY
- Professional Relations and Research
  Institute, Inc.   617/927-8330   MA
- Ruggles Services Corp.   804/353-9529   VA
- Shea Management, Inc.   412/782-1624   PA
- Smith, Bucklin & Associates, Inc.   202/857-1100   DC
- Society and Association Services Corp.   703/790-1745   VA
- Thomas Associates, Inc.   216/241-7333   OH
- A.P. Wherry & Associates, Inc.   216/226-7700   OH

LOBBYING AND PACs

If the major involvement of most individuals with associations is writing a check for annual membership dues, where does all the money go? The money goes toward renting office space and supporting staffs engaged in a variety of activities in addition to seeing that members receive their membership cards and certificates, magazines, and newsletters. For trade and professional associations, their activities center on promoting the common interests of members.

Most large associations are organized to lobby Federal, state, and local governments. Full-time staffs engage in numerous activities aimed at congressional committees, executive departments, and regulatory agencies to both protect and promote their members' interests. These activities include:

- Providing information to officials on the organization's position on various issues; sometimes this includes drafting legislation for congressional committees and writing policy papers for agencies.
- Testifying before committees.
- Monitoring the day-to-day actions of Congress, agencies, and other lobbying groups.
- Mobilizing constituent support for or against government candidates with money and campaign workers. The National Rifle Association (NRA), for example, is reputed to have the capability to organize virtually overnight mass mailings to its 3,000,000-plus members.
- Assisting favored congressional candidates with money, campaign workers, and votes.
- Developing networks, coalitions, and alliances with other associations in support of various policy positions.

Trade and professional associations, whether they operate at the Federal, state, or local levels, are affected by the legislative process. Trade unions, for example, are very active at the state level to ensure that state legislatures avoid passing right-to-work legislation which would significantly undermine union membership. State bar associations lobby to fix legal fees and prevent members from advertising. Local Chambers of Commerce are active at City Hall to ensure that local ordinances are conducive to a positive business climate. The National Rifle Association (NRA) and the National Association of Manufacturers (NAM) continuously lobby for legislation in favor of their members.

Since the 1970s, a new form of association activity has developed in the form of Political Action Committees (PACs). First initiated by the American Medical Association in 1961, today approximately 3500 PACs funnel funds into the campaigns of favored congressional and presidential candidates as well as representatives at the state and local levels. PACs are normally associated with particular associations. They provide job opportunities in addition to the regular associational staff positions. We examine the case of PACs in Chapter 24.

WORK AND COMPENSATION

Most associations consist of members, a Board of Directors, numerous committees, and a professional staff. Committees, such as education and trade show, are especially important to day-to-day operations. Committees are used to mobilize members' expertise and involve members in promoting the activities of the association.

The work of associations requires a variety of skills from handling mass mailings to drafting legislation and conducting training programs. Public relations and writing skills are highly valued. Most associations need individuals who are good at performing the following functions:

- *Maintain communication with members and government officials:* write newsletters, edit magazines, develop press releases, maintain mailing lists, issue special reports and publications.

- *Develop proposals and legislation:* issue information and position papers to members of Congress and agency personnel, and draft legislation.

- *Expand contacts with influential groups and individuals:* network by telephone, letter, and personal visits to develop supportive relations between the association and important others.

- *Respond to inquiries:* answer questions, conduct research, and supply materials.

- *Organize meetings:* manage all logistics involved in organizing the annual membership meeting, executive board meetings, and special meetings.

- *Conduct training:* identify training needs, organize instructors and participants, develop brochures and training materials, and entertain.

Above all, staff members must have strong communication skills and enjoy working with people. The nature of association work also requires one to be flexible in dealing with the day-to-day work of the association. Being membership-driven organizations, staff personnel must be willing to be responsive to members' needs.

Depending on the size of the association, the work environment stresses the importance of managing communication and networking. Individuals who have strong written and oral communication skills as well as good interpersonal and networking skills are highly valued. Many individuals who work for associations have previously worked on Capitol Hill where they acquired such skills in the offices of Representatives. At the same time, many Capitol Hill employees have previously worked for associations. Because of the complementary nature of associational and congressional work, employees tend to develop working relations with each other which result in a revolving door between personnel in associations and on Capitol Hill. If you have Capitol Hill experience, especially in drafting legislation and networking, you will be very marketable with associations.

Salaries with associations vary. Large and well established associations tend to pay better than small associations. In a 1984 survey of top executive salaries with associations in Washington, D.C., Columbia Books found the salary range to be from $25,500 to $250,000, with the average salary being $98,500. Overall, however, salaries with associations are modest by most standards. Entry-level positions are often in the $14,000 to $18,000 range, with most professional positions paying in the mid 20s to the low 30s.

While compensation is not great, the benefits are relatively good. Association work does provide an exciting work environment for many people and leads to other career opportunities. The jobs are relatively secure, and most people work for an association for about three years before moving on to another association. For others, association work is a necessary stepping stone to Capitol Hill and consulting work with government agencies. And for others, association work is an excellent stepping stone to working for member organizations of the association and consulting firms that primarily work in the private sector. The name of the game is getting contacts for networking your way to better job and career opportunities.

LOCATING ASSOCIATIONS

Several useful information sources are available for identifying associations appropriate for your job and career interests. The single, most comprehensive source for surveying various types of associations is the four-volume *Encyclopedia of Associations*. Found in the reference section of most libraries, the *Encyclopedia* provides names, addresses, telephone numbers, and annotated descriptions of nearly 20,000 national and international organizations. The *Encyclopedia* classifies all associations into the following categories:

1. Trade, Business, and Commercial Organizations
2. Agricultural Organizations and Commodity Exchanges
3. Legal, Government, Public Administration, and Military
4. Scientific, Engineering, and Technical Organizations
5. Educational Organizations
6. Cultural Organizations
7. Social Welfare Organizations
8. Health and Medical Organizations
9. Public Affairs Organizations
10. Fraternal, Foreign Interest, Nationality, and Ethnic Organizations
11. Religious Organizations
12. Veteran, Hereditary, and Patriotic Organizations
13. Hobby and Avocational Organizations
14. Athletic and Sports Organizations
15. Labor Union Associations and Federations
16. Chambers of Commerce
17. Greek Letter and Related Organizations

The following examples — two of the largest and most powerful interest groups — outline the type of information found in the listings of the *Encyclopedia:*

ASSOCIATIONS IN THE ENCYCLOPEDIA

NATIONAL ASSOCIATION OF MANUFACTURERS (NAM)
1776 F St., N.W.   Phone: (202) 626-3700
Washington, DC 20006   Alexander B. Trowbridge, Pres.
Founded: 1895. *Members:* 13,000. *Staff:* 220. Manufacturers; cooperating are non-manufacturers having a direct interest in or relationship to manufacturing. Represents industry's view on national and international problems to government. Maintains public relations program. Reviews

current and proposed legislation, administrative rulings and interpretations, judicial decisions and legal matters affecting industry. Sponsors Human Resources Forum (human relations and labor-management problems). Maintains numerous policy groups: Human Resources Management; International Economic Affairs; Regulations; Resources and Innovation; Taxation and Fiscal Policy. Affiliated with 150 local and state trade associations of manufacturers through National Industrial Council of 110 manufacturing trade associations. *Publications:* Enterprise, monthly; also publishes Directory of Officers, Directors and Committees, reports, bulletins, and legal studies. *Convention/meetings:* annual.

**NATIONAL RIFLE
ASSOCIATION OF AMERICA** (Firearms) (NRA)
1600 Rhode Island Ave., N.W.   Phone: (202) 828-6000
Washington, DC 20036   Harlon B. Carter, Exec. V.Pres.
Founded: 1871. *Members:* 3,000,000. *Staff:* 350. *State Groups:* 54. *Local Groups:* 12,000. Target shooters, hunters, gun collectors, gunsmiths, police officers, and others interested in firearms. Promotes rifle, pistol, and shotgun shooting, hunting, gun collecting, home firearm safety, and wildlife conservation. Encourages civilian marksmanship. Educates police firarms instructors. Maintains national and international records of shooting competitions; sponsors teams to compete in world championships. Maintains comprehensive collection of antique and modern firearms. Bestows awards; compiles statistics; sponsors research and education programs; maintains speakers bureau and museum. Operates library of 1000 volumes; lobbies on firearms issues. *Divisions:* Field Services; General Operations; Institute for Legislative Action; Public Education; Publications. *Publications:* (1) The American Hunter, monthly; (2) The American Marksman, monthly; (3) The American Rifleman, monthly; (4) Monitor, bimonthly. *Convention/Meeting:* annual – 1986 April 25-29, New Orleans, LA; 1987 April 24-28, Reno, NV.

You should also consult the *National Trade and Professional Associations of the United States* directory (Columbia Books, Inc.,

1350 New York Avenue, NW, Suite 207, Washington, D.C. 20005, Tel. 202/737-3777). This is an excellent resource for locating 3,400 national trade associations and 2,300 professional and learned societies. Each organization is annotated and listed alphabetically as well as by subject and geographical area. Alphabetical listings appear as follows:

ASSOCIATIONS IN NATIONAL DIRECTORY

AMERICAN MANAGEMENT ASSOCIATIONS (1923)
135 West 50th St., New York, NY 10020
President & Exec. Officer: Thomas R. Horton
Members: 78,000   *Staff:* 700
Annual Budget: over $5,000,000   *Tel:* (212) 586-8100
Hist. Note: Merger (1973) of the American Management Ass'n (1923), the American Foundation for Management Research (1960), the Internat'l Management Ass'n (1956), the Presidents Ass'n (1961) and the Soc. for Advancement of Management (1912), the oldest society in the U.S. devoted to all types of management education. Maintains a Washington Office.
Publications:
Comp. Flash. m
Compensation Review. q
Management Review. m
Organization Dynamics. q
Personnel. m.
The President. m
Supervisory Management. m.
Supervisory Sense. m
Annual Meetings. New York City, in September.

AMERICAN MEDICAL ASSOCIATION (1847)
535 North Dearborn St., Chicago, IL 60610
Exec. V. President: James H. Sammons, M.D.
Members: 250,000   *Staff:* 1,000
Annual Budget: over $5,000,000 *Tel.* (312) 645-5000
Hist. Note: Established in Philadelphia in 1847 and incorporated in Illinois in 1897. Principal spokesman for the U.S. medical profession with about 2000 local and regional medical societies. Maintains a Washington office. It and its affiliates support num-

ous political action committees throughout the country. Has an annual budget of over $100 million. Members: $330/year.

Publications:
American Medical News. w. adv.
American Journal of Diseases of Children. m. adv.
Archives of Dermatology. m. adv.
Archives of General Psychiatry. m. adv.
Archives of Internal Medicine. m. adv.
Archives of Neurology. m. adv.
Archives of Ophthalmology. m. adv.
Archives of Otolaryngology. m. adv.
Archives of Pathology and Laboratory Medicine. m. adv.
Archives of Surgery. m. adv.
The Citation. bi-w.
Journal of the American Medical Ass'n. w. adv.
Legislative Roundup. w. (during congressional sessions).

Annual Meetings: Semi-annual meetings; Summer and Winter

Under the Subject Index, all organizations specialized in a particular functional area are grouped together. If, for example, you are interested in all associations dealing with nuclear energy, you will find the following organizations listed under the "Nuclear Energy" subject category:

NUCLEAR ENERGY ASSOCIATIONS

- American Association of Physicists in Medicine
- American College of Nuclear Medicine
- American Nuclear Energy Council
- American Nuclear Insurers
- American Nuclear Society
- American Osteopathic College of Nuclear Medicine
- Atomic Industrial Forum
- Bureau of Explosives
- Clinical Ligand Assay Society
- Health Physics Society
- Institute of Nuclear Materials Management
- Institute of Nuclear Power Operations
- International Association for Hydrogen Energy

- Mutual Atomic Energy Liability Underwriters
- National Council on Radiation Protection and Measurements
- National Lead Burning Association
- National Records Management Association
- Pipe Fabrication Institute
- Professional Reactor Operator Society
- Radiation Research Society
- Society of Nuclear Medicine
- Universities Research Association

Columbia Books also publishes a useful directory of organizations in Washington, D.C. Revised each year, *Washington 86* lists 3,400 key public and private organizations and the 15,000 who lead them in the Washington area. The book's 17 chapters outline the governmental, business, labor, political, cultural, educational, religious, and social power structure of Washington, D.C. An index also identifies individuals with multiple affiliations and responsibilities with the various organizations.

Another excellent resource is the *Washington Information Directory* published by the Congressional Quarterly Inc. All libraries should carry this volume in their reference section. The *Directory* classifies various government-related functions into 16 categories:

1. Communications and Media
2. Economics and Business
3. Education and Culture
4. Employment and Labor
5. Energy
6. Equal Rights: Minorities, Women
7. Government Personnel and Services
8. Health and Consumer Affairs
9. Housing and Urban Affairs
10. Individual Assistance Programs
11. International Affairs
12. Law and Justice
13. National Security
14. Natural Resources, Environment, and Agriculture
15. Science, Space, and Transportation
16. Congress and Politics

Each category is further subdivided into functional areas. Within each subdivision the *Directory* lists agency, congressional, and nongovernmental organizations most concerned with the government function and agency. Each listing includes the name, address, telephone number, and a short annotation. For example, under the "Tourism" subdivision of the "Economics and Business" category, the following governmental and non-governmental listings appear among seven others:

GOVERNMENT-ASSOCIATION LINKAGES IN THE DIRECTORY

Agency

U.S. Travel and Tourism Administration (Commerce Department), Main Commerce Bldg. 20230; 377-0136. Donna Tuttle, under secretary.
Prepares and distributes abroad materials to promote travel to the United States (VISIT USA program). Works with states and cities to provide information to foreign travel agencies on destinations in the United States, including accommodations, transportation, recreational facilities, and sight-seeing attractions.

Congress

House Energy and Commerce Committee, Subcommittee on Commerce, Transportation, and Tourism, 151 HOB Annex #2 20515 (2nd and D Sts. S.W.); 226-3160. James J. Florio (D N.J.), chairman; Gregory E. Lawler, staff director and chief counsel. Jurisdiction over legislation affecting tourism.

Non-governmental

American Society of Travel Agents, 440 MacArthur Blvd., N.W. 20007; 965-7520. Joe Hallissey, chairman.
Membership: representatives of the travel industry. Works against fraud, misrepresentation, and other unethical practices. Offers training programs for travel agents. Consumer affairs department offers help for anyone with a travel complaint or industry problem. Library open to the public by appointment.

Another useful reference source is *The Professional and Trade Association Job Finder*. This book identifies career services offered by various types of associations:

1. Professional and Trade Associations
2. Women's Organizations
3. Labor Unions
4. Employment Clearinghouses, Skills Registries, and Job Banks
5. Community Agencies
6. Apprenticeships
7. State and Local Government Agencies

Under the "Professional and Trade Association" section, for example, you will find this type of information:

**NATIONAL ASSOCIATION OF HOUSING
AND REDEVELOPMENT OFFICIALS** (NAHRO)
2600 Virginia Avenue, NW
Washington, DC 20037   202/333-2020
Career information is available. Semi-monthly *NAHRO Monitor* newsletter publishes available positions.

By surveying this book you will quickly identify key contact points for gaining access to job listings, personnel offices, newsletters, job banks, and journals which are organized to provide career and job information on each organization. The real advantage of this resource is that it provides important contact information for finding employment with both the association and member organizations. Many trade and professional organizations will list positions through their association newsletter, placement office, or job bank. Thus, this publication can provide access to nearly 30 million jobs.

Another useful source of information are telephone directories in any city, but especially in state capitals and Washington, D.C. Most associations have listed telephone numbers. Look under the alphabetical listing for these key words:

- American
- Association
- Education
- Institute

- International
- National
- Society
- United

At least 70 percent of all associations begin their names with these key words. Also, try the Yellow Pages. In some communities these organizations will be listed under "Associations." Once you get a telephone number, call the organization for information. Most will be happy to send you a packet of information, including a sample brochure, magazine, newsletter, and application form.

STRATEGIES

Finding employment with associations should follow the job search strategies we outlined in Part II. By consulting the information sources in the *Professional and Trade Association Job Finder* you will locate the major sources for job vacancy listings, ranging from newsletters to computerized job banks. Many associations will place ads in local newspapers in either the classified or business sections, depending on the professional level of the position. You should monitor these job listings and respond with letters, resumes, and telephone calls. But do not spend all your time with these formal job listing sources.

Your most effective job search strategy will be networking. Contact associations for information, advice, and referrals. You can do this by:

1. Contacting the placement service of associations for job listings and counseling.
2. Joining the association and attending their regularly scheduled meetings where you can meet and talk to association members about their needs, your skills, and future job vacancies with this and other associations.
3. Introducing yourself to individuals who work for associations.
4. Responding to classified ads for association positions.
5. Sending a copy of your resume and a cover letter to the head of the association.

Associations operate similarly to other organizations. Once they have a vacancy, they want to fill it as soon as possible. If they have your resume on file and someone knows you personally, your chances of getting called for a job interview and offered a job will be good.

One useful source on job search strategies are special workshops and seminars designed to assist individuals in developing effective job hunting skills and job leads for associations. Georgetown University in Washington, D.C. sponsors a two-day, five-hour "Careers in Associations" seminar ($55) as part of their Professional Development Program (202/625-3001). The Open University (202/966-9606) in Washington, D.C. also presents a similar two-evening course every month ("Getting Your First Association Job," $35) as does First Class (202/797-5102). Such seminars are led by individuals who work for associations and thus they can provide you with the latest tips on who is hiring whom among associations in the Washington, D.C. Metropolitan area and elsewhere.

LISTINGS, PLACEMENTS, AND NETWORKS

Individuals who work for associations can keep abreast of employment opportunities with various associations by consulting a few organizations and publications specializing in job listings and referrals. The American Society of Association Executives (ASAE) is the largest professional association of association executives. It maintains a Washington staff of 100 individuals who assist 13,000 members. ASAE publishes a magazine, maintains a resume referral system, and provides executive search services for all types of positions — not just executive level ones. You can contact them at:

> American Society of Association Executives
> 1575 Eye St., NW
> Washington, DC 20005
> Tel. 202/626-2750 (Placement)
>   202/626-2742 (Information)

The Greater Washington Society of Association Executives provides similar services. It publishes an annual association salary survey as well as a directory of their 2,300 members: *Who's Who in Association Management*. Contact them at:

> Greater Washington Society of Association Executives
> 1133 15th St., NW, Suite 1110
> Washington, DC 20005
> Tel. 202/429-9370

The U.S. Chamber of Commerce also can provide job assistance. Over 14,000 associations belong to this organization. It maintains a free job referral service for professionals. For information on this and other services, contact:

U.S. Chamber of Commerce
1615 H St., NW
Washington, DC 20062
Tel. 202/659-6000

Two organizations publish useful newspapers and maintain job services for associations. *Association Trends*, a weekly newspaper ($60), also maintains a job referral service. This publication goes to 6,000 associations throughout the United States with a readership of over 25,000. You want to pay particular attention to two sections in this newspaper: "Executive Changes" and "Moves and Changes." The newspaper reports on who leaves which association and thus identifies potential job vacancies. The "Moves and Changes" section identifies associations moving office locations from one city to another. Normally, these associations have immediate staffing needs since most of their employees will not move with the association. *Trends* also maintains a "Free Resume" service. For $52 and 10 copies of your resume, they will place a 30-word classified ad of the job you want in their Washington, New York, or Chicago editions for three consecutive weekly issues. When associations respond to your ad, *Trends* sends them a copy of your resume. The association then contacts you directly for more information or schedules you for an interview. Your only cost for this service is the $52 and 10 resumes. *Trends* will keep your file active for three months. You can get information on this publication and service by writing or calling:

Association Trends
4948 St. Elmo Ave., #306
Bethesda, MD 20814
Tel. 301/652-8666

The United States Association Executive also publishes a weekly newspaper which includes a classified section with association job listings. You will want to monitor various sections relevant to your job search, especially "Executive Changes," "Classifieds," and various calendars of meetings. You can list your desired position in the "Job Seeker" section of the Classifieds. This is a free service to subscribers. Non-subscribers can use the service by sending $60 and five copies of their resume to the Association. This fee also automatically gets you a one-year subscription to the newspaper.

Your ad will run up to 42 words in three consecutive weekly issues. Employers request your resume through the Association service. For more information on this service and subscription, contact:

United States Association Executive
4341 Montgomery Avenue
Bethesda, MD 20814
Tel. 301/951-1881

Chapter Twenty - Two
NONPROFIT ORGANIZATIONS

Numerous nonprofit organizations also provide job opportunities for those interested in public service careers. A truly diverse group of organizations, they come in various types, forms, sizes, and interest orientations. They range from public assistance and utilities organizations to single-issue consumer advocacy groups. Most are organized to perform a needed public service or promote a particular cause.

TYPES OF ORGANIZATIONS

Nonprofit organizations are by no means easy to classify. As legal entities, many of the trade and professional associations discussed in Chapter 21 have nonprofit status. However, these are not nonprofit organizations in terms of their major orientation – monetary gain.

Nonprofit organizations generally are organizations with a clear public service mission. Primarily nongovernmental entities, they are incorporated under state laws, exempt from Federal taxes, and legally structured to receive tax deductible gifts and contributions. The governance structure cannot receive private financial gain from the organization. While many such organizations make money, the money must be directed to promote a public purpose.

Several types of nongovernmental and quasi-governmental organizations are good examples of public nonprofit organizations:

- Consumer advocacy groups focused on influencing public policy
- Public assistance organizations with programs designed to assist various community groups
- Religious and charitable groups
- Medical and hospital groups
- Civil rights groups
- Public utilities groups
- Arts and museum groups
- Women's groups
- Public affairs groups

Many educational groups also are nonprofits, but groups such as the American Federation of Teachers (AFT), the National Education Association (NEA), and the American Association of University Professors (AAUP) are best viewed as professional associations; they combine membership, professional representation, lobbying, and political action functions.

Nonprofit organizations generally receive funding through public donations, corporate gifts, fund raising activities, grants, and endowments. Foundations are a major funding source for these organizations. Given the public nature of such funding, staff members of many nonprofit organizations are paid relatively low salaries for their levels of responsibility. In many cases, staff positions with nonprofit organizations are primarily volunteer positions. This is especially true for nonprofit organizations at the local level.

SKILLS NEEDED

Nonprofit organizations hire all types of individuals. They especially need people with good communication, organization, public relations, program development, and fund raising skills. Because of the need to continuously find funding sources, individuals with fund raising skills are highly valued. Fund raising skills include writing grant proposals, soliciting donations, and expanding membership rolls.

Finding employment with nonprofit organizations is usually easier than getting a job with trade and professional organizations and consulting firms. This is due in part to the fact that nonprofit organizations tend to hire generalists and pay lower salaries than these other types of organizations.

RESOURCES AND CONTACTS

Your search for nonprofit organizations should begin in the library. Several books are available on various aspects of nonprofit organizations, from directories of nonprofit organizations at the national and local levels to how-to guides for improving the internal management and resources of these organizations. A new book on careers in nonprofit organizations provides useful guidance on how to enter this field: Terry W. McAdam, *Careers in the Nonprofit Sector: Doing Well By Doing Good* (Washington, D.C.: The Taft Group, 1986). This book outlines job search strategies appropriate for nonprofit organizations as well as lists the largest nonprofits in the country. Other resources are available on nonprofit organizations with international orientations. We include information on these organizations and appropriate resources in Chapter 28.

The most comprehensive listing of nonprofit organizations is a publication issued by the Internal Revenue Service: *Cumulative List of Organizations* (IRS: Publication 78). Updated and reissued annually, this directory lists over 250,000 charitable, fraternal, and private foundation organizations which qualify for tax deductible contributions. Although the IRS claims this list is not all inclusive, after you examine more than 1200 pages of these organizations, you quickly lose interest in looking for additional nonprofits not listed in this resource! Organizations are listed alphabetically and include the organization's name and its city and state location. You will need to do additional research to get the street address and telephone number for individual organizations as well as identify the mission, size, and staff of these organizations.

You also should examine the *Encyclopedia of Associations.* It includes contact and descriptive information on most nonprofit organizations with regional and national offices. The sections on Educational, Cultural, Social Welfare, Health and Medical, and Public Affairs Organizations will yield numerous names and addresses on several such organizations. For example, the following consumer organization appears in the "Public Affairs Organizations" section:

CITIZEN/LABOR ENERGY COALITION (Consumer)
(C/Lec)
600 W. Fullerton Pkwy.   Phone: (312) 975-3680
Chicago, IL 60614   Robert Brandon, Exec. Dir.
Founded: 1978. *Members*: 200. *Staff*: 40. *State Groups*: 15.
Public interest groups including trade union, senior citizen, consumer, environmental, neighborhood, housing, religious, and minority group organizations. Goals are: to meet the

power of the oil companies and utilities; to fight to hold down energy prices and utility rates; and to win a national energy policy for the development of jobs and safe, clean, renewable sources of energy. Activities include working on national issues such as oil and gas pricing and on local issues such as consumer utility legislation, and helping to organize citizen opposition to utility rate hikes and shut-offs. Lobbies in Washington, DC; conducts conferences and local training seminars for community leaders; compiles statistics. Sponsors Energy Action Educational Project (see separate entry). *Committees:* Political Action. *Publications:* Citizen Power, quarterly; also publishes pamphlet and policies brochure.

Several professional organizations provide assistance for individuals seeking employment with nonprofit organizations. The Society for Nonprofit Organizations is the only national society organized to promote nonprofit organizations. Its 3000 member organizations constitute an important professional network of nonprofit executives and directors. The Society publishes a biweekly newspaper and regularly conducts workshops, provides technical assistance, and publishes resources for strengthening nonprofit organizations. You can contact this organization at the following address and phone number:

> Society for Nonprofit Organizations
> 6314 Odana Rd., Suite 1
> Madison, WI 53719
> Tel. 608/274-9777

The Taft Group, one of the nation's leading information and professional service firms for nonprofit organizations, provides numerous resources and services for individuals seeking employment with these organizations. In addition to publishing *Careers in the Nonprofit Sector*, the Taft Group provides executive search services for individuals seeking positions in development, marketing, and public relations. If you are interested in executive level positions, you may want to subscribe to their newsletter, *The Nonprofit Executive,* which provides the latest information on executive level developments. You can contact this organization by writing or calling:

> The Taft Group
> 5130 MacArthur Blvd., N.W.
> Washington, DC 20016
> Tel. 202/966-7086

LOCAL LEVEL NONPROFITS

Nonprofit organizations are most prevalent at the local level. In every city you will find numerous community service organizations. Frequently referred to as community-based organizations, these nonprofit groups provide a variety of social services in the areas of health, education, culture, recreation, rehabilitation, youth, senior citizen services, and local economic development. One of the largest such groups is the United Way which raises funds to provide general, programmatic, and emergency grants to other community service groups.

Local nonprofit organizations come in many types. In most large communities you should be able to locate a directory of community service organizations through your local government, United Way, or other community organization. Check the reference section of your local library for such a directory. These directories usually include three types of nonprofit organizations which comprise the local public service network: governmental, quasi-governmental, and nongovernmental. The United Black Fund Inc. of Greater Washington, D.C., for example, publishes a *Directory of Community Service Organizations in the Washington Metropolitan Area* (1343 H St., N.W., Washington, D.C. 20005, Tel. 202/628-3354 or 628-8043). The index lists nearly 1,000 community-based nonprofit organizations for the Washington, D.C. Metropolitan area in the following generic categories also relevant to other communities:

CATEGORIES OF
LOCAL NONPROFIT ORGANIZATIONS

- Abortion
- Adoption
- Advocacy
- Adult Education
- Alcoholics, Service to
- Ambulance Services
- Animal Care
- Bail Bond
- Birth Certificates
- Child Abuse
- Children Services
- Clothing Distribution
- Community Planning and Development

- Food Distribution
- Foreign Born, Service to Fund Raising and Charitable Organizations
- Furniture Storage and Distribution
- Group Homes, Adult
- Group Homes, Children
- Handicapped, Services to
- Health Organizations
- Hearing and Speech Impaired
- Hospitals and Clinics
- Household Goods, Storage, and Distribution

- Consumer Information and Protection
- Correctional Services
- Counseling Services
- Credit Unions
- Culture and Arts, Media Arts
- Culture and Arts, Performing Arts
- Culture and Arts, Services to the Field
- Culture and Arts, Training and Education
- Culture and Arts, Visual Arts
- Day Care
- Deaf, Services to
- Death Certificates
- Disease Control
- Discrimination Complaints
- Drug Abuse Prevention
- Economic Development
- Education, Alternative
- Education, Basic and Vocational
- Education, Remedial
- Emergency Assistance
- Housing Assistance
- Legal Assistance
- Libraries and Museums
- Maternity Homes
- Mental Health
- Parks and Recreation Services
- Pre-Natal Care
- Public Assistance
- Reading Assistance
- Referral Services
- Regional Agencies
- Research
- Senior Citizens, Services to
- Social Security Assistance
- Spanish Speaking, Services to
- Thrift Shops
- Transportation for the Elderly
- Transportation for the Handicapped
- Transportation, Public
- Veterans, Services to
- Visually Impaired, Services to
- Volunteer Services
- Women, Services to
- Youth Organizations

If you are interested in working with a drug rehabilitation program, you will find 15 organizations with programs and services under the "Drug Abuse Prevention" category:

- Alcohol and Drug Abuse Control Coordinating Office
- Alexandria Methadone Treatment Center
- Bureau of Rehabilitation of the National Capitol Area
- Drug Intervention Counseling Action Program
- Family Service Counseling for the Deaf
- Family Services of Prince George's County
- Last Renaissance
- Latin American Youth Center
- Narcotics Treatment Administration (NTA)
- Palmer Park Counseling Center
- Rap, Inc.
- Shiloh Baptist Church Human Service Center

Southeast Enrichment Center
Surrattsville Community Counseling Center
Washington Area Council on Alcoholism and Drug Abuse
(WACADA)

Within this category, you will find brief annotated descriptions of each program.

STRATEGIES

Once you identify a nonprofit organization appropriate for your interests and skills, contact the organization by letter or telephone. Keep in mind that most nonprofit organizations have two tiers of decision-making: Board of Directors and staff. Hiring decisions may be made by one or the other or both levels, depending on the organization. Let the people at both levels know you are interested in working for them. For small nonprofits, schedule an appointment with the head of the organization or a member of the Board. For large nonprofits, you need to contact both the personnel office and individual hiring personnel within the various organization's units. Chances are you will have no problem being hired for a volunteer position as long as you are willing to help raise funds and organize activities. A full-time paid staff position will be more difficult to find. Nonetheless, make your contacts, conduct informational interviews, leave your resume with key people, and follow-up on referrals and interviews. If you engage in enough of these job search activities, you should be able to find the job you want.

REALISTIC EXPECTATIONS

Except with the largest nonprofit organizations headquartered in Washington, D.C. and New York City, career opportunities with nonprofit organizations are the least financially rewarding public service careers. For example, while the head of an association may earn $85,000 a year, the head of a similar sized nonprofit organization may only earn $30,000 a year. Furthermore, these organizations often lack good management practices, because their staff members lack managerial expertise and have limited funds to acquire the necessary management training and consulting services; some are organizational nightmares run by well-meaning but administratively inept individuals. Governing boards are often weak, and the organizations are frequently involved in difficult political situations.

While these characteristics of nonprofit organizations may be negatives for many job seekers, they are positives for others who seek unique and personally rewarding challenges. Since many of these groups are poor — surviving by a hand-to-mouth existence through a combination of public donations, foundation grants, and government funding — many staff positions may be volunteer positions. Nonetheless, the work of these organizations is personally very rewarding for many people who are oriented to making a difference in the lives of others. Because nonprofit organizations pay staff members much less than other public organizations, you will find it is much easier to break into public sector work through these organizations.

Requiring fewer skills and limited experience, work in nonprofit organizations is open to people who are willing to devote their time and effort to the cause. Thus, they are excellent organizations in which to acquire public service experience as well as for networking with government agencies, associations, foundations, and local elites. Indeed, most nonprofit organizations are governed by a volunteer Board of Directors consisting of community leaders. As a staff member, you are responsible for day-to-day operations to these individuals. You will meet with these individuals and develop contacts with other community elites who provide funding for the organization. In the long run, these individuals may be helpful in advancing your career with other organizations.

Chapter Twenty-Three
FOUNDATIONS AND RESEARCH ORGANIZATIONS

Foundations and research organizations provide job opportunities for individuals with specialized organizational and subject-matter skills. They tend to seek well educated and experienced professionals. The work of these organizations supports the service activities of both governmental and nongovernmental organizations. Most are nonprofit organizations.

FOUNDATIONS

Foundations primarily provide funding for nonprofit organizations pursuing particular social, economic, and cultural programs. Nearly 22,000 foundations operate at both the national and local levels throughout the 50 States. While most of the large foundations (4,063 with assets of $1 million or more or give at least $100,000 a year) have national and international orientations, a large number of smaller foundations operate primarily at the local level. These latter groups are often too small to support a full-time staff and thus look toward community foundations to administer their programs and funds. Indeed, during the past decade there has been a major growth in community foundations which provide funding for community-based nonprofit organizations.

Every large city has several local foundations engaged in providing grants to educational institutions and social service programs. In Washington, D.C., for example, the largest foundation is the Public Welfare Foundation (2600 Virginia Avenue, N.W., Room 505, Washington, D.C. 20037, Tel. 202/965-1800) with assets of $108,600,000. In 1982 this foundation provided 224 grants totalling $5,009,200, ranging from a high of $125,000 to a low of $1,500. Its five largest grants went to The Community Board Program ($125,000), Warren Wilson College ($90,000), Population Institute ($75,000), Environmental Defense Fund ($75,000), and Partners of the Americas ($70,000). These and other large foundations require full-time staffs to administer the grant process.

Foundations provide job opportunities for individuals with specialized skills. Like other nonprofit organizations, foundations have a two-tiered decision-making structure consisting of a Board of Trustees and an administrative staff. The staff positions primarily involve managing foundation funds, reviewing proposals, awarding grants, and administering programs. These activities require skilled professionals who can work well with grantees and board members. They require strong communication, analytical, and management skills.

Since most foundations are small, they have a limited number of staff positions. Therefore, your best job search strategy is to conduct research on these organizations and make personal contacts with either the staff or trustees. A good starting point for conducting research is *The Foundation Directory*, published by The Foundation Center in New York City. Found in most library reference sections, this book lists information on over 4,000 foundations with assets of more than $50 billion. While this represents only 18.5 percent of all foundations, these foundations account for 93 percent of all foundation assets and 85 percent of all grant dollars awarded each year by all foundations. The *Directory* is organized alphabetically and by State and fields of interest. For example, the following information is included for two of the largest foundations:

FOUNDATIONS IN THE DIRECTORY

LILLY ENDOWMENT, INC.
2801 North Meridian Street
P. O. Box 88068
Indianapolis, IN 46208   (317) 924-5471
Incorporated in 1937 in Indiana
Donor(s): J. K. Lilly, Sr., Eli Lilly, J. K. Lilly
Purpose and Activities: "The promotion and support of religious, educational, or charitable purposes." Giving

emphasizes projects that depend on private support, with a limited number of grants to government institutions and tax-supported programs. Special interest in innovative programs that seek to produce positive changes in human society, promote human development, strengthen independent institutions, encourage responsive government at local, state, and national levels, and improve the quality of life in Indianapolis and Indiana. Grants for cultural programs limited to Indianapolis and Indiana. No grants in the fields of health care, biological and physical science research, housing, transportation, or environment, for the establishment of endowment funds, scholarships, production of films or other mass media, or for research on population. No grants to individuals. Report published annually.

Financial Data (yr. ended 12/31/82):
Assets, $779,036,055 (M); expenditures, $47,104,611, including $42,277,363 for 310 grants (high: $5,000,000; low: $5,100).

Officers: Thomas H. Lake, Chairman and President; James T. Morris, Robert A. Johnson, Executive Vice-Presidents; Laura A. Bornholdt, Vice-President, Education; Robert W. Lynn, Vice-President, Religion; William M. Goodwin, Secretary-Treasurer.

Directors: Otis R. Bowen, M.D., Byron P. Hollett, Eli Lilly II, Eugene F. Ratliff, Margaret Chase Smith, Herman B. Wells, Richard D. Wood.

Write: James T. Morris, Executive Vice-President.

THE ROCKEFELLER FOUNDATION
1133 Avenue of the Americas
New York, NY 10036   (212) 869-8500
Incorporated in 1913 in New York.

Donor(s): John D. Rockefeller, Sr.

Purpose and Activities: "To promote the well-being of mankind throughout the world." Concentrates its activities on fields of fundamental importance to mankind through the following six program areas: 1) agricultural sciences, 2) population sciences, 3) health sciences, 4) international relations, 5) equal opportunity, and 6) arts and humanities. Programs are carried out through the awarding of grants and fellowships, the operation of field programs, and the dissemination of knowledge through publications and close association with the media. No grants for personal aid to individuals; for appraising or subsidizing cures or inventions; for the establishment of local hospitals, churches, schools, libraries, or welfare agencies, or for their building and operating funds; for financing altruistic movements involving private profit; for supporting propaganda or attempts to influence legislation; or for investing in securities on a philanthropic basis. Report published annually.

Financial Data (yr. ended 12/31/81):

Assets, $883,200,092 (M); gifts received, $7,630; expendutures, $50,883,521, including $28,855.071 for 550 grants (high: $1,461,000; low: $1,500), $11,440,784 for 6 programs and $2,289,143 for 220 fellowships.

Officers: Richard W. Lyman, President; Laurence D. Stifel, Vice-President and Secretary; Nan S. Robinson, Vice-President for Administration; Jack R. Meyer, Treasurer.

Trustees: Clifton R. Wharton, Jr., Chairman; Robert V. Roosa, Vice-Chairman; W. Michael Blumenthal, John Brademas, Harold Brown, Kenneth N. Dayton, John R. Evens, James C. Fletcher, Herman E. Gallegos, James P. Grant, Tom Johnson, Vernon E. Jordan, Jr., Lane Kirkland, Mathilde Krim, Eleanor Holmes Norton, Victor H. Palmieri, Jane C. Pfeiffer, Alice M. Rivlin, Nevin S. Scrimshaw, Elernor B. Sheldon, Billy Taylor, James D. Wolfensohn.

Write: Laurence D. Stifel, Vice-President and Secretary.

The "Fields of Interest" index of the *Directory* classifies each foundation by purpose and activity:

- Accounting
- Adult Education
- Africa
- Aged
- Agriculture
- Alcoholism
- Animal Welfare
- Anthropology
- Archaeology
- Architecture
- International Law
- International Studies
- Israel
- Italy
- Japan
- Journalism
- Labor
- Language and Literature
- Latin America
- Law and Justice

- Arms Control
- Arts
- Asia
- Australia
- Belgium
- Biochemistry
- Buildings & Equipment
- Business Administration
- Canada
- Cancer
- Caribbean
- Chemistry
- Child Development
- Child Welfare
- Citizenship
- Civic Affairs
- Civil Rights
- Communications
- Community Development
- Community Funds
- Conservation
- Crime & Law Enforcement
- Cultural Programs
- Dentistry
- Dermatology
- Drug Abuse
- Ecology
- Economics
- Education
- Education - Building Funds
- Education - Minorities
- Education, Early Childhood
- Educational Associations
- Education Research
- Elementary Education
- Energy
- Engineering
- Environment
- Europe
- Exchange Programs
- Family Services
- Fellowships
- Fine Arts
- France

- Leadership Development
- Legal Education
- Leprosy
- Libraries
- Marine Sciences
- Medical Education
- Medical Research
- Medical Sciences
- Mental Health
- Mexico
- Middle East
- Military Personnel
- Minorities
- Museums
- Music
- Native Americans
- Nursing
- Nutrition
- Ophthalmology
- Peace
- Performing Arts
- Pharmacy
- Philippines
- Physical Sciences
- Poland
- Political Science
- Population Control
- Population Studies
- Professorships
- Psychiatry
- Psychology
- Public Administration
- Public Policy
- Race Relations
- Recreation
- Rehabilitation
- Religion
- Religion - Missionary Programs
- Religion, Christian
- Religion, Jewish
- Relition, Protestant
- Religion, Roman Catholic
- Rural Development
- Safety

- Freedom
- Government
- Greece
- Handicapped
- Health
- Health Services
- Heart Disease
- Heroism
- Higher Education
- Historic Preservation
- History
- Hospitals
- Hospitals - Building Funds
- Hotel Administration
- Housing
- Humanities
- Immigration
- Insurance Education
- Intercultural Relations
- International Affairs
- International Development
- Schistosomiasis
- Scholarships
- Science and Technology
- Scotland
- Seamen
- Secondary Education
- Social Sciences
- Social Services
- Sociology
- South Pacific
- Speech Pathology
- Student Loans
- Theological Education
- Transportation
- United Kingdom
- Urban Affairs
- Venezuela
- Vocational Education
- Welfare
- Wildlife
- Women
- Youth

The Foundation Center also supports several foundation depositories or libraries throughout the United States. Each depository maintains comprehensive collections of information on foundation activities. If you are seriously interested in working for a foundation, you should visit one of these depositories to familiarize yourself with foundation operations.

RESEARCH ORGANIZATIONS

Approximately 7,500 research organizations provide job opportunities for individuals with specialized research skills. Most of these organizations conduct public related research. Many of them function as public think-tanks, generating public policy options based upon research findings. While the largest number of research organizations are university research centers, thousands of other groups are primarily nonprofit research organizations. They receive their funding through a variety of public sources: government contracts, foundation grants, corporate philanthropy, individual donations, parent institutions, local revenue, membership fees, and sales of books, reports, journals, and other products. Salaries with research organizations tend to be better than those with most nonprofit organizations. They are most comparable to university faculty salaries, which are similar to association and government salaries.

The major sources for developing job leads on research organizations is the *Research Center Directory*, published by Gale Research Company in Detroit. Found in most library reference sections, this comprehensive volume classifies nearly 7,500 research organizations into the following categories:

1. Agriculture, Home Economics, and Nutrition
2. Astronomy
3. Business, Economics, and Transportation
4. Conservation
5. Education
6. Engineering and Technology
7. Government and Public Affairs
8. Labor and Industrial Relations
9. Law
10. Life Sciences
11. Mathematics
12. Physical and Earth Sciences
13. Regional and Area Studies
14. Social Sciences, Humanities, and Religion
15. Multidisciplinary Programs
16. Research Coordinating Offices

Typical entries provide useful contact information and annotated descriptions of activities engaged in by these organizations. The following examples are for three of the largest and most important public affairs-related research organizations:

RESEARCH ORGANIZATIONS IN THE DIRECTORY

AMERICAN ENTERPRISE INSTITUTE (AEI)
1150 Seventeenth Street N.W.   Phone: (202) 862-5800
Washington, DC 20036   Founded: 1943
William J. Baroody, Jr., President
Governance: Independent nonprofit, nonpartisan research and educational organization, with its programs and studies monitored by panels of distinguished scholars, an academic advisory board, and a program priorities advisory committee. Supported by contributions from foundations, corporations, and individuals. Staff: 150 persons.

Research Activities and Fields: Government regulation, economics, health, energy, foreign affairs, law, and legislation. Assists policymakers, scholars, businessmen, the press, and the public by providing objective analyses of national and international issues and fostering competition of ideas. Sponsors televised debates and meetings featuring discussions among experts on major public issues.

Publications and Services: Research results published in legislative and special analyses, books, periodicals, and a series of evaluative, foreign and defense, domestic affairs, and AEI studies. Publications: Economist (monthly), Public Opinion (bimonthly), and Regulation (bimonthly). Holds annual Public Policy week in December. Televised programs made available in audio and video cassettes. Maintains a library of 8,000 volumes and 350 periodicals.

BROOKINGS INSTITUTION
1775 Massachusetts Avenue, N.W.   Phone: (202) 797-6000
Washington, DC 20036   Founded: 1916
Bruce K. MacLaury, President
Governance: Independent nonprofit research organization. Supported by endowment, industry, philanthropic foundations, and contracts with U.S. Government. Staff: 50 research professionals, 145 others.

Research Activities and Fields: Economics, government, foreign policy, and social sciences, including studies on economic growth and stability, taxation, international economics, econometrics, industrial organization and regulation, economics of human resources, government leadership and management, the public service, the Congress, public administration, national security policy, international economic policy, and U.S. relations with northeast Asia and the Soviet Union. Research facilities available, upon application, to visiting scholars whose work is related to purposes of the Institution.

Publications and Services: Research results published in books, pamphlets, and professional journals. Publications: Annual Report, Brookings Papers on Economic Activity (semiannually), The Brookings Review (quarterly), and Reprint Series (irregularly). Maintains a library of 80,000 volumes in economics, political science, and foreign policy; Laura Walker, librarian.

URBAN INSTITUTE (UI)
2100 M Street, N.W.   Phone: (202) 223-1950
Washington, DC 20037   Founded: 1968
William Gorham, President
Governance: Independent nonprofit research organization. Supported by state and local governments, foundations, individuals, and corporate philanthropy. Staff: 86 research professionals, 27 supporting professionals, 42 others. Volume of research: 1983 — $10,000,000.
Research Activities and Fields: Domestic, social, and economic affairs, including multidisciplinary studies on governance and management, health policy, housing and community development, human resources, income security and pension, international activities, public finance, productivity and economic development, and social services. Also conducts research programs on employment and training, women and family policy, minorities and social policy, state and local governments, and transportation and community impact.
Publications and Services: Research results published in books, booklets, and project reports. Publications: Policy and Research Report (three times yearly), Annual Report, supplements and summaries of reports, papers, reprints, and other communications of the Institute. Maintains a library of 26,000 volumes on urban affairs; Camille Motta, librarian.

Many of the larger research organizations will advertise for personnel through their personnel offices or professional associations. You should monitor job listings in newspapers, especially the *Washington Post* and *The Chronicle of Higher Education*, as well as contact both the personnel offices and key individuals within the organizations. The personal contact will be your best strategy. Since these organizations tend to hire subject matter specialists, you should contact individuals in the organizations who share your research expertise. Fellow professionals normally will be happy to provide you with job-related information and referrals. Also, be sure to contact your professional association for job leads. They may maintain a placement service which regularly includes job listings for research organizations.

Chapter Twenty-Four

POLITICAL SUPPORT, INFLUENCE, AND MANAGEMENT GROUPS

Our final set of peripheral organizations consists of an assortment of political support, influence, and management groups primarily centered in and around Washington, D.C. and state capitals. Consisting of Political Action Committees, political parties, lobbyists, lawyers, and political consultants, these groups primarily focus their activities on legislative and executive organizations. In contrast to most other peripheral groups, individuals working with these organizations are deeply involved in the political process of elections, campaign finance, legislative power, and executive influence.

The groups discussed in this chapter constitute a network of related organizations offering numerous job opportunities for individuals interested in nonelected political careers. Furthermore, they provide alternative career paths for individuals on Capitol Hill, in regulatory agencies, and with law firms. While many of the jobs we discussed earlier in government and among peripheral organizations are relatively apolitical, the jobs examined in this chapter lie at the heart of the American political process. These jobs follow the ebb and flow of politics, can be extremely rewarding both financially and personally, and are the glamour, glitter, and glory of the high road of politics and power. Most of these jobs require many years of experience on Capitol Hill, in the legal profession, and among influential political networks. They go to a uniquely talented group of individuals — many of whom are political junkies. However, administrative support positions with these organizations may require very little experience and thus are good entry points for acquiring experience in these fascinating professions.

POLITICAL ACTION COMMITTEES

Political Action Committees (PACs) are a relatively new phenomenon on the American political scene. The first PAC was established in 1961 by the American Medical Association: the American Medical Political Action Committee (AMPAC). In 1963 the National Association of Manufacturers provided seed money to establish the Business-Industry Political Action Committee (BIPAC). Today, nearly 8,250 PACs ostensibly raise money and contribute to the election campaigns of officials at the state and national levels. The pacesetting AMPAC and BIPAC remain two of the most influential PACs.

Most major corporations, labor unions, and lobbying groups have their own PACs. Others contribute to PACs which represent the interests of numerous groups. All PACs are either sponsored by or connected to corporations, labor organizations, membership groups, and trade associations.

The purpose of PACs is clear: raise and spend money on elected officials. They are organized as campaign finance arms of particular trade and professional associations or industries, such as AMPAC. Other PACs are organized as collective campaign finance organizations for several trade and professional associations and interest groups, such as BIPAC. The majority of PACs "invest" in incumbent candidates who are expected to look favorably on the interests of contributors. At times they target incumbents for defeat in expectation a newly elected official they helped fund will favor their interests.

A new type of PAC is one associated with a particular political candidate but is classified and legally functions as a multi-candidate PAC. The rise of this hybrid type of PAC is most closely associated with Vice-President George Bush's PAC: The Fund For America's Future. In 1986 this became the largest PAC of any potential 1988 presidential candidate — $3.9 million in resources, 24 staffers, and 9 consultants. Functioning similar to a miniature presidential campaign organization, The Fund For America's Future in early 1986 was headed by the deputy campaign manager of the Reagan-Bush '84 committee; the political director was the former head of Reagan-Bush voter registration; four regional political directors were hired; full-time staff were hired in Iowa and Michigan and were planned for

New Hampshire; and the staff was rounded out with three research-ers, consultants, professional fund raisers, and direct-mail specialists. Ostensibly an unaffiliated PAC, The Fund For America's Future allocated less than 4 percent of its funds to other candidates (*Washington Post*, February 5, 1986: A3). For all intents and purposes, this PAC is Vice-President Bush's financial and organizational launching pad for the 1988 presidential campaign. This new type of PAC most likely will become a pacesetter for PACs in the late 1980s. Closely affiliated with particular candidates, it opens a new element in the ever expanding revolving door of PACs, Capitol Hill staffs, political parties, lobbyists, political consultants, and trade associations.

Most PACs are multi-candidate organizations. Funded primarily by associations and industries, they funnel funds into the campaigns of particular individuals rather than into political parties. In so doing, these organizations require staff members who are talented in raising contributions, networking among the powerful, and targeting funds into particular campaigns. In addition, PACs such as BIPAC maintain two divisions. A political action division raises and targets funds. A political education division engages in public education programs favorable to the activities of PACs and business associations. This second division requires individuals with strong research and public relations skills.

PACs vary in how they hire personnel. Since they require experienced political fund raising skills, many work exclusively with a particular employment agency or executive search firm to locate key personnel. Others rely on word-of-mouth for recruiting key people from associations and Capitol Hill. Many PACs advertise in newspapers but only for part-time administrative support positions.

The world of PACs is a fascinating yet relatively uncharted employment arena. If you have the necessary skills and motivation, you will need to do a great deal of research on individual PACs as well as network into the proper informal channels which yield employment opportunities with these groups. If you know very little about PACs, read Larry J. Sabato's excellent, well-research book on this subject: *PAC Power: Inside the World of Political Action Committees* (New York: W. W. Norton). Next, contact the Public Records section of the Federal Election Commission (FEC):

> Federal Election Commission
> 999 E Street, N.W.
> Washington, D.C. 20463
> Tel. 202/376-3140
> Toll free: 800/424-9530

The Commission oversees the activities of PACs to make sure they conform with Federal laws. Consequently, the FEC compiles a great deal of information on the location and size of PACs. In particular, you should purchase the FEC's latest editions of "Gross Receipts and Expenditures" ($4.00) and "Non-Party Political Committees — Alphabetical Index" ($10.00). These two documents will provide you with the names, addresses, contact person, affiliations, and total receipts and expenditures of all PACs registered with the FEC. For a $14.00 investment you will have 8,250 PACs at your fingertips!

A few PACs listed in the FEC documents also appear with descriptive information in the *Encyclopedia of Associations*. The BIPAC entry, for example, is annotated in the following manner:

BUSINESS-INDUSTRY POLITICAL ACTION COMMITTEE (BIPAC)
1747 Pennsylvania Ave., N.W.   Phone: (202) 833-1880
Washington, DC 20006   Joseph J. Fanelli, Pres.
Founded: 1963. Businessmen/women and other individuals who are concerned with "the steadily increasing trend toward centralization of our government and domination of the economy and the individual." Describes itself as "the political arm of the business community." Not affiliated with any political party, it provides direct campaign support to U.S. congressional candidates who favor limited government, sound fiscal policies and the American system of free competitive enterprise. Conducts political education briefings, seminars, and conferences for the business community. *Publications:* (1) Politikit, monthly; (2) Politics, quarterly; also publishes Directory of Business-Related Political Action Committees, newsletters, reports, and research studies.

The two FEC documents will provide you with basic comparative data for targeting a job search on particular PACs. In 1986, according to FEC data, the 25 largest PACs were:

LARGEST PACs, 1986

Committee	Receipts	Expenditures
• National Conservative Political Action Committee	$3,956,189	$4,090,258
• Realtors Political Action Committee	2,582,518	988,944
• American Medical Association Political Action Committee	2,088,189	920,911
• National Congressional Club	1,740,000	2,183,260
• The Fund for America's Future, Inc.	1,452,932	392,919
• Democratic-Republican Independent Voter Education Committee (Drive Committee)	1,432,969	685,640
• The Fund for a Conservative Majority (AKA Young America Campaign)	1,361,833	1,398,664
• National Education Association Political Action Committee	1,322,057	341,717
• Citizens For the Republic	1,277,892	977,791
• Auto Dealers for Free Trade PAC	1,201,625	407,173
• UAW - V - CAP (UAW Voluntary Community Action Program)	1,094,242	304,383
• Committee on Letter Carriers Political Education (Letter Carriers Political Action)	985,128	304,320
• Marine Engineers' Beneficial Association Political Fund AKA (MEBA Political Action)	962,388	384,096
• Transportation Political Education League	934,756	681,627
• CWA-COPE Political Contributions Committee	842,009	597,027
• Machinists Non-Partisan Political League	827,916	281,468
• National Association of Life Underwriters Political Action Committee	789,628	652,063
• American Federation of State, County, and Municipal Employees — P.E.O.P.L.E., Qualified	784,358	517,898
• Republican Majority Fund	779,589	1,089,846

• League of Conservation Voters	741,496	721,850
• Campaign for Prosperity	733,241	637,501
• Build Political Action Committee of the National Association of Home Builders	718,188	496,429
• Committee for Thorough Agricultural Political Education of Associated Milk Producers	714,455	577,374
• Active Ballot Club, A Dept. of United Food and Commercial Workers International Union	710,814	384,731
• Marine Engineers Beneficial Association Retirees Group Fund AKA (MEBA Retirees Group)	668,058	735,076

The financial size and rankings of these PACs will change during election years. PACs with the largest staffs also tend to be the ones with the largest amount of receipts and expenditures. AMPAC, for example, has a full-time staff of 48.

POLITICAL PARTIES

Political parties offer job opportunities for individuals interested in working at the heart of the political arena. The Democratic and Republican parties alone consist of thousands of relatively independent party organizations at the national, state, and local levels. While many of them are staffed by volunteers, many also have part-time and full-time paid positions.

Both the Republican and Democratic parties maintain full-time staffs at the national and state levels to provide assistance to local party organizations and individual candidates. The size of these staffs will vary depending on the electoral process. In 1986, for example, the Republican National Committee had a staff of approximately 400; the Democratic National Committee had a staff of 100. During presidential election years, the parties will enlarge their staffs considerably with temporary and part-time employees, many of whom are hired to staff phone banks. Altogether, political parties do not generate a large number of full-time paid positions.

Several political parties hire individuals for a variety of staff positions. Political parties with some staff presence include:

POLITICAL PARTY STAFFS

Party	Staff Size	Telephone Number
• Citizens	2	202/659-8878
• Coalition for a Democratic Majority	4	202/466-4700
• College Republican National Committee	15	202/662-1330
• Conservative Party	5	212/689-8400
• Democratic Congressional Campaign Committee	25	202/789-2920
• Democratic Governors Association	2	202/797-6644
• Democratic National Committee	100	202/797-5900
• Fund for a Democratic Majority	6	202/546-2282
• Libertarian Party	5	713/686-1776
• National Black Republican Council	2	212/863-8628
• National Federation of Democratic Women	3	202/797-5900
• National Federation of Republican Women	8	202/863-8770
• National New Democratic Coalition	6	202/483-4805
• National Republican Congressional Committee	88	202/479-7000
• National Republican Heritage Groups Council	3	202/662-1345
• Republic Governors Association	8	202/863-8620
• Republican National Committee	400	202/863-8500
• Republican National Hispanic Assembly of the United States	4	202/662-1355
• Republicans Abroad	2	202/484-6652
• Republicans Abroad International	3	202/662-1390
• Socialist Labor Party of America	11	415/494-1532
• Young Democrats of America	2	202/797-5900
• Young Republican National Federation	6	202/484-6680

Of all the political parties, the Republican Party has the largest number of organizations and staff positions. This is in part due to the fact that the Republican Party is more centralized and disciplined than the Democratic Party.

Since the political process tends to be highly decentralized and centered around individual candidates for political office, state and national party organizations primarily provide support and assistance to thousands of party members and organizations at the local level. They do this through public education, consulting, technical assistance, and training activities. The funding of individual political campaigns, however, is centered around PACs and the fund raising activities of individual candidates. Given the decentralized nature of political parties, national and state political party jobs vary from fund raising to organizing meetings and conducting training. The Democratic and Republican National Committees each have a personnel office which can provide information on job vacancies. However, the hiring process with these and other political parties is very much an informal networking and word-of-mouth process. You can submit your resume to the personnel office, but your best strategy will be to make contacts with key individuals within the organizations.

The networking strategies outlined in previous chapters, especially Chapter Eight, are most appropriate for gaining entry into these organizations. Whom you know becomes important to your networking approach. The more names you collect and drop as well as referrals you receive will strengthen your job search campaign with these organizations.

LOBBYISTS AND LAWYERS

While most large associations maintain full-time lobbyists and legal counsels on their staffs, other organizations function as lobbyists for various groups, including foreign governments. Variously termed political consultants, government relations firms, public relations and public affairs consulting firms, these are professional lobbying firms. They gather information, provide legal counsel, and lobby legislators and executive agencies for their clients. In short, they pedal information, advice, and influence to and for those willing to pay the price.

Given the multiple roles of lobbyists, the largest group consists of lawyers. Many have previous Capitol Hill experience as congressional staff or committee members. A significant number have been former Administrative Assistants, Legislative Assistants, and Press Secretaries for members of Congress. After all, much of their lobbying work involves legislators and the legislative process. Their intimate Capitol Hill knowledge and contacts prove invaluable in this profession. They monitor impending laws and regulations for their clients as well as push for or against laws and regulations which would affect them. They are the protectors and catalysts for the billions of dollars in government subsidies that go to their clients. Therefore, legal skills and the personal connections the legal field affords these individuals are central to this process.

Lobbyists are associated with law firms, professional lobbying organizations, or freelance as independent consultants. Many former Representatives leave the legislature to join such firms or develop their own clientele. Their major skill is their ability to gain access to key decision-makers. In Washington, D.C. alone, there are approximately 40,000 lawyers; 25,000 of them actively practice their profession. Of these, approximately one-fourth are in the lobbying business. Many of them are associated with law firms which hire paralegals and other support staff to conduct research and writing.

If you are interested in lobbying, keep in mind this is primarily an area dominated by lawyers who are well connected in both the corporate and government worlds. Their organizations do hire nonlawyers for support staff positions. However, this is strictly an informal, word-of-mouth hiring culture. A great deal of secrecy surrounds their organizations and activities. Therefore, you must know the right people, and the more influential people are the ones who can provide you with the necessary connections and access.

If you don't know the right people, try conducting library and networking research which will help develop your connections. Congressional lobbyists are required by law to register with Congress. Representatives of foreign governments must register with the Department of Justice. Consequently, a great deal of data is available on who does what for whom in the lobbying business. One of the easiest ways to locate information on these firms is to consult the latest annual edition of *Washington Representatives* (Washington, D.C.: Columbia Books). This directory lists all registered lobbyists and law firms representing interest groups. It also includes a Foreign Interests Index which lists lobbyists registered as agents of individual foreign governments. For example, two of the largest and most influential professional lobbying firms during the Reagan Administration have been Gray and Company and Black, Manafort, and Stone, Inc. The *Washington Representatives* directory provides inside information on firms as described in the following examples:

———— PROFESSIONAL LOBBYING FIRMS ————

GRAY AND CO.
3255 Grace St., N.W., Washington, DC 20007
Tel.: 202/333-7400
Background: A public relations and public affairs consult-
ant firm. The full name of the company is Gray and
Company Public Communications International, Inc.
Members of firm representing client organizations: John
Berard; Joan R. Braden; Lawrence Brady; Lauri J. Fitz;
Ronna A. Freiberg; Robert Keith Gray; Adonis E. Hoff-
man; Niels Holch; Gary Hymel; Stephen M. Johnson;
Joseph H. Kramer, III; John Lengel; Neil C. Living-
stone; Frank Mankiewicz; Mark Robertson; Jeffrey B.
Trammell; Robert V. Witeck; Steven M. Worth. (NOTE:
The directory provides background information on
some staff members. For example, Mr. Hymel was
former Administrative Assistant to Speaker Thomas
P. O'Neill, Jr.; Mr. Johnson was former Press Secretary
for U.S. Senators John Culver and Gaylord Nelson;
Mr. Mankiewiez was former President of the National
Public Radio)
Clients: American Express Co.; American Flagships;
American Iron and Steel Institute; American Maritime
Association; ASARCO; Browning-Ferris Industries, Inc.;
Budd Co.; Canadian Asbestos Information Centre;
Electronic Industries Association of Japan; Govern-
ment of Haiti; HTB Corporation; Independent Bankers
Association of America; International Brotherhood of
Teamsters, Chauffeurs, Warehousemen and Helpers of
America; Government of Japan; Joint Maritime Con-
gress; Government of Korea; Estee Lauder Inc.; Life
Care Services Corporation; Martin-Baker Aircraft Co.,
Ltd.; Motorola, Inc.; Mutual of Omaha Insurance Co.;
National Broadcasting Co.; Prince Talal bin Abdul Aziz
al Saud; Quixote Corporation; Santa Fe International
Corp.; Shaklee Corporation; Stroh Brewery; Tobacco
Institute; Government of Turkey; United States Bank-
note Corp.

BLACK, MANAFORT, AND STONE, INC.
324 N. Fairfax St., Alexandria, VA 22314
Tel. 703/683-6612

> *Background:* A political consulting and government relations firm.
>
> *Members of firm representing client organizations:* Wayne L. Berman; Charles R. Black; Van R. Boyette; Matthew Freedman; Paul J. Manafort; Nicholas A. Panuzio; Linda Pinegar; Robin D. Roberts; Roger J. Stone.
>
> *Clients:* Banco Central de la Republica Dominica; Government of Barbados; Citizens for Reagan; Government of the Dominican Republic; International Medical Centers; News Corporation, Ltd.; Salomon Brothers; Embassy of Saudi Arabia; Solar Energy Association; Squibb Corp.; Government of St. Lucia; Suburban Propane Gas Corp.; Tosco Corp.

While these firms tend to have good access to the Republican Administration, they are organized to be in the lobbying business over the long-term regardless of who occupies the White House. Consequently, drawing their staffs from both political parties enables them to work well with either Democratic or Republican Administrations. Nonetheless, should a Democratic Administration take control of government in the 1988 presidential elections, these two firms would loose some of their access to top decision-makers. Other firms – primarily with Democratic connections – might emerge as the most influential lobbying groups. For example, one of the newest and fastest growing firms in 1985 was Michael K. Deaver and Associates. Mr. Deaver left the White House in 1985 to cash in on his numerous connections with the Republican Administration – while his connections were still in place. His new firm became an instant success with several million dollars in contracts with foreign and domestic clients. However, Deaver and Associates may well be a "flash organization" – set up only for short-term financial gain based upon a unique set of connections with powerful Republicans. If a Democratic Administration comes to power in 1988, Mr. Deaver should be able to walk away from this business with a few million dollars in his bank account.

Lobbyists also have their own professional association. The American League of Lobbyists has 250 members with a single staff member. Contact them at:

The American League of Lobbyists
1133 15th St., NW
Washington, DC 20005
Tel. 202/429-9440

POLITICAL CONSULTANTS

Political consultants specialize in providing information and advice on how to best run political campaigns and organizations. They work with PACs, political parties, lobbyists, and special interest groups. Most have a great deal of experience and are extremely talented both politically and technically. The better known groups are Patrick Caddall's polling organization, Cambridge Survey Research, and Richard Viguerie's conservative direct-mail fund raising group, Richard A. Vigerie Company. These organizations tend to be associated with a particular political group and perform key political functions: fund raising, campaign strategy, media coverage, and political information. Most use the latest technology to improve the political positions of their clients.

If you are interested in working for these firms, you should begin by reading several books on political consulting. One of the best is another well written and researched book by Larry J. Sabato: *The Rise of Political Consultants* (New York: Basic Books). It includes an examination of the history, roles, and organization of these groups as well as a listing of the major political consulting firms classified into four types of consulting skills and services: general, polling, media, and direct-mail. Dr. Sabato also identifies firms by party affiliation, ideological leaning, scope, and specialty.

Your best job search strategy with these firms again is networking. Few of these firms advertise for personnel. They locate personnel through word-of-mouth and through direct contacts with individuals who self-market themselves.

Except for administrative support positions, keep in mind that these firms hire individuals with a great deal of experience and skills. Like so many others who work the political arena, these individuals live work-driven life styles of the political junkie. Dr. Sabato best captures their skills and life styles in his revealing study of these political operatives:

> . . . consultants are hard-working professionals: very bright and capable, politically shrewd and calculating, and impressively articulate. They travel tens of thousands of miles every year, work on campaigns in a dozen or more states simultaneously, and eat, breathe, and live politics. They are no less political junkies than the candidates they serve.

Political consultants also have their own association or belong to specialty associations which can provide you with information and advice on entering this field. The 572 members of the American Association of Political Consultants tend to be generalists and media professionals. Contact them at:

> American Association of Political Consultants
> One Mercantile Center, Suite 2612
> St. Louis, MO 63101
> Tel. 314/436-4185

Political consultants specializing in polling tend to join one of these associations:

> American Association of Public Opinion Research
> P. O. Box 17
> Princeton, NJ 08542
> Tel. 609/924-8670
>
> Council of American Survey Research Organizations
> Three Upper Devon Belle Terre
> Port Jefferson, NY 11777
> Tel. 516/928-6954
>
> National Council on Public Polls
> Box 183
> Princeton, NJ 08540
> Tel. 609/924-6570

PART VI

GOING INTERNATIONAL

Many Americans prefer working in the international arena on public-related issues ranging from political communication to assisting the poor in Third World countries. Indeed, nearly 2.5 million Americans live abroad. Approximately 50 percent of them reside in Third World countries. Many of these individuals have chosen either short-term or long-term international careers. Many become expatriates who will live the remainder of their lives abroad. Nearly 150,000 work for the Federal government; another 300,000 work for private industry.

Public affairs-related international jobs and careers follow several patterns. Some individuals acquire their initial work and international experience as Peace Corps volunteers. After Peace Corps many volunteers join the U.S. Agency for International Development, the State Department, nonprofit international organizations, or the United Nations. Other individuals complete a graduate level program in international relations and find employment with the Defense Department or the United Nations. Others prefer working for church missions, private development organizations, newspapers, or educational institutions.

In this final section we outline basic job alternatives and strategies for individuals interested in working in the public international arena. We focus on the interests of two groups of people. First, many individuals want to begin their careers working abroad on public-related issues and thus need guidance on what to do in order to land a job. Second, many individuals who work in the United States wish to work abroad for a few years and thus need assistance on acquiring short-term international employment. Except for some expatriates who have chosen to permanently live abroad, most Americans working abroad will eventually come home to settle into other careers. This part, as well as the other chapters throughout this book, will help these returnees find employment with public service organizations.

Chapter Twenty-Five

OPPORTUNITIES AND STRATEGIES IN THE INTERNATIONAL ARENA

Public service jobs and careers in the international arena are more than just another form of employment. For many people, they involve an important life style where one's job and personal life merge into a unique form of worklife. They frequently involve a life style where it is difficult to separate one's work and income from one's personal and family situation. Resettling Cambodian refugees, feeding the starving in Ethiopia, demonstrating a new irrigation pump in Indonesia, or responding to a political coup d'etat in Guatemala are experiences unlike any found in jobs and careers in the United States.

Challenging, exciting, and sometimes dangerous, international jobs are particularly appealing for certain types of individuals. For many, these jobs are both personally and financially rewarding. Some individuals become international nomads, addicted to travel and living in unfamiliar societies and cultures. Indeed, for those who have lived and worked abroad, it is often difficult to communicate to others the uniqueness, excitement, and satisfaction of the international experience. For others, international work can be a trying experience, best abandoned and forgotten.

Living and working abroad is required for only certain types of international jobs. Other international jobs are based in the United States. For example, many international agencies and organizations maintain both field and headquarter operations; headquarters are

373

often located in Washington, D.C., New York City, or San Francisco. An international career with these organizations involves rotation between field and headquarter locations or occasional travel to field sites abroad.

MYTHS AND REALITIES

International work has a certain lure and mysticism which was once reserved for itinerate missionaries, anthropologists, and soldiers of fortune of decades ago. There are probably more myths about international work than of any other type of work. Among these myths are:

1. International employment pays extremely well compared to salaries in the States.
2. International jobs are very challenging and interesting.
3. International work involves exciting and sometimes exotic travel.
4. International development work is personally rewarding because of the positive changes one is able to make in the lives of others.
5. International life styles are better than back home.

Like many other jobs, international employment has its ups and downs. The following realities more accurately reflect situations many individuals encounter in this employment arena:

1. *The financial rewards of international employment vary greatly.* Some jobs — especially international consulting — pay very well. Jobs with nonprofit organizations pay poorly. For those living abroad, special financial benefits are often offset by additional expenses incurred in trying to maintain a certain life style as well as lost opportunities for supplementing income, such as appreciation on property in the States.

2. *Some international jobs are exciting, but many are dull and boring.* The excitement tends to come from the life style which involves traveling and learning about other cultures, eating different foods, meeting new and different people, and encountering unique events. Foreign Service

Officers often end up stamping travel documents in some dreadful, hot and dirty capital city where the most exciting things to happen are to receive a letter from home, take a trip outside the country, acquire a new videotape, or check into a first-class hotel which has hot water and air conditioning. These are the events that make international work interesting for many people. They are often the subjects of peoples' "war stories" about "how it was when we lived and worked abroad."

3. *Travel is definitely a benefit for many individuals who have international jobs.* However, the excitement of travel often wears off after age 40, after the third move in five years, after the tenth flight in a single year, and after the third lost suitcase and another terrifying taxicab ride from another chaotic airport. On the other hand, young, inexperienced, and single people tend to disproportionately enjoy the novelty of international travel. Like all novelties, this one can wear off after a while.

4. *International development work is personally rewarding for individuals who can make a difference in the lives of others.* But development work also is one of the most frustrating areas of international work. Few changes actually take place; the process tends to be very political; and development work fails more often than it succeeds. Individuals working for the USAID missions in Third World countries, for example, are more likely to be preoccupied with obligating aid funds and putting out brush fires on problematic USAID projects than in making progress in development. For many people, development work becomes more of a personal ego trip than one of concrete long-term accomplishments. Satisfaction comes more from "mingling with the natives" — speaking the local language, eating the local foods, laughing at the local jokes, and receiving the exaggerated status accorded to well-educated American development workers.

5.   *International life styles vary considerably.* Living
     abroad can mean a large and comfortable home
     with servants and a good international school for
     one's children. But such comforts are often offset
     by daily inconvenience of transportation and
     communication, by poor health and recreation
     facilities, by cultures which are at best remembered
     rather than lived, and by the unemployed spouse
     situation. In many countries one spends a great
     deal of time on the basics of living, such as shop-
     ping for food and getting from point A to point B.
     Local health facilities may be rudimentary or
     downright dangerous. And one's spouse is likely
     to be unemployed – a recurring and extremely
     serious problem for two-career couples who have
     chosen to live abroad and then find international
     living a tremendous strain on their marriage, often
     ending in divorce. Local cultures may place con-
     straints on women. Consequently, adverse living
     conditions may result in a low level of work out-
     put and little professional development. For
     families with teenage children, the international
     life style often becomes a serious liability because
     good international high schools are found in only
     a few countries. At this point in life, many people
     are anxious to return to the States or be trans-
     ferred to a country which has a good international
     school. Others get tired of international living.
     Added to these adverse conditions are safety con-
     siderations attendant with the continuing rise of
     international terrorism and anti-Americanism.
     Consequently, the international life style is not for
     everyone nor is it for some people at particular
     stages in their lives.

MOTIVATION

The myths and realities provide a glimpse into some of the
distinct advantages and disadvantages which motivate individuals
to pursue international work. The major advantages are:

1.   *Money:* Many international positions pay excellent
     salaries which may be exempt from Federal, state,

and local taxes (first $80,000 is exempt from Federal taxes if one lives abroad for at least 11 consecutive months). This tax break applies to international consultants who live abroad. Federal government employees working abroad, however, are not exempt from Federal taxes, and many consultants must pay taxes to their countries of residence. But given additional housing and living adjustment benefits, as well as lower costs of living in many countries, some individuals do very well financially.

2. *Adventure:* Especially for young, inexperienced, and single individuals, international work can be very exciting. Working in Latin America, Africa, and Asia is for some people one of the last great frontiers. New places and different cultures become extremely life enriching experiences.

3. *Pursue a cause:* Several public causes can be pursued through international employment. Many individuals want to promote U.S. foreign policy, international peace, population planning, and rural development. Numerous government agencies, private development organizations, religious groups, and nonprofit organizations are organized to pursue such causes.

4. *New Challenges:* International work does offer new and unusual challenges, from basic living to getting a job done. Individuals often find such work challenges their basic assumptions about people as well as work itself.

5. *Life style:* Many individuals are motivated to work in the international arena because of the life style. The work itself brings them into contact with new and interesting cultures; the work may change constantly; and they are given an extraordinary amount of status and authority not found with most jobs in the United States.

Those who work long-term in the international arena often find the advantages outweigh the disadvantages. In addition, many long-term international workers don't know what else they could or would do if they left this employment arena.

ORIENTATION

International work is not for everyone. Most organizations working in this arena identify a particular type of individual who is best suited for international work. These people tend to have the following characteristics:

1. *Adaptability and flexibility:* willing to adapt to changing circumstances and adjust to the norms of the situation.

2. *Tolerance and empathy:* listen to others, understand their behavior, accept different behaviors as legitimate, and tolerate ambiguities.

3. *Sensitivity to cultural differences:* adjust to cultural differences without going "native"; maintain one's own identity.

4. *Patience and perseverance:* balance the America work ethic of getting things done now with work cultures that place higher value on maintaining power and good interpersonal relations rather than punctuality and productivity.

5. *Humor:* maintain a sense of humor especially in situations which are sometimes frustrating; don't take oneself too seriously.

6. *Curiosity:* be open to new experiences and learning.

7. *Facility in foreign languages:* especially for individuals living and working abroad, they should have some ability to learn a second or third language.

While these characteristics are common among many individuals who work in the international arena, there is also a negative side to them. Indeed, there is a fine line between being tolerant, sensitive, and patient, and being useless on the job. Some individuals adjust *too* well and thus accomplish little or nothing other than "enjoy" their international life styles. For many professionals who are very job-oriented, international employment can take a serious toll on their professional development.

ORGANIZATIONAL ALTERNATIVES

Numerous public-oriented organizations provide a host of alternative international job opportunities for enterprising job seekers. The major such organizations are:

1. *Federal, state, and local government agencies:* Most Federal executive agencies have international interests and functions. The U.S. Congress and legislative agencies are deeply involved in international issues. Many state governments are very active in promoting international trade and tourism. Some cities even hire international experts to promote trade, tourism, and foreign investment in local economic development.

2. *Contracting and consulting firms:* Several specialized consulting firms compete for Federal government contracts to perform a variety of international tasks, such as designing projects, providing support services, and implementing development projects abroad. The major funding sources for these firms are the U.S. Agency for International Development (USAID) and the World Bank.

3. *International organizations:* Numerous international and regional organizations, such as the United Nations and the Organization of American States, are structured to promote world peace, international cooperation, economic development, and social welfare.

4. *Nonprofit organizations:* A variety of organizations are designed to promote particular international causes. These include: nonprofit charitable and social welfare organizations such as

CARE and Project Hope. Other organizations are primarily private development organizations engaged in promoting particular types of development projects in population planning, health, education, energy, and rural development. Religious organizations are active in promoting health, education, and welfare services in developing countries. Several foundations specialize in funding nonprofit organizations throughout the world.

5. *Trade and Professional Associations:* Thousands of trade and professional associations have international interests, including members and affiliated offices. Most of these associations are headquartered in New York City or Washington, D.C.

STRATEGIES AND RESOURCES

Each of the following chapters outline useful job search strategies for each type of organization. The chapters present basic job search information. Whever possible we identify key resources so you can follow up in locating the details on employment opportunities with specific organizations.

In general, your best overall job search strategy is to research each organization and custom-design your resumes and letters as well as your networking strategies around the interests, concerns, and language of the organizations you wish to pursue. Your first step should be to read a few useful books on international employment and then begin researching various organizations through key directories in the library. A good starting point are several of the following major books on international employment, most of which are updated regularly. Since few libraries have these books, we have included order information on them in our resource section.

┌─── **USEFUL RESOURCES ON INTERNATIONAL JOBS** ───┐

Careers in International Affairs, Linda L. Powers (Washington, D.C.: Georgetown University, 1986). This newly revised and hard-to-find volume is perhaps the best overview of international job opportunities available anywhere. It provides contact names, addresses, and phone numbers as well as annotated descriptions of 10 types of international organizations.

The Overseas List: Opportunities for Living and Working in Developing Countries, David M. Beckmann, Timothy J. Mitchell, and Linda L. Powers (Minneapolis: Augsburg Publishing House, 1985). An excellent examination of Third World job opportunities. The book stresses a religious theme in finding employment with a variety of organizations focused on Third World development work. It includes a separate chapter on finding employment with church missions abroad.

How to Get a Job Overseas, Curtis W. Casewit (New York: Arco, 1984). One of the most comprehensive and readable books on all types of international jobs. Includes special chapters on job strategies, educators, youth, skilled craftspeople, writers, artists, volunteers, travel, international organizations, intelligence agencies, and health.

International Jobs: Where They Are, How to Get Them, Eric Kocher (Reading, MA: Addison-Wesley, 1984). Divides the international job market into seven organizational arenas, addresses questions on education, and provides useful job search strategies, including sample resumes and letters.

Guide to Careers in World Affairs (New York: Foreign Policy Association, 1986). Provides an overview of alternative careers in world affairs. Addresses careers in private nonprofit organizations, the Federal government, international organizations, and international business, banking, and finance. Includes names and addresses.

Work, Study, Travel Abroad, 1986-1987, Margorie Aloff Cohen (New York: St. Martin's, 1986). Sponsored by the Council on International Educational Exchange and published biannually, this guide is especially useful for young people who wish to work and travel abroad. It includes part-time and volunteer work and is organized by geographic regions and countries. Includes useful tips on visas, study programs, and travel along with personal testimonies of life on the road.

Work Your Way Around the World, Susan Griffith (Cincinnati: Writer's Digest Books, 1986). Designed for the global traveller, this book is the guide for the young living on a shoestring who seek the unusual but fascinating world of short-term employment for bank-rolling their passion for travel. Organized by region and countries and includes names, addresses, and maps.

The Prentice-Hall Global Employment Guide, James N. Powell (Englewood Cliffs, NJ: Prentice-Hall, 1983). Reveals where today's jobs are in the U.S., overseas, and in government. Includes practical exercises and sample resumes. Out of print but found in libraries.

Several other books, brochures, and listing services focus on teaching abroad. Two of the best and most comprehensive books are:

Teach Overseas: The Educator's World-Wide Handbook and Directory of International Teaching in Overseas Schools, Colleges, and Universities, Steve Webster (New York: Maple Tree Publishing, 1984). Contains 432 pages of valuable and hard-to-find information, including names and addresses, on teaching opportunities in each of over 200 countries and territories.

Educators' Passport to International Jobs: How to Find and Enjoy Employment Abroad, Rebecca Anthony and Gerald Roe (Princeton, NJ: Peterson's Guides, 1984). Provides an overview of the process of preparing for overseas employment, surviving the experience, and returning home. Includes sample resumes and letters as well as names and addresses.

A useful booklet on this same topic is Irvin D. Soloman's *Make It Happen: A Comprehensive Guide and Directory for Americans Wishing to Teach Overseas* (Casselberry, FL: Impact Communication, 1985).

Several job listing services also are available for individuals interested in international employment. However, you must be careful since many of these services are big rip-offs. You will see classified ads in numerous publications on "Jobs Overseas," "Teach Overseas," or "International Jobs." Some of these ads produce useful books and brochures, but many are nothing more than a list of contact names and addresses − often dated − which can be readily found in your library. In fact, many of the "Teach Overseas" ads result in a listing of Department of Defense Dependent Schools or a $10 per country listing of contact names and addresses which are easily found in Webster's *Teach Overseas* book or by calling the Teacher Recruitment Section of the Department of Defense Dependents Schools (202/325-0885) for a free listing of overseas schools under the Department of Defense.

Many groups have developed international job listings. Some of the better known ones include:

Job Opportunities Bulletin. Published bimonthly, this listing includes job vacancy announcements from employers as well as advertisements from individuals seeking jobs in international development with all types of organizations. To subscribe for one year, send $15 to the New TransCentury Foundation, 1724 Kalorama Rd., NW, Washington, D.C. 20009. You can also advertise your availability to potential employers for $35.

ODN Opportunities Catalog. Published by the Overseas Development Network, the *Catalog* includes internship, employment, and research opportunities for individuals first entering the international field. Send $15 to Catalog Orders, Overseas Development Network, P. O. Box 2306, Stanford, CA 94305.

Employment Abroad. Publishes international career information and maintains an employment registry. Write or call: Council on International Educational Exchange, 205 E. 42nd Street, New York, NY 10017, Tel, 212/661-1414.

International Employment Opportunity Digest. Lists current job openings. Write: Employment International, P. O. Box 29217, Indianapolis, IN 46229.

Friends of World. Publishes job listings for teachers as well as provides employment services for nurses. Write or call: Friends of World, P. O. Box 1049, San Diego, CA 92112, Tel. 714/690-4311.

Overseas Jobworld. Provides career information on overseas job opportunities. Write: Overseas Jobworld, Box 645 — WW, Union City, CA 94587.

Foreign and Domestic Teachers' Bureau. Maintains a listing of foreign teaching opportunities. Write: Foreign and Domestic Teachers' Bureau, Box 1063, Vancouver, WA 98666.

Several international organizations, such as InterAction, CODEL, PACT, and NCIH, also provide job listings and advice. We have included information on these employment sources in the appropriate chapters of this section.

Several executive search firms also specialize in finding individuals for international positions. However, most of these firms will work with private businesses which are not oriented toward public affairs. Nonetheless, you might contact these firms by telephone or letter. Indicate your interest and send them a resume. An excellent guide to these firms is another hard-to-find volume which we include in our resource section: *International Directory of Executive Recruiters* (Fitzwilliam, NH: Consultants News, regularly updated).

Other sources of international job leads include the classified ads in major newspapers, especially the Sunday editions of *The New York Times* and *The Washington Post*. All types of international groups will list job vacancies in these newspapers. Also, be sure to monitor job listings with professional associations and in *The Chronicle of Higher Education, The National Job Market,* and the *National Employment Business Weekly* of the *Wall Street Journal*.

But your single best job search strategy will be your networking efforts in the international arena. Talk to people in the international field, get referrals, and follow-up with informational interviews, resumes, letters, and telephone calls. People working in the international field tend to have a certain comradery not found in many other employment fields. The fact that someone works, or is interested in working, in this field often leads to instant assistance. For one does not have to know someone to know that there is something very special about having worked in the international field, especially if the work involved living abroad for a lengthy period of time. International experience creates a unique common bond among many individuals who otherwise have little in common.

Chapter Twenty-Six
UNITED STATES GOVERNMENTS

The largest number of international job opportunities in the United States are found with various agencies of the Federal government. Approximately 50,000 Federal civilian employees work abroad. Another 500,000 U.S. military work in overseas U.S. installations.

But these numbers represent less than half of all government employees working in international affairs. The majority of international public affairs jobs are based in the United States. These jobs either provide support for agency field operations or they direct international operations from U.S.-based offices. Each agency has some international interest and staff themselves accordingly. At the same time, since many state and local governments are involved in international affairs, they too need international staff expertise.

In this chapter we outline the basics for locating international opportunities with various government agencies at all levels. While many of the jobs are based in the United States and require occasional travel abroad, many other international jobs require residence in foreign countries and rotation from one field site to another as well as between field and headquarter offices. For example, the U.S. Information Agency (USIA) has 8,600 employees of whom 3,400 work in the U.S. They provide support for field operations consisting of 4,200 foreign nationals hired by USIA.

FEDERAL EXECUTIVE AGENCIES

The Federal government hires all types of individuals for international positions, ranging from highly-skilled intelligence specialists to clerk-typists. Most positions deal with international politics, economics, administrative, commercial, and information affairs as well as all support services required to perform the international activities.

The distinction between what is an international or a non-international job is not always clear. For example, one may be employed as a Department of State librarian in charge of maintaining an excellent international resource collection. While this position involves a great deal of knowledge and skill concerning international affairs, it does not involve overseas travel nor the use of foreign languages. Yet, the position could lead to other international positions requiring overseas travel and the use of foreign languages.

For our purposes, we consider any position which to some degree involves international affairs to be an international position. This broad definition includes Foreign Service Officers, Peace Corps volunteers and staff, U.S. Agency for International Development employees, as well as thousands of individuals in other agencies promoting U.S. foreign, military, economic, and social goals in both policy and support staff positions at the Federal, state, and local levels. Some agencies and positions are primarily oriented toward foreign policy whereas others are primarily concerned with promoting domestic policies through the use of international resources.

Executive Office of the President

The Executive Office of the President, while employing fewer than 600 individuals altogether, has a few international positions. The major offices with such positions include:

- Council of Economic Advisors
- National Security Council
- Office of Management and Budget
- Office of Science and Technology
- Office of the United States Trade Representative
- White House Office

Executive Departments

- ***Department of Agriculture***
  — Foreign Agricultural Service

- Office of International Cooperation and Development
- Economics and Statistics Service (International Economic Division)
- Agricultural Market Service
- Animal and Plant Health Inspection Service
- Forest Service (International Forestry Staff)
- Office of Transportation
- Science and Education Administration
- World Food and Agricultural Outlook and Situation Board
- *Department of Commerce*
  - International Trade Administration
  - Foreign Commercial Service
  - Bureau of the Census
  - National Oceanic and Atmospheric Administration
  - Bureau of Economic Analysis
  - United States Travel Service
  - Maritime Administration
  - National Bureau of Standards
  - National Telecommunications and Information Administration
  - Office of Products Standards Policy
  - Patent and Trademark Office
- *Department of Defense and Related Agencies*
  - Office of the Assistant Secretary for International Security Affairs
  - Office of the Undersecretary of Defense for Research and Engineering
  - Army Material Development and Readiness Command
  - Planning and Policy Directorate of the Organization of the Joint Chiefs of Staff
  - Office of the Secretary of Defense

  NOTE: Department of Defense maintains a special service to assist individuals with overseas employment: Department of Defense Automated Overseas Employment Referral Program (DOD AOEFP)

  - Defense Advanced Research Projects Agency
  - Defense Intelligence Agency
  - Defense Security Assistance Agency
  - Department of Defense Dependents Schools
  - National Security Agency/Central Security Service
- *Department of Education*
  - Office of International Education
  - Office of the Administrator of Education for Overseas

Dependents
- *Department of Energy*
  - Office of International Energy Affairs
  - Assistant Secretary for Defense Programs
  - Assistant Secretary for Policy and Evaluation
  - Economic Regulatory Administration
  - Energy Information Administration
  - Office of Energy Research
- *Department of Health and Human Services*
  - Office of International Health
  - Social Security Administration (Division of International Operations and Office of International Policy)
  - National Institutes of Health (Fogarty International Center)
  - National Center for Health Statistics
  - Alcohol, Drug Abuse, and Mental Health Administration
  - Center for Disease Control
- *Department of Housing and Urban Development*
  - Office of International Affairs
- *Department of Interior*
  - Office of Territorial and International Affairs
  - Bureau of Mines
  - U.S. Geological Survey
  - Bureau of Land Management
  - Ocean Mining Administration
  - U.S. Fish and Wildlife Service
  - National Park Service
  - Water and Power Resources Service
- *Department of Justice and Related Agencies*
  - *Department of Justice*
    - Antitrust Division
    - Civil Division
    - Criminal Division
    - Office of the Deputy Attorney General
    - Office of Intelligence Policy Review
    - Foreign Claims Settlement Commission of the United States
  - *Drug Enforcement Administration* (DEA)
    - Office of Intelligence
  - *Federal Bureau of Investigation* (FBI)
  - *Immigration and Naturalization Service* (INS)
- *Department of Labor*
  - Bureau of International Labor Affairs
  - Bureau of Labor Statistics

- *Department of State*
  - U.S. Foreign Service
  - All other offices
- *Department of Transportation*
  - Office of International Policy and Programs
  - Federal Aviation Administration (Office of International Aviation Affairs)
  - Federal Highway Administration
  - Saint Lawrence Seaway Development Corporation
  - U.S. Coast Guard (Office of Public and International Affairs)
- *Department of Treasury*
  - Office of the Assistant Secretary for International Affairs
  - United States Custom Service
  - Office of International Tax Affairs
  - International Revenue Service (Office of International Operations; Foreign Tax Assistance Staff)
  - Office of the Comptroller of the Currency

Independent Agencies

- *Central Intelligence Agency*
- *Civil Aeronautics Board*
  - Bureau of International Affairs
- *Consumer Product Safety Commission*
  - Office of International Affairs
- *Environmental Protection Agency*
  - Office of International Activities
- *Export-Import Bank of the United States*
- *Federal Communications Commission*
  - Office of Science and Technology (International Staff)
  - Common Carrier Bureau (International Conference Staff)
  - International Facilities Office
- *Federal Maritime Commission*
- *Federal Reserve System*
  - Division of International Finance
  - Division of Banking Supervision and Regulation
  - Federal Open Market Committee
- *General Services Administration*
  - National Archives and Records Service
- *Inter-American Foundation*
- *National Aeronautics and Space Administration*

  – Office of International Affairs
- *National Science Foundation*
  – Division of International Programs
- *Nuclear Regulatory Commission*
  – Office of International Programs
- *Panama Canal Commission*
- *Peace Corps*
- *Securities and Exchange Commission*
  – Corporate Finance Division
  – Enforcement Division
  – Market Regulation Division
- *Smithsonian Institution*
  – Office of International Activities
  – Office of Fellowships and Grants
  – Office of Museum Programs
  – International Exchange Service
  – Traveling Exhibition Service
  – Woodrow Wilson International Center for Scholars
- *U.S. Arms Control and Disarmament Agency*
- *U.S. Information Agency*
- *U.S. International Development Cooperation Agency*
  – Agency for International Development
  – Overseas Private Investment Corporation
- *U.S. International Trade Commission*
- *U.S. Postal Service*
  – Office of International Postal Affairs

Commissions, Committees, Advisory Groups

A final group of Federal executive employers which hire international specialists are the various commissions, committees, and advisory groups established by the president or Congress. Most of these groups are attached to particular departments or agencies. Some are permanent whereas others function for only one or two years. Examples of such groups include:

- Agricultural Policy Advisory Committee for Trade Negotiations (U.S. Department of Agriculture)
- Committee on Foreign Investment in the United States
- East-West Foreign Trade Board
- Japan-United States Friendship Commission
- U.S. National Commission for UNESCO (Department of State)

Your best strategy for getting a job with these groups is to monitor their formation through the *Congressional Record* and the *Federal Register*. As soon as you learn of the impending formation of a group, contact the individuals responsible for establishing the group. Schedule an appointment for an informational interview, and leave a copy of your resume with the individual you interviewed.

Overseas Staffs and Recruitment

Most executive agencies do not maintain overseas staffs. Agencies with overseas staffs sometimes recruit individuals locally, normally among staff spouses and talented expatriates, and through central personnel offices in Washington, D.C. Overall, however, most recruitment for international jobs with Federal agencies is done in the United States. Indeed, given the Washington-bias of Federal agencies, it is difficult to find employment with agencies if you are abroad, even though a vacancy is available for which you are highly qualified. Most agencies prefer recruiting individuals in the States and then transferring them to field sites.

The major agencies maintaining overseas staffs and conducting some in-country recruitment are:

- Department of Defense
- Department of State
- Peace Corps
- U.S. Agency for International Development
- U.S. Information Agency

Hiring Systems and Strategies

Hiring procedures and practices vary among executive agencies. Several agencies are exempted from the competitive service, whereas others follow OPM rules and regulations. Exempted services have their own hiring procedures. The Department of State, for example, follows the European pattern of a career and rank personnel service. Responsible for promoting U.S. foreign policy, the Foreign Service employs over 7,000 people as Foreign Service Officers and Specialists. Special recruitment and selection procedures define entry into the Foreign Service. Each December approximately 12,000 individuals sit for the written Foreign Service examination to gain entry into the Department of State (Foreign Service Officers), the U.S. Information Agency (Foreign Service Information Officers), and Department of Commerce (Foreign Service Commercial Officers).

Once selected, most Foreign Service Officers spend the rest of their career in the Foreign Service. Their "tour" involves being transferred to several of the 230 embassies and consulates the U.S. maintains throughout the world as well as moves from one type of position to another. Rather than being hired as specialists for a particular position, they are hired as international specialists who move through the ranks. The "ranks" consist of many positions requiring different types of skills and knowledge.

The U.S. Agency for International Development (USAID) is structured similarly to the Foreign Service. In fact, the majority of USAID positions are designated as Foreign Service positions. At the same time, nearly 40 percent of USAID positions are civilian (GS positions and thus follow OPM procedures). USAID maintains two personnel offices — a civilian and Foreign Service — which are located in Rosslyn, Virginia. If you want to work for USAID, you must decide which personnel system you want to enter. If your choice is Foreign Service, then your career will take a different pattern from that of the civilian-based civil service.

The Peace Corps is a good example of another type of personnel system. Peace Corps is one of the most unique agencies created in the Federal government. In many respects its volunteers are the "real" international workers. They learn local languages and work in the field with foreign counterparts. No other Federal employees work to the same extent at the field level and literally get their hands dirty in international development work. However, entry into the Peace Corps is extremely competitive today. Each year Peace Corps receives more than 13,500 applications for fewer than 3,500 volunteer positions. Once selected, the typical Peace Corps tour is two years; some volunteers extend an additional year. Altogether, there are approximately 6,000 volunteers working in 61 countries throughout the Third World.

Most Peace Corps staff positions are largely limited to individuals with Peace Corps volunteer experience. In addition, staff positions have a built-in time limit. To discourage the growth of a traditional, conservative, and entrenched bureaucracy, Congress placed a statutory time limit on employment with Peace Corps: staff members cannot work more than five consecutive years with the Agency. Consequently, Peace Corps members are hired for two and one-half year tours, which may be extended to a second tour for a total of five years of service. After the second tour, they must leave the Agency. Many staff members look for employment with other Federal agencies doing international development work. Indeed, the Department of State alone has 1,000 former Peace Corps volunteers and staff members on its staff. USAID has become one of

the major recruiters and employers of former Peace Corps employees.

While some executive agencies may follow other recruitment
patterns, most executive departments adhere to the competitive
civil service system associated with OPM. Positions are classified and
announced, and candidates submit SF-171's and supporting documents to the agency personnel office. Since most hiring decisions
are decentralized to agencies, you must follow the formal Federal
hiring procedures and informal job search strategies as outlined in
Chapters 16 and 17.

Employment with offices in the Executive Office of the President, independent agencies, committees, and commissions follow
more independent hiring patterns. Most of these agencies and offices
have their own internal hiring procedures. Therefore, it is best to
directly contact their personnel offices to learn about vacancy
announcements and the best procedures for applying for particular
positions.

Keep in mind that both formal and informal hiring systems
operate in the case of most agencies. Your research and networking
activities will provide you with the necessary knowledge and contacts to gain entry into these agencies.

Your best sources of information for researching these organizations will be:

KEY REFERENCE WORKS

Books

- *Careers in International Affairs*
- *International Jobs*
- *The Overseas List*

Directories

- *The Federal Yellow Book*
- *Directory of Federal Executives*
- *U.S. Government Manual*

Each of these books and directories provides names, addresses, and
telephone numbers for locating the right offices and individuals you
should contact for employment information.

CONGRESS

Both Congress and legislative agencies hire a variety of international specialists. Within Congress, international positions are found with the same groups outlined in Chapter 18 for general public employment: congressional committee staffs and personal staffs of Senators and Representatives.

Committee Staffs

International positions on committee staffs are limited in number and are primarily found on the two most important committees dealing with international issues:

- Senate Foreign Relations Committee
- House Foreign Affairs Committee

Other committees and subcommittees in the House of Representatives also deal with international matters and thus hire individuals with some international background. The relevant committees include:

- Agriculture Committee
- Appropriations Committee
- Armed Services Committee
- Banking, Finance, and Urban Affairs Committee
- Energy and Commerce Committee
- Government Operations Committee
- Science and Technology Committee
- Ways and Means Committee

On the Senate side, several committees deal with similar international issues:

- Agriculture and Forestry Committee
- Appropriations Committee
- Armed Services Committee
- Banking, Housing, and Urban Affairs Committee
- Commerce Committee
- Finance Committee
- Government Affairs Committee

Both the House and Senate have various joint committees which also offer international employment opportunities. The major such committees include: Joint Economic Committee and the Joint Committee on Taxation.

Personal Staffs

Not all Representatives hire international specialists on their personal staffs. Those that usually do have major responsibilities on the committees and subcommittees which deal with international issues. Therefore, you need to first identify who sits on which international committee, and then contact their staffs for information on international positions. Most of these staff positions will involve conducting research, writing reports, and drafting legislation on committee-related matters.

Contact information on the various congressional committees and personal staffs can be found in *Congressional Yellow Book, Congressional Directory, Congressional Staffing Directory,* and *The American Almanac of Politics.* Follow the same strategies for finding an international job on these staffs as you would for finding any type of staff position (Chapter 18).

Legislative Agencies

Most legislative agencies also have international interests and thus hire international specialists. The major agencies and offices include:

- *Congressional Budget Office*
  – National Security and International Affairs Division
- *General Accounting Office*
  – International Division
- *Library of Congress*
  – Congressional Research Service
  – Office of Research Services (Office of the Director for Area Studies)
- *Office of Technology Assessment*

The *Directory of Federal Executives* provides the names and telephone numbers of key individuals to contact in each of these legislative agencies and offices.

STATE AND LOCAL GOVERNMENTS

International opportunities with state and local governments are both relatively unknown and widely overlooked among most international specialists. This is in part due to the expectation that only the Federal government engages in foreign policy and international affairs.

During the past two decades, state and city governments have increasingly become involved in international affairs. Many have their own foreign policies involving:

- Trade promotion
- Tourism
- Local economic development
- Immigration

Florida, for example, maintains a state tourism agency which attempts to promote travel to Florida among European tourists. Virginia Beach maintains sister city relationships and promotes foreign industrial investment in the city through their Department of Economic Development. In certain areas, regional economic development authorities and tourism boards perform international functions for several units of government.

State and local governments offer unique international opportunities. They combine local economic issues with international development activities. For individuals who want to be involved in international affairs but wish to avoid many of the negative aspects of international careers — such as living abroad and transfers — these positions may be ideal.

Finding an international job with state and local governments requires a great deal of research and initiative on your part. No directories or books outline state and local agencies with opportunities in international affairs. Hence, your best approach will be to identify which city or state governments you would like to work with and then research the organizations to find the offices involved in international affairs. Both the national and local branches of the World Affairs Council may be helpful in uncovering international positions with these governmental units. Also, consult the resources and directories outlined in Chapters 14 and 15 on state and local governments to identify relevant offices. The same job search strategies outlined in those chapters will assist you in landing an international job at the state and local levels.

Chapter Twenty-Seven
INTERNATIONAL ORGANIZATIONS

Numerous international organizations offer job opportunities for talented international specialists. Most of these organizations are either directly tied to the United Nations or function as regional military, political, economic, and social organizations.

Since historically the United States has played a major role in developing international organizations and continues as a major funding source, many Americans have been employed with these groups. Yet, American participation in the day-to-day administration of international organizations is normally limited by specific hiring quotas imposed on all member nations related to population and financial contribution criteria. As a result, only certain positions requiring specific expertise will be open to American job seekers. In this sense, employment with many international organizations is very political in terms of both hiring for a position and retaining a job in competition with eager job seekers from the United States and other countries.

In this chapter we provide a brief overview of employment alternatives with numerous international organizations. Each organization has its own hiring system which you must understand in order to be effective in landing a job. Most important of all, each organization has a particular political environment which may or may not meet your criteria for a rewarding international job or career.

THE UNITED NATIONS

The United Nations is the largest single employer of international specialists. Its bureaucracy consists of nearly 50,000 individuals who work in over 600 duty stations throughout the world. Less than 10 percent of the UN civil servants are Americans.

The United Nations consists of a central organization and a loose collection of relatively autonomous specialized agencies and organizations. Given both the centralized and decentralized nature of the United Nations, all specialized agencies and related organizations recruit their own personnel. The United Nations, in effect, consists of more than 25 different hiring systems.

Organizations

The United Nations consists of six major organizational units and numerous specialized and autonomous agencies, standing committees, commissions, and other subsidiary bodies. The six principal organs are the:

- General Assembly
- Security Council
- Economic and Social Council
- Trusteeship Council
- International Court of Justice
- Secretariat

While job opportunities are available with all of these organs, the most numerous jobs are found with the Economic and Social Council and the UN Secretariat.

The Economic and Social Council is under the General Assembly. It coordinates the economic and social work of the United Nations and numerous specialized agencies, standing committees, commissions, and related organizations. The work of the Council involves international development, world trade, industrialization, natural resources, human rights, status of women, population, social welfare, science and technology, crime prevention, and other social and economic issues.

The Economic and Social Council is divided into a headquarters staff in New York City and five regional economic commissions:

- Economic Commission for Africa (Addis Ababa)
- Economic and Social Commission for Asia and
  the Pacific (Bangkok)

- Economic Commission for Europe (Geneva)
- Economic Commission for Latin America (Santiago)
- Economic Commission for Western Asia (Beirut)

Each Commission maintains a large staff of specialists. Furthermore, they promote the work of several standing committees and commissions which also have their own staffs. The Committee for Co-Ordination of Investigations of the Lower Mekong Basin (Mekong Committee), for example, was established in 1957. Under the Economic and Social Commission for Asia and the Pacific (ESCAP) and headquartered in Bangkok, this Committee has provided job opportunities for numerous consultants and full-time professionals. Indeed, some individuals have made a life-long career of working with the Mekong Committee.

Specialized or intergovernmental agencies are autonomous organizations linked to the United Nations by special intergovernmental agreements. In addition, they have their own membership, budgets, personnel systems, legislative and executive bodies, and secretariats. The International Atomic Energy Agency (IAEA), for example, consists of 35 member nations. It is administered by a professional staff of 619 and a general services staff of 941 which is headquartered in Vienna, Austria. The Economic and Social Council coordinates the work of these organizations with the United Nations as well as with each other. Altogether, there are 15 specialized agencies:

- Food and Agriculture Organization (FAO)
- International Atomic Energy Agency (IAEA)
- International Bank for Reconstruction and
  Development (IBRD or World Bank)
- International Civil Aviation Organization (ICAO)
- International Development Association (IDA)
- International Finance Corporation (IFC)
- International Labour Organization (ILO)
- International Maritime Organization (IMO)
- International Monetary Fund (IMF)
- International Telecommunication Union (ITU)
- United Nations Educational, Scientific and Cultural
  Organization (UNESCO)
- Universal Postal Union (UPU)
- World Health Organization (WHO)
- World Intellectual Property Organization (WIPO)
- World Meteorological Organization (WMO)

Several other major organizations also are attached to the Economic and Social Council as well as the Secretariat. These consist of:

- General Agreement on Tariffs and Trade (GATT)
- International Sea-Bed Authority
- Office of the United Nations Disaster Relief Co-Ordinator (UNDRO)
- United Nations Centre for Human Settlements (HABITAT)
- United Nations Children's Fund (UNICEF)
- United Nations Conference on Trade and Development (UNCTAD)
- United Nations Development Programme (UNDP)
- United Nations Environment Programme (UNEP)
- United Nations Fund for Population Activities (UNFPA)
- United Nations High Commissioner for Refugees (UNHCR)
- United Nations Industrial Development Organization (UNIDO)
- United Nations Institute for Training and Research (UNITAR)
- United Nations Observer Mission and Peacekeeping Forces in the Middle East
- United Nations Relief and Works Agency for Palestine Refugees in the Near East (UNRWA)
- United Nations Research Institute for Social Development (UNRISD)
- World Food Council (WFC)
- World Food Programme (WFP)

The UN Secretariat employs nearly 3,000 international civil servants from 130 countries. Most are stationed at the United Nations headquarters in New York City. The Secretariat is the central "bureaucracy" in charge of carrying out the day-to-day work of the United Nations.

The largest UN agencies — those employing at least 1,500 individuals — consist of the following:

- United Nations
- Food and Agriculture Organization
- World Health Organization
- United Nations Development Program

- World Bank
- UNESCO
- International Labor Organization
- UNICEF
- International Monetary Fund

Employment Alternatives

The United Nations and related specialized agencies and organizations hire all types of professionals and general service staff as full-time, permanent staff, technical assistance experts, and consultants. Major positions include engineers, lawyers, accountants, doctors, lawyers, researchers, translators, interpreters, demographers, guides, and typists. The UN also hires technical assistance experts who are then loaned to Third World governments. Except for general service staff positions, most UN jobs require highly educated and experienced professionals.

Many United Nations jobs are exciting. They involve traveling to interesting places, working with highly intelligent and competent professionals, and dealing with important international problems and issues. At the same time, many UN offices have acquired characteristics of Third World and Byzantine bureaucracies. They spend much of their time in meetings, which produce little or nothing except for a great deal of memos and reports requiring further meetings. Bureaucratic intrigue, power struggles, and manuevers to take over others' positions characterize the daily work of some UN offices.

Competition for UN positions is keen for several reasons. UN jobs pay extremely well compared to comparable jobs in the U.S. Federal government or in any national government. Indeed, competition is most keen and the personnel process is most political among professionals from Third World countries — especially those from India, Pakistan, and Bangladesh — who cannot find comparable professions and pay elsewhere. For many of them, working for the United Nations, specialized agencies, or related organizations is extremely important to financing their life styles which frequently include plush homes, servants, private schools, and one or two Mercedes.

Hiring Practices

The hiring process is largely decentralized within the United Nations and among the specialized agencies and related organizations. Therefore, you must directly contact each agency for job vacancy information as well as network with your resume by conducting informational interviews. If you are interested in working for the UN Secretariat in New York City, contact the following offices for information on job vacancies:

> United Nations
> Recruitment Programs Section
> Office of Personnel Services
> New York, NY 10017

Most agencies and organizations will have a personnel office which issues job vacancy announcements. Bulletin boards outside personnel offices or cafeterias often include the latest vacancy announcements.

For technical assistance positions, you should contact the following office for information:

> Technical Assistance Recruitment Service
> Department of Technical Cooperation
> United Nations
> New York, NY 10017

The U.S. Department of State provides a recruitment and job referral service for individuals interested in working for the UN, specialized agencies, and related organizations. The Bureau of International Organization Affairs identifies qualified Americans who are then referred for UN assignments. Most candidates should have specialized and advanced academic degrees and several years of recent international experience. The categories of positions covered include: public information personnel; computer programmers; military personnel; administrative posts; legal posts; translators; interpreters; summer employment; clerical personnel; UN guides; intern programs; political affairs posts; telecommunication posts; economists; and UN volunteers. The Bureau maintains a computerized roster of qualified professional candidates whose backgrounds are matched against the qualifications specified in UN vacancy announcements. To get on this roster and be referred, send a detailed resume to:

> Staffing Management Officer
> Office of UN System Recruitment
> Bureau of International Organizational Affairs
> Department of State — Room 3536
> Washington, DC 20520
> Tel. 202/647-3396

You can write or call this office for information on the UN and the referral system. Ask for their "Fact Sheet" on employment with international organizations and "United Nations People." The "Fact Sheet" includes names and addresses of various UN agencies to which you can apply directly for vacancies. Consequently, you may want to get on the State Department roster as well as apply directly to UN agencies and offices for positions.

The United Nations uses a special application form – the UN Personal History Form P-11 (UN P-11) – which is similar to the SF-171. Be sure to complete this form and submit it along with a targeted resume for most UN positions.

Your most effective job search strategy will be to target particular agencies and organizations. Personnel offices will provide vacancy announcements and information on the formal hiring process, but you must make contact with the hiring personnel in the operating units. Do informational interviewing so you can uncover vacancies for which you may qualify. You will want to learn about the political environment of offices in order to avoid both wasting your time on positions which are wired and landing what may quickly become a terrible job!

REGIONAL ORGANIZATIONS

Several international regional organzations also provide job opportunities. Most of these organizations are designed to promote regional security and economic and social development. The major regional organizations are:

- African Development Bank
- Andean Group
- ANZUS
- Arab Bank for Economic Development in Africa (BADEA)
- Arab Fund for Economic and Social Development (AFESD)
- Arab Monetary Fund
- Asian Development Bank (ADB)
- Association of Southeast Asian Nations (ASEAN)
- Bank for International Settlements (BIS)
- Benelux Economic Union
- Caribbean Community and Common Market (CARICOM)
- Central American Common Market (CACM)
- The Colombo Plan for Co-operative Economic and Social Development in Asia and the Pacific

- The Commonwealth
- Communaute Economique de 1 'Afrique de 1 'Quest (CEAO)
- Conseil de 1 'Entente
- Co-operation Council for the Arab States of the Gulf
- Council for Mutual Economic Assistance (CMEA)
- Council of Arab Economic Unity
- Council of Europe
- Economic Community of West African States (ECOWAS)
- The European Communities
- European Free Trade Association (EFTA)
- The Franc Zone
- Inter-American Development Bank (IDB)
- International Bank for Economic Co-operation (IBEC)
- International Investment Bank
- International Olympic Committee
- Inter-Parliamengary Union
- Islamic Development Bank
- Latin American Integration Association (ALADI)
- League of Arab States
- Nordic Council
- Nordic Council of Ministers
- North Atlantic Treaty Organization (NATO)
- Organization Commune Africaine et Mauricienne (OCAM)
- Organization for Economic Co-operation and Development (OECD)
    - International Energy Agency
    - OECD Nuclear Energy Agency (NEA)
- Organization of African Unit (OAU)
- Organization of American States (OAS)
- Organization of Arab Petroleum Exporting Countries (OAPEC)
- OPEC Fund for International Development
- South Pacific Commission (SPC)
- South Pacific Forum
    - South Pacific Bureau for Economic Co-operation (SPEC)
- Southern African Development Co-ordination Conference (SADCC)
- Western European Union (WEU)

While the U.S. Department of State can provide information on jobs with some of these regional organizations, you must contact the organizations directly for detailed job information. Keep in mind that U.S. participation on the staffs of these organizations will be limited and, in some cases, nonexistant. Furthermore, most regional organizations hire highly educated, skilled, and experienced professionals. Expect the hiring processes to be somewhat political in most cases.

USEFUL RESOURCES

Before contacting individuals in the international organizations for informational interviews, you should collect basic data on the organizations. Most libraries have the following annual directories for researching these organizations:

- *Yearbook of the United Nations*
- *Europa Year Book*
- *Yearbook of International Organizations*

The *Yearbook of the United Nations* provides detailed information on the operations of each UN agency.

The *Europa Year Book* gives details on the United Nations as well as other political, economic, and commercial institutions throughout the world. This two-volume directory classifies international organizations into 21 categories:

- Agriculture, Food, Forestry, and Fisheries
- Aid and Development
- Arts and Culture
- Economics and Finance
- Education
- Government and Politics
- Industrial and Professional Relations
- Law
- Medicine and Health
- Posts and Telecommunications
- Press, Radio, and TV
- Religion
- Science
- Social Sciences and Humanities Studies
- Social Welfare
- Sports and Recreation
- Technology
- Tourism
- Trade and Industry

- Transport
- Youth and Students

The following types of information are found in the "Aid and Development" and "Government and Politics" sections:

ENTRIES IN EUROPA YEAR BOOK

Committee for Co-ordination of Investigations of the Lower Mekong Basin: c/o ESCAP, United Nations Bldg., Rajadamnern Ave, Bangkok 10200, Thailand; aims to develop the resources of the lower Mekong basin, including hydroelectric power, irrigation, navigation, fisheries, and food production; contributions pledged by the end of 1983 amounted to US $520.5m., from member states, co-operating countries, and the UN and other international agencies. Mems: Laos, Thailand and Viet-Nam; 26 co-operating countries. Exec. Agent: Galal Magdi.

International Union of Local Authorities: Wassenaarseweg 45, 2596 CG The Hague, Netherlands; tel. (070) 244032; f. 1913 to promote local government, improve local administration and encourage popular participation in public affairs. Functions include organization of conferences, seminars, and biennial international congress; servicing of specialized committees (municipal insurance, wholesale markets, European affairs, technical); research projects; comparative courses for local government officials, primarily from developing countries; development of intermunicipal relations to provide a link between local authorities of all countries; maintenance of a permanent office for the collection and distribution of information on municipal affairs. Members in over 65 countries. Pres. H. Koshnick (FRG); Sec.-Gen. J. G. Van Putten. Publs. *Local Government* (monthly newsletter), *Bibliographia* (bi-monthly), *Planning and Administration* (2 a year), preparatory reports and proceedings of conferences, reports of study groups.

The *Yearbook of International Organizations* compiles similar information on over 20,000 organizations. It provides annotated descriptions on all "international" organizations. These are organizations whose membership is comprised of at least 60 member nations.

This directory includes all organs, specialized agencies, and related organizations of the United Nations; other international organizations; and individual country profiles of organizations. A typical entry in this directory appears as follows:

Society for International Development (SID)
SG: Ponna Wignaraja, palazzo Civilta del Lavoro, 1-00144 Roma, Italy. T. (06) 591 7897 - (06) 592 5506. C. SOCINTDEV Rome. Tx 612339 GBG for SID.
North South Round Table Secretariat: Suite 501, 1717 Massachusetts Ave NW, Washington, DC 20036. USA. T. 234 8701 C. OVERCON
United Nations Representative: Arthur Goldschmidt, 544 E. 86th Street, New York, NY 10028.
Aims: Encourage, support and facilitate the creation at the local, national, regional, and international level of a sense of community among individuals and organizations committed to development; promote international *dialogue* understanding and cooperation for *social development* and *economic development* that furthers the well-beings of all peoples and of a more equitable system of international relations; advance the science, processes and art of social and economic development through educational means including research, publication and discussion; provide support and services for national development constituencies which facilitate the foregoing. *Structure:* The form of the Chapter may vary from country to country, but each serves as an independent forum engaged in promoting the process of dialogue, and development education. International Secretariat in Rome since 1977, with a unit in Washington, DC. *Languages:* English, French, Spanish, Arabic. *Staff:* 7 full-time professional and administrative 2 part-time; 3 interns. *Finance:* Members' dues (income-rated). Contributions from private, public, international government, and non-governmental organizations.

You also should acquire annual reports from individual organizations. The World Bank, for example, publishes a comprehensive annual report on its organization, mission, and accomplishments which is required reading for anyone interested in working for this organization. In addition, the World Bank has a publications program which produces numerous special reports and books each year. You can get copies of these reports and publications by writing to or calling the Publications Division of various organizations.

Most libraries also will have books about international organizations as well as magazines and journals published by different offices within the organization. Reference librarians can usually identify these publications for you.

Chapter Twenty-Eight
PERIPHERAL INSTITUTIONS

Although international organizations and Federal agencies have the greatest visibility in the international arena, numerous other organizations pursue public-related international interests. These peripheral institutions consist of consulting firms; trade and professional associations; nonprofit organizations; foundations; and research organizations.

Several of the peripheral institutions and organizations discussed in Chapters 20-24 also could be included in this chapter. These organizations have international interests and interface in both the U.S. domestic and international arenas. However, organizations with a primary orientation toward international work are the subjects of this chapter.

CONSULTING FIRMS

Several consulting firms are organized to acquire contracts with Federal agencies and international organizations. These include huge firms such as Coopers and Lybrand, which does contract work with both public and private institutions and maintains an international staff of 30,000 in 97 countries; medium-sized firms with staffs of 10 to 50 individuals; and one or two-person firms which primarily rely on short-term contracts with a single agency or office.

The World Bank, United Nations, and several Federal agencies are the major funding sources for these consulting firms. Federal agencies most frequently using international contractors are the U.S. Agency for International Development, Department of Agriculture, Department of State, Department of Defense, and the Central Intelligence Agency.

The U.S. Agency for International Development, for example, is one of the largest dispensers of government contracts to large, small, and minority consulting firms. Since USAID is primarily organized to obligate funds for development projects in Third World countries, numerous consulting firms in the United States and abroad are recipients of USAID funding. The contracts deal with every conceivable type of development project. USAID, for example, classifies all contractors according to 16 activity categories:

- Accounting and Financial Management
- Agriculture
- Architecture and Engineering
- Cooperative Development
- Data Processing
- Development Administration
- Education/Human Resources
- Energy Systems
- Environmental Protection and Natural Resources Management
- Health
- Housing and Urban Programs
- Library and Information Sciences
- Management Consulting
- Nutrition Planning and Analysis
- Project Design and Analysis/Evaluation
- Rural Development

A USAID contracting officer is assigned to each category. This individual issues solicitations, negotiates, and regularly communicates with the firms doing work under USAID contracts.

USAID does business with nearly 2,000 contractors in the United States and abroad. While many job opportunities are available with U.S. firms, additional opportunities are available with firms located in Third World countries which receive "Host Country Contracts" — a rather controversial and problem-ridden way USAID does business. As part of USAID's emphasis on decentralization and capacity building, more and more USAID contracts are earmarked for consulting firms in Third World countries. Since many of these firms lack basic capabilities to develop proposals and implement projects, some will hire experienced Americans to help them get and manage USAID contracts. The contracting officer attached to each USAID mission should have a list of these local firms, which usually will be available upon request or through a Freedom of Information inquiry.

USAID publishes a wealth of information on U.S. and European-based firms which receive contracts as well as have special relationships with the Agency. Indeed of all Federal agencies, this one is a job hunter's paradise. The *Current Technical Services Contracts and Grants* directory, for example, is issued by the Support Division of USAID's Office of Acquisition and Assistance Management. This lengthy document identifies most firms receiving contracts and grants from USAID each fiscal year. It includes a statistical summary, a regional directory, and a state and country listing of contractors and grantees. Each contract is identified by contract number, contract name, contract term, dollar amount, contract description, and address of contractor. If you conduct a basic analysis of this document, you will acquire some very useful information for your job search. For example, in the period October 1, 1983 to September 30, 1984, firms in five states received the largest dollar value of USAID contracts and grants:

Location of Firms	Total Amount
District of Columbia	$576,362,957
New York	$445,202,533
Maryland	$127,396,085
Virginia	$106,047,061
California	$90,635,870

Hundreds of firms are located throughout the United States — not just in these five states. Not surprising, firms in and around Washington, D.C. — the so-called Beltway Bandits — received the largest number of USAID contracts, totalling nearly $1 billion.

A useful feature of this key USAID document is the index. It identifies which firms received the largest number of contracts and grants during the fiscal year. For example, during Fiscal Year 1984 over 1400 foundations, universities, firms, and nonprofit organizations received USAID contracts and grants. Of these, 30 organizations received 10 or more contracts or grants:

USAID CONTRACTORS/GRANTEES RECEIVING 10 OR MORE CONTRACTS	
Firms/ Organizations	Number of Contracts/ Grants Awarded
• Academy for Educational Development	13
• Adventist Development and Relief Agency International	11
• The Asia Foundation	12
• Associates in Rural Development	10
• Catholic Relief Services	28
• Checchi Company/Louis Berger International, Inc.	10
• CARE	23
• Cooperative Housing Foundation	12
• Coopers and Lybrand	14
• Development Alternatives, Inc.	29
• Development Associates, Inc.	17
• University of Hawaii	10
• Institute for Development Anthropology, Inc.	11
• International Science and Technology Institute, Inc.	17
• Johns Hopkins University	10
• Arthur D. Little, Inc.	14
• Management Sciences for Health	18
• Population Council	10
• Pragma Corporation	11
• Price Waterhouse	22
• Research Triangle Institute	13
• Ronco Consulting Corporation	22
• Save the Children Federation	14
• John Snow Public Health Group, Inc.	12
• South-East Consortium for International Development	12
• Sun Research, Inc.	13
• Technical Support Services, Inc./Advanced Technology, Inc.	10
• Tibbetts-Abbett-McCarthy-Stratton	13
• Urban Institute/Robert R. Nathan Associates, Inc.	14
• Volunteers in Technical Assistance, Inc.	11

The names and addresses of these firms, as well as hundreds of individuals who also received USAID contracts and grants, are included in the section entitled "State/Country Listing of Contracts and Grants." This document is required reading for anyone interested in identifying firms doing international contracting and consulting work. The names and addresses constitute the single best directory for international networking. You can get a free copy of this document by requesting it through the Support Division of USAID's Office of Acquisition and Assistance Management (Tel. 703/235-9110).

Another useful annual USAID document is required reading: *Directory of AID Indefinite Quantity Contracts.* This document identifies all firms which have a "special" relationship with USAID. The Indefinite Quantity Contract, or IQC, is a unique contracting mechanism which enables USAID to acquire short-term technical services — normally for 120 days or less — by issuing a "work order" to firms which qualify as eligible for IQCs. In other words, the IQC limits competition to a few USAID approved firms. This special contracting mechanism and agency-contractor relationship ostensibly saves USAID time and avoids lengthy and sometimes difficult negotiation procedures. At the same time, the IQC is highly valued by many firms. These are bread-and-butter contracts which regularly pay salaries and overhead and keep full-time staffs and associates employed especially during periods between large contracts. If you contact firms with IQC status, you may find they have work in your skill and interest areas.

The IQC directory identifies every firm which has this special relationship with USAID. In addition, it classifies firms according to the 16 contracting categories, identifies the size and status of firms, provides descriptions of each firm, and includes contact information — USAID contracting officers and technical personnel as well as representatives from the firm. The 1984 directory identified the following firms with IQC status:

FIRMS WITH SPECIAL USAID CONTRACTING RELATIONSHIP

Firm	Size/Type	Telephone

1. Accounting and Financial Management

• Birch and Davis Associates, Inc.	Small/8(a)	301/589-6760
• Coopers and Lybrand	Large	202/223-1700
• Executive Management Systems, Inc.	Small	703/525-8025
• Watson, Rice and Co.	Small/8(a)	202/628-0833
• Arthur Young and Co.	Large	202/828-7000

2. Agriculture

• ABA International	Small	808/523-5479
• Checchi and Co.	Large	202/452-9700
• Consortium for International Development	Nonprofit	602/745-0455
• Development Alternatives, Inc.	Small	202/833-8140
• Development Associates, Inc.	Large	703/979-1000
• Development Planning and Research Associates, Inc.	Small	913/539-3565
• Devres, Inc.	Small	202/797-9610
• Experience, Inc.	Large	202/659-3864
• International Agricultural Development Service	Large	212/869-8500
• A. L. Nellum & Associates, Inc.	Small/8(a)	202/862-9300
• Pragma Corporation	Small	703/237-9303
• Resources Development Associates	Small	916/622-8841
• Ronco Consulting Corporation	Small	202/785-2791

3. Architecture and Engineering

• Burns and McDonnell Engineering Co.	Large	816/333-4375
• Ebasco Services Inc.	Large	212/839-2689
• Jordan/Avent and Associates	Small/8(a)	415/989-1025
• Lozano, White and Associates	Small/8(a)	617/868-6344
• Moffatt and Nichol, Engineers	Small	213/426-9551
• James M. Montgomery Consulting Engineers, Inc.	Large	213/796-9141
• Stone and Webster Engineering Corp.	Large	617/973-0597
• Teleconsult, Inc.	Small	202/466-3250

- Tippetts-Abbett-McCarthy-
  Stratton   Partnership   212/867-1777

4. *Cooperative Development Service*

• Agricultural Cooperative Development, Inc.	Nonprofit	202/638-4661
• Cooperative Housing Foundation	Nonprofit	202/887-0700
• Cooperative League of the USA	Nonprofit	202/872-0550
• National Rural Electrification Cooperative Assoc.	Nonprofit	202/857-9500
• World Council of Credit Unions	Nonprofit	202/828-4500

5. *Data Processing Services*

• Automated Dataron, Inc.	Small/8(a)	301/277-9575
• Infodata Systems, Inc.	Small	703/578-3430
• Pinkerton Computer Consultants, Inc.	Large	703/820-5571

6. *Development Administration*

• Clapp and Mayne, Inc.	Small	809/723-9797
• Development Alternatives, Inc.	Small	202/673-9100

7. *Education/Human Resources Services*

• Academy for Education Development	Nonprofit	202/862-1900
• Creative Associates, Inc.	Small/8(a)	202/966-5804
• Development Associates, Inc.	Large	703/979-0100
• Wu P'I, Inc.	Small/8(a)	617-864-2042

8. *Energy Systems Services*

• Associates in Rural Development	Small	802/658-3890
• Louis Berger International, Inc./ TRW Energy Engineering Division	Large/ Joint Venture	202/466-4000
• Center for Energy and Environmental Research	Research Ins.	809/767-0350
• Development Sciences, Inc.	Small	617/888-0101
• Energy/Development International	Small	516/751-5400
• The Futures Group/Burns and Roe, Inc.	Large/ Joint Venture	516/677-4000

- Arthur D. Little, Inc.   Large   617/864-5770
- MetaSystems, Inc.   Small   617/868-8660
- Midwest Research Institute   Nonprofit 816/753-7600
- Sheladia Associates, Inc.   Small/8(a) 301/779-4313
- Synergic Resources Corporation   Small/8(a) 215/667-2160

9. Environmental Protection and Natural Resources

- International Science and
  Technology Institute, Inc.   Small/8(a) 202/466-7290
- Resources Development Associates   Small   916/622-8841
- Tippetts-Abbett-McCarthy-Stratton   Large   212/867-1777

10. Health (subdivided into Handpump Technology Services, Planning and Delivery Systems Services, Rural Water Supply and Sanitation Services, Tropical Disease Services)

- Development Associates, Inc.   Large   703/979-0100
- Georgia Technical
  Research Institute   Nonprofit 404/894-3851
- International Science and
  Technology Institute, Inc.   Small/8(a) 202/466-7290
- Management Sciences for Health   Nonprofit 617/482-9450
- Pragma Corporation   Small   703/237-9303
- John Snow Public Health
  Group, Inc.   Small   617/482-9485
- Tippetts-Abbett-McCarthy-Stratton   Large   212/867-1777
- University Research Corporation   Large   202/654-8338
- Westinghouse Health Systems   Large   301/992-3100

11. Housing and Urban Programs

- Abeles, Schwartz, Haeckel and
  Silverblatt, Inc.   Small   212/475-3030
- Comprehensive Marketing Systems   Small/8(a) 202/393-6800
- Research Triangle Institute   Nonprofit 919/541-6365
- Resource Applications, Inc.   Small/8(a) 701/282-7833
- Resources for Action   Small   301/365-2457
- Rivkin Associates, Inc.   Small   202/337-3100
- Technical Services (TSS)   Joint   202/462-9107
  Advanced Technology   Venture 701/442-4000
- The Urban Institute/Robert T.   Joint   202/223-1950

Nathan Associates	Venture	202/393-2700
• U.S. League of Savings Institutes/	Joint	
Institute of Financial Education	Venture	312/644-3100

12. Library and Information Science Services

| • King Research, Inc. | Small | 301/881-6766 |
| • MAXIMA Corporation | Small/8(a) | 301/951-9330 |

13. Management Consulting Services

• Booz-Allen and Hamilton, Inc.	Large	301/951-2200
• Ferguson, Bryan and Associates	Small/8(a)	202/682-3100
• The Granville Corporation	Small/8(a)	202/638-4550
• Management Analysis Center (MAC)/	Large/	202/343-6500
First Washington		
Association (FWA)	Joint Venture	202/331-7376
• Meridian Corporation	Small	703/998-0927

14. Nutrition Planning and Analysis Services

• Community Systems Foundation	Large/	
	Nonprofit	313/761-1357
• Development Associates, Inc.	Large/8(a)	703/979-0100
• Management Services for Health	Nonprofit	617/482-9450
• Sigma One Corporation	Small/8(a)	919/828-5501
• John Snow Public Health		
Group, Inc.	Small	617/482-9485

15. Project Design and Analysis/Evaluation Services

• Abt Associates, Inc.	Large	617/492-7100
• Barnett and Engle	Small	203/226-0118
• Checchi and Co./Louis Berger	Large/	
International, Inc.	Joint Venture	202/452-9700
• Development Alternatives, Inc.	Small	202/783-9110
• Development Associates, Inc.	Large	703/979-0100
• International Science and		
Technology Institute, Inc.	Small/8(a)	202/466-7290
• Ronco Consulting Corporation	Small	202/785-2791

16. Rural Development Services

| • Development Alternatives, Inc. | Small | 202/783-9110 |

- Development Associates, Inc.   Large   703/979-0100
- Devres   Small   202/797-9610
- Institute for Development
  Anthropology   Small   607/772-6244
- Multinational Agribusiness
  Systems, Inc.   Small   703/527-4300
- Robert R. Nathan Associates, Inc.   Large   202/393-2700
- A. L. Nellum and Associates   Small/8(a)   202/862-9300
- TransCentury Corporation   Large   202/328-4478

This document is available in the main USAID library in Rosslyn, Virginia. You can purchase it by sending $22.67 to the USAID Document Information Handling Facility:

> AID/DIHF
> 7222 47th St., Suite 100
> Chevy Chase, MD 20815
> Tel. 301/951-7191

USAID is the only agency we know which compiles such comprehensive and informative documents on contractors. Other agencies either do not organize this data or they refuse to release it to the public, except through a Freedom of Information request.

Information on some of the firms we identified — names, addresses, telephone numbers, and annotated descriptions — is found in two useful directories:

- *Careers in International Affairs*
- *The Consultants and Consulting Organizations Directory*

In addition, you should monitor firms receiving Federal government contracts by regularly reviewing the "Contract Awards" section of the *Commerce Business Daily* as well as the *Federal Register*.

Several minority firms also receive contracts with Federal agencies, but they are less visible to the public. Known as "8(a) firms," these ostensibly disadvantaged businesses qualify for non-competitive contracts. Agencies can reserve certain projects and activities for 8(a) firms. Indeed, many prefer using this contracting mechanism, because it expedites agency spending without requiring a lengthy competitive procurement process for obligating funds. Since agencies keep lists of these firms, contact their contracting office for the names of the 8(a) firms they are using for noncompetitive contracts. The contracting office may or may not willingly release this information and thus you may need to request it through the Freedom of Information Act. These firms can provide excellent job opportunities, because they often take on projects for which they lack sufficient full-time expertise. They may need additional qualified professionals to plan and implement projects.

International consulting firms should be approached in the same manner we outlined for consulting firms in Chapter 20. Conduct your research; call for information; arrange informational interviews; get your resume in their hands and files; and follow-up with telephone calls, letters, and personal visits.

If you are interested in doing independent consulting, your best strategy will be to network with government employees who are responsible for contracting-out services. In many cases, agencies prefer giving certain work to individuals rather than incurring the overhead costs involved with contracting-out to an established firm. In addition, agencies can avoid lengthy competitive procedures and maintain closer control when they contract directly with individuals for amounts less than $10,000 or use a special category of contracts — the Personal Services Contract (PSC) — for larger amounts. Many individuals have been able to create consulting jobs for themselves by proposing to agency personnel new projects requiring their expertise.

You should be aware of one category of contracts frequently used in international consulting: Personal Service Contracts. These contracts are convenient ways for an agency to acquire specific expertise as well as additional personnel without disturbing personnel ceilings or increasing the agency payroll. Individuals are hired on one to three year contracts to perform specific services within the agency. Normally these positions are announced in the *Commerce Business Daily* and appear similar to classified employment ads. The following announcement appeared in the *CBD* during 1985:

> **HONDURAS: PROGRAM OPERATIONS SPEC-IALIST.** The USAID/H is accepting CV's (curriculum vitae) and private data from qualified individuals to fill the position of program operations specialist. The position involves assisting the USAID in the analysis, planning, budgeting, monitoring, and implementation of US economic assistance program in Honduras. These programs include economic support funds, development assistance, housing guarantees, and PL 480 Titles I, II, and III. Qualifications include a master degree in business administration, economics, or a similar discipline. Fluency in Spanish/

English at R3, S2 IAW the Foreign Service Institute's standards. Have considerable and proven USAID program office experience relating to the programming, monitoring, reporting, and implementation of the aid program, and a thorough knowledge of aid goals and major programs including NBCCA recommendations. No formal sol will be issued. CV's and biodata from individuals only will be accepted. The contractual relationship will be personal services (PSC) between the USG and the selected individual. Interested applicants should submit CV and salary history NLT mid-Dec. 85. (The Agency for International Development, Contracting Officer, c/o American Embassy, Teguigalpa, Honduras, or USAID Honduras APO Miami, FL 34022)

While agencies are required to announce their intent to conclude a Personal Services Contract, often the positions are "wired" for individuals who already have worked for the agency — especially a former employee who has retired or started a consulting business — or who helped develop a project for the agency and thus created his or her own full-time consulting position with the agency.

TRADE AND PROFESSIONAL ASSOCIATIONS

Many of the major trade and professional associations outlined in Chapter 21 are organized primarily as international associations to promote members' interests among international organizations and national governments.

There are literally thousands of international trade and professional associations. Under the key word "International," the *Encyclopedia of Associations* lists over 3,300 such associations; the key word "World" generates another 675 international associations. The major international trade and professional associations include:

INTERNATIONAL TRADE AND PROFESSIONAL ASSOCIATIONS

U.S.-Based Trade and Professional Associations

- Aereospace Industries Associations of America
- Aircraft Owners and Pilots Association
- Airline Pilots Association International
- American Bankers Association
- American Chemical Society
- American Insurance Association
- American Iron and Steel Institute
- American Management Association
- American Paper Institute
- American Petroleum Institute
- American Plywood Association
- American Political Science Association
- American Society of International Law
- Chamber of Commerce of the United States
- Electronic Industries Association
- Foreign Credit Insurance Association
- International Studies Association
- Motor Vehicle Manufacturers Association of the U.S., Inc.
- National Association of Manufacturers
- National Education Association
- National Foreign Trade Council
- National Geographic Society

Trade Unions

- AFL-CIO
- Aluminum Workers International Union
- Amalgamated Clothing and Textile Workers Union
- Communications Workers of America
- International Association of Machinists and Aerospace Workers
- United Automobile, Aerospace and Agricultural Implementation Workers International Union
- United Food and Commercial Workers International Union
- United Mine Workers
- United Steelworkers

International Trade and Professional Organizations

- International Air Transport Association
- International Chamber of Commerce
- International Co-Operative Alliance
- Council of the Americas
- Foreign Policy Association
- National Association of Foreign Student Affairs
- National Council for U.S.-China Trade
- Transafrica
- U.S.-U.S.S.R. Trade and Economic Council
- Young President's Organization

Detailed information on these and other international trade and professional associations is found in the following directories:

- *Careers in International Affairs*
- *Encyclopedia of Associations*
- *Europa Year Book*
- *National Trade and Professional Associations of the U.S.*
- *Yearbook of International Organizations*

These directories provide the necessary names, addresses, telephone numbers, and annotated descriptions to get you started in the proper direction for locating job opportunities with these associations. In addition, be sure to monitor vacancy announcements, and use the placement services outlined in Chapter 21, especially those available through the American Society of Association Executives, the *United States Association Executive*, and *Association Trends*.

NONPROFIT ORGANIZATIONS

The nonprofit category of international organizations includes organizations frequently referred to as Non-governmental Organizations (NGO's) or Private Voluntary Organizations (PVO's) which are primarily oriented toward promoting a particular international issue or cause. In contrast to the domestic nonprofit organizations outlined in Chapter 22, international nonprofits operate almost solely in the international arena. They span a broad spectrum of issues and causes:

- foreign affairs
- education
- energy
- economic development
- population planning
- food
- social welfare
- health
- children and youth

- relief
- human rights
- religion
- rural development
- cultural exchange
- water resources
- housing
- community development

Non-profit organizations such as the International Voluntary Service, Catholic Relief Service, and CARE provide similar development services as the U.S. Peace Corps. The Population Council's involvement in family planning and health issues affects all other development issues in Third World countries. The World Affairs Councils function to increase the awareness of Americans concerning international issues. The Council for International Exchange of Scholars (Fulbright-Hays) and Meridian House International focus on promoting educational and cultural exchanges.

The major non-profit international organizations which hire international specialists for headquarter and field locations and have full-time staffs of at least 20 and an annual budget exceeding $4 million include:

LARGEST INTERNATIONAL NONPROFIT ORGANIZATIONS

- Africare
- Agricultural Cooperative Development International
- American Friends Service Committee
- American Institute for Free Labor Development
- American Jewish Joint Distribution Committee
- Association for Voluntary Sterilization
- Cooperative for American Relief Everywhere, Inc. (CARE)
- Catholic Medical Mission Board
- Catholic Relief Services
- Christian Children's Fund, Inc.
- Church World Service
- Direct Relief International
- Family Planning International Assistance
- Food for the Hungry
- Foster Parents Plan International
- Heifer Project International

- Holt International Children's Services
- The Institute of Cultural Affairs
- Interchurch Medical Assistance, Inc.
- International Eye Foundation
- International Executive Service Corps
- International Human Assistance Programs, Inc.
- International Planned Parenthood Federation
- International Rescue Committee
- Lutheran World Relief
- MAP International
- Mennonite Economic Development Associates, Inc.
- Overseas Education Fund
- Partnership for Productivity International
- Pathfinder Fund
- People to People Health Foundation, Inc.
- Population Council
- Salvation Army
- Save the Children Federation, Inc.
- United Methodist Committee on Relief
- Volunteers in Technical Assistance (VITA)
- World Concern
- World Relief
- World Vision International

When conducting research on international nonprofit organizations, you should examine the *Encyclopedia of Associations, Yearbook of International Organizations,* and USAID's *Current Technical Service Contracts and Grants* directory. Two excellent books also examine many of these organizations: *Careers in International Affairs* and *The Overseas List.* USAID also publishes two useful directories on nonprofit organizations:

- *Voluntary Foreign Aid Programs* (Washington, DC: USAID, Food for Peace and Voluntary Assistance Bureau, Private Voluntary Cooperation Office, Tel. 703/235-1689 to receive a copy)

- *Directory of Development Resources* (Washington, DC: USAID, Bureau of Science and Technology; Tel. 301/951-7191 for order information from AID/DIHF)

Several other books and directories focus specifically on nonprofit international organizations. These include:

- *US Non-Profit Organizations in Development Assistance Abroad* (New York: Technical Assistance Information Clearing House). Also known as the TAICH Directory. Includes 535 nonprofits. The best of the directories, it is now out-of-print but available in many large libraries.

- *Overseas Development Network (ODN) Opportunities Catalog* (Cambridge, MA: Overseas Development Network). Describes 52 development organizations offering internships, research, and employment opportunities for students. To join ODN, write or call: Overseas Development Network, P. O. Box 1430, Cambridge, MA 02238, Tel. 617/858-3002. For correspondence, write or call: SIDO, ODN Clearinghouse Project, Box 2306, Stanford, CA 94305, Tel. 415/497-9262.

- *US Voluntary Organizations and World Affairs* (New York: Center for War/Peace Studies)

- *Technical Assistance Programs of US Non-Profit Organizations* (New York: American Council of Voluntary Agencies for Foreign Service)

Several organizations provide clearinghouse, job listing, and placement services for individuals interested in working for nonprofit international organizations. Among these are:

- **InterAction: American Council for Voluntary International Action** (200 Park Avenue S., New York, NY 10003, Tel. 212/777-8210 or 2101 L St. NW, Suite 916, Washington, DC 20037, Tel. 202/822-8429). Consisting of a coalition of over 100 U.S. private and voluntary international organizations, InterAction provides information and advice on employment with nonprofit international organizations. This is one of the best international networks available.

- **The New TransCentury Foundation** (1724 Kalorama Rd., NW, Washington, DC 20009, Tel. 202/328-

4486). Publishes a bimonthly "Job Opportunities
Bulletin" for international specialists ($15 for annual
subscription), maintains a Talent Bank ($40 to reg-
ister), and hosts job conferences.

- *CODEL* (Coordination in Development, 79 Madison
  Ave., New York, NY 10016, Tel. 212/685-2030).
  Clearinghouse for over 40 church-related agencies
  working abroad.

- *PACT* (Private Agencies Collaborating Together,
  77 U.N. Plaza, New York, NY 10017, Tel. 212/
  597-6222). Consortium of 19 nonprofit agencies
  working abroad.

If you are in the field of international health, you are fortunate
to have a career-aware professional organization and a new service
available to assist you in locating health organizations and job
opportunities. The National Council for International Health (NCIH)
promotes international health through numerous educational services
and publishes the *International Health News* and *Directory of Health
Agencies*. In addition, NCIH is developing one of the most unique
job and career services – a data base and directory of international
health organizations. It is creating the first computerized directory
and Bulletin Board of private, nonprofit, educational, and industrial
health organizations. When completed, the data base will include
nearly 2000 international health organizations with several useful
classifications for job seekers. Individuals and organizations can
access this data on-line as well as receive computer print-outs of
specific types of organizations. The data base also generates a useful
Bulletin Board of job vacancies. The Bulletin Board becomes fully
operational in March 1986; the directory is targeted for completion
in December 1986. Both services are regularly updated. For information on these services, contact:

> The National Council for International Health
> 1101 Connecticut Ave., NW, Suite 605
> Washington, DC 20036
> Tel. 202/833-5900

Use the same strategies for landing a job with an international
nonprofit organization as you would for any nonprofit organization
(Chapter 22). This essentially involves networking, informational
interviews, and moving your resume and name among key people

associated with these organizations at both the staff and board levels. Many of the nonprofit international organizations will be organized with headquarters in the United States, especially New York City and Washington, D.C., and field operations in developing countries. While most nonprofits hire through headquarters, many also hire individuals in the field. Your research on each organization will determine which job search strategy is most appropriate for a particular organization.

FOUNDATIONS AND RESEARCH ORGANIZATIONS

Several foundations and research organizations either focus solely on the international arena or maintain an international division or section. You will need to consult the *Foundation Directory* and the *Research Center Directory* (Chapter 23) to identify the appropriate organizations.

Foundations vary in their approach to the international arena. Some foundations operate similarly to nonprofit development assistance organizations by maintaining full-time staffs at both headquarter and field locations. Other foundations primarily dispense grants to nonprofit organizations engaged in international development. The major foundations primarily funding international development include:

- Carnegie Corporation of New York
- China Medical Board of New York
- Edna McConnell Clark Foundation
- Ford Foundation
- W.K. Kellogg Foundation
- Lilly Endowment, Inc.
- Rockefeller Brothers Fund
- Rockefeller Foundation

Research organizations focusing on public international issues include several types of organizations. Some research organizations are special research units of universities or are part of graduate degree programs. Several consulting firms also conduct research as a major part of their work. Therefore, international research organizations will include both consulting firms previously outlined in this chapter and Chapter 20 and the research organizations identified in Chapter 23. Some of the major research firms conducting international research include:

- American Enterprise Institute
- The Aspen Institute
- The Brookings Institute
- Carnegie Endowment for International Peace
- Center for Strategic and International Studies
- The Chicago Council on Foreign Relations
- The Conference Board
- Council on Foreign Relations
- East-West Center
- Economic Growth Center
- Government Research Corporation
- The Heritage Foundation
- The Hoover Institution
- Hudson Institute
- Institute for Policy Studies
- Institute of War and Peace Studies
- International Development Research Centre
- International Management and Development Institute
- Rand Corporation
- SRI (Stanford Research Institute) International

Each of these foundations and research organizations have staff positions for highly skilled specialists. When seeking employment with these organizations, use the same job search strategies we outlined in Chapters 20 and 23.

PART VII

TAKING
EFFECTIVE ACTION

Understanding without action is a waste of time. And buying a how-to book without implementing it is a waste of money. Many people read how-to books, attend how-to seminars, and do nothing other than read more books and attend more seminars. While these activities become forms of therapy for some individuals, they should lead to positive actions for you.

From the very beginning of this book we stressed the importance of both understanding how the public sector operates and developing appropriate job search strategies for getting the job you want. We make no assumptions nor claim any magic is contained in this book. Rather, we have attempted to assemble useful information to help individuals realistically approach a public sector job search. Individual chapters examined specific job search skills, such as writing resumes and conducting informational interviews, as well as outlined specific structures and opportunities among Federal, state, and local governments and the peripheral institutions of trade and professional associations, consulting firms, nonprofit organizations, foundations, research organizations, and political support groups along with similar institutions in the international arena. We have done our part in getting you to the implementation stage. What happens next is your responsibility.

Assuming you have a firm understanding of each job search skill and how to relate them to each public sector institution, what

429

do you do next? The next steps involve *hard work*. Just how motivated are you to seek public sector employment or change your
career within the public sector? Our experience is that individuals
need to be sufficiently motivated to make the first move and do it
properly. If you go about your job search half-heartedly — you just
want to "test the waters" to see what's out there for you — don't
expect to be successful. You must be committed to achieving specific
goals. Make the decision to properly develop and implement your
job search and be prepared to work hard in achieving your goals.

Once you've convinced yourself to take the necessary steps to
finding a job or changing and advancing your career, you need to
find the *time* to properly implement your job search. This requires
setting aside specific blocks of time for identifying your motivated
skills, developing your resume, writing letters, making telephone
calls, and conducting the necessary research and networking required
for success. This takes time. If you are a busy person, like most
people, you simply must make the time. Practice your own versions
of time management and cutback management. Get better organized,
give some things up, or cut back on all your activities. If, for example, you can set aside one hour each day to devote to your job
search, you will spend seven hours a week or 28 hours a month on
your search. However, you should and can find more time than this
for these activities. Time and again we find successful job hunters
are ones who routinize a job search schedule and keep at it. They
make contact after contact, conduct numerous informational interviews, submit many applications and resumes, and keep repeating
these activities in spite of encountering rejections. They learn that
success is just a few more "nos" and informational interviews away.

You may find it useful to commit yourself in writing to achieving job search success. This is a very useful way to get both motivated and directed for action. Complete the following job search
contract and keep it near you — put it in your briefcase or on your
desk.

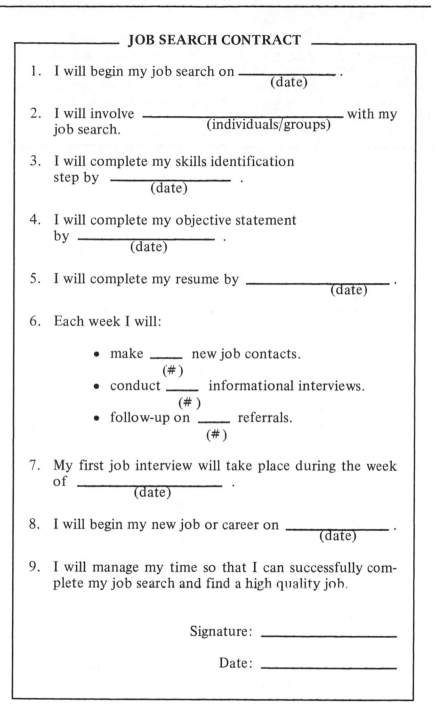

JOB SEARCH CONTRACT

1. I will begin my job search on _____ .

(date)

2. I will involve _____ with my
    (individuals/groups)
    job search.

3. I will complete my skills identification
    step by _____ .
    (date)

4. I will complete my objective statement
    by _____ .
    (date)

5. I will complete my resume by _____ .
    (date)

6. Each week I will:

    - make _____ new job contacts.
      (#)
    - conduct _____ informational interviews.
      (#)
    - follow-up on _____ referrals.
      (#)

7. My first job interview will take place during the week
    of _____ .
    (date)

8. I will begin my new job or career on _____ .
    (date)

9. I will manage my time so that I can successfully com-
    plete my job search and find a high quality job.

    Signature: _____

    Date: _____

In addition, you should complete weekly performance reports. These reports identify what you actually accomplished rather than what your good intentions tell you to do. Make copies of the following performance and planning report form and use one each week to track your actual progress and plan your activities for the next week:

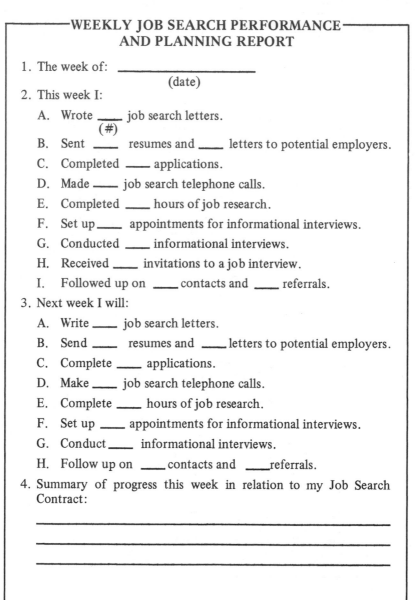

WEEKLY JOB SEARCH PERFORMANCE
AND PLANNING REPORT

1. The week of: _____
   (date)

2. This week I:

   A. Wrote ____ job search letters.
      (#)

   B. Sent ____ resumes and ____ letters to potential employers.

   C. Completed ____ applications.

   D. Made ____ job search telephone calls.

   E. Completed ____ hours of job research.

   F. Set up ____ appointments for informational interviews.

   G. Conducted ____ informational interviews.

   H. Received ____ invitations to a job interview.

   I. Followed up on ____ contacts and ____ referrals.

3. Next week I will:

   A. Write ____ job search letters.

   B. Send ____ resumes and ____ letters to potential employers.

   C. Complete ____ applications.

   D. Make ____ job search telephone calls.

   E. Complete ____ hours of job research.

   F. Set up ____ appointments for informational interviews.

   G. Conduct ____ informational interviews.

   H. Follow up on ____ contacts and ____ referrals.

4. Summary of progress this week in relation to my Job Search Contract:

   _____

   _____

   _____

If you fail to meet these written commitments, issue yourself a revised and updated contract. But if you must do this three or more times, we strongly suggest you quit kidding yourself about your motivation and commitment to find a job. Start over again, but this time consult a professional who can provide you with the necessary structure to make progress in finding a job.

A professional may not be cheap, but if paying for help gets you on the right track and results in the job you want, it's money well spent. Do not be "penny wise but pound foolish" with your future. If you must seek professional advice, be sure you are an informed consumer according to our "shopping" advice in Chapter Five.

The public sector as outlined in this book is a fascinating arena for employment. You may not get rich monetarily by working in this arena, but many people are personally richer for having pursued public goals. If your primary goal is to pursue money, the public sector will frustrate you. But if your goals are to pursue an interest, practice a skill, or promote a worthwhile cause, the public sector offers unlimited opportunities. Contrary to popular perceptions, this public sector is not stagnant nor declining. It remains dynamic and offers some of the most exciting employment opportunities found anywhere. You should open yourself to these opportunities by taking the necessary actions for achieving a successful job search in the public sector. We have done our part to get you started. Now it is your turn to translate this book into successful action!

APPENDICES

A.   FEDERAL EMPLOYMENT BY CITY, STATE, AND BRANCH OF GOVERNMENT

B.   TYPES OF RESUMES

C.   JOB SEARCH LETTERS

D.   GOVERNMENT JOB LISTING SERVICES

E.   ASSOCIATIONS OF LOCAL GOVERNMENT EMPLOYEES

F.   ASSOCIATIONS OF STATE GOVERNMENT EMPLOYEES

G.   FEDERAL JOB INFORMATION CENTERS (FJICs)

H.   FEDERAL PERSONNEL OFFICES AND JOB HOTLINE SERVICES

I.   FEDERAL AND POSTAL EMPLOYEE UNIONS AND ORGANIZATIONS

Appendix A

FEDERAL EMPLOYMENT BY CITY, STATE, AND BRANCH OF GOVERNMENT

Federal employees work in numerous metropolitan areas throughout the United States as well as abroad. While primarily full-time employees of executive agencies in the competitive service, they also work in the legislative and judicial branches of government; many are part-time or temporary employees and members of the exempted services. The three largest agencies – Department of Defense, U.S. Postal Service, and the Veterans Administration – are well represented in every state, with the largest number found in the Washington, D.C. Metropolitan area and the states of California, Texas, and New York. Regardless of where you live, Federal employees are located nearby. Your local telephone book under "United States Government" will list the names and telephone numbers of various Federal agencies in your area. You might want to contact a few Federal employees to learn more about life in the public service.

Employment data is available through the U.S. Office of Personnel Management or in Joseph Young's (ed.), *Federal Employees' Almanac* (Falls Church, VA: Federal Employees' Almanac, annual publication issued in January).

435

FEDERAL CIVILIAN EMPLOYMENT BY STANDARD
METROPOLITAN STATISTICAL AREA, DECEMBER 31, 1984

Abilene, TX	992	Columbus, OH	14,622
Akron, OH	2,294	Corpus Christi, TX	2,337
Albany, GA	3,167		
Albany-Schenectady-Troy, NY	9,331	Dallas, TX	21,612
Albuquerque, NM	11,288	Davenpt-Rock Is-Moline, IA-IL	10,511
Alexandria, LA	2,333	Dayton-Springfield, OH	24,805
Allentown-Bethlehem, PA-NJ	2,031	Denver, CO	32,192
Altoona, PA	801	Des Mones, IA	5,226
Amarillo, TX	1,802	Detroit, MI	30,110
Anaheim-Santa Ana, CA	11,865	Dothan, AL	3,848
Anchorage, AK	7,603	Duluth, MN-WI	1,797
Ann Arbor, MI	3,183		
Anniston, AL	6,787	El Paso, TX	7,712
Appleton-Oshkosh-Neenah, WI	899	Erie, PA	1,423
Asheville, NC	2,446	Eugene-Springfield, OR	1,969
Athens, GA	1,375	Evansville, IN-KY	1,004
Atlanta, GA	34,381		
Atlantic City, NJ	2,711	Fargo-Moorhead, ND-MN	1,968
Augusta, GA-SC	6,994	Fayetteville, NC	6,730
Austin, TX	9,308	Fayetteville-Springdale, AR	942
		Flint, MI	1,319
Bakersfield, CA	9,498	Florence, AL	3,253
Baltimore, MD	51,501	Fort Collins-Loveland, CO	1,552
Bangor, ME	953	Ft. Laudrdl-Hylwd-Pmpn Bch.,FL	4,066
Baton Rouge, LA	2,023	Fort Myers-Cape Coral, FL	1,017
Battle Creek, MI	4,039	Fort Smith, AR-OK	1,088
Beaumont-Port Arthur, TX	1,432	Fort Walton Beach, FL	4,644
Bellingham, WA	601	Fort Wayne, IN	1,898
Bergen-Passaic, NJ	5,691	Fort Worth-Arlington, TX	10,922
Billings, MT	1,683	Fresno, CA	8,030
Biloxi-Gulfport, MS	7,272		
Binghamton, NY-PA	1,155	Gainesville, FL	2,743
Birmingham, AL	8,575	Galveston-Texas City, TX	905
Bismarck, ND	980	Gary-Hammond, IN	1,879
Boise City, ID	3,543	Grand Forks, ND-MN	1,078
Boston, MA	36,895	Grand Rapids, MI	2,499
Boulder-Longmont, CO	2,554	Great Falls, MT	1,277
Bremerton, WA	18,746	Green Bay, WI	786
Bridgeport-Milford, CT	1,996	Grnsboro-Wnst Sal-High Pt., NC	4,430
Brockton, MA	2,349	Greenville-Spartanburg, SC	1,830
Brownsville-Harlingen, TX	1,012		
Buffalo, NY	8,373	Hagarstown, MD	1,364
Burlington, VT	1,280	Harrisbg-Lebanon-Carlisle, PA	17,287
		Hartford, CT	6,352
Canton, OH	1,310	Honolulu, HI	25,522
Casper, WY	748	Houston, TX	22,942
Cedar Rapids, IA	961	Hntngton-Ashlnd,WV-KY-OH	2,534
Champaign-Urbana-Rantoul, IL	2,368	Huntsville, AL	15,314
Charleston, SC	17,289		
Charleston, WV	1,802	Indianapolis, IN	17,173
Charlot-Gastonia-Rk Hl, NC-SC	5,059	Iowa City, IA	1,419
Charlottesville, VA	1,084		
Chattanooga, TN-GA	8,734	Jackson, MS	4,688
Chicago, IL	59,208	Jacksonville, FL	14,247
Cincinnati, OH-KY-IN	13,998	Jacksonville, NC	3,069
Clarksvlle-Hopkinsvlle, TN-KY	2,983	Jersey City, NJ	11,578
Cleveland, OH	19,151	Jhnsn City-Kngspt-Brstl, TN-VA	3,291
Colorado Springs, CO	6,914	Johnstown, PA	1,070
Columbia, MO	2,120		
Columbia, SC	6,792	Kalamazoo, MI	966
Columbus, GA-AL	4,929	Kankakee, IL	318

Kansas City, MO-KS	28,221	Provo-Orem, UT	810
Kileen-Temple, TX	7,131	Pueblo, CO	1,371
Knoxville, TN	9,199		
		Raleigh-Durham, NC	6,785
Lake County, IL	6,977	Reading, PA	948
Lakeland-Winter Haven, FL	1,078	Redding, CA	1,022
Lancaster, PA	1,290	Reno, NV	2,759
Lansing-East Lansing, MI	2,248	Richland-Kennewick-Pasco, WA	1,024
Laredo, TX	729	Richmond-Petersburg, VA	14,781
Las Cruces, NM	4,580	Riverside-San Bernardino, CA	16,452
Las Vegas, NV	4,722	Roanoke, VA	3,225
Lawrence-Haverhill, MA-NH	2,966	Rochester, NY	5,104
Lawton, OK	4,136	Rockford, IL	1,045
Lexington-Fayette, KY	5,284		
Lincoln, NE	2,490	Sacramento, CA	27,712
Little Rock-N Little Rock, AR	8,051	Saginaw-Bay City-Midland, MI	1,685
Lorain-Elyria, OH	1,142	St. Cloud, MN	1,594
Los Angeles-Long Beach, CA	68,969	St. Louis, MO-IL	35,835
Louisville, KY-IN	10,026	Salem, OR	1,501
Lubbock, TX	1,876	Salem-Glouster, MA	1,612
		Salinas-Seaside-Monterey, CA	6,116
Macon-Warner Robins, GA	16,442	Salt Lake City-Ogden, UT	27,727
Madison, WI	3,625	San Antonio, TX	37,564
Manchester, NH	2,079	San Diego, CA	34,769
Medford, OR	1,479	San Francisco, CA	33,636
Melbourne-Titusvl-Palm Bay,FL	4,876	San Jose, CA	11,740
Memphis, TN-AR-MS	15,658	San Juan, PR	7,701
Miami-Hialeah, FL	15,719	Snta Barb-Snta Maria-LMPC,CA	3,626
Mdlsex-Somerset-Hunterdon, NJ	5,546	Santa Fe, NM	1,493
Milwaukee, WI	10,484	Santa Rosa-Petaluma, CA	1,278
Minneapolis-St Paul, MN-WI	19,522	Sarasota, FL	826
Mobile, AL	2,593	Savannah, GA	2,534
Monmouth-Ocean, NJ	14,489	Scranton-Wilkes-Barre, PA	9,144
Montgomery, AL	5,571	Seattle, WA	19,990
		Shreveport, LA	3,667
Nashville, TN	9,007	Sioux City, IA-NE	879
Nassau-Suffolk, NY	19,813	Sioux Falls, SD	1,830
New Haven-Meriden, CT	4,420	South Bend-Mishawaka, IN	1,144
New London-Norwich, CT-RI	3,773	Spokane, WA	3,584
New Orleans, LA	14,796	Springfield, IL	1,986
New York, NY	83,957	Springfield, MO	1,646
Newark, NJ	19,619	Springfield, MA	5,784
Niagara Falls, NY	1,286	Stamford, CT	1,341
Norflk-Va Bch-Newprt News, VA	53,189	Stockton, CA	5,365
		Syracuse, NY	4,496
Oakland, CA	29,338		
Oklahoma City, OK	28,450	Tacoma, WA	8,366
Olympia, WA	728	Tallahassee, FL	1,248
Omaha, NE-IA	7,928	Tampa-St. Petersburg-Clrwtr, FL	13,690
Orange County, NY	3,772	Terre Haute, IN	1,094
Orlando, FL	5,251	Texarkana, TX-AR	7,274
Oxnard-Ventura, CA	9,536	Toledo, OH-MI	2,502
		Topeka, KS	3,288
Panama City, FL	2,586	Trenton, NJ	3,079
Parkersburg-Marietta, WV-OH	1,740	Tuscon, AZ	6,208
Pensacola, FL	9,228	Tulsa, OK	4,538
Peoria, IL	1,871	Tuscaloosa, AL	1,591
Philadelphia, PA-NJ	69,332		
Phoenix, AZ	14,563	Utica-Rome, NY	4,242
Pine Bluff, AR	1,919		
Pittsburgh, PA	16,977	Vallejo-Fairfield,Napa, CA	14,036
Portland, ME	1,655	Vancouver, WA	2,398
Portland, OR-WA	13,930		
Portsmth-Dover-Rochstr, NH-ME	10,158	Waco, TX	2,739
Poughkeepsie, NY	1,927	Washington, DC-MD-VA	356,238
Providence, RI	4,997	W Palm B-Boca Ratn-Dlra B,FL	3,068

Wichita, KS	4,317	Yakima, WA	1,137
Wichita Falls, TX	1,963	York, PA	1,165
Wilmington, DE-NJ-MD	4,613	Youngstown-Warren, OH	1,893
Worcester, MA	1,503	Yuba City, CA	1,086

——— FEDERAL CIVILIAN EMPLOYMENT BY MAJOR ——— GEOGRAPHIC AREA, STATES AND SELECTED AGENCY DECEMBER 31, 1984

	All[1] Agencies	Per- cent	Depart- ment of Defense	U.S. Postal Service	Veter- ans Ad- minis- tration	All Other Agen- cies
Total, All Areas	2,950,199	100.0	1,052,904	715,268	245,460	936,567
Outside United States. .	143,922	4.9	100,577	3,077	2,475	37,793
United States.	2,806,277	95.1	952,327	712,191	242,985	898,774
District of Columbia . .	215,926	7.3	18,299	10,176	6,635	180,816
Fifty States.	2,590,351	87.8	934,028	702,015	236,350	717,958
Washington,D.C. SMSA .	356,238	12.1	87,280	18,620	6,745	243,593
District of Columbia . .	215,926	7.3	18,299	10,176	6,635	180,816
Counties of Maryland . .	69,490	2.4	20,334	4,436	41	44,679
Counties and Indepen- dent Cities of Virginia	70,822	2.4	48,647	4,008	69	18,098
Alabama	59,771	2.0	27,050	7,641	4,682	20,398
Alaska	13,882	0.5	4,112	1,923	129	7,718
Arizona.	34,565	1.2	10,055	8,286	3,306	12,918
Arkansas	18,260	0.6	4,463	4,822	3,941	5,034
California	307,257	10.4	134,954	82,595	23,905	65,803
Colorado	50,511	1.7	14,084	10,886	2,854	22,687
Connecticut	21,323	0.7	4,666	11,033	2,553	3,071
Delaware	4,997	0.2	1,803	1,685	780	729
Florida	90,972	3.1	30,102	31,596	10,668	18,606
Georgia.	80,210	2.7	37,449	14,284	5,114	23,363
Hawaii	26,768	0.9	21,228	2,392	220	2,928
Idaho	9,800	0.3	1,229	2,056	595	5,920
Illinois	101,407	3.4	22,078	42,560	12,257	24,512
Indiana	39,226	1.3	14,529	13,907	4,018	6,772
Iowa	18,240	0.6	1,402	9,020	3,204	4,614
Kansas	23,398	0.8	6,888	7,505	3,360	5,645
Kentucky	35,128	1.2	14,002	7,755	3,341	10,030
Louisiana.	32,062	1.1	9,065	9,566	4,133	9,298
Maine.	17,365	0.6	10,793	3,544	1,195	1,833
Maryland.	128,753	4.4	41,762	12,678	3,151	71,162
Massachusetts	56,341	1.9	12,321	22,373	7,857	13,790
Michigan	54,392	1.8	12,654	24,277	6,251	11,210
Minnesota	29,478	1.0	2,667	14,036	4,859	7,916
Mississippi	24,244	0.8	10,650	4,573	3,228	5,793
Missouri	66,441	2.3	20,408	17,910	6,088	22,035

Montana	11,289	0.4	1,175	2,142	667	7,305
Nebraska	14,991	0.5	3,802	5,194	2,049	3,946
Nevad.	9,312	0.3	1,965	2,397	942	4,008
New Hampshire	6,707	0.2	1,501	2,925	731	1,550
New Jersey.	71,985	2.4	28,542	29,542	4,539	9,452
New Mexico	25,169	0.9	10,093	2,996	1,611	10,469
New York	153,806	5.2	18,922	76,546	21,431	36,907
North Carolina	43,337	1.5	15,558	12,707	4,829	10,243
North Dakota	7,513	0.3	1,735	2,071	670	3,037
Ohio	88,222	3.0	33,527	30,480	9,061	15,154
Oklahoma	46,326	1.6	24,739	8,247	2,714	10,626
Oregon	27,443	0.9	3,075	7,326	2,826	14,206
Pennsylvania.	126,720	4.3	55,499	36,867	8,956	25,398
Rhode Island	9,201	0.3	4,225	2,900	1,120	956
South Carolina	32,696	1.1	20,311	5,669	2,796	3,920
South Dakota	9,132	0.3	1,309	2,105	1,885	3,833
Tennessee	57,089	1.9	7,073	11,804	7,044	31,168
Texas.	163,109	5.5	64,528	42,142	15,576	40,863
Utah	35,717	1.2	22,106	3,403	1,740	8,468
Vermont	4,474	0.2	555	1,807	880	1,232
Virginia.	155,038	5.3	106,166	14,373	5,912	28,587
Washington	64,088	2.2	29,563	12,146	4,552	17,827
West Virginia	14,713	0.5	1,538	4,298	2,895	5,982
Wisconsin	25,731	0.9	2,845	11,879	5,295	5,712
Wyoming.	6,470	0.2	988	1,200	877	3,405
Unspecified State	35,292	1.2	2,274	36	3,063	29,919

[1] Excludes employees in the Central Intelligence Agency, and the National Security Agency.

—— SUMMARY OF FEDERAL CIVILIAN EMPLOYMENT——

Employment Categories	Average Employment to Date August 1985		CY 1985
	Total	%	
Total Civilian Employment[1]	3,065,770	100.00	3,016,659
Full-time	2,773,535	90.47	2,721,750
With permanent appointments	2,520,690	82.22	2,507,147
With temporary and indefinite appointments	252,845	8.25	214,603
Part-time (regularly scheduled)	208,786	6.81	216,376
Intermittent	83,449	2.72	78,533
U.S. Citizens	2,996,020	97.72	2,947,411
Non U.S. citizens	69,750	2,28	69,247
United States, Total	2,918,390	95.19	2,871,222
Washington, D.C., Metropolitan Area	356,289	11.62	354,614
Outside Washington, D.C., Metropolitan Area	2,562,101	83.57	2,516,608
Overseas, Total	147,380	4.81	145,437
U.S. Citizens	81,951	2.67	80,578
Non U.S. Citizens	65,429	2.13	64,859
Territories	17,418	.57	16,981
U.S. Citizens	17,291	.56	16,850
Non U.S. Citizens	127	—	131

Foreign Countries	129,962	4.24	128,455
U.S. Citizens	64,660	2.11	63,728
Non U.S. Citizens	65,302	2.13	64,727
Executive Branch, Total	3,007,489	98.10	2,959,249
Related to ceiling	2,971,620	96.93	2,926,835
Full-time with permanent appointments	2,484,367	81.04	2,470,395
Other	487,253	15.89	456,440
Excluded from ceiling	35,869	1.17	32,414
Full-time, total	2,716,724	88.61	2,665,945
Type of position occupied:			
In permanent positions	2,508,133	81.81	2,501,839
In temporary positions	208,591	6.80	164,106
Type of appointment:			
With permanent appointments	2,487,931	81.15	2,473,227
With temporary and indefinite appointments	228,793	7.46	192,718
Part-time (regularly scheduled)			
Total	207,969	6.78	215,448
With permanent appointments	173,662	5.66	172,891
With temporary and indefinite appointments	34,307	1.12	42,557
Intermittent, total	82,796	2.70	77,856
Competitive service, total	1,745,522	56.94	1,733,298
Permanent appointments	1,638,509	53.45	1,643,646
Temporary and indefinite appointments	107,013	3.49	89,652
Excepted and Senior Executive Services, total	1,261,967	41.16	1,225,951
Permanent appointments	1,031,733	33.65	1,011,430
Temporary and indefinite appointments	230,234	7.51	214,522
Legislative Branch, Total	39,996	1.30	39,667
Full-time	39,269	1.28	38,839
Part-time (regularly scheduled)	354	.01	446
Intermittent	373	.01	383
Judicial Branch, total	18,285	.60	17,743
Full-time	17,542	.57	16,967
Part-time (regularly scheduled)	463	.02	483
Intermittent	280	.01	294

[1] Excludes Central Intelligence Agency and National Security Agency. August 1985 and July 1985 totals include employees exempted from personnel ceilings in the Youth Programs and Worker Trainee Opportunities Program: August 1985 – 35,872 in all areas; 35,263 in the United States; and 5,050 in the Washington, D.C., metropolitan area. July 1985 – 40,365 in all areas; 39,720 in the United States; and 5,143 in the Washington, D.C., metropolitan area.

Appendix B
TYPES OF RESUMES

The following examples are the most frequently used types of resumes. Except for the traditional chronological resume – which you should avoid – you may want to develop similar resumes for certain job search situations. We use the same fictitious individual in our examples to demonstrate how one person's qualifications can be presented in these different formats.

The *traditional chronological resume* presents a hodge-podge of disconnected information on an individual's background. A chronology of history is the major organizing principle for this resume. Displaying individual weaknesses rather than strengths, it lacks a job objective, includes extraneous information, and presents negatives. The layout also is unattractive.

The *improved chronological resume* stresses skills and accomplishments but organizes this critical information chronologically. Using a functional skills vocabulary to highlight individual positions, all important information comes first; inclusive dates are placed at the end of each position summary to satisfy employers' need for chronological information. This type of resume is ideal for individuals with extensive work experience and who are applying for positions directly related to their previous work experience. Employers, especially those in the public sector, prefer this type of chronological resume.

The *combination resume* stresses skills and accomplishments

441

("Areas of Effectiveness") in relation to a skills–outcome objective and includes a chronological work history section. A personal statement appears at the end to communicate a distinctive personal quality. A second page, "Supplemental Information," is attached to further strengthen the resume and provide more specific information on the functional skills and work history categories.

Functional resumes primarily stress one's objective, education, skills, and accomplishments. Work history is purposefully absent because an individual either lacks specific work experience or is interested in entering a new work field. This type of resume should only be used if you are first entering the job market or are making a major career change where a chronology of your past work experience would be a negative on the resume. For employers, these resumes are primarily poetic promises of future performance rather than documents of actual work performance from which one can make judgments for predicting future accomplishments.

The *resume letter* is designed to target a particular position by stressing one's skills and accomplishments in direct relation to a specific position. Resume letters are used to specifically address employer's needs when a resume is inadequate for dealing with certain specifics. If an employer requests a resume based on this letter, you must be prepared to send one of the other types of resumes along with a cover letter.

For examples of other resumes, both typeset and typewriter produced in different formats, see Krannich and Banis, *High Impact Resumes and Letters*.

Traditional Chronological Resume

RESUME

Sarah Taylor
2720 Euclid Drive
Philadelphia, Pennsylvania 19110

Weight: 125 lbs.
Height: 5'7"
Born: August 3, 1953
Health: Good
Marital Status: Married with two children

EDUCATION

1979-1980: M.A., Public Administration, Temple University, Philadelphia, Pennsylvania.
1971-1975: B.A., Political Science, State University of New York, Plattsburg.
1967-1971: High School Diploma, Furniss High School, Philadelphia, Pennsylvania.

WORK EXPERIENCE

9/2/83 to 4/3/86: Planning Analyst, Department of Planning, City of Philadelphia. Responsible for housing plans. Terminated due to major cuts in municipal planning budget.
2/4/81 to 6/4/83: Research Associate, Coalition for Community Service Agencies, Philadelphia, Pennsylvania. Responsible for developing reports. Resigned to seek a government job.
4/2/79 to 11/21/81: Waitress, The Do Drop Inn, Philadelphia, Pennsylvania. Part-time while attending college.
6/5/76 to 11/14/78: Clerk Typist, Office of Admissions, State University of New York, Plattsburg. Part-time while attending college.

PROFESSIONAL AFFILIATIONS

American Society for Public Administration
American Planning Association
Daughters of the American Revolution
National Rifle Association

HOBBIES

I like to paint, garden, and jog.

REFERENCES

David Stoffer, Chief, Department of Planning, City of Philadelphia, Pennsylvania 19130, (315)721-6131.
Dr. Alice White, Professor, Department of Public Administration, Temple University, Philadelphia, Pennsylvania 19118, (215)719-3100.

Improved Chronological Resume

———————— SARAH TAYLOR ————————
2720 Euclid Drive
Philadelphia, Pennsylvania 19110   215/721-1982

OBJECTIVE: A research and public relations position with an
                association, where strong communication, research, and
                analytical skills will be used for furthering the goals
                of the association.

EXPERIENCE: Planning Analyst, City of Philadelphia, Pennsylvania.
                Developed community-wide plans for public housing and
                conducted research in response to requests for zoning
                variances. Regularly met with community groups to
                identify housing needs, communicate city's policies, and
                advise on policies and procedures. Wrote policy papers
                and reports for city council as well as issued press
                materials on city planning issues. Worked closely with
                citizen groups, landlords, contractors, and lawyers
                representing interests of various local groups.
                Developed a new information system for responding
                quickly to requests for planning information. 1983-1986.

                Research Associate, Coalition for Community Service
                Agencies, Philadelphia, Pennsylvania.
                Conducted research, analyzed data, wrote reports, and
                lobbied government agencies at both the local and
                state levels on various aspects of community service
                organizations. Research involved interviewing
                government officials and representatives of community
                service groups. Several reports were responsible for
                providing greater public assistance to strengthen
                community service organizations at the local level.
                Reports cited by supervisor as "outstanding contributions
                to making community service organizations a central issue
                on the local government agenda." 1981-1983.

EDUCATION: M.A., Public Administration, Temple University,
                Philadelphia, Pennsylvania, 1980.

                B.A., Political Science, State University of New York,
                Plattsburg, New York, 1975.

REFERENCES: Available upon request.

Combination Resume

——————— SARAH TAYLOR ———————
2720 Euclid Drive
Philadelphia, Pennsylvania   215/721-1982

OBJECTIVE: A research and public relations position with an
                    association, where strong communication, research, and
                    analytical skills will be used for furthering the goals
                    of the association.

AREAS OF EFFECTIVENESS

RESEARCH: Conducted 22 research projects on various aspects of
                    planning and community service groups. Developed
                    research design, conducted field interviews, and
                    analyzed data. Research resulted in several reports
                    which were responsible for changing local government
                    policies. Consistently cited by supervisors as making
                    "outstanding" contributions to both understanding and
                    action.

PUBLIC   Developed press releases, issued reports, and met
RELATIONS: regularly with community groups, government officials,
                    contractors, and the press. Devised an innovative
                    information system to respond quickly to requests for
                    information.

COMMUNICATION: Authored numerous position papers and major reports
                    on public policy issues for government agencies and
                    community groups. Frequent speaker before community
                    organizations. Conducted several briefings for
                    supervisors, city council members, and the press.

WORK HISTORY: Planning Analyst, City of Philadelphia, Pennsylvania,
                    1983-1986.

                    Research Associate, Coalition for Community Service
                    Agencies, Philadelphia, Pennsylvania, 1981-1983.

EDUCATION: M.A., Public Administration, Temple University,
                    Philadelphia, Pennsylvania, 1980.

                    B.A., Political Science; State University of New York,
                    Plattsburg, New York, 1975.

PERSONAL: Enjoy developing innovative approaches to public issues
                    which involve research, writing, and frequent contact
                    with government officials and community groups.

Combination Resume – continued

CONTINUING EDUCATION AND TRAINING

- Completed 15 graduate level hours of research and communication courses directly related to the public service.
- Recently attended several workshops on strengthening research, communication, and community relations skills:

    "Survey Research Methods in Local Government," International City Manager Association, June 4-6, 1986.

    "Briefing Techniques," American Management Associations, September 8-9, 1985.

    "Public Speaking," Greater Philadelphia Chamber of Commerce, February 20-21, 1985.

    "Effective Report Writing for Public Employees," November 12-13, 1984.

    "Planning as a Community Process," American Planning Association, March 21-25, 1984.

MAJOR RESEARCH CONDUCTED AND REPORTS AUTHORED

- "Making Community Service Organizations Work More Effectively," Coalition for Community Service Agencies, 1982.
- "Serving the Community: A Practical Manual for Working With Government and Other Community Organizations," Coalition for Community Service Agencies, 1983.
- "Planning Our Housing Future: A Comprehensive Approach to Balanced Growth," City of Philadelphia, 1984.
- "City Planning Research: A Manual for Conducting Survey Research in the City of Philadelphia," City of Philadelphia, 1985.

PROFESSIONAL AFFILIATIONS

- American Society for Public Administration
- American Society of Association Executives
- Toastmasters International

EDUCATIONAL HIGHLIGHTS

- Working toward Ph.D. in Public Policy with concentration on policy formation and community management.
- Earned 4.0/4.0 grade point average in graduate studies.

Functional Resume

SARAH TAYLOR

| 2720 Euclid Drive | Philadelphia, PA 19110 | 215/721-1982 |

OBJECTIVE: A research and public relations position with an
             association, where strong communication, research, and
             analytical skills will be used for furthering the goals
             of the association.

EDUCATION: M.A., Public Administration, Temple University,
             Philadelphia, Pennsylvania, 1980.

             B.A., Political Science, State University of New York,
             Plattsburg, New York, 1975.

MAJOR   Research
STRENGTHS:
             Conducted 22 research projects on various aspects of
             planning and community service groups. Developed
             research design, conducted field interviews, and
             analyzed data. Research resulted in several reports
             which were responsible for changing local government
             policies. Consistently cited by supervisors as making
             "outstanding" contributions to both understanding and
             action.

             Public Relations

             Developed press releases, issued reports, and met
             regularly with community groups, government officials,
             contractors, and the press. Devised an innovative
             information system to respond quickly to requests for
             information.

             Communication

             Authored numerous position papers and major reports
             on public policy issues for government agencies and
             community groups. Frequent speaker before community
             organizations. Conducted several briefings for
             supervisors, city council members, and the press.

PERSONAL: Enjoy developing innovative approaches to public issues
             which involve research, writing, and frequent contact
             with government officials and community groups.

Resume Letter

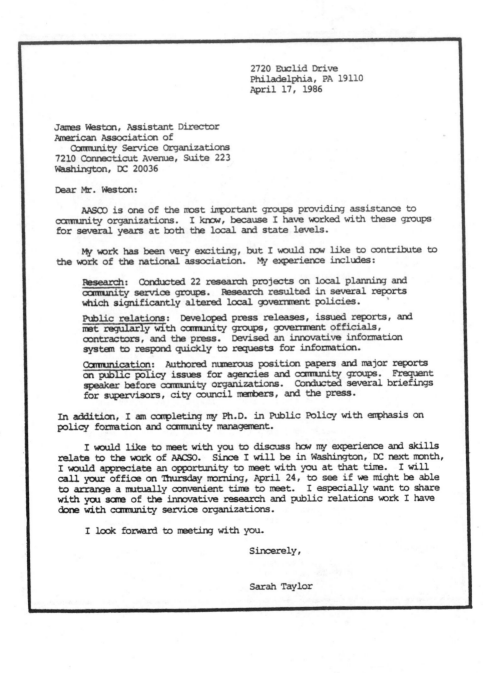

                                        2720 Euclid Drive
                                        Philadelphia, PA 19110
                                        April 17, 1986

James Weston, Assistant Director
American Association of
    Community Service Organizations
7210 Connecticut Avenue, Suite 223
Washington, DC 20036

Dear Mr. Weston:

    AASCO is one of the most important groups providing assistance to
community organizations. I know, because I have worked with these groups
for several years at both the local and state levels.

    My work has been very exciting, but I would now like to contribute to
the work of the national association. My experience includes:

    Research: Conducted 22 research projects on local planning and
    community service groups. Research resulted in several reports
    which significantly altered local government policies.

    Public relations: Developed press releases, issued reports, and
    met regularly with community groups, government officials,
    contractors, and the press. Devised an innovative information
    system to respond quickly to requests for information.

    Communication: Authored numerous position papers and major reports
    on public policy issues for agencies and community groups. Frequent
    speaker before community organizations. Conducted several briefings
    for supervisors, city council members, and the press.

In addition, I am completing my Ph.D. in Public Policy with emphasis on
policy formation and community management.

    I would like to meet with you to discuss how my experience and skills
relate to the work of AACSO. Since I will be in Washington, DC next month,
I would appreciate an opportunity to meet with you at that time. I will
call your office on Thursday morning, April 24, to see if we might be able
to arrange a mutually convenient time to meet. I especially want to share
with you some of the innovative research and public relations work I have
done with community service organizations.

    I look forward to meeting with you.

                                        Sincerely,

                                        Sarah Taylor

Appendix C
JOB SEARCH LETTERS

The following are examples of the major types of letters you will most frequently write during your job search. An example of a resume letter is not included because it is a subject of Appendix B.

The *cover letter* can be used to respond to a classified ad. Following the principles of providing "cover" for advertising your resume, this letter mainly highlights interests. The writer takes the initiative to contact the employer by requesting an interview.

The *approach letters* respond to two different situations. The first letter is written in response to a referral. The second example goes "cold turkey" — with no prior contacts or introductions. In each case, the writers are requesting only information and advice; they are careful to avoid any hint they are looking for a job through this individual.

The *thank-you letters* are written for several different situations: post-job interview, post-informational interview, job rejection, and job offer acceptance. Each letter should communicate enthusiasm and thoughtfulness. Try to avoid using standard thank-you letter language. Make your letter express *you* rather than a model of a good letter.

You will find other occasions for writing letters which are not included in our examples. These might include sending a thank-you letter in response to information received over the telephone or through the mail or when declining a job offer or terminating employment for another job. See Krannich and Banis, *High Impact Resumes and Letters*, for examples of other types of letters.

Cover Letter

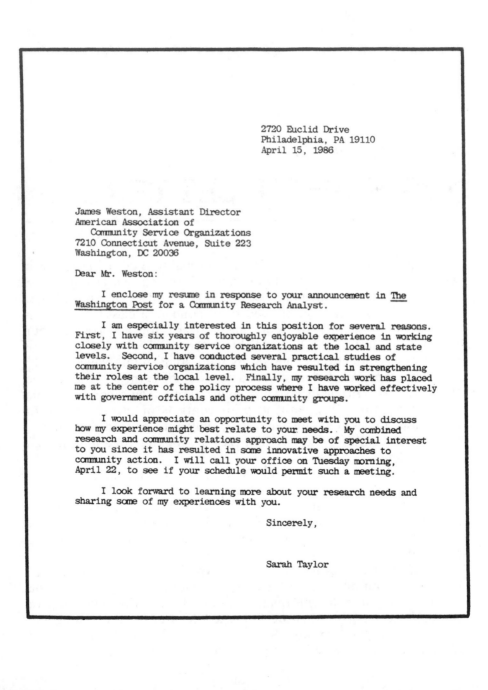

2720 Euclid Drive
Philadelphia, PA 19110
April 15, 1986

James Weston, Assistant Director
American Association of
 Community Service Organizations
7210 Connecticut Avenue, Suite 223
Washington, DC 20036

Dear Mr. Weston:

I enclose my resume in response to your announcement in The
Washington Post for a Community Research Analyst.

I am especially interested in this position for several reasons.
First, I have six years of thoroughly enjoyable experience in working
closely with community service organizations at the local and state
levels. Second, I have conducted several practical studies of
community service organizations which have resulted in strengthening
their roles at the local level. Finally, my research work has placed
me at the center of the policy process where I have worked effectively
with government officials and other community groups.

I would appreciate an opportunity to meet with you to discuss
how my experience might best relate to your needs. My combined
research and community relations approach may be of special interest
to you since it has resulted in some innovative approaches to
community action. I will call your office on Tuesday morning,
April 22, to see if your schedule would permit such a meeting.

I look forward to learning more about your research needs and
sharing some of my experiences with you.

Sincerely,

Sarah Taylor

Approach Letter: Referral

2720 Euclid Drive
Philadelphia, PA 19110
April 8, 1986

James Weston, Assistant Director
American Association of
   Community Service Organizations
7210 Connecticut Avenue, Suite 223
Washington, DC 20036

Dear Mr. Weston:

    Alice White suggested that I contact you about my interest in community service organizations. She enthusiastically mentioned you as one of the best people to talk to about careers in this public service field.

    I am leaving local government after three years of progressively responsible experience in community planning where I worked extensively with community service organizations. But before I decide to seek a career in this field as well as relocate, I believe I would benefit greatly from your experience and insights into this field. Your advice would be very helpful at this stage in my career.

    I will be in Washington during the week of April 21-25. Would it be possible for us to meet briefly to discuss my career plans? I have several concerns you might be most helpful in clarifying. I will call your office on Tuesday morning, April 15, to see if your schedule would permit such a meeting.

    I look forward to learning from your experience.

               Sincerely,

               Sarah Taylor

Approach Letter: Cold Turkey

2720 Euclid Drive
Philadelphia, PA 19110
April 8, 1986

James Weston, Assistant Director
American Association of
    Community Service Organizations
7210 Connecticut Avenue, Suite 223
Washington, DC 20036

Dear Mr. Weston:

I have been most impressed by your work with community service organizations in Philadelphia. Indeed, the recent article appearing in Association Trends on your promotion to assistant director of AACSO stressed what I learned a long time ago here in Philadelphia—you have an exceptional talent to get the local organizations to work together in pursuing the national agenda of AACSO. Congratulations on a well deserved promotion!

Your public service career with community service organizations is one I hope to emulate. After six enjoyable years of working with these organizations at the local and state levels, I am convinced I want to pursue a long-term career in this field and especially from a much broader national perspective. My research and public relations work with these groups may also be of interest to you.

Would it be possible for us to meet briefly to discuss my career interests in this field? I believe your advice would be most valuable in helping me better define my future with community service organizations.

I will be in Washington, DC during the week of April 21-25. Perhaps your schedule would permit a meeting during that week. I will call your office on Tuesday morning, April 8, to see if such a meeting would be possible.

I look forward to meeting you and learning from your experiences.

Sincerely,

Sarah Taylor

Thank-You Letter: Post-Informational Interview

```
                                   2720 Euclid Drive
                                   Philadelphia, PA 19110
                                   April 24, 1986



James Weston, Assistant Director
American Association of
    Community Service Organizations
7210 Connecticut Avenue, Suite 223
Washington, DC 20036

Dear Mr. Weston:

     Our meeting yesterday was truly informative and extremely
useful in helping me clarify various concerns regarding careers
with community service organizations.  Your experience and
knowledge of this field is most impressive.

     I want to thank you again for taking the time from your
busy schedule to meet with me.  Your suggestions for strengthening
my resume were very helpful.  I am how revising the resume in
light of your thoughtful advice.  I will sent you a copy of the
revised resume next week.

     Following your advice, I will contact Marilyn Plante tomorrow
to see if she might have or know of any opportunities for someone
with my interests and qualifications.  I will give her your
regards.

     I hope to have a chance to meet with you again sometime.

                              Sincerely,



                              Sarah Taylor
```

Thank-You Letter: Post-Job Interview

2720 Euclid Drive
Philadelphia, PA 19110
April 30, 1986

James Weston, Assistant Director
American Association of
  Community Service Organizations
7210 Connecticut Avenue, Suite 223
Washington, DC 20036

Dear Mr. Weston:

I want to thank you again for the opportunity to interview for the Community Research Analyst position. You and your staff were most helpful in clarifying many questions about this position and AACSO.

Our meeting further convinced me that this position is ideally suited for my interests, skills, and experience. My prior research and public relations work with community service agencies at the local and state levels has prepared me well for this position. I am committed to giving AACSO my very best effort.

I look forward to meeting with you again to further discuss my candidacy.

                              Sincerely,

                              Sarah Taylor

Thank-You Letter: Job Rejection

```
                                    2720 Euclid Drive
                                    Philadelphia, PA 19110
                                    April 29, 1986



James Weston, Assistant Director
American Association of
    Community Service Organizations
7210 Connecticut Avenue, Suite 223
Washington, DC 20036

Dear Mr. Weston:

     I want to thank you again for considering me for the
Community Research Analyst position.  Although I am disappointed
with the outcome, I appreciated the opportunity and learned a
great deal about AACSO.  I am especially pleased with the
highly professional manner in which you and your staff conducted
the interview.

     Please keep me in mind for future vacancies.  I have a strong
interest in AACSO which will certainly continue in the future.
I believe I could contribute a great deal to AACSO.  I am sure
I would work well with you and your staff.

     Best wishes.

                                    Sincerely,


                                    Sarah Taylor
```

Thank-You Letter: Job Offer Acceptance

2720 Euclid Drive
Philadelphia, PA 19110
May 3, 1986

James Weston, Assistant Director
American Association of
     Community Service Organizations
7210 Connecticut Avenue, Suite 223
Washington, DC 20036

Dear Mr. Weston:

I am pleased to accept your offer and look forward to joining AACSO later this month.

The Community Research Analyst position is ideally suited to my interests, skills, and experience. I will give you and AACSO my very best effort.

I understand I will begin work on May 14. Please contact me if I need to complete any paper work prior to this starting date.

Thank you again for your consideration and confidence.

Sincerely,

Sarah Taylor

Appendix D
GOVERNMENT JOB LISTING SERVICES

The following publications and services are the major resources available on national and regional job listings for individuals interested in government employment. More than 100 additional sources are available in publications of specialized national, regional, and state professional associations. For a more complete listing of resources, especially among state level professional associations, see Daniel Lauber, *The Compleat Guide to Jobs in Planning and Public Administration* and the *Encyclopedia of Associations.*

Affirmative Action Register: Warren H. Green, Inc., 8356 Olive Blvd., St. Louis, MO 63132, Tel. 314/991-1335.

APWA Reporter: American Public Works Association, 1313 E. 60th St., Chicago, IL 60637, Tel. 312/947-2520.

The City-County Recruiter: Clearinghouse for Government Personnel, P. O. Box 2400, Station "B", Lincoln, NE 68502.

ICMA Newsletter: International City Management Association, 1120 G St., NW, Washington, DC 20005, Tel. 202/626-4600.

The Job Finder: A Checklist of Openings for Administrative and

Governmental Research Employment in the West: Western Government Research Association, c/o Center for Public Policy and Administration, California State University, 1250 Bellflower Blvd., Long Beach, CA 90840, Tel. 213/498-5419.

JobMart: American Planning Association, 1313 E. 60th St., Chicago, IL 60637, Tel. 312/955-9100.

Jobs Available: A Listing of Employment Opportunities in the Public Sector: P.O. Box 1040, Modesto, CA 95353.

Mountain Plains States' Job Bank: Mountain Plains States' Job Bank, Utah League of Cities and Towns, Suite 305, 10 W. Broadway, Salt Lake City, UT 84101, Tel. 801/364-4143.

NAHRO Monitor: National Association of Housing and Redevelopment Officials, 260 Virginia Ave., NW, Washington, DC 20037, Tel. 202/333-2020.

New England Administrative, Professional, Technical Job Bank: New England Municipal Center, Pettee Brook Offices, P. O. Box L, Durham, NH 03824, Tel. 603/868-5000.

Public Administration Times: American Society for Public Administration, 1225 Connecticut Ave., NW, Washington, DC 20036, Tel. 202/785-3255.

The State Recruiter: Clearinghouse for Government Personnel, P. O. Box 2400, Station "B", Lincoln, NE 68502.

Appendix E

ASSOCIATIONS OF LOCAL GOVERNMENT EMPLOYEES

The following associations primarily serve local government employees. However, some associations also include state and Federal employees as well as quasi-government employees because they are organized along professional lines which cross-cut levels of government. A similar membership situation concerns the state and Federal associations and organizations outlined in Appendices F and I. Therefore, you may want to examine several organizations relevant to these other levels of government.

AMERICAN ASSOCIATION OF SCHOOL ADMINISTRATORS: 1801 North Moore St., Arlington, VA 22209, Tel. 703/528-0700.

AMERICAN PLANNING ASSOCIATION: 1313 East 60th St., Chicago, IL 60637, Tel. 312/955-9100.

AMERICAN PUBLIC HEALTH ASSOCIATION: 1015 15th St., NW, Washington, DC 20005, Tel. 202/789-5600.

AMERICAN PUBLIC POWER ASSOCIATION: 2301 M St., NW, 3rd Floor, Washington, DC 20037, Tel. 202/775-8300.

AMERICAN PUBLIC TRANSIT ASSOCIATIONS: 1225 Connecticut Ave., NW, Suite 200, Washington, DC 20036, Tel. 202/838-2800.

AMERICAN PUBLIC WELFARE ASSOCIATION: 1125 15th St., NW, Suite 300, Washington, DC 20005, Tel. 202/293-7550.

AMERICAN PUBLIC WORKS ASSOCIATION: 1313 East 60th St., Chicago, IL 60637, Tel. 312/667-2200.

AMERICAN SOCIETY FOR PUBLIC ADMINISTRATION: 1120 G St., NW, Suite 500, Washington, DC 20005, Tel. 202/393-7878.

AMERICAN WATER WORKS ASSOCIATION: 6666 West Quincy Ave., Denver, CO 80235, Tel. 303/794-7711.

INTERNATIONAL ASSOCIATION OF ASSESSING OFFICERS: 1313 East 60th St., Chicago, IL 60637, Tel. 312/947-2064.

INTERNATIONAL ASSOCIATION OF FIRE CHIEFS: 1329 18th St., NW, Washington, DC 20036, Tel. 202/833-3420.

INTERNATIONAL CITY MANAGEMENT ASSOCIATION: 1120 G St., NW, Suite 300, Washington, DC 20005, Tel. 202/626-4610.

INTERNATIONAL INSTITUTE OF MUNICIPAL CLERKS: 160 N. Altadena Drive, Pasadena, CA 91106, Tel. 213/795-6153.

INTERNATIONAL PERSONNEL MANAGEMENT ASSOCIATION: 1850 K St., NW, Suite 870, Washington, DC 20006, Tel. 202/833-5860.

MUNICIPAL FINANCE OFFICERS ASSOCIATION: 180 North Michigan Ave., Chicago, IL 60601, Tel. 312/977-9700.

NATIONAL ASSOCIATION OF COUNTIES: 440 1st St., NW, 8th Floor, Washington, DC 20001, Tel. 202/393-6226.

NATIONAL ASSOCIATION OF HOUSING AND REDEVELOPMENT OFFICIALS: 2600 Virginia Ave., NW, Suite 404, Washington, DC 20037, Tel. 202/333-2020.

NATIONAL ASSOCIATION OF REGIONAL COUNCILS: 1700 K St., NW, 13th Floor, Washington, DC 20006, Tel. 202/457-0710.

NATIONAL ASSOCIATION OF REGULATORY UTILITY COM-MISSIONERS: 1102 ICC Building, P. O. Box 684, Washington, DC 20044, Tel. 202/628-7324.

NATIONAL ASSOCIATION OF TOWNS AND TOWNSHIPS: 1522 K St., NW, Suite 730, Washington, DC 20005, Tel. 202/737-5200.

NATIONAL INSTITUTE OF MUNICIPAL LAW OFFICERS: 1000 Connecticut Ave., NW, Suite 800, Washington, DC 20036, Tel. 202/466-5424.

NATIONAL LEAGUE OF CITIES: 1301 Pennsylvania Ave., NW, Washington, DC 20004, Tel. 202/626-3010.

NATIONAL MUNICIPAL LEAGUE: 55 West 44th St., New York, NY 10036, Tel. 212/730-7930.

NATIONAL RECREATION AND PARK ASSOCIATION: 3101 Park Center Drive, Alexandria, VA 22302, Tel. 703/820-4940.

NATIONAL SCHOOL BOARDS ASSOCIATION: 1055 Thomas Jefferson St., Suite 600, Washington, DC 20007, Tel. 202/337-7666.

U.S. CONFERENCE OF MAYORS: 1620 Eye St., NW, Washington, DC 20006, Tel. 202/293-7330.

Appendix F

ASSOCIATIONS OF STATE GOVERNMENT EMPLOYEES

The following associations and organizations are primarily organized to serve the professional interests of state government employees. But similar to many organizations included in Appendix E for local government employees and in Appendix I for Federal employees, many of the following organizations include members from other levels of government. The American Society for Public Administration, the International Personnel Management Association, and the National Association of Schools of Public Affairs and Administration, for example, cross-cut employees at all levels, including many from the private sector and abroad.

ACADEMY FOR STATE AND LOCAL GOVERNMENT: 400 North Capitol St., NW, Suite 349, Washington, DC 20001, Tel. 202/638-1445.

AMERICAN ASSOCIATION OF STATE HIGHWAY AND TRANSPORTATION OFFICIALS: 444 North Capitol St., NW, Suite 225, Washington, DC 20001, Tel. 202/624-5810.

ASSOCIATION OF STATE AND INTERSTATE WATER POLLUTION CONTROL ADMINISTRATORS: 444 N. Capitol St., NW, Suite 330, Washington, DC 20001, Tel. 202/624-7782.

ASSOCIATION OF STATE AND TERRITORIAL HEALTH OFFICIALS: 1311A Dolly Madison Blvd., Suite 3A, McLean, VA 22101, Tel. 703/556-9222.

ASSOCIATION OF STATE AND TERRITORIAL SOLID WASTE MANAGEMENT OFFICIALS: 444 N. Capitol St., NW, Suite 343, Washington, DC 20001, Tel. 202/624-5828.

CONFERENCE OF CHIEF JUSTICES: 300 Newport Ave., Williamsburg, VA 23185, Tel. 804/253-2000.

CONFERENCE OF STATE COURT ADMINISTRATORS: 300 Newport Ave., Williamsburg, VA 23185, Tel. 804/253-2000.

COUNCIL OF STATE COMMUNITY AFFAIRS AGENCIES: 444 North Capitol St., NW, Suite 251, Washington, DC 20001, Tel. 202/393-6435.

COUNCIL OF STATE GOVERNMENTS: Iron Works Pike, P. O. Box 11910, Lexington, KY 40578, Tel. 606/252-2291.

COUNCIL OF STATE HOUSING AGENCIES: 400 N. Capitol St., NW, Suite 295, Washington, DC 20001, Tel. 202/628-8880.

COUNCIL OF STATE PLANNING AGENCIES: 400 N. Capitol St., NW, Suite 291, Washington, DC 20001, Tel. 202/624-7726.

EDUCATION COMMISSION OF THE STATES: 300 Lincoln Tower Building, 1860 Lincoln St., Denver, CO 80295, Tel. 303/861-4917.

FEDERATION OF TAX ADMINISTRATORS: 444 North Capitol St., NW, Suite 334, Washington, DC 20001, Tel. 202/624-5890.

NATIONAL ASSOCIATION OF STATE ALCOHOL AND DRUG-ABUSE DIRECTORS: 444 North Capitol St., NW, Suite 530, Washington, DC 20001, Tel. 202/783-6868.

NATIONAL ASSOCIATION FOR STATE INFORMATION SYSTEMS: Iron Works Pike, P. O. Box 11910, Lexington, KY 40578, Tel. 252-2291.

NATIONAL ASSOCIATION OF SECRETARIES OF STATE: Iron Works Pike, P. O. Box 19910, Lexington, KY 40578, Tel. 606/252-2291.

NATIONAL ASSOCIATION OF STATE AUDITORS, COMP-TROLLERS, AND TREASURERS: Iron Works Pike, P. O. Box 11910, Lexington, KY 40578, Tel. 606/252-2291.

NATIONAL ASSOCIATION OF STATE BOARDS OF EDUCA-TION: 444 North Capitol St., NW, Suite 526, Washington, DC 20001, Tel. 202/624-5844.

NATIONAL ASSOCIATION OF STATE BUDGET OFFICERS: 444 North Capitol St., NW, Suite 3428, Washington, DC 20001, Tel. 202/624-5382.

NATIONAL ASSOCIATION OF STATE COMPTROLLERS: Iron Works Pike, P. O. Box 11910, Lexington, KY 40578, Tel. 606/252-2291.

NATIONAL ASSOCIATION OF STATE DEPARTMENTS OF AGRICULTURE: 1616 H. St., NW, Washington, DC 20006, Tel. 202/628-1566.

NATIONAL ASSOCIATION OF STATE MENTAL HEALTH PROGRAM DIRECTORS: 1001 Third St., SW, Suite 114, Washington, DC 20024, Tel. 202/554-7807.

NATIONAL ASSOCIATION OF STATE PURCHASING OFFI-CIALS: Iron Works Pike, P. O. Box 11910, Lexington, KY 40578, Tel. 606/252-2291.

NATIONAL ASSOCIATION OF STATE TREASURERS: Iron Works Pike, P. O. Box 11910, Lexington, KY 40578, Tel. 606/252-2291.

NATIONAL ASSOCIATION OF TAX ADMINISTRATORS: 444 North Capitol St., NW, Suite 334, Washington, DC 20001, Tel. 202/625-5890.

NATIONAL CENTER FOR STATE COURTS: 300 Newport Ave., Williamsburg, VA 23185, Tel. 804/253-2000.

NATIONAL CONFERENCE OF COMMISSIONERS ON UNIFORM STATE LAWS: 645 North Michigan Ave., Chicago, IL 60611, Tel. 312/321-9710.

NATIONAL CONFERENCE OF LIEUTENANT GOVERNORS:

Iron Works Pike, P. O. Box 11910, Lexington, KY 40578, Tel. 606/252-2291.

NATIONAL CONFERENCE OF STATE GENERAL SERVICE OFFICERS: Iron Works Pike, P. O. Box 11910, Lexington, KY 40578, Tel. 606/252-2291.

NATIONAL CONFERENCE OF STATE LEGISLATURES: 1125 17th St., 15th Floor, Denver, CO 80202, Tel. 303/623-6600.

NATIONAL GOVERNORS' ASSOCIATION: 400 North Capitol St., NW, Suite 250, Washington, DC 20001, Tel. 202/624-5300.

NATIONAL STATE AUDITORS ASSOCIATION: Iron Works Pike, P. O. Box 11910, Lexington, KY 40578, Tel. 606/252-2291.

STATE AND TERRITORIAL AIR POLLUTION PROGRAM ADMINISTRATORS: 444 North Capitol St., NW, Suite 306, Washington, DC 20001, Tel. 202/624-7864.

STATE AUDITOR COORDINATING COUNCIL: Iron Works Pike, P. O. Box 11910, Lexington, KY 40578, Tel. 606/252-2291.

Appendix G

FEDERAL JOB INFORMATION CENTERS (FJICs)

The following Federal Job Information Centers function as regional and subregional offices of the U.S. Office of Personnel Management. If you write to them for information, insert the building, street, and city address found in the list below in the following address format:

> Federal Job Information Center
> U.S. Office of Personnel Management
> (building)
> (street address)
> (city, state, zip code)

However, you will find it more useful and convenient to either call or visit the center nearest you for information on Federal jobs within the area and to obtain the necessary application forms.

ALABAMA: Southerland Building, 806 Governors Dr., SW, Huntsville, AL 35801, Tel. 205/453-5070.

ALASKA: Federal Building and U.S. Courthouse, 700 C Street, Box 22, Anchorage, AK 99513, Tel. 907/271-5821.

ARIZONA: 522 N. Central Ave., Phoenix, AZ 85004, Tel. 602/261-4736.

ARKANSAS: Federal Building, Rm. 3421, 700 W. Capitol Ave., Little Rock, AR 72201, Tel. 501/378-5842.

CALIFORNIA: Linder Building, 845 South Figueroa St., Los Angeles, CA 90017, Tel. 213/688-3360; Federal Building, 650 Capitol Mall, Sacramento, CA 95814, Tel. 916/440-3441; 880 Front St., San Diego, CA 92188, Tel. 714/293-6165; Federal Building, Rm. 1001, 450 Golden Gate Ave., San Francisco, CA 94102, Tel. 415/556-6667.

COLORADO: 1845 Sherman St., Denver, CO 80203, Tel. 303/837-3509.

CONNECTICUT: Federal Building, Rm. 717, 450 Main St., Hartford, CT 06103, Tel. 203/244-3096.

DELAWARE: None. Contact offices in nearby states.

DISTRICT OF COLUMBIA: 1900 E St., NW, Washington, DC 20415, Tel. 202/737-9616.

FLORIDA: Federal Building, 80 N. Hughey Ave., Orlando, FL 32801, Tel. 305/420-6148.

GEORGIA: Richard B. Russell Federal Building, 75 Spring St., SW, Atlanta, GA 30303, Tel. 404/221-4315.

GUAM: 238 O'Hara St., Rm. 308, Agana, GU, 96910, Tel. 344-5242.

HAWAII: Federal Building, Room 1310, 300 Ala Moana Blvd., Honolulu, HI 96850, Tel. 808/546-7108.

IDAHO: None. Contact offices in nearby states.

ILLINOIS: Dirksen Building, Rm. 1322, 219 S. Dearborn Street, Chicago, IL 60604, Tel. 312/353-5136.

INDIANA: U.S. Courthouse and Federal Building, 46 E. Ohio St., Rm. 123, Indianapolis, IN 46204, Tel. 317/269-7161 or 7162.

IOWA: 210 Walnut St., Rm. 191, Des Moines, IA 50309, Tel. 515/284-4546.

KANSAS: One-Twenty Building, Rm. 101, 120 S. Market St., Wichita, KS 67202, Tel. 316/269-6106. If in the counties of Johnson, Leavenworth, or Wyandotte, call 816/374-5702.

KENTUCKY: Federal Building, 600 Federal Pl., Louisville, KY 40202, Tel. 502/582-5130.

LOUISIANA: F. Edward Herbert Building, 610 South St., Rm. 103, New Orleans, LA 70130, Tel. 504/589-2764.

MAINE: None. Contact offices in nearby states.

MARYLAND: Edward A. Garmatz Federal Building, 101 W. Lombard St., Baltimore, MD 21201, Tel. 962-3822. If in the DC Metro area, contact the District of Columbia office.

MASSACHUSETTS: 3 Center Plaza, Boston, MA 02108, Tel. 617/223-2571.

MICHIGAN: 477 Michigan Ave., Rm. 595, Detroit, MI 48226, Tel. 313/226-6950.

MINNESOTA: Federal Building, Fort Snelling, Twin Cities, MN 55111, Tel. 612/725-3355.

MISSISSIPPI: 100 W. Capitol St., Suite 335, Jackson, MS 39201, Tel. 601/960-4586.

MISSOURI: Federal Building, Rm. 134, 601 E. 12th St., Kansas City, MO 64106, Tel. 816/374-5702; 915 Olive St., Rm. 400, St. Louis, MO 63101, Tel. 314/425-4285.

MONTANA: None. Contact offices in nearby states.

NEBRASKA: U.S. Courthouse and Post Office Building, Rm. 1010, 215 N. 17th St., Omaha, NE 68102, Tel. 402/221-3815.

NEVADA: None. Contact offices in nearby states.

NEW HAMPSHIRE: Federal Building, Rm. 104, Daniel and Penhallow Streets, Portsmouth, NH 03801, Tel. 703/436-7720, ext. 762.

NEW JERSEY: Peter W. Rodino, Jr. Federal Building, 970 Broad St., Newark, NJ 07102, Tel. 201/645-3673. If in Camden, call 215/597-7440.

NEW MEXICO: Federal Building, 421 Gold Ave., SW, Albuquerque, NM 87102, Tel. 505/766-5583.

NEW YORK: Jacob K. Javits Federal Building, 26 Federal Plaza, New York, NY 10278, Tel. 212/264-0422; U.S. Courthouse and Federal Building, 100 S. Clinton St., Syracuse, NY 13260, Tel. 315/423-5660.

NORTH CAROLINA: Federal Building, 310 New Bern Avenue, P. O. Box 25069, Raleigh, NC 27611, Tel. 919/755-4361.

NORTH DAKOTA: None. Contact offices in nearby states.

OHIO: Federal Building, Lobby, 200 West 2nd St., Dayton, OH 45402, Tel. 513/225-2720 or 2654.

OKLAHOMA: 200 NW 5th St., Rm. 205, Oklahoma City, OK 73102, Tel. 405/231-4948.

OREGON: Federal Building, North Lobby, 1220 SW 3rd St., Portland, OR 97204, Tel. 503/221-3141.

PENNSYLVANIA: William J. Green, Jr. Federal Building, 600 Arch St., Philadelphia, PA 19106, Tel. 215/597-7440; Federal Building, Rm. 168, Harrisburg, PA 17108, Tel. 717/782-4494; Federal Building, 1000 Liberty Ave., Pittsburgh, PA 15222, Tel. 412/644-2755.

PUERTO RICO: Federico Degetau Federal Office Building, Carlos E. Chardon St., Hato Rey, PR 00918, Tel. 809/753-4209, ext. 209.

RHODE ISLAND: Federal and Post Office Building, Rm. 310, Kennedy Plaza, Providence, RI 02903, Tel. 401/528-4447.

SOUTH CAROLINA: Federal Building, 334 Meeting St., Charleston, SC 29403, Tel. 803/724-4328.

SOUTH DAKOTA: None. Contact offices in nearby states.

TENNESSEE: Federal Building, 167 N. Main St., Memphis, TN

38103, 901/521-3956.

TEXAS: Rm. 6B4, 1100 Commerce St., Dallas, TX 75242, Tel. 214/767-8035; 701 San Jacinto St., Houston, TX 77002, Tel. 713/ 226-2376; 643 E. Durango Blvd., San Antonio, TX 78206, Tel. 512/229-6600.

UTAH: None. Contact offices in nearby states.

VERMONT: None. Contact offices in nearby states.

VIRGINIA: Federal Building, Rm. 220, 200 Granby Mall, Norfolk, VA 23510, Tel. 804/441-3355. If in DC Metro area, contact District of Columbia office.

WASHINGTON: Federal Building, 915 Second Ave., Seattle, WA 98174, 206/442-4365.

WEST VIRGINIA: Federal Building, 500 Quarrier St., Charleston, WV 25301, Tel. 304/343-6181, ext. 226.

WISCONSIN: None. Contact offices in nearby states.

WYOMING: None. Contact offices in nearby states.

Appendix H

FEDERAL PERSONNEL OFFICES AND JOB HOTLINE SERVICES

Each agency maintains a personnel office to which you should address your inquiries concerning job vacancies and applications. However, some agencies maintain several personnel offices. The Department of Agriculture, for example, is an extremely decentralized agency. Each of its services has a separate personnel office.

The following personnel offices are located in the Washington, D.C. Metropolitan area. Many agencies located within the 10 Federal regions also maintain personnel offices. Several of the personnel offices listed below also maintain a 24-hour "Dial a Vacancy" line. By calling a number, you will get a recorded message listing the latest agency vacancies as well as indications of eligibility status and instructions for submitting an application. In most cases we have included the telephone number for the personnel office in charge of disseminating job vacancy information. In some cases, especially where several personnel offices are found within a single agency, we have included the telephone number of the director of the personnel office. You can call that number to get information on whom you should contact within the agency.

AGENCY	Personnel Office	"Dial a Vacancy"
ACTION	202/634-9261	202/634-1000
Administrative Office of U.S. Courts	202/393-1640	
Agency for International Development	202/632-1850	202/632-3942
Agriculture, Department of	202/447-5625	202/447-2108
Arms Control and Disarmament Agency, U.S.	202/632-2034	
Bureau of Engraving and Printing	202/964-7955	
Central Intelligence Agency	703/351-2028	
Civil Aeronautics Board	202/673-5250	
Commerce, Department of	202/377-4285	
Commission on Civil Rights	202/376-8332	
Commodity Future Trading Commission	202/254-3275	
Congressional Budget Office	202/226-2621	
Consumer Product Safety Commission	202/492-6660	
Defense, Department of (civilian)	202/694-9487	
• Air Force, Department of	202/697-9336	
• Army, Department of	202/695-3881	202/694-1812
• Navy, Department of	202/692-4139	202/696-4450
Defense Contract Audit Agency	202/274-7325	
Defense Logistics Agency	703/274-6000	703/274-7372
Education, Department of	202/245-8366	202/245-8404
Energy, Department of	202/252-4333	202/252-4338
Environmental Protection Agency	202/382-3144	202/755-5055
Equal Employment Opportunity Commission	202/634-4921	
Executive Office of the President	202/395-3766	
Export-Import Bank of the U.S.	202/566-8834	
Farm Credit Administration	202/883-4136	
Federal Aviation Administration	202/426-3229	202/426-1662
Federal Bureau of Investigation	202/252-7960	202/252-7031
Federal Communications Commission	202/632-7120	202/632-7106
Federal Deposit Insurance Corporation	202/389-4301	
Federal Election Commission	202/523-4108	
Federal Emergency Management Agency	202/646-2500	
Federal Energy Administration	202/961-7255	
Federal Energy Regulatory Commission	202/357-8071	

Federal Home Loan Bank Board	202/377-6054	
Federal Labor Relations Authority	202/382-0751	
Federal Maritime Commission	202/523-5773	
Federal Mediation and Conciliation Service	202/653-5260	
Federal Reserve System	202/452-3880	
Federal Trade Commission	202/523-3986	
General Accounting Office	202/275-5540	202/275-6017 202/275-6361
General Services Administration	202/566-0085	
Government Printing Office	202/275-2951	
Health and Human Services, Department of	202/443-1986	
Housing and Urban Development, Department of	202/755-5408	202/755-4303
Interior, Department of	202/343-2154	202/343-2154 202/343-7742
Internal Revenue Service	202/376-0497	202/566-3901
International Trade Commission	202/523-0182	
Interstate Commerce Commission	202/275-7288	
Justice, Department of	202/633-4615	202/633-3121
Labor, Department of	202/523-6677	
Library of Congress	202/287-5627	202/287-5295
Merit Systems Protection Board	202/653-7120	
National Aeronautics and Space Administration	202/755-3054	
National Bureau of Standards	202/912-3555	
National Capital Planning Commission	202/724-0206	
National Credit Union Administration	202/357-1156	
National Endowment for the Arts	202/682-5405	
National Endowment for the Humanities	202/786-0415	
National Gallery of Art	202/737-4215	202/842-6298
National Guard Bureau	202/756-1213	
National Institute of Health	301/443-1230	301/443-2282
National Labor Relations Board	202/254-9106	
National Oceanic and Atmospheric Administration	202/377-4285	301/443-8274
National Park Service	202/343-4648	
National Science Foundation	202/357-7868	
National Security Agency	301/859-6444	
National Transportation Safety Board	202/382-6718	
Nuclear Regulatory Commission	202/492-7400	
Office of Management and Budget	202/395-3765	

Office of Personnel Management	202/632-5400	
Overseas Private Investment Corporation	202/632-8618	
Panama Canal Commission	202/634-6441	
Peace Corps	202/376-2550	
Pension Benefit Guaranty Corporation	202/254-4779	
Postal Rate Commission	202/789-6840	
Postal Service	202/523-2081	
Railroad Retirement Board	202/751-4570	
Securities and Exchange Commission	202/272-2550	
Selective Service System	202/724-0435	
Small Business Administration	202/653-6563	
Smithsonian Institution	202/357-2465	202/357-1450
		202/357-1452
State, Department of	202/632-0850	202/433-4930
Supreme Court of the United States	202/479-3404	
Tax Court of the United States	202/376-2724	
Tennessee Valley Authority	615/632-3341	
Transportation, Department of	202/426-2550	202/566-2540
U.S. Information Agency	202/486-2618	202/485-2854
Veterans Administration	202/389-2459	
Voice of America	202/485-8062	

Appendix I

FEDERAL AND POSTAL EMPLOYEE UNIONS AND ORGANIZATIONS

AMERICAN FEDERATION OF GOVERNMENT EMPLOYEES, AFL-CIO: 80 F St., NW, Washington, DC 20001, Tel. 202/737-8500.

AMERICAN POSTAL WORKERS UNION, AFL-CIO: 817 14th St., NW, Washington, DC 20005, Tel. 202/842-4200.

AIR TRAFFIC CONTROL ASSOCIATION, INC.: 2020 N. 14th St., Suite 410, Arlington, VA 22201, Tel. 703/522-5717.

ASSOCIATION OF FEDERAL INVESTIGATORS: 1612 K St., NW, Suite 506, Washington, DC 20006.

BLACKS IN GOVERNMENT: 1424 K St., NW, Suite 604, Washington, DC 20005, Tel. 202/638-7767.

THE FEDERAL BAR ASSOCIATION: 1815 H St., NW, Suite 408, Washington, DC 20006, Tel. 202/638-0252.

FEDERAL CRIMINAL INVESTIGATORS ASSOCIATION: P. O. Box 676, Oakton, VA 22124.

FEDERAL EMPLOYEE ASSOCIATIONS/GOVERNMENT EMPLOYEE ASSOCIATION: P. O. Box 32766, San Antonio, TX 78216, Tel. 512/349-4397.

FEDERAL EXECUTIVE AND PROFESSIONAL ASSOCIATION: 15535 New Hampshire Ave., Silver Spring, MD 20904, 301/384-2616.

FEDERAL FIREFIGHTERS ASSOCIATION: 240 N. Cottage Rd., Sterling, VA 22170, Tel. 703/450-6179.

FEDERAL LAW ENFORCEMENT OFFICERS ASSOCIATION: 106 Cedarhurst Ave., Selden, NY 11784, Tel. 516/698-0719.

FEDERAL MANAGERS ASSOCIATION: 2300 S. 9th St., Arlington, VA 22204, Tel. 703/892-4408.

FEDERAL POLICE OFFICERS ASSOCIATION: P. O. Box 46191, Mount Clemens, MI 48046, Tel. 313/466-4673.

FEDERALLY EMPLOYED WOMEN: 101 Vermont Ave., NW, Suite 821, Washington, DC 20005, Tel. 202/638-4404.

INTERNATIONAL ASSOCIATION OF MACHINISTS AND AERO-SPACE WORKERS — GOVERNMENT EMPLOYEES DEPARTMENT: 1300 Connecticut Ave., NW, Washington, DC 20036, Tel. 202/857-5235.

INTERNATIONAL PERSONNEL MANAGEMENT ASSOCIATION: 1617 Duke St., Alexandria, VA 23314, Tel. 703/549-7100.

NATIONAL ALLIANCE OF POSTAL AND FEDERAL EMPLOYEES: 1628 11th St., NW, Washington, DC 20001, Tel. 202/939-6325.

NATIONAL ASSOCIATION OF AERONAUTICAL EXAMINERS: P. O. Box 352, Dulzura, CA 92017.

NATIONAL ARMY AND AIR TECHNICIANS ASSOCIATION: 2002 Route 541, Burlington, NJ 08016, Tel. 609/387-8162.

NATIONAL ASSOCIATION OF CIVIL SERVICE EMPLOYEES: 7185 Navajo Rd., Suite D, San Diego, CA 92119, Tel. 619/464-1014.

NATIONAL ASSOCIATION OF FEDERAL VETERINARIANS: 1522 K St., NW, Suite 836, Washington, DC 20005, Tel. 202/223-3590.

NATIONAL ASSOCIATION OF GOVERNMENT EMPLOYEES: 285 Dorchester Ave., Boston, MA 02127, Tel. 617/268-5002.

NATIONAL ASSOCIATION OF LETTER CARRIERS, AFL-CIO: 100 Indiana Ave., NW, Washington, DC 20001, Tel. 202/393-4695.

NATIONAL ASSOCIATION OF POSTAL SUPERVISORS: 490 L'Enfant Plaza, SW, Suite 3200, Washington, DC 20024, Tel. 202/484-6070.

NATIONAL ASSOCIATION OF POSTMASTERS: 4212 King St., Alexandria, VA 22302-1595, Tel. 703/671-6800.

NATIONAL ASSOCIATION OF RETIRED FEDERAL EMPLOY-EES: 1533 New Hampshire Ave., NW, Washington, DC 20036, Tel. 202/234-0832.

NATIONAL COUNCIL OF JEWISH GOVERNMENT EMPLOYEE ORGANIZATIONS: 45 E. 33rd St., Suite 603, New York, NY 10016, Tel. 212/689-2015.

NATIONAL FEDERATION OF FEDERAL EMPLOYEES: 1016 16th St., NW, Washington, DC 20036, Tel. 202/862-4400.

NATIONAL LEAGUE OF POSTMASTERS: 1023 North Royal St., Alexandria, VA 22314, Tel. 703/548-5922.

NATIONAL RURAL LETTER CARRIERS ASSOCIATION: 1445 Duke St., Alexandria, VA 22314, Tel. 703/684-5545.

NATIONAL TREASURY EMPLOYEES UNION: 1730 K St., NW, Washington, DC 20006, Tel. 202/785-4411.

OVERSEAS EDUCATION ASSOCIATION: 1201 16th St., NW, Washington, DC 20036, Tel. 202/822-7850.

PROFESSIONAL ENGINEERS IN GOVERNMENT: 1420 King St., Alexandria, VA 22314, Tel. 703/684-4322.

PROFESSIONAL AIRWAYS SYSTEMS SPECIALISTS: 444 N. Capitol St., NW, Suite 840, Washington, DC 20001, Tel. 202/347-6065.

SENIOR EXECUTIVES ASSOCIATION: P. O. Box 7610, Ben

Franklin Station, Washington, DC 20044, Tel. 202/535-4328.

UNITED STATES "SKY MARSHAL" ASSOCIATION: 11 Hunton St., Staten Island, NY 10304, 718/979-0403.

SUBJECT INDEX

NAME AND ORGANIZATIONAL INDEX

||||||||||||||||||||||||||||||||||||||||||||||||||||||||||||||||||||||||||||||||||

PUBLIC EMPLOYMENT RESOURCES

||||||||||||||||||||||||||||||||||||||||||||||||||||||||||||||||||||||||||||||||||

Call or write IMPACT PUBLICATIONS to receive the latest issue of their comprehensive, illustrated, and annotated catalog of nearly 800 career resources.

The following resources, many of which are recommended throughout the book, are available directly from IMPACT PUBLICATIONS. Complete the following form, or list the titles desired by order number, and send your order to:

> IMPACT PUBLICATIONS
> 10655 Big Oak Circle
> Manassas, VA 22111
> Tel. 703/361-7300

All prices include shipping and handling. You are entitled to a $1.00 discount on each single title or $2.00 on two or more titles, plus a 10% discount on all orders of $100 or more, if you include the bonus coupon appearing at the end of the order form with your prepaid order. Orders from individuals should be prepaid by check, money-order, Visa or MasterCard number.

Qty.	Code	TITLES	Price	TOTAL

APPROACHES TO CAREER SUCCESS

Qty.	Code	TITLES	Price	TOTAL
_____	5-BA	Molloy's Live For Success	$10.95	_____
_____	6-IM	Moving Out of Education	$24.95	_____
_____	88-PH	Reach Out And Sell Someone	$7.95	_____
_____	1-IM	Re-Careering in Turbulent Times	$8.95	_____
_____	2-SC	The Robert Half Way to Get Hired	$12.95	_____
_____	2-FF	Telesearch	$7.95	_____
_____	1-KH	Training for Life	$18.95	_____
_____	1-WA	Up Your Career	$12.95	_____
_____	9-TS	Where Do I Go From Here With My Life?	$11.95	_____
_____	10-BF	Wishcraft: How to Get What You Really Want	$7.95	_____
_____	1-KH	Your Career: Choices, Chances, Changes	$18.95	_____

TESTING AND ASSESSMENT

_____	45-AR	Career Aptitude Tests	$10.95 _____
_____	35-SS	Discover What You're Best At	$11.95 _____
_____	1-EA	Employability Inventory	$8.95 _____
_____	46-AR	How to Pass Employment Tests	$8.95 _____
_____	17-TS	The New Quick Job Hunting Map	$4.95 _____
_____	8-SS	Test Your Management I.Q.	$8.95 _____

JOB LISTING NEWSPAPERS

_____	1-JM	National Job Market (1 year subscription — 26 issues)	$125.00 _____
_____	1-FS	Federal Career Opportunities (6, 12, or 26 issues)	$36.00/$70.00/$146.00 _____

RESOURCE MATERIALS AND DIRECTORIES

_____	8-GP	900,000 Jobs Annually	$11.95 _____
_____	6-WD	Internships: 16,000 Opportunities	$14.95 _____
_____	1-IE	The National Directory of Internships	$17.95 _____
_____	3-CB	National Trade and Professional Associations	$47.95 _____
_____	10-GP	The Professional and Trade Association Job Finder	$14.95 _____
_____	4-CB	Washington Representatives	$47.95 _____
_____	5-CB	Washington (annual)	$42.95 _____

RESUMES, LETTERS, INTERVIEWS, SALARIES

_____	1-AV	American Almanac of Jobs and Salaries	$14.95 _____
_____	2-IM	High Impact Resumes and Letters	$8.95 _____
_____	3-IM	Interview for Success	$8.95 _____
_____	4-SC	Salary Strategies	$14.95 _____
_____	21-TS	Sweaty Palms: Being Interviewed	$9.95 _____

DRESS, APPEARANCE, ETIQUETTE

_____	10-BA	Color Wonderful	$11.95 _____
_____	11-SM	Executive Etiquette	$9.95 _____
_____	3-SC	The Executive Look	$12.95 _____
_____	6-PT	The Professional Image	$10.95 _____

PUBLIC EMPLOYMENT

_____106-PH	101 Challenging Government Jobs for College Graduates	$14.95	_____
_____ 1-WB	The 171 Reference Book	$18.95	_____
_____ 1-TS	Capitol Jobs	$7.95	
_____ 1-WK	Career Choices: Law	$7.95	_____
_____ 2-WK	Career Choices: Political Science and Government	$7.95	_____
_____ 1-TG	Careers in the Nonprofit Sector	$21.95	_____
_____ 1-ST	Careers in Secret Operations	$9.95	_____
_____ 3-GP	Careers in State and Local Government	$12.95	_____
_____ 1-PC	The Compleat Guide to Jobs in Planning and Public Administration	$10.95	_____
_____ 4-IM	The Complete Guide to Public Employment	$14.95	_____
_____ 14-AR	The Complete Guide to U.S. Civil Service Jobs	$6.95	_____
_____ 65-AR	Directory of Employment Opportunities in the Federal Government	$26.95	_____
_____ 14-AR	General Test Practice for 101 U.S. Jobs	$7.95	
_____ 2-JM	How to Get a Federal Job (Video — specify Beta or VHS format)	$71.00	_____
_____ 1-FH	How to Get a Federal Job or Survive a RIF	$16.95	_____
_____ 5-IM	Moving Out of Government	$14.95	_____
_____ 5-NT	Opportunities in Counseling and Guidance	$11.95	_____
_____ 6-NT	Opportunities in Federal Government Careers	$11.95	_____
_____ 7-NT	Opportunities in Fire Protection Services	$11.95	_____
_____142-NT	Opportunities in Government Service	$11.95	_____
_____ 8-NT	Opportunities in Law Careers	$11.95	_____
_____ 9-NT	Opportunities in Law Enforcement and Criminal Justice	$11.95	_____
_____ 10-NT	Opportunities in Paralegal Careers	$11.95	_____
_____ 11-NT	Opportunities in Recreation and Leisure	$11.95	_____
_____134-NT	Opportunities in State and Local Government	$11.95	_____
_____ 72-AR	You as a Law Enforcement Officer	$9.95	_____
_____ 12-NT	Your Career in Court Administration	$9.95	_____
_____ 13-NT	Your Career in Law Enforcement	$9.95	_____
_____ 14-NT	Your Career in Local, State and Federal Government	$9.95	_____

INTERNATIONAL JOBS AND CAREERS

_____	1-GT	Careers in International Affairs	$12.95 _____
_____	1-WD	The Directory of Overseas Summer Jobs	$10.95 _____
_____	9-PE	The Educator's Passport to International Jobs	$11.95 _____
_____	21-SS	Foreign Jobs	$11.95 _____
_____	1-FP	Guide to Careers in World Affairs	$8.95 _____
_____	13-AR	How to Get a Job Overseas	$8.95 _____
_____	1-GO	Jobs in Japan	$11.95 _____
_____	10-WD	Kibbutz Volunteer	$10.95 _____
_____	2-MM	Living Overseas	$11.95 _____
_____	1-IC	Make It Happen	$8.95 _____
_____	2-WD	Summer Jobs in Britain	$10.95 _____
_____	1-MT	Teach Overseas	$14.95 _____
_____	2-SM	Work, Study, Travel Abroad	$8.95 _____
_____	3-WD	Work Your Way Around the World	$12.95 _____
_____	3-NT	Your Career in the Foreign Service	$9.95 _____
_____	4-NT	Your Career in the International Field	$9.95 _____

CONSULTING

_____	47-WI	Cashing in on the Consulting Boom	$14.95 _____
_____	46-WI	How to Become a Top Consultant	$21.95 _____
_____	13-WI	How to Succeed as an Independent Consultant	$22.95 _____
_____	26-WI	Marketing Your Consulting and Professional Services	$21.95 _____

OPPORTUNITIES FOR WOMEN AND MINORITIES

_____	13-BR	Back to Work: A Career Guide for the Returnee	$8.95 _____
_____	5-GP	Directory of Special Opportunities for Minority Group Members	$22.95 _____
_____	4-GP	Directory of Special Opportunities for Women	$21.95 _____
_____	4-MG	Displaced Homemakers	$7.95 _____
_____	7-AC	Getting Ahead	$9.95 _____
_____	3-MM	High-Tech Career Strategies for Women	$9.95 _____
_____	7-GP	Minority Organizations	$32.95 _____
_____	1-SS	What to Do With the Rest of Your Life	$14.95 _____
_____	20-NT	Women in Government	$11.95 _____

OPPORTUNITIES IN MAJOR METROPOLITAN AREAS

_____	1-HM	The Best Towns in America	$11.95	_____
_____	1-AD	The Boston Job Bank	$11.95	_____
_____	2-AD	The Greater Atlanta Job Bank	$11.95	_____
_____	3-AD	The Greater Chicago Job Bank	$11.95	_____
_____	1-SY	How to Get a Job in Chicago	$15.95	_____
_____	14-TS	How to Get a Job in Houston	$11.95	_____
_____	2-SY	How to Get a Job in Dallas/Ft. Worth	$15.95	_____
_____	3-SY	How to Get a Job in Los Angeles	$15.95	_____
_____	5-SY	How to Get a Job in New York City	$15.95	_____
_____	4-AD	The Metropolitan New York Job Bank	$11.95	_____
_____	5-AD	The Metropolitan Washington, D.C. Job Bank	$11.95	_____
_____	6-AD	The Northern California Job Bank	$11.95	_____
_____	7-AD	The Northwest Job Bank	$11.95	_____
_____	8-AD	The Ohio Job Bank	$11.95	_____
_____	9-AD	The Pennsylvania Job Bank	$11.95	_____
_____	10-AD	The Southern California Job Bank	$11.95	_____
_____	11-AD	The Southwest Job Bank	$11.95	_____
_____	12-AD	The Texas Job Bank	$11.95	_____

RETIREMENT AND CAREERS AFTER 60

_____	48-WI	The Arthur Young Preretirement Book	$18.95	_____
_____	1-CS	Comfort Zones: A Practical Guide for Retirement Planning	$14.95	_____
_____	2-CT	Managing Retirement	$19.95	_____
_____	36-SS	Success Over Sixty	$10.95	_____
_____	2-ST	Writing for Pleasure and Profit in Retirement	$8.95	_____

EXECUTIVE SEARCH AND HEADHUNTERS

_____	2-CO	Directory of Executive Recruiters	$25.95	_____
_____	37-SS	The Directory of Executive Search Firms	$12.95	_____
_____	29-WI	The Headhunter Strategy	$18.95	_____
_____	17-AM	How to Answer A Headhunter's Call	$18.95	_____
_____	50-WI	How to Get A Headhunter to Call	$21.95	_____
_____	3-CO	International Directory of Executive Recruiters	$32.95	_____

• Virginia residents add 4% state sales tax. . . . . _____

TOTAL _____

I enclose my check or money order for $ _____ made payable to
IMPACT PUBLICATIONS.

Please charge $ _____ to my credit card: ☐ Visa   ☐ MasterCard

Card # _____ Expiration Date _____

Signature _____ Date _____

SPECIAL BONUS OFFER

Include this coupon with your prepaid order
and receive a $1.00 discount on any single
title; $2.00 on two or more titles. Receive an
additional 10% discount on all prepaid orders
of $100.00 or more.

NAME _____

DATE _____